Nashville
SINCE THE 1920s

Nashville

SINCE THE 1920s

Don H. Doyle

THE UNIVERSITY OF TENNESSEE PRESS
KNOXVILLE

COPYRIGHT © 1985
BY THE UNIVERSITY OF TENNESSEE PRESS / KNOXVILLE.
ALL RIGHTS RESERVED.
MANUFACTURED IN THE UNITED STATES OF AMERICA.

*The paper in this book meets the guidelines for
permanence and durability of the Committee on Production Guidelines
for Book Longevity of the Council on Library Resources.
Binding materials have been chosen for durability.*

Library of Congress Cataloging in Publication Data

Doyle, Don Harrison, 1946–
  Nashville since the 1920s.
  Bibliography: p.
  Includes index.
  1. Nashville (Tenn.)—History. I. Title.
F444.N257D694 1985   976.8'55   85-3262
ISBN 0-87049-470-8 (alk. paper)

FOR
*Carrie,
and her future*

CONTENTS

MAPS, ILLUSTRATIONS, AND TABLES ix
PREFACE xiii

1. Renaissance in Athens 3
2. Coming in from the Country 30
3. Boss Howse and the Reformers 64
4. A New Deal for Nashville 85
5. Into the Sunbelt 108
6. Music City, Athens, Protestant Vatican 143
7. Integrating the Government 179
8. Integrating the People 222
9. Century III 261

APPENDIX A: Population and Race, Nashville and Davidson County, 1860–1980 273
APPENDIX B: Nashville Bank Clearings, 1915–1980 274
APPENDIX C: Nashville's Labor Force, 1950, 1980 275
APPENDIX D: Municipal Revenues and Expenditures, 1938–1971 276
APPENDIX E: Mayors of Nashville, 1915–1983 277
NOTES 279
ESSAY ON SOURCES 312
INDEX 320

MAPS, ILLUSTRATIONS, AND TABLES

Figure 1. The Fugitives in 1923	11
Figure 2. The Vanderbilt Agrarians	16
Figure 3. The original Parthenon	19
Figure 4. The Parthenon under construction, c. 1926	19
Figure 5. Lula Naff at Ryman Auditorium	23
Figure 6. Arthur Henkel and the Nashville Symphony	25
Figure 7. Nashville Conservatory of Music faculty, 1928	25
Figure 8. Conservatory dancers at the Parthenon	27
Figure 9. Willis D. Weatherford, c. 1910	33
Figure 10. Commercial students at night school	39
Figure 11. Office workers at National Life	39
Figure 12. Women office workers outside National Life	41
Figure 13. Map of the Bethlehem House area	43
Figure 14. The homes of the poor	47
Figure 15. Christmas at Bethlehem House	52
Figure 16. Fisk social science students	54
Figure 17. A sewing class at Wesley House	54
Figure 18. Churches of the poor	57
Figure 19. Scene from a religious street meeting	61
Figure 20. Another scene from a religious street meeting	62
Figure 21. "Southern Chivalry" extends the vote to women	70
Figure 22. Map: Nashville, 1927	79
Figure 23. Mayor Hilary Howse with Huey Long	82
Figure 24. Hilary Howse's funeral procession	84
Figure 25. FDR in Nashville, 1934	88
Figure 26. WPA workers on Church Street	91
Figure 27. American Airlines at Berry Field	91
Figure 28. Percy Warner Park	93

Figure 29. Hilary Howse High School — 93
Figure 30. The new courthouse — 95
Figure 31. Cheatham Place public housing — 98
Figure 32. Tom Little cartoons of TVA's coming to Nashville — 107
Figure 33. The celebration of TVA's arrival in Nashville — 107
Figure 34. Dedication of the Vultee Aircraft plant — 111
Figure 35. The Vultee Aircraft plant, 1947 — 111
Figure 36. Soldiers at Union Station — 114
Figure 37. V-J Day downtown — 116
Figure 38. Mayor Cummings and Silliman Evans, Sr. — 117
Figure 39. James G. "Jimmy" Stahlman — 118
Figure 40. Downtown in the early 1930s — 122
Figure 41. Downtown, c. 1940 — 122
Figure 42. Capitol Hill slum clearance, 1954 — 123
Figure 43. Capitol Hill in smoke — 123
Figure 44. Auto traffic on Broadway — 124
Figure 45. Aerial view, Capitol Hill — 127
Figure 46. Another aerial view, Capitol Hill — 128
Figure 47. Grand Ole Opry at the Dixie Tabernacle — 145
Figure 48. Roy Acuff — 147
Figure 49. Kitty Wells with the Ernest Tubb tour bus — 148
Figure 50. Hank Williams — 150
Figure 51. Owen Bradley — 152
Figure 52. Francis Preston of BMI — 155
Figure 53. Music City, U.S.A., Hall of Fame display — 155
Figure 54. Vanderbilt fraternity protest — 163
Figure 55. Charles S. Johnson of Fisk — 167
Figure 56. Beverly Briley and Litton Hickman — 188
Figure 57. Mayor Cummings stumping for reelection, 1951 — 189
Figure 58. Thomas Cummings and Ben West — 189
Figure 59. Suburban tract housing — 192
Figure 60. Suburban home sale — 192
Figure 61. Map: Nashville and suburbs, 1960 — 196
Figure 62. First charter commission, 1958 — 201
Figure 63. Second charter commission, 1962 — 208
Figure 64. Anti-Metro posters, 1962 — 213
Figure 65. Henry "Good Jelly" Jones in the anti-Metro campaign — 213
Figure 66. Congressman Richard Fulton — 219
Figure 67. "Pay Your Poll Tax Now" — 226
Figure 68. Poll scene at city election, 1947 — 226
Figure 69. City-County Democratic Civic League, 1950 — 227
Figure 70. Map: Nashville residential segregation, 1940 — 231
Figure 71. Black poverty amid prosperity — 232
Figure 72. Map: Nashville residential segregation, 1960 — 233

Figure 73. Z. Alexander Looby and Avon Williams, Jr.   236
Figure 74. Caldwell School, September 9, 1957   240
Figure 75. School desegregation, 1957   240
Figure 76. Hattie Cotton School after bombing   241
Figure 77. John Kasper under arrest   241
Figure 78. Sit-in at Walgreen's   247
Figure 79. James M. Lawson, Jr., addressing a meeting   247
Figure 80. A silent protest march   250
Figure 81. Confrontation at Cross Keys   253
Figure 82. Picketing the Krystal Grill   253
Figure 83. National Guard troops in North Nashville   256
Figure 84. Anti-busing rally   259
Figure 85. Founders Day, December 23, 1979   267
Figure 86. Mayor Richard Fulton on Settlement Day   267
Figure 87. Settlement Day, April 24, 1980   269

TABLES

Table 1. Nashville's Female Labor Force by Race, 1920, 1940   36
Table 2. Nashville's Religious Affiliations, 1926, 1936   58
Table 3. Nashville's Higher Education Industry, 1950, 1960, 1970   159

PREFACE

This is the second of two books I have written on the history of Nashville during its second century. The first, *Nashville in the New South, 1880–1930,* began with the celebration of the 1880 centennial and ended fifty years later with the collapse of Caldwell and Company and the onset of the Great Depression. This volume returns to the 1920s to explore the cultural and social history of that crucial time, and it ends with the bicentennial celebration in 1980.

In writing this book I have aimed at exploring all of Nashville's history, from intellectual and cultural life to political events and economic development, from wealthy business elites to laborers and slum dwellers. Alas, the coverage could not always be even, nor is this by any means the definitive history of Nashville in this period. Many aspects of the city's recent past remain to be explored, and I hope this book will prove a useful point of departure for those historians who follow.

Though this book focuses on the history of a single city, it will also serve as a window through which to view changes occurring elsewhere in urban America, and especially the South. In 1920 more than 70 percent of southerners lived in rural areas; by 1980 almost that same proportion (67 percent) lived in urban places. The Northeast, the most urbanized section of the nation, had passed approximately the same thresholds of urbanization three-quarters of a century earlier, between 1850 and 1900. After World War II the southern lag that had left the region forty to fifty years behind the rest of the nation began to close rapidly. Urban growth, industrial development, and rising personal income were only a few measures of economic prosperity that shifted southward and cityward in these decades.

With that economic transformation came vast changes in the politics and race relations of the South. Cities like Nashville were vanguards for all the changes required of the South during what historian Charles Roland called this "improbable era." The cities were the magnets that drew migrants from the country. Out of the cities came a new generation of political leaders devoted to planning and to the use of government as an instrument for economic development and social improvement. It was in the cities also that the South worked out a new basis for race relations and dismantled the system of segregation and racism that had obstructed the progress of the entire region. Nashville was only one of the urban crucibles in which southern society was being remade, and it was one whose story illuminates an important part of the region's experience in these years.

This book opens in the 1920s when Nashville witnessed agonizing conflicts between the legacy of local and regional traditions and the modern world of radios, movies, automobiles, factories, skyscrapers, and heady prosperity that rushed into the city during and after the first world war. Intellectuals at the universities and common folk coming in from the country were contemplating choices between these two worlds, as people were throughout much of the South. The tension inherent in this contest between regional traditions and urban modernity provides a theme that runs through Nashville's history during this period. It emerges in the essays of the Vanderbilt Agrarians, in the persistence of fundamentalist religion among rural migrants to the city, in the plaintive lyrics of country music, and, in more recent times, in the conflict between urban renewal and preservation of historic buildings. That tension was not as acute in a city like Birmingham or Atlanta, where progress usually took precedence over tradition. Nor would it be as intense in Charleston or Savannah, where tradition more often has prevailed. In Nashville the contest was at once more sharply defined and more ambiguous in its outcome. It is that ambiguity, I believe, that makes Nashville such an interesting part of the world.

In writing any scholarly book, an author incurs many debts to those who help the cause, but this book involves more than the usual number. I am grateful to the Century III Commission for sponsoring this project as part of the city's bicentennial celebration in 1980. Susan Cox, a staff assistant to the commission and a former student of mine, first alerted me to the commission's interest in a book on Nashville's history, and I thank her for her early service on my behalf. I am especially grateful to May Dean Eberling, a member of the commission and its Historical Records Committee, who understood the importance of a scholarly history to the bicentennial and the need for sufficient time and support to carry out the project. The Century III Commission allowed me full freedom to write an objective history of the city and gave me all the time I needed to complete it. They secured funds from the Metropolitan Council to begin the project and, toward the end, supplied funds from the many generous donations made by private corporations and individuals to the bicentennial celebration.

The principal financial support came from the National Endowment for the Humanities (NEH), Division of Research Grants, which awarded me a grant under their program in State, Local, and Regional History. This grant allowed me to hire research assistants and to cover far more of Nashville's history than I could have done alone. One consequence of this, however, was that the slim single volume I had projected to complete within two or three years grew into two books that required over five years to complete. I am grateful to NEH for giving me the extra time and for cooperating at all stages of the project.

Sandy Evans, executive director of Century III, administered the grant before the commission disbanded, and I thank her for that. Robert Horton and his Office of Intergovernmental Affairs took over in 1981. I am grateful to Loretta Conners, of that office, for her cheerful and efficient handling of all the bookkeeping duties. Finally, Mimi Hayes, of the Department of Finance, took over those duties in the summer of 1983, and I am thankful for her excellent service to the project.

Several research assistants worked on aspects of this book at various times over the course of four years. Some I have already mentioned in connection with the first volume. John Rumble researched a number of topics explored in this volume, and his knowledge of the country music industry in Nashville was particularly helpful to my understanding of that subject. Roz McGee researched the newspapers of the 1930s and 1940s and shared her knowledge of local politics and power in ways that helped me enormously. James Summerville was indispensable to the successful completion of this volume. He performed numerous tasks, from newspaper research to tracking down photographs, and he kept me going when the end seemed nowhere in sight. Betty Grimes helped with the research and interviews on desegregation and the civil rights movement. Doug Flamming assisted me with the final stages of manuscript preparation. I am grateful to all of these research assistants for their dedication to the project.

There were dozens of other scholars, amateur historians, interested citizens, and busy office workers who took the time to help me understand the history of Nashville. Some offered hints on sources, others offered tantalizing gossip on local personalities, still others admonished me to either include—or delete—aspects of their ancestors' past in the book I was writing. I cannot thank all of them, but I do wish to express my gratitude to Sam Shannon of Tennessee State University, who read portions of the manuscript and generously shared his knowledge of many aspects of Nashville's history. Herschel Gower offered several useful tips on cultural life in Nashville during the 1920s. Pat Miletich lent me her notes on settlement house workers and steered me toward some useful sources. Bobby Grubb, formerly of Wartrace, Tennessee, shared her experience as a country girl coming into the city and inspired my interest in that subject. Several other people volunteered their time and their personal memories to enhance my understanding of the social history of the interwar years. I am particularly grateful to E. B. Williams, Robbie Sanford, Camilla Caldwell, and John Hardcastle for their gracious cooperation. Robert Horton shared his vast knowledge of the history of Metro and local politics in two lengthy and highly informative interviews.

I have benefited enormously over the past several years from teaching (and learning from) my students at Vanderbilt who took my undergraduate seminar on Nashville history. I have tried to cite every student paper that was of direct relevance to the subjects I wrote about, but I learned so much from helping them explore the history of this community, I owe them collectively my sincere thanks.

Several people read early drafts of chapters, and all helped me improve the final product. Mills Thornton read the chapter on desegregation and offered numerous suggestions for improving it. Other parts of the manuscript were read in early draft by Betsie Hancock, Marilyn Doyle, James Summerville, and Sam Shannon. Robert Horton offered his helpful criticism of the chapter on metropolitan consolidation. Charles F. Bryan, Jr., Louise Davis, and May Dean Eberling, as representatives of the Century III Commission, also examined an early draft of the manuscript. David Goldfield and Carl Abbott read the manuscript for the University of Tennessee Press and offered numerous suggestions for improving it. I am sincerely grateful to all these readers for their helpful suggestions, and I absolve them from any blame for the errors and omissions that inevitably remain.

Books like this would be impossible without libraries to store the written documents of the past and librarians who know how to retrieve them. My special thanks to the staff of the Vanderbilt University Library (recently renamed the Jean and Alexander Heard Library) and to the Tennessee State Library and Archives, particularly Marylin Bell, for her able assistance. The Nashville Room of the Ben West Public Library is a rich trove of material for Nashville historians, and I am grateful to Mary Glenn Hearne and Hershel Payne for their cheerful cooperation in aiding this project. Don Belcher of the Research Division of the Nashville Area Chamber of Commerce cordially offered the services of his staff to help my research efforts.

Some of this book was written during a most pleasant year on leave at the Charles Warren Center at Harvard University. I am grateful to Steve Thernstrom and Pat Denault, and to the staffs of the Weidner and Littauer libraries at Harvard, for all they did to make my work easier.

The manuscript for this book, and the earlier volume I wrote on Nashville, was done with the word-processing facilities of the Vanderbilt University Computer Center. I am very grateful for the friendly assistance all the staff offered me in so many ways during the course of preparing this book.

The photographs for this volume came from a variety of locations and with the aid of several skilled photographers. Annette Morrison of the *Tennessean* library graciously opened the rich collection of photographs deposited there since the late 1930s. Larry Reid was extraordinarily helpful in tracking down photographs and arranging for duplication. My thanks to Frank Empson of the *Tennessean* for permission to use the photographs and to Forchion Bellamy for reproducing them. Edwin C. P'Pool reproduced several photographs from the Nashville Room collections in addition to others I brought to him. Leslie Pritikin prepared the illustrations from the Tennessee State Library and Archives. Bracey Holt at the Methodist Publishing House reproduced several photographs from their collections, and I thank him for his careful work. Thanks also to Wesley Paine of the Parthenon Art Gallery for lending me a photographic negative. Steve McHugh and Jim Baird of National Life and Accident Insurance Company generously helped me locate photographs and provided copies for my use.

The staff of the University of Tennessee Press has been delightful to work with. Special thanks are due to Mavis Bryant, Katherine Holloway, and to Barbara Reitt of Reitt Editing Services.

This book is dedicated to my oldest daughter, Carrie, who at seventeen is, quite naturally, more interested in the future than the past. But she has lived most of her life in Nashville (and all her life with a historian as her father), so she knows how much the past decides the future.

—Nashville
July 1984

Nashville
SINCE THE 1920s

RENAISSANCE IN ATHENS

Before the 1920s Nashville's claim as the Athens of the South rested precariously on its constellation of colleges more than its indigenous cultural and intellectual life. There were also numerous literary and intellectual societies, including the Round Table, Old Oak, and Coffee House, small town-and-gown men's clubs that had been meeting and discussing papers since the 1880s. It was women who were the most ardent champions of cultural life in Nashville. The Centennial Club, organized in 1905 and devoted generally to civic uplift and cultural improvement, was the most prominent and active woman's club. The Query Club, the Review Club, and the Nashville Art Association, among others, were also available to wealthy and middle-class women interested in promoting culture. All fostered interest in literature and the arts and produced an experienced corps of strong-minded women who saw it as their duty to refine the materialistic world their husbands and sons were building in the city.[1]

But Nashville and its universities had not nurtured strong literary and artistic traditions of their own since antebellum times, which in the 1920s took on the aura of a lost golden age in the eyes of some.[2] Serious music and theater appeared occasionally at the Ryman Auditorium and Vendome Theater, but this was culture imported from the Northeast or Europe. Other musical performances outside the churches were limited, by and large, to recitals at Ward-Belmont's School of Music.

Because of its several colleges, Nashville probably was richer in cultural amenities and intellectual diversions than many American cities its size, particularly in the less affluent South. Rival cities like Memphis, Birmingham, or Atlanta may have overshadowed Nashville in their commercial and industrial might, but perhaps for that reason, none cultivated the arts and letters that Nashville boasted. Nashville, in fact, was an oasis in a region H. L. Mencken satirized in 1917 as the "Sahara of the Bozart." "Down there a poet is now almost as rare as an oboe-player, a drypoint etcher or a metaphysician, ... Critics, musical composers, painters, sculptors, architects ... there is not even a bad one between the Potomac mud-flats and the Gulf. Nor an historian ... sociologist ... philosopher ... theologian ... scientist."[3]

Mencken's acerbic attack on the South was unfair, cruel, and partly true. He exaggerated the dearth of indigenous intellectual and artistic creativity within the region, and his ridicule began just at the inception of the renaissance in southern literature, a movement that would set the pace for American writing in coming years. Mencken may even deserve credit for embarrassing the South into its cultural revival. Nashville was one of the centers of that awakening during the 1920s, and before the decade ended, literature, poetry, music, dance, theater, painting, architecture—all had come alive and brought Nashville closer than ever to its boast as the Athens of the South.

THE FUGITIVES

The most distinctive component of the Nashville renaissance was a group of poets and intellectuals who became known as the Fugitives, after the poetry magazine they published in the 1920s. The Fugitives' poetry earned them lasting respect in American letters, but they are best known for two intellectual movements that stemmed from them, or certain of their members. The first was the New Criticism, which emphasized close textual analysis of language and structure rather than scholarly research on the author's life and historical context. In the coming years this approach radically transformed the way literature was taught and studied in America. The other intellectual spin-off from the Fugitives was Agrarianism, a critique of modern society and its faith in scientific progress in particular. This was a philosophical movement quite distinct from the Fugitives' poetry but linked to it through four key intellectual leaders and through a common interest in reviving southern culture and self-respect. Agrarianism became a revival of southern sectionalism and a counterattack on the cultural and economic imperialism of the North. In the end, Agrarianism probably had fewer converts, and less clear success, than the New Criticism, but in its implications it was of broader significance to the South and to modern America.

Nashville in the 1920s was the perfect setting for these intellectual movements to take root. Not that the city, or even Vanderbilt University, cherished the Fugitives and the Agrarians. On the contrary, it was the indifference and even the hostility of the community toward these men — and their ambivalence toward Nashville and Vanderbilt — that shaped their ideas and made them what they were. In recent times the Fugitives and Agrarians have been so lionized in Nashville, and particularly at Vanderbilt, it is easy to forget the antagonism they felt toward the city and university. But it is hard to imagine such intellectual movements occurring any other place or any other time than at Vanderbilt, in Nashville, during the 1920s. They were the product of a special place and time.

"After the war," Allen Tate wrote, "the South again knew the world, but it had a memory of another war; with us, entering the world once more meant not the obliteration of the past but a heightened consciousness of it; so that we had . . . a double focus, a looking two ways, which gave a special dimension to the writings of our school."[4] The South in the 1920s, historian George Tindall observed, "had reached a historical watershed, . . . it stood between two worlds, one dying and the other struggling to be born."[5] In Nashville that new world was rushing in on a wave of economic prosperity. It had begun during World War I with the coming of the DuPont powder plant. After the war the city's insurance companies, banks, and brokerage firms flourished. One of them, Caldwell and Company, specialized in marketing bonds for southern counties and cities eager to finance new road-paving projects and other improvements. Rogers Caldwell — the "J. P. Morgan of the South" — had built a financial empire worth one-half billion dollars in the process. ("We Bank on the South" was the company's slogan.) Beyond Union Street downtown (the "Wall Street of the South," according to local boosters) a new flock of manufacturers was building plants around the city. Textiles, clothing, hosiery, shoe, and other factories — several migrating from the North — came to Nashville in the 1920s, and the Chamber of Commerce welcomed them with yeasty rhetoric about the city's progressive spirit and its cheap, docile labor force, made up, they invariably added, of native, Anglo-Saxon stock.

Thousands of young people, some uprooted by the war, others by the agricultural depression that followed it, streamed into Nashville to enlarge the city's labor force. They forsook rural life for better jobs, bright city lights, fast cars, baseball, dance halls, restaurants, and movies. Some rode the wave of prosperity that rolled through Nashville in the 1920s; others sank into miserable poverty in the slums of the city. Aside from human suffering, one of the most visible contradictions to the comforts of modern urban life was a heavy pall of soft coal smoke belching forth from the factory smokestacks and furnace chimneys, blackening the sky and smudging every building. Nashville in the 1920s presented an unusual opportunity to witness the tension between rural tradition and urban modernity.

Out at Vanderbilt many were striving to make the university useful to the New South that the boosters downtown were fashioning.

Having finally severed its ties to the Methodist church in 1914, Vanderbilt was building strong links to the business elite in Nashville and the South in this period. Under Chancellor James H. Kirkland, Vanderbilt revamped its curriculum, dropped the Greek and Latin requirements, introduced new programs in chemistry, "commercial science," and sociology, and rebuilt the medical school. When the Scopes trial in Dayton exposed Tennessee to ridicule in the northern press in 1925, Kirkland announced that Vanderbilt's "answer to Dayton" was to build more scientific laboratories and a new school of religion. He had already launched a $4-million endowment campaign and now appealed to northern benefactors to invest in the education of the benighted South that was revealed in the Dayton "monkey trail."[6] The liberal arts college and its humanities departments were now a smaller part of Kirkland's modern university. But one of the chancellor's most powerful allies was Edwin Mims, chairman of the English department. Mims, who came to Vanderbilt in 1912, was a thoroughgoing New South progressive, a leader in the liberal Commission on Interracial Cooperation (CIC) and an advocate of economic progress and social engineering. His book *The Advancing South*, published in 1926, was another "answer to Dayton," a refutation of the backward South depicted in reports on the Scopes trial. Mims became a popular speaker with northern audiences and with local advocates of the New South.[7]

Mims and Kirkland were praised for their opposition to the South of fundamentalism and narrow conservatism, but the Fugitives and, later, the Agrarians thought them all too subservient to the businessmen downtown and to their faith in modern progress. It was no accident that the rebellion against the New South began among professors and students in the English department, where Mims's autocratic rule was formidable.[8] Mims, to his credit, had hired a constellation of bright, young professors who, in turn, drew together some extraordinary talent among the undergraduate and graduate students at Vanderbilt. There were sixteen people involved at one time or another in the Fugitives and twelve who formed the Agrarians, but the ones of most lasting importance, and the only ones involved in both groups, were John Crowe Ransom, Donald Davidson, Allen Tate, and Robert Penn Warren.

Like so many in Nashville at that time, all four came from small, rural communities to pursue their futures in the metropolis of Middle Tennessee. They came from that earnest, high-minded, small-town middle class of schoolteachers, preachers, merchants, and the like that had sent so many of its sons to Nashville since the Civil War. It was from this same element of rural society in Middle Tennessee that the city's leading businessmen, industrialists, bankers, and insurance executives had been drawn since the late nineteenth century. But unlike their fellow rural migrants who became the most ardent promoters of the New

South, these young men who came to Nashville were to become its most sensitive critics.

Ransom was born in Pulaski, Tennessee, in 1888, the son of a Methodist minister. He came to Nashville as a boy to attend the Bowen School and entered Vanderbilt when he was only fifteen. He had to leave to teach school for a time, graduated in 1909, and was then awarded a Rhodes scholarship to study classical literature and philosophy at Oxford for three years. Though he never took any graduate degrees in English, he was hired by Mims to teach English at Vanderbilt in 1914.[9]

Among Ransom's first serious students at Vanderbilt was Donald Davidson, who had been born in the small country town of Campbellesville, Tennessee, not far from Ransom's birthplace. Davidson's father was a schoolteacher, and later a school principal, imbued with the spirit of uplift through education. He gave his son the middle name Grady to honor the Atlanta prophet of the New South (his son "discarded it in early college days"). Like Ransom, Davidson worked his way through Vanderbilt by teaching school. In 1919 Davidson joined the Vanderbilt English department.[10]

Allen Tate was born in Winchester, Kentucky, in 1899. Tate's father was a peripatetic businessman who constantly moved his family to follow new jobs. His mother was a proud descendant of Tidewater Virginia aristocracy. They personified the turmoil between the new and the old South, Tate later mused. After entering Vanderbilt in 1918, he quickly earned a reputation as a brilliant, somewhat arrogant protégé.[11]

Robert Penn Warren came from Guthrie, Kentucky, just north of the Tennessee border. He grew up on a farm with his father, a frustrated writer-turned-banker, and his grandfather, a Confederate veteran who held his grandson spellbound with tales of the war and local history. Warren came to Vanderbilt in 1921, when he was only sixteen years old, originally intending to become a chemical engineer. But he became entranced by Ransom and Davidson and in his sophomore year decided to study poetry.[12]

The Fugitive group brought these four and several other Vanderbilt students and professors together with people outside the campus, including members of Nashville's Jewish community. The catalyst for this unlikely fusion of country southern boys and urban Jews was Sydney Mttron Hirsch, a brilliant, eccentric mystic who was frustrated in his own grand ambitions to become a writer. Hirsch had no formal education. He had run away from home as a young man, joined the Navy and traveled throughout Europe and Asia. In Paris and New York, Hirsch had come to know many of the leading figures in the world of art and literature, including Gertrude Stein and Edward Arlington Robinson. He had a fascination with the historical evolution of words and their meanings, and he could easily command an audience with his esoteric allusions to the classics, Oriental philosophy, mythology, and philosophy. Hirsch liked to expound on his enchanting theory that he was one of the seven mystic seers in the world who alone had the power to understand the hidden meaning of life. These gifted few could teach only those who, through some mystical process, were drawn to them—an idea that must have flattered his young admirers as much as Hirsch himself. It was also Hirsch's belief that those who were to understand the inner meaning of life must suffer, must live outside the comforts of this world, must wander apart from society, like fugitives—an image he was fond of invoking.

Hirsch had already made an impact on the Nashville cultural scene with an extravagant Greek pageant, staged in front of the Parthenon in May 1913. "The Fire Regained" had a cast of six hundred, including the wife of former governor Benton McMillan, and a chorus of five hundred. Some three hundred sheep, one thousand pigeons, and eight horses (for the climactic chariot race) filled out the cast. Somehow Hirsch had persuaded the Nashville Retailers Association to sponsor the pageant (his brother-in-law was a prominent member). It became the event of the season, and special trains brought people from miles around to see it. Before the scheduled six performances were over, an estimated five thousand people had seen the pageant.[13] Hirsch stayed on in Nashville, preparing for a renowned literary career, supported by relatives. Worldly, exotic, and more than willing to share his time with young Vanderbilt students who came by initially to see his sister, Goldie, Sydney Hirsch must have seemed simply wonderful to the eager young men who gathered on the balcony of his apartment near campus for long afternoon and evening discussions.

It was Stanley Johnson, later one of the Fugitive group, who first met Hirsch and introduced his friend Donald Davidson to him in the summer of 1915. Johnson enjoyed arguing with Hirsch; Davidson watched in awe, his head swimming with ideas. The two young men brought their professor, Ransom, into the discussions, thinking he could keep up more easily with this mystic sage. Other students, William Yandell Elliott and Alec Brock Stevenson, joined them, and they began to meet frequently through the summer and into the academic year. Hirsch drew his audience into a world of ideas quite remote from the conventional offerings in the Vanderbilt classrooms, and he impressed on them the profound importance of the intellectual's mission.

The group dispersed during World War I while Ransom and Davidson both served in the army; then, by the spring of 1920, they reconvened at Vanderbilt and took up the same informal meetings. More students and faculty joined the group now: Allen Tate, Walter Clyde Curry, Merrill Moore, William Frierson; later Jesse Wills, Ridley Wills, and Robert Penn Warren—all Vanderbilt students, except for Curry, who was a professor in the English department. Laura Riding, James Marshall Frank, and Alfred Starr all were non-Vanderbilt people who joined the group. Hirsch by this time had suffered an undetermined spinal injury that left him an invalid (it fit his theory that inner knowledge required suffering, and his argument that all poets must be maimed).[14] He moved in with his brother-in-law, James Marshall Frank, a well-to-do business man with an interest in intellectual matters. Frank joined the group, and it began meeting at the Franks' home on Whitland Avenue, in a pleasant suburban neighborhood about two miles west of Vanderbilt.

The discussions in this early period focused on no particular topic but ranged widely over any number of philosophical questions and literary or artistic issues, usually under Hirsch's leadership. Ransom by this time had become deeply involved in writing poetry, and in the fall of 1921 he brought some of his work to the group for their criticism. Soon the meetings began to focus solely on the mutual criticism and discussion of one another's poetry and writing. They began bringing carbon copies of the poems and distributing them before a reading to facilitate discussion. This was the seedbed of the New Criticism, with its close attention to structure and the analysis of inner meanings, all influenced by Sydney Hirsch's fascination with the remote origins of words and their hidden significance.

It was Hirsch's idea to start a magazine to publish the poems, and by April 1922 the first issue of *The Fugitive* appeared in Nashville bookstores. In later years the fame of its young authors and the New Criticism was such that it is difficult to recall just how limited a success this magazine was at the time. It lasted only three and one-half years before it folded in December 1925, partly because of the authors' preoccupations but also because of slow subscription sales limited almost entirely to Nashville. Outside the city the magazine received some favorable critical notice (H.L. Mencken liked it and offered the backhanded compliment that it constituted "the entire literature of Tennessee"). But it was a commercial failure in New York bookstores, where little magazines had to find a market to survive.[15]

At Vanderbilt the response to the Fugitives ranged from cold indifference to ridicule and hostility. Chancellor Kirkland refused to pay the one-dollar subscription fee. Edwin Mims had already offered his firm advice as chairman that they forget the whole idea of publishing their own poetry magazine. For all his progressive views on the New South, Mims was quite old-fashioned when it came to scholarly standards. He felt that writing poetry was a poor substitute for scholarship on the great authors and their works. Furthermore, Mims wanted his faculty to publish in established journals and with respected publishers in the North, not begin their own provincial magazine destined, so he thought, to obscurity.[16] Later, after the success of the Fugitive group, it is true that Mims spoke with some pride of their accomplishments. But at the same time, he used his power as head of the English department against some of them, and by the late 1930s most had left Vanderbilt.[17]

But Mims's opposition to the Fugitives was not, at this point, due to any philosophical disagreements on the New South. Indeed, the initial posture of the Fugitives was decidedly modern and self-consciously nonsouthern. The Fugitives were young men determined to break with the confining sentimentality that characterized most southern literature. The foreword to the first issue of the magazine announced the death of this "moonlight and magnolias" tradition. The Fugitive, it stated, "flees from nothing faster than from the high-caste Brahmins of the Old South."[18] The Fugitives were warning their audience, in a slightly brash manner, that they were not trading on Old South genealogy or nostalgia. But aside from this distaste for sentimental, local-color themes, there was no coherent ideology or point of view that bound the poems of the Fugitives. The themes were usually personal and introspective, not aimed at prescribing solutions to social problems. Some in the group, like Tate, were more open to the trends of modern literature and experimentation, but others were inclined to be more respectful of traditional literature and the classics. Whatever their views on modernism, "they did not regard themselves as Southern poets, Old or New."[19]

By December 1925 the magazine ended, and many members of the Fugitive group left Nashville. For those who stayed, the meetings at the Franks continued for three more years before they, too, ended. The Fugitives' hour was brief and, at the time, not a conspicuous event in American literary history. The Fugitives would take on greater importance because of the individual careers of a few writers that were launched at their meetings and because of another, wholly separate intellectual movement that crystallized in the Agrarians five years after the demise of *The Fugitive*.

THE AGRARIAN DEFENSE OF THE SOUTH

As the magazine was closing, a marked shift in intellectual focus was already occurring among some of the key members of the group. Ransom, Davidson, Tate, and Warren all took their own intellectual journeys between about 1925 and 1930, but they arrived on common ground obsessed by southern history and southern tradition as the central focus of their philosophy. The first three, especially Davidson, took up a conservative defense of a mythic, traditional southern way of life and joined it to an aggressive attack on the modern, liberal faith in

Figure 1. The Fugitives in 1923. *Top, from left:* Merrill Moore, Donald Davidson, Sidney Mttron Hirsch, Stanley P. Johnson, William C. Frierson. *Middle row, from left:* James M. Frank, John Crowe Ransom, William Yandell Elliott, Walter Clyde Curry. *Bottom row, from left:* Jesse Ely Wills, Allen Tate, Alec B. Stevenson, Ridley Wills. *Tennessean,* May 27, 1923. Reproduced by Tennessee State Library and Archives (hereafter TSLA).

reason, progress, and technology, which they saw emanating from the North.

For Ransom the journey began sometime after the Scopes trial. His book *God Without Thunder* (1929) was a vindication of the mythological religious view of the world against the abstractions of modern science and rationalism—a contest that had been dramatized at Dayton.[20] For Tate it came in Greenwich Village, where he had gone in 1924 to seek his fame as a writer. While working on his "Ode to the Confederate Dead," perhaps his most famous poem, he discovered a deep well of southern tradition within him and began to explore its philosophical meaning.[21] Davidson's rediscovery of southern tradition found its first expression in a 1926 essay, "The Artist as Southerner" and in his collection of poems *The Tall Men*, a tribute to the heroic pioneers of Tennessee and a condemnation of their weak, modern descendants in Nashville. It was, he later said, "intended to be a dramatic visualization of a modern Southerner, trapped in a distasteful urban environment, subjecting the phenomena of the disordered present to a comparison with the heroic past."[22] Warren turned to his southern roots during his years of graduate study in Berkeley, New Haven, and then in Oxford, England, on a Rhodes scholarship. His first book, a biography of John Brown, the radical abolitionist, was an exploration of Northern intolerance of the South.

According to Davidson, it was the famous Scopes, or "monkey," trial in Dayton, Tennessee, in the summer of 1925 that sparked the kindling of southern sentiment they had gathered into a fiery defense of the South. In Davidson's eyes the trial became a nationally publicized attack on the South and its traditions. H.L. Mencken reported from Dayton that it was "the bunghole of the United States, a cesspool of Baptists, a miasma of Methodism, snake-charmers, phony real-estate operators, and syphilitic evangelists."[23] Behind the ridicule of H.L. Mencken, the acerbic comments of defense lawyer Clarence Darrow, and the prejudice of the national press, Davidson and Ransom saw the arrogant assumption of the modern, liberal ideal that scientific rationalism must prevail over mythic religion. The Scopes trial came to be seen as but one battle in a prolonged historic struggle of the industrial North to destroy the agrarian South.[24]

Vanderbilt's official answer to Tennessee's humiliation at Dayton was to push the "advancing South" faster toward the northern model, to "build more laboratories," as Kirkland put it—and with northern money at that! It was a measure of how undefined Ransom and Davidson's views on these issues were that Edwin Mims actually approached them one day and asked if they would write letters and essays disassociating Vanderbilt from the antievolution law on trial in Dayton. Ransom not only refused but launched into a spirited defense of the fundamentalists' position.[25]

Davidson, who became the most ardent and unwavering polemicist among the four, now understood that the southern tradition he was exploring as a poet required a powerful response by aggressive social critics. "No real defense was being made," he later recalled of the anti-southern attack in the 1920s. "A kind of wholesale surrender was in progress at the upper levels of Southern society." "The South must be defended," he and the others decided, "in historical terms as it was entitled to be defended." But this was no task for introspective Fugitives, aloof from the issues of the day.[26] It would require intellectuals as citizens engaged in battle over the very soul of the South.

"I have been going through a spiritual 'Secession,'" Davidson wrote to Tate in 1927. "I am delighted at your own new annunciation of the True Southern Spirit. . . . " Nashville, Davidson determined, would be his bastion for the coming battle. "My America is here or nowhere." "As to the organic decay . . . there's less of it in these parts (Nashville, especially) than elsewhere in the South." He warned Tate, ". . . I tell you, I am very much stirred up."[27]

The others were stirred up also, and they laid plans to unite their efforts, to present a collective counterattack against the "leviathan" of the industrial North and the unexamined assumptions that supported industrial society. They compared their strategy more than once to Robert E. Lee's "aggressive defense" of the Confederacy and his bold invasion of Pennsylvania (unmindful, apparently, of the disastrous outcome at Gettysburg).[28] By the summer of 1929 the plans had crystallized, and Davidson called on Tate to join in the "big fight," to put together a collection of "openly partisan documents . . . written by native Southerners of our mind . . . [and] intended to come upon the scene with as much vigor as is possible. . . ."[29]

The result was *I'll Take My Stand: The South and the Agrarian Tradition*, by Twelve Southerners, published in November 1930. Eight of the twelve authors were from outside the Fugitive group, but most had been connected to Vanderbilt in some way. Frank Lawrence Owsley, a historian at Vanderbilt, contributed "The Irrepressible Conflict," which explained the Civil War as the result of an intolerant industrial North determined to destroy the southern way of life. Lyle H. Lanier, a former student and psychology professor at Vanderbilt, wrote "A Critique of the Philosophy of Progress." Herman Clarence Nixon taught history (later political science) at Vanderbilt. His essay, "Whither the Southern Economy," examined the persistence of agriculture in the South and urged the region to resist the "conquest" of industrialism. Andrew Nelson Lytle, a former student of Ransom and Davidson at Vanderbilt, wrote "The Hind Tit," surely the most provocative of the twelve essays. It evoked a warm image of the culture of the common folk in the South and a plea to preserve it against the incursions of the modern world. "Throw out the radio and take down the fiddle from the wall," he urged the rural southerner. "Forsake the movies for the play-parties and the square dance."[30] John Donald Wade was teaching in the English department at Vanderbilt when he wrote "The Life and Death of Cousin Lucius," a piece of historical fiction about southern traditions since the Civil War. Henry Blue Kline, a former graduate student in English at Vanderbilt, contributed a biographical sketch. John Gould Fletcher was an Arkansas poet who wrote on education for the anthology. Stark Young, a Mississippi playwright and critic, wrote the concluding essay, "Not in Memorium, But in Defense," an appeal to preserve the best in southern culture. Of the twelve authors only Fletcher and Young had no connection with Vanderbilt.

It was the four former Fugitives—Ransom, Davidson, Tate, and Warren—whose essays were among the most searching. Warren's "The Briar Patch," on the southern Negro, was almost rejected because it was too liberal. It defended segregation but urged southerners to do more to ensure equality for blacks within that system. Tate's essay on religion argued for the necessity of mythology as the basis of faith and rejected the liberal theology of modern society. Southerners could regain the religious tradition they had lost only by some form of undefined "violent and revolutionary" action aimed at "cutting away the overgrowth and getting back to the roots."

Davidson's essay, "A Mirror for Artists," explored the fundamental antagonism of modern industrial society toward art and the humanistic tradition. It depicted the South as the last American refuge for preserving the European heritage of the arts as an integral part of life. He called upon southern writers and artists to reclaim the southern tradition—as artists and as citizens in opposition to the threat of industrialism. Ransom's "Reconstructed but Unregenerate" amplified the idea that southern agragrian life was continuous with the older European way. It was northern industrial society, with its unbridled materialism, that had deviated from the mainstream of western culture, not the agrarian South.

Ransom also wrote the unsigned "Statement of Principles" introducing the twelve essays and laying out the common points of attack the book was intended to advance. It supplied the best single statement of the Agrarian philosophy. Industrial society, Ransom explained, was ruled by the cult of applied science that prevails without serious question as to its effect on human happiness. The economic disorder and social inequalities that inevitably attend industrialism will, in their excesses, lead to regulation by the state and eventually to communism (some of the authors originally wanted to title the book *Tracts Against Communism*). Industrial society was also aesthetically ruinous. It has no tolerance for mythical religion or art, nor for the gentle graces of manners and human intimacy—it was, in short, dehumanizing.

The agrarian way of life, Ransom, offered "does not stand in particular need of definition." Here Ransom exposed the central weakness of the Agrarians' stand. They were superb at attacking the industrial leviathan and pointing out all its corruption, spoilage, and ominous dangers. When it came to defining Agrarian society—much less outlining a program for achieving it—the authors fell back on an evocation of the South as the model. It was an image of the South that existed only in a mythical past, one with none of the wrenching poverty, disease, or class and racial oppression that had so tragically shaped southern life. But to point out the lack of reality in their image, as their critics so frequently did, may miss the point. These were men who understood the power of myths to take hold of people's lives. As for the corollary charge of impracticality, the Agrarians, it is true, failed to offer any specific program of action. But they were attempting to take the first, and perhaps more important step, in raising the very idea that choices were possible, that industrialism, progress, science, or modernism by whatever name need not be embraced thoughtlessly.

The book appeared simultaneously with the collapse of the once-powerful financial empire of Caldwell and Company, which brought the Depression full force to Nashville. The Agrarians' attack on northern industrialism and its New South collaborators, though aimed at the robust economy of the 1920s, might have taken on deeper—perhaps even prophetic—importance during the economic crisis of the 1930s. On the other hand, conditions of widespread unemployment, bank foreclosures, and dustbowl migrations were not the most opportune for questioning the value of materialism or progress. Nor did the expansion of the New Deal, with its welcomed relief programs and Tennessee Valley Authority, invite southern skepticism about the intrusion of federal authority in regional affairs.

Some critics took the book seriously and even credited it with raising provocative questions about the future of the South, but most dismissed the Agrarians as hopeless reactionaries, "neo-confederates," whose ideas were totally irrelevant to the realities of the contemporary South. H. L. Mencken wrote "left to the farmers of Tennessee, [the Agrarians] would be clad in linsey-woolsey and fed on sidemeat, and the only books they could read would be excessively orthodox."[31] Even the student magazine at Vanderbilt, *Masquerader*, lampooned the Agrarians in an editorial and a cover cartoon showing Davidson, Tate, and Ransom as farmers protecting the tree of civilization from the pests of modern technology.[32] The events of the 1930s and the critical response to the Agrarian manifesto encouraged some of the authors to modify and even abandon the stand they took in 1930.[33] It was left to Ransom and Davidson to defend the Agrarian point of view at several public debates throughout the South and, with Tate, in a stream of articles and books elaborating themes laid out in *I'll Take My Stand*.[34]

Another collective effort appeared in *Who Owns America?*, coedited

Figure 2. The Vanderbilt Agrarians Donald Davidson, Allan Tate, and John Crowe Ransom defending the "tree of Civilization" from the pests of modern technology, as depicted in an irreverent cartoon on the cover of a student magazine. *Masquerader* 10 (Dec. 1933), Vanderbilt University Library (hereafter VUL) Special Collections, reproduced by Vanderbilt University Photographic Archives.

in 1936 by Tate and Herbert Agar, with essays by several of the Agrarians. But this book took the cause into more cosmopolitan channels by joining southern agrarianism to the ideas of English Distributists.[35] Ransom had seriously pursued studies of economic theory and had a keen interest in subsistence farming as a practical solution to America's ills. But he finally abandoned the cause and returned to the life of a poet and literary critic when he left Vanderbilt in 1937 for Kenyon College in Ohio. By 1945 he publicly renounced his agrarian stand.[36]

Now Davidson carried on what was virtually a lost cause. His collection of essays *The Attack on Leviathan* appeared in 1938, a full defense of his Agrarian stand. As editor of the *Tennessean* book page and author of a weekly column entitled "The Spyglass" (later "Critic's Almanac"), Davidson enjoyed a popular forum from which to address the citizens of Nashville. He was ambivalent about the city and its business classes in particular. In his poems and essays Davidson savaged Nashville, with its smoke and grime, its shallow culture, and its boosters willing to sell their souls for another shoe factory or textile plant. In a 1936 essay Davidson recalled the Nashville he had come to as a young college student in 1910: "To country boys in 1910, the cities were . . . shining, glorious places, ... Now the New Jerusalem of my college days no longer glitters." In summer, he complained, the streets of downtown Nashville broil the pedestrian because "all the shade trees were cut away to make room for store fronts and modern paving."[37] In winter the "smoke of its engines and furnaces hangs over the city for months; it stops up the lungs, it blackens books, it soils public buildings." As the central city decays and people leave for the suburbs, "civilization has gone," Davidson lamented, "and in its place . . . more commercial greed than ever, less honor, less public spirit, less religion, less of the grace and beauty of life."[38]

The same damning tone was evident earlier in *The Tall Men*, his 1927 collection of poems. The narrator is a Nashville suburbanite commuting downtown by streetcar:

> And my soft proud body is borne on the smooth
> Parallel rails into a city hoarse
> With nine o'clock which brings the swivel-chair
> And to the hungry brain the pelt of typewriters.

In "Fire on Belmont Street," the prize-winning poem that concludes *The Tall Men*, Davidson depicts "some plump burgher of Nashville—some devout Rotarian or Kiwanian perhaps" rushing to a fire in a suburban neighborhood built on the graves of Indians whose land is now despoiled. The fire is the revenge of nature

> On this gray city, blinded, soiled, and kicked
> By fat blind fools. . . .[39]

Davidson could also be encouraging in his praise of Nashville and its progress in the arts. Perhaps no individual in Nashville, and certainly none in the Fugitive or Agrarian groups, did more than Davidson to promote the cultural renaissance of Nashville. He was even willing to credit businessmen with the city's cultural revival in the 1920s. "We might as well be realists," he wrote uncharacteristically in 1928: "The key is in the hands of the business men." "Under their touch art takes courage, and independent opinion thrives."[40] He called on the business leaders of Nashville and the South to preserve the very traditions they and the New South threatened to destroy.

In these instances Davidson seemed to understand the fundamental contradiction of a culture in which business leaders and business values could be at once the enemies and the saviors of intellectual and artistic life. It is an American paradox that even the most avaricious *nouveaux riches* feel compelled to somehow legitimize their claim to social status by supporting universities, museums, symphonies and otherwise patronizing the arts. The artists and intellectuals who depend on the philanthropy of wealthy capitalists, in turn, are expected to cultivate values or advance humanistic ideas at odds with the utilitarianism and materialism that rules the business world. Surely the Agrarians who attacked the leviathan from Vanderbilt—a university named after its principal benefactor, a New York railroad tycoon who won his fortune in part by aiding the Yankee war to destroy the Old South—understood this paradox better than most.

A PARTHENON FOR ART

Nashville in the 1920s was a fascinating example of the alliance between commerce and culture. The city experienced a broad-based revival in nearly all aspects of the arts. The perfect symbol of the city's cultural aspirations was the Parthenon, built originally as the Gallery of Fine Arts for the Tennessee Centennial Exposition of 1897. Nashville's citizens refused to allow it to be torn down, as the other temporary buildings were after the exposition closed. But years of exposure decayed the plaster and lathe structure and made it unsafe for further use. In 1920 the Park Commission, which included Nashville's most prominent and wealthy citizens, decided to reconstruct it with a new, aggregate concrete that would weather the ages. Nashville's Parthenon was an exact-scale replica of the original in Athens, with sculptures on the frieze reproduced from moldings of the Elgin marbles and finished by local artists, George J. Zolnay, Belle Kinney, and Leopold Scholz. The outside was completed in 1925, the interior six years later.

Even before it was finished the Parthenon became the scene of nu-

Figure 3. The original Parthenon, built for the Tennessee Centennial Exposition in 1897, was a temporary structure in bad repair by 1920 when the new structure was begun. Photograph by C. Wexell, courtesy of Jewish Federation Archives and the Parthenon.

Figure 4. The Parthenon of Nashville under construction, c. 1926. Courtesy of Wilbur Creighton, of Foster & Creighton Company, the general contractors on the project.

merous artistic events, from touring exhibits of paintings to dance recitals on the portico. "Its influence flows with perfect harmony into the cultural life of a half-submerged people whose latent hereditary interests, always artistic, have been awakened by its radiant influence," observed one proud Nashvillian.[41] Besides swelling local pride, the reconstruction of the Parthenon brought favorable attention in the national press. The *New York Times* proclaimed the "Glory of ancient Greece has been reproduced to enrich modern life. . . ."[42] The *Literary Digest*, quoting a snobbish French observer, referred to it as "an expression of reverence for European intellectuality."[43] *The Outlook* played on the conflict between the city's cultural affectations and the belching coal smoke of an "Athenian Pittsburgh" but applauded the effort: "on the rising tide of its commercial progress it builds its Parthenon."[44] Donald Davidson commented on the same theme with more bite in his poem "On a Replica of the Parthenon":

> Why do they come? What do they seek?
> Who build but never read their Greek?

The city's coal smoke blackens the statues on the pediment,

> And gods, like men, to soot revert.
> . . . .
> But what blind motion, what dim last
> Regret of men who slew their past
> Raised up this bribe against their fate.

These men who "slew their past" seemed eager to restore some replica of it and infuse it with cultural importance. The Parthenon became the repository of the newly organized Nashville Museum of Art, a permanent gallery of art established for the first time in the city. Its predecessor, the Nashville Art Association, had been founded in 1883. On a small endowment it managed to support classes, lectures, and music recitals, but as of 1911 the association's dreams of a permanent art collection had resulted in the purchase of only one painting. Under the first administration of Mayor Hilary Howse (1909–15) the creation of a city Art Commission gave more financial support for the arts, but this was abandoned by the economy-minded reformers who followed Howse. With the reconstruction of the Parthenon the Park Commission decided to turn its basement floor into a gallery, at least until a more suitable gallery could be established. The Nashville Museum of Art was organized in 1924 with Mrs. James C. Bradford as director.[45] In 1925, because of the efforts of the Centennial Club, a traveling exhibit from the Grand Central Art Galleries in New York was displayed in the still unfinished interior of the Parthenon. The show, which stayed for two weeks and was "thronged each day," stirred great pride and much talk of the need for a permanent collection of art and a museum separate from the Parthenon in Nashville. "Nashville's big business men and club leaders," one magazine reported, "are expressing their belief that a permanent art gallery is a great civic asset."[46] Within two years an anonymous donation (from a "former Tennessean") of an art collection valued at $100,000 was announced. This gift, the *Tennessean* proclaimed, "will probably do more than any other attribute . . . in making the . . . 'Athens of the South' a reality for Nashville."[47]

NASHVILLE'S MUSICAL SOUL

The music world also came alive in Nashville in the 1920s. For years before World War I, trained musicians and an appreciative audience had been cultivated in several of the city's schools. The most accomplished in this regard was Ward-Belmont, a prestigious woman's school that drew talent from all parts of the South. Its School of Music (later known as the Conservatory of Music and opened to men as well as women) sponsored a steady round of lectures, student and faculty recitals, and performances by outstanding visiting musicians and singers. The Ward-Belmont faculty included several who were to become vital elements of the Nashville music scene of the 1920s: Frederick Arthur Henkel, organist and pianist; Kenneth D. Rose, violinist; Lawrence Goodman, pianist; and Signor Gaetano Salvatore de Luca, vocalist. Several of its students also won fame outside Nashville as singers and musicians.[48]

Another long-standing influence on Nashville musical taste was the Ryman Auditorium and its manager, Lula C. Naff. Beginning in 1904 Miss Naff was hired to book a variety of cultural events, from lyceum lectures to opera and vaudeville shows. In 1914 she leased the Ryman on her own and became an aggressive promoter of the arts in Nashville. When Irish tenor John McCormack insisted on a guarantee of $3,000 in 1916, she promptly borrowed against a second mortgage on her house to get the cash, nailed up posters all over town, pushed the newspapers to promote the event, and filled the house. Her role as Nashville's cultural impresario was launched that night. Over the years she brought to the city the best talent she could muster, convinced that Nashville audiences would pay top dollar for high quality. The city's good rail connections and central location made it a logical stopover for one-night stands by touring performers, and Naff earned Nashville a reputation for profitable performances. In any given season she learned to mix a variety of acts that might include the great opera soloist Enrique Caruso, a Gilbert and Sullivan musical, minstrel shows, comedy acts, vaudeville, and New York plays.[49] The 1924 season, reviewed by George Pullen Jackson in the *Banner*, included John Phillip Sousa and his band, Metropolitan Opera star Giuseppe de Luca, pianist Vladimir de Pachmann, contralto Ernestine Schumann-Heink, Paul Whiteman, the "jazz king" and his orchestra, the world renowned violinist Jasha Heifetz, two visiting performances by the St. Louis Symphony orchestra, opera by Feodor Chaliapin, Shakespearean drama from actor Fritz Lieter, two marionette shows, and several lyric opera performances, including *Madam Butterfly* and *Rigoletto*.[50]

The Ryman was importing all types of culture while Ward-Belmont was exporting some its best student talent. In the 1920s Nashville developed homegrown cultural institutions drawing on local talent and catering to local audiences. This movement toward musical self-sufficiency ran parallel to the southern renaissance in literature, to which the Fugitives and Agrarians had contributed. But it also bore striking resemblance to the campaigns of local boosters to "Buy Nashville-Made Goods" and "Sell Nashville to Itself." It was remarkable how the 1920s rhetoric of economic growth and civic improvement flowed smoothly into campaigns for cultural uplift.[51]

This booster spirit was vividly illustrated in the drive to organize the Nashville Symphony Orchestra in 1920. When news arrived that a symphony was being organized in Meridian, Mississippi, the *Tennessean* twitted local pride by asking: "IS NASHVILLE TO BE OUTDONE BY A LITTLE JERK-WATER TOWN IN THE BACKWOODS OF THE COTTON BELT?"[52] Early in 1920 a group of local amateur and professional musicians formed an orchestra and began practicing. Later that year a Nashville Symphony Society organized and elected as its president and symphony manager George Pullen Jackson, a Vanderbilt professor and music critic for the *Banner*.[53] An orchestra of sixty musicians ("100 percent Nashville"), with F. Arthur Henkel as their conductor, began its first season that fall. It represented "Nashville's unexpressed yearning for a higher and nobler self-expression . . . [a] rediscovery of Nashville's soul." The symphony was organized "not by snobs, not by those who would buy elsewhere a commercialized brand of 'culture' and engraft it on us, but by a small group of Nashville's self-sacrificing lovers of the highest and best in music, and believers in the tenet that all things that are truly good for a people come through self development." The business interests who sponsored the symphony were promised that it would "do much to center the attention of people of culture and worth elsewhere on Nashville."[54]

After playing in Ryman Auditorium, then the Vendome Theater, for the first five years, the symphony moved in 1925 into the spacious new quarters of the War Memorial Auditorium.[55] The symphony struggled against low subscriptions, no endowment, and a rising deficit. By its seventh season the future was uncertain. The symphony still lacked a broad-based audience. David R. Gebhart, chairman of the Department of Music at Peabody, blamed a southern tradition that assigned music appreciation only to "little children and young ladies."

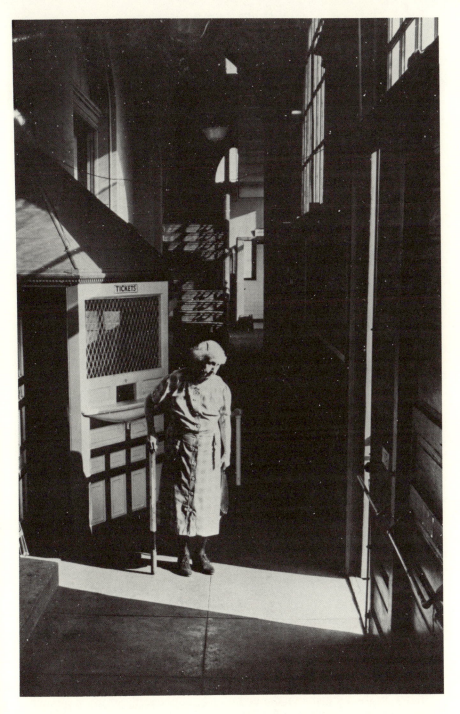

Figure 5. Lula C. Naff, the impresario of the Ryman Auditorium, in the lobby of the Ryman sometime in her—and the Ryman's—declining years. Nashville Room, Ben West Public Library.

Nashville, he pointed out, was particularly deficient in supporting music education in the public schools, so the ability to overcome this legacy in coming generations was seriously hampered.[56] But appeals to local pride kept the symphony afloat, and subscriptions increased. By 1928 Charles Mitchell, the new president of the Symphony Society, reported with satisfaction, "the taste of Nashville people for orchestral music had decidedly grown. . . ."[57]

As the symphony was struggling to get on its feet in 1927, Nashville musicians and business leaders launched the Nashville Conservatory of Music. Directed by Signor de Luca, who soon left Ward-Belmont, the conservatory aimed at nothing less than "making Nashville the musical center of the South. . . ." The conservatory had the backing of the most powerful and wealthy men in the city, including Joel Cheek, the Maxwell House coffee magnate who was a major patron of music in this period, James G. Stahlman and Luke Lea, publishers of the *Banner* and the *Tennessean*, respectively, and the leading bankers, insurance executives, and businessmen in Nashville. They put the conservatory on a solid business footing with a stock subscription of $250,000, which sold readily in the business community. The money was used to build a new "fully-equipped and beautifully furnished" building on West End Avenue across from Vanderbilt, and to hire a professional faculty of "nationally-known artist instructors."

Signor de Luca was the man who inspired Nashville's business leaders in this musical venture. During nine years at Ward-Belmont, de Luca enjoyed remarkable success with his students and brought national attention to Nashville. Joseph T. MacPherson ("Nashville's Own Son," the *Tennessean* crowed) went from de Luca's schooling to a triumphal engagement with the Metropolitan Opera Company in New York. After his first season with the Met he returned to a city bursting with pride. Mayor Hilary Howse presented him the key to the city, and he entertained a packed house in Ryman Auditorium with his arias.[58] Another student, James Melton, won popular fame as a radio singer with "Roxy's Gang." Signor de Luca's experiment with a civic opera, the Home Talent Grand Opera in 1925, was considered a "triumph" in the eyes of local music lovers.[59]

By the fall of 1928 de Luca had drawn to Nashville an accomplished faculty of fourteen people from the musical centers of Europe and the North. The conservatory offered training in voice, piano, and dance.[60] The instructors in dance were Louise Smith and Sarah Jeter, who had opened their own dance studio on Eighteenth Avenue the year before. Jeter had trained in Chicago and New York, and had studied with Ted Shawn in the Denishawn dance he had popularized. Smith, a pianist, was a dance accompanist who had trained at Ward-Belmont, where Jeter also had taught earlier. Both returned to Nashville with cosmopolitan

Figure 6. Arthur Henkel and some members of the Nashville Symphony in a 1927 opera production. Francis Robinson Collection, Vanderbilt University Photographic Archives.

Figure 7. The faculty of the new Nashville Conservatory of Music, September 1928. *Front row, from left:* Wanda Labunska, Verna Brackinreed, Erich Sorantin, G. S. de Luca (Director), Wiktor Labunski, Louise S. Smith. *Second row:* Eduard Loessel, Evalyne MacNevin, Marguerite Shannon, Sarah C. Jeter, C. P. Bartolini, May Herbert Dalton. *Third row:* F. Arthur Henkel, Sydney Dalton, Browne Martin. Jeter-Smith Collection, Nashville Room, Ben West Public Library.

experience, and they introduced a generation of young Nashville women to the art of dance.[61]

With the talent assembled at the conservatory, Nashville was assured of a steady supply of well-trained musicians and singers. The city's aspirations to become the musical center of the South, given the weak competition from other southern centers, seemed a realistic goal for music lovers. At this time the rise of "hillbilly music," which eventually put Music City, U.S.A. on the map, was far from the minds of Signor de Luca and his wealthy patrons.

THE NASHVILLE STAGE

The renaissance of the 1920s also inspired new interest in the theater. The Ryman, the Vendome, the Princess, and other theaters had booked visiting plays, musicals, vaudeville acts, and minstrel shows for years, but local talent was rarely exposed to public performances. The Stagecrafters, organized in 1906, was an amateur drama club that put on occasional plays for charities.[62] Beginning sometime after 1910 the movie craze threatened to displace the stage, even its popular vaudeville acts. Loew's Vendome Theater, one of the most popular downtown, converted to the screen after World War I, and Nashville's stage lights began to dim.

In the fall of 1920 the Orpheum Theater billed stage plays by the Hazel Burgess Players, a small stock company directed by Albert Lando, who planned to use Nashville as a base for road trips to towns throughout Middle Tennessee. Anne Rankin, cultural reporter for the *Tennessean*, urged Nashville to support the effort: "Shall the intelligence of a community like ours grow dull . . . its interests sink to apathy, and its taste decay, because the picture screen is its only stimulant?" But the company apparently failed commercially in a short time.[63]

Elsewhere in America playwrights, drama devotees, and self-appointed guardians of popular morals were fighting the movie craze and the more vulgar products of vaudeville. They produced new plays and organized community little theaters; others simply denounced the movies and vaudeville. The Drama League of America (organized nationally in 1910) sent a representative to Nashville in 1921 to organize a local affiliate. She spoke before the Centennial Club and appealed to the women of Nashville to counter the "insidious and dangerous influence" of the "faulty and often time [sic] immoral productions" that appeared on the screen and stage. By that fall a local Drama League had formed. H.B. Schermerhorn, a Vanderbilt professor and director of the Stagecrafters, was elected first president of the league, and the two organizations joined hands to promote legitimate theater in Nashville.[64]

Figure 8. Nashville Conservatory dance students at the Parthenon, 1929. *From left:* Claudia Whitson, Clara Collier, and Marian Curell. Jeter-Smith Collection, Nashville Room, Ben West Public Library.

It was not until 1926, however, that Nashville (rebuked in the *Tennessean* as "long neglectful of the drama") organized its own Little Theater. Lark Taylor, a Vanderbilt drama teacher, and Pauline Townsend, of Ward-Belmont, went to the business community for support. Harry Sudekum, part owner of a movie house chain, donated use of the Hillsboro Theater for the Little Theater's trial season beginning in April 1926.[65] When the Drama League joined forces with the new theater group that fall, the company was reorganized as the Little Theater Guild, and Ramon Savitch replaced Taylor as director.[66] The Little Theater struggled to gain an audience with entertaining comedies, only to be chided by critics in the *Tennessean* and the *Banner*. Donald Davidson, critic for the *Tennessean*, wrote: "We cannot ever be satisfied merely with light, healthy comedy, if we really, as a community, have any serious interest in the drama."[67] But the more demanding plays did not help the box office, and the Little Theater continued to search for the right mix of drama and entertainment.[68]

In the spring of 1927, with the Nashville renaissance at full tide, Donald Davidson looked with some satisfaction at the cultural progress of his city: "not since the Civil War tragically interrupted the older Southern civilization has there been a year more rich in evidence that we are artistically awake and active in all the fields which give meaning and beauty to life." The orchestra had completed its seventh season with encouraging signs of maturity. Nashville artists were returning from "metropolitan triumphs." The Fisk Jubilee Singers and Vanderbilt Glee Club offered several concerts, and a civic opera "done entirely by local talent" climaxed the musical season. The Little Theater Guild had arrived the year before to redeem "us from the theatrical poverty which we have endured since the movies came to feed us treacle and spectacular titillations." The Nashville Art Association was promoting an art museum and assembling its own collection. The lovers of literature and poetry were treated to lectures of visiting authors sponsored by the Centennial Club and by Vanderbilt's Cole lecture series. Moreover, books and poems were pouring forth from local writers. "Everywhere and every day," Davidson exclaimed, "I meet people who are projecting or writing novels, poems, plays, biographies, histories, articles, essays. Ideas are in the air."

"It is all very well for our business friends to think of these enterprises in terms of advertising . . . ," Davidson went on. "But . . . such undertakings exist for themselves and for ourselves. . . ." "In our older Southern civilization we were self-sufficient: . . . Our prosperity should mean that we return to that condition and practice a provincialism of the high-minded sort which made Athens great."[69]

Within a few years of Davidson's encouraging report the prosperity of the 1920s and the artistic luxuries it allowed were swept away by the Great Depression. Those who saw the arts as a counterforce to modern materialism and business values were now forced to realize just how dependent art was on business. Davidson lost his job with the *Tennessean* following the collapse of Caldwell and Company. The symphony folded in 1930, not to be revived until 1946. The Conservatory of Music came to an end in 1936 after the death of Signor de Luca. The Little Theater ended in 1932 (to be reincarnated in the Community Playhouse in 1935). The plans for an art museum were raised again in the 1930s, but they died quietly amidst the pressing claims for other public services.[70]

The Parthenon, reconstructed with modern concrete to endure the ages, was finished inside as the Depression settled on the city. It was at once the proud symbol of Nashville's boast as the Athens of the South and the most durable reminder of the renaissance in intellectual and cultural life that flourished for a time amid the coal smoke and material prosperity of Nashville in the 1920s.

COMING IN FROM THE COUNTRY

While the Nashville renaissance was enlivening the musical, artistic, and literary arts in the 1920s, on another level the character of the city was being shaped by a flood of migrants from the country. Oblivious to the debate between the Agrarians and the modernists, swarms of country folk throughout Tennessee and the South voted with their feet, and they voted to pull up their agrarian roots and head for the city. Many of them thrived in the urban environment and embraced its ways with enthusiasm, rarely looking back at the rural life they had left behind. Others became mired in Nashville's slums and vice districts, and they must have wondered why the city had seemed so appealing.

As the city filled with newcomers, the social welfare agencies, schools, churches, and civic organizations reached out to absorb them into the community. The Commercial Club, for example, sponsored Know Nashville Day in May 1920, and the Chamber of Commerce followed in 1925 with a thirty-nine-week campaign to Sell Nashville to Itself. Thousands of pamphlets, posters, and lapel buttons, along with a stream of newspaper columns, all strained to instill a sense of local patriotism among Nashville's burgeoning population.[1] For rural migrants in the South, these and other efforts were the equivalent of the Americanization programs that the foreign-born faced in the cities of the North.

THE GREAT SOUTHERN MIGRATION

They came in droves from small country towns and from isolated farms. Most came from within roughly a one-hundred-mile radius of

Nashville that extended to the Cumberland Plateau on the east and the Highland Rim on the west, north into southern Kentucky and south below the Alabama border. The cityward migration was more intense closer to the urban magnet and along the rail lines and highways that connected the rural hinterland with the metropolis of Middle Tennessee. Some came into the city in steps, first from the farm to one of the small country towns or county seats, from there into Nashville. Most had visited Nashville on weekend shopping trips or while going to football games at Vanderbilt, baseball games at Sulphur Dell, or perhaps a performance at the Grand Ole Opry.

The rural migrants typically were young people, able to pick up roots, with little to risk and much to gain. They were more often young women who filled Nashville's burgeoning demand for female workers in stores, banks, insurance companies, offices, and factories. These young migrants left the country to escape a depressed farm economy plagued by declining prices and transformed by a process of mechanization that favored large-scale farmers (who could afford the new tractors) and displaced the mule-and-plow farmer. They left families that had too many children and not enough land. They left also to find some freedom from confining families, churches, and rural neighbors who disapproved of the modern fashions that invaded rural hinterlands by way of radios, movies, popular magazines — fashions that youth were embracing with enthusiasm in the 1920s. Blacks left for all these reasons and more — the limited educational opportunities, poor social services, and oppressive race relations that characterized most rural counties.

The migrants came to the city, first of all, for economic opportunity. The city offered jobs in offices, stores, banks, or in factories, laundries, and private homes as servants. Compared with farm work, the hours were short, wages good, and the work light. They came to the high schools and the night schools and the business schools that emerged to offer vocational training to a new, urban work force. They came also for the movies, the automobiles, the restaurants, and the ice cream; some came for the delicious variety of sins the city offered to adventurous country youth. They came to experience all these exciting aspects of the city with thousands of others their own age.

Brothers, cousins, friends, and new acquaintances who had come in earlier from the country eased the migrant's passage into the city way of living. They shared housing with newcomers, vouched for them on job applications, and introduced them to the urban world. More visible forms of aid to the rural migrant appeared in a variety of institutions — from night schools and boarding homes to settlement houses, welfare agencies, fundamentalist churches, and political machines — all adapted in their own way to serve the waves of country immigrants.

Defenders of rural society watched the flight to the city with great alarm, and they devised an array of responses to the popular World

War I song: "How're you goin' to keep 'em down on the farm?" "The present universal cry of 'keep the boy on the farm,'" one federal official advised, "can and should be expanded into a great public sentiment for making country life more attractive in every way." He recommended "modern social, educational, and other opportunities."[2] But others realized that the invasion of modern life in the form of better schools, automobiles, good roads, radios, and movies only made the young people want city life more. John Washington Butler (later the author of Tennessee's "monkey law" against teaching evolution), writing to the *Macon County Times* in 1922, blamed the public schools for teaching young people "to hate manual labor such as farm work." "They want to be clerks, bookkeepers and stenographers and wear biled [boiled] shirts all the time and loud neckties and collars so high they have to jump to spit over the top of them. They want to get in what they call society . . . in the cities, and marry some society belle who thinks eggs grow on trees and that butterflies make the butter."[3] A letter to the *Carthage Courier* complained that the Old Hickory Silk Mills (DuPont's rayon plant) were draining the Cumberland counties of their young labor force, leaving behind nothing but old men and women, with churches and schools nearly deserted.[4] The elders complained, but the young people kept coming into the city.

The great migration of country people into the city is one of the central themes in the social history of Nashville and the South. Before World War I the flow of foreign immigrants across the Atlantic fed the great cities of the North while southern urbanization was being generated primarily by the migration of its own rural population from country to city. The South consequently lagged behind the North in urban growth. With World War I and the immigration restriction laws that followed it, the relentless surge of American urban growth was now due to a massive shift from farm to city. The South, with its large, prolific rural population, became a major supplier of urban migrants. Many of these migrants, blacks in particular, left the region for the industrial cities of the North and the West. But a large segment of the southern rural exodus flowed into the cities of the South.[5]

Nashville offers an unusually good historical window on the process of rural migration and urban adaptation, for it was scrutinized by dozens of sociologists and their students at several of the city's colleges. Nashville's pioneer in sociological surveys was Willis D. Weatherford, who came to Vanderbilt in 1897 from a rural Methodist background in Texas. Weatherford began his career with the YMCA during his years at Vanderbilt before he graduated from the Divinity School in 1902. Weatherford went to work for the YMCA full time and became devoted to improving understanding between the races in the South. He wrote *Negro Life in the South* in 1910 and was active in the Southern Sociological Congress that met in Nashville in 1912 to promote scientific

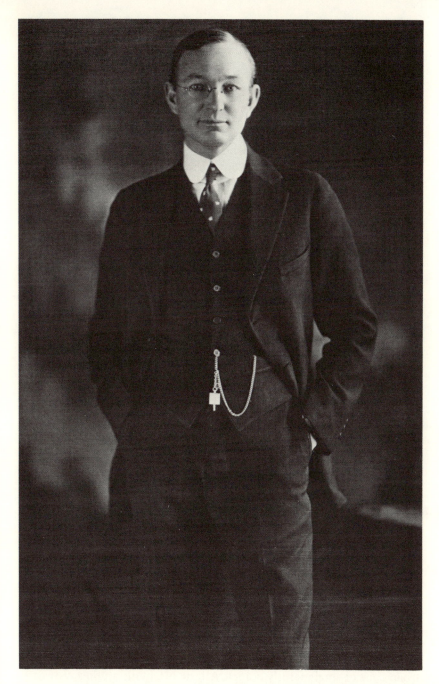

Figure 9. Willis D. Weatherford, c. 1910, a Methodist social reformer, cofounder of the Commission on Interracial Cooperation, a principal organizer of the YMCA Graduate School, and later a faculty member at Fisk University. He and his students conducted numerous surveys of Nashville's poor black community and promoted modern social welfare programs in the city. Courtesy of Willis D. Weatherford, Jr.

welfare and social reform. After World War I, he and Will Alexander, a Methodist minister in Atlanta, organized the Commission on Interracial Cooperation. In 1919 Weatherford founded the YMCA Graduate School in Nashville. Designed to train YMCA workers throughout the South, Weatherford's school became a center for the sociological approach to poverty and racial degradation. It served as a vital connecting link for the new sociologists who came to Vanderbilt, where Walter Krueger and Walter J. Reckless taught, to Fisk, where Charles S. Johnson conducted his research, and to Scarritt College.[6]

The studies that came out of all these schools in the 1920s and 1930s were influenced by the "new sociology" that had emerged at the University of Chicago under the leadership of Robert Park, Ernest Burgess, and others. Park and the "Chicago School" of urban sociology understood the process of urbanization to be pulling rural migrants out of a deeply rooted folk culture, organized around the family and kin group and knit together by a system of shared religious and social values that were passed with little change from one generation to the next. The city, into which these folk cast their lives, required a massive adjustment on their part. Urban society, in Park's view, was the antithesis of folk society: large, anonymous, and highly heterogeneous. In urban society, people met as strangers in narrowly segmented, impersonal roles. Among those who failed to adjust to urban society the sociologists found traumatic social "disorganization." Youth rebelled against the archaic values of their parents and fell into patterns of truancy, delinquency, and youth gangs. Young women, forced by economic circumstances, resorted to prostitution. Gambling, alcoholism, drug abuse, filth, violence, and grinding poverty were among the symptoms of disorganization that the sociologists identified with the experience of rural folk entering the urban world.[7]

The new sociologists joined their theory of social breakdown and adjustment to a theory of the physical evolution, or ecology, of the modern city. Beneath the jumbled disorder of rapid urban growth they saw an organic selection that produced several neatly defined concentric zones within the city. The expanding central business district created on its edges a zone of blight and poverty in rooming houses and dilapidated mansions abandoned by the wealthy. Beyond this zone of disorganization working-class families found small homes and apartments in close proximity to the factories and warehouses while the wealthier middle-class families retreated to a purely residential suburban zone of single-family homes. All the Nashville studies were careful to map the exact location of the "selected area" under scrutiny and to describe its particular "moral environment" and "social characteristics."[8] Nashville's topography and racial segregation defied the kind of neat concentric-circle model that the Chicago School sociologists had invented, but the pattern was similar.

The sociologists often exaggerated the degree of social disorganization and underestimated the inner resources of the urban migrants and poor. But the social surveys they left behind have preserved a picture of the rural migrant and the urban poor that would have been otherwise impossible for the historian to reconstruct. Together with the interviews of migrants, who tell the story from their own perspective, these materials can illuminate an important part of that picture.

The exact number of migrants that came into Nashville can only be estimated in terms of net migration figures from one federal census to the next. One demographer estimated the net gain from migration to Davidson County during the 1920s at 29,286, about 53 percent of the total population growth, the remainder being due to natural increase. In the 1930s Nashville's growth slowed, and net migration to the county was estimated at 16,389, or about 48 percent of the total county growth. The racial makeup of this migration changed also: about 83 percent of the net migration gain was white during the 1920s; in the next decade, when the black northward migration slowed, only 64 percent was white.[9]

Whatever the numbers of net migration gain, they leave out the thousands more who came and left within the decade, many en route to the North, to neighboring cities in the South, or back to the farms. The movement to the city was also followed by frequent moves within the city, meaning that many neighborhoods, especially poor and working-class neighborhoods, were constantly churning with newcomers. Vanderbilt sociologist Walter Reckless traced a random sample of 7,000 adult males in Nashville from 1926 to 1936 and found that only 13 percent remained at the same address throughout the decade. More than half left the city altogether, and the rest (25 percent) had moved within the city.[10] October 1 every year (a tradition going back to the 1870s) was "moving day" in Nashville, when leases were up and thousands of renters found new quarters. In 1923, the *Tennessean* estimated, about 50,000 Nashvillians would change their addresses on this single day.[11]

THE MIGRANT GIRL

Within this volatile population, there was a special concern for the young migrant woman who made up a large part of the migration. Beginning in World War I the Nashville job market for white women expanded rapidly, particularly occupations as stenographers, office clerks, store saleswomen, and as textile or clothing factory workers. The 1920 census (see table 1) showed that women made up roughly one-third of the work force. Almost half of Nashville's working women were in do-

Table 1: Nashville's Female Labor Force by Race, 1920, 1940

	All Women		Black Women		All Women, as Percentage of Occupation Group	
	1920	1940	1920	1940	1920	1940
Manufacturing	18%	18%	8%	4%	18%	29%
Transportation, communication	3	3	—	—	7	12
Trade, sales	7	15	1	5	14	27
Public service	—	4	—	—	—	27
Professional service	8	15	3	10	47	61
Finance, insurance	—	5	—	1	—	38
Clerical	15	—	1	—	47	—
Domestic, personal service	49	38	85	78	76	75
Other	—	4	—	1	—	—
Total	100%	100%	100%	100%	32%	37%
N	17,929	23,581	9,106	8,946	17,929	23,581

SOURCE: Department of Commerce, Bureau of Census, *Fourteenth Census of the United States* . . . , 4, *Population, 1920, Occupation* (Washington, D.C., 1923), 129, 1149; idem, *Sixteenth Census of the United States: 1940, Population*, 2, *Characteristics of the Population*, pt. 6 (Washington, D.C., 1943), 723–35.

NOTE: Due to rounding, totals do not always add to exactly 100%.

mestic and personal service (usually waitresses), and most of these were black women. Factory labor occupied almost one-fifth of the female work force, another 15 percent were office clerical workers, 7 percent sales clerks, and another 8 percent in professions, mainly teaching. By 1940 women claimed 37 percent of the city's work force. Now about 38 percent of women workers were in domestic and personal service, still a predominantly black stratum. The percentage in manufacturing climbed very slightly, but more women were found in the professions and clerical office work. Black women found jobs as domestic servants, cooks, and laundresses but were mostly shut out from sales and office work, except in black-owned businesses.

Expanding job opportunities and increased pay were the principal magnets drawing women into the Nashville workforce. Wages, which averaged $6.92 a week for all Nashville women in 1913, were rising steadily and by 1923 were $12.58 and still climbing.[12] By 1930 the "girl migration to the city" produced a large female surplus in the Nashville population.[13] Most came from farms or small towns within forty-five to sixty miles of Nashville. They often left behind single-parent families who had more than average numbers of children. Some came with the idea that they would help support the family by sending savings back home or at least reduce the burden on their families by supporting themselves. Their fathers were usually farmers or small-town craftsmen whose economic fortunes were diminishing. Over half the girls in one study had completed high school and had ambitions for jobs or more education that could be fulfilled only in the city.[14]

"When I first came to Nashville," one twenty-two-year-old migrant explained, "I was supposed to be on a visit, but all the time I was looking for work. . . . I tried department stores, printing houses and several other different places." Her mother refused to let her go at first, and she stayed on at the farm, but "all the time I was thinking and planning of going off to work."[15] Another, the youngest in a family of five children, took a secretarial course at home and brought her new skills to the city to help the family with her income, ". . . and too I wanted to have freedom and make my own way in the world." Still another, the fourth of nine children from a "once-wealthy and aristocratic family, who had suffered misfortune as a result of drink," came to Nashville to teach and satisfy her "desires for travel and cultural pursuits."[16] Robbie Sanford, a young girl growing up near Nolensville, recalled that she "just plain had a fight with my father and left." She headed for Nashville, the city she had visited with her parents on shopping excursions. "Where else was there to go?"[17]

Some of the migrant girls followed an older relative, or were "country cousins," of a Nashville family, with whom they could live upon arriving. But many found their first housing in the several semicharity boarding homes that sprang up to meet the needs of this migrant female work force. The YWCA on Seventh Avenue North and Union, the Central Church of Christ Home for Girls at Fifth and Commerce, McGannon Hall at Eighth and Union, King's Daughters Home on Seventh between Union and Cedar (now Charlotte), and the Russell Street Church of Christ Home for Girls in East Nashville were the largest of the homes. All except the YWCA were organized in the 1920s.[18] These homes offered inexpensive housing and meals in a strictly regulated moral environment that must have reassured the girl's parents back home, but it may have cramped her own quest for romance and adventure in the city. It was often to escape the confinement of these homes that the better paid clerical workers moved out of them a year or two after arriving in the city. They found a room in one of the dozens of private boarding homes or set up an apartment with girlfriends.[19]

The dreams of a private room or apartment, movies, and restaurants that had lured young women into the city often eluded unskilled workers. There were many jobs open to white women with no work experience and limited education. Black women had to find employment as domestic servants and laundresses, occupations that were poorly paid (about $8 a week, plus meals in 1929) and shunned by native white women. Unskilled white women could get jobs in the textile and hosiery mills and the clothing and shoe factories that were expanding in Nashville during the 1920s. Factory girls earned about $11 a week in 1929, but the hours were long (nine to ten hours a day, less on Saturday), the work was grinding, and the factory neighborhoods were away from the amenities of the downtown. Others found jobs waiting tables in restaurants for wages under $8.50, plus tips and some meals. Another ready avenue of employment for young, unskilled white girls was behind the counters of department stores and five-and-dime stores, which paid about $10.75 a week in 1929. These low-wage, unskilled jobs were usually taken by younger women, fresh to the city, with no experience or skills to offer in the job market.[20]

The better paying jobs, and the more appealing work settings, were in the offices of the city's stores, banks, insurance companies, and professional offices. Here higher wages, averaging $16.30 a week in 1929, combined with the chance for periodic raises, and the attraction of working in a clean, quiet office in the downtown, made office work a desirable goal for the aspiring working woman. Employers found in the rural migrant an eager worker, accustomed to long hours on the farm and more easily satisfied with wages and working conditions. Some companies made a practice of recruiting country girls in preference to their city counterparts and relied on an informal network of friends, relatives, and church ties to recruit new workers. Nashville Bank and Trust, for example, drew heavily from Van Leer, Cumberland Furnace, and other small country towns west of Nashville. Life and Casualty Insurance Company had a reputation for preferring country girls from the Church of Christ, who often stayed at the Home for Girls the church sponsored at Fifth and Commerce.[21]

But office work required specific skills in stenography, typing, or bookkeeping, and many country girls had no opportunity to acquire this kind of training back home. In answer to their needs, several small business or secretarial schools were organized to train this new female office work force. Watkins Institute, named after its founder Samuel Watkins, had offered practical education for adults since it opened in 1889. During the 1920s it offered courses in stenography, typing, arithmetic, bookkeeping, and English to give the aspiring working woman (or man) an opportunity to train for a better paid office job or acquire a high school diploma.[22] The 1935 City Directory listed Dickinson Secretarial Institute in the Arcade ("shorthand and typing in 30 days"), the Draughon Practical Business College, Nashville Business College, Fall's Business College, and several more.[23]

Many young women carefully plotted their steps in career advance-

Figure 10. Commercial students at a night school sponsored by the Centenary Methodist Institute. Hundreds of young women, and many men, lifted themselves into better paying office jobs through this brand of education. *World Outlook* (Nov. 1939), reproduced by the Methodist Publishing House.

Figure 11. Office workers at National Life and Accident Insurance Company in the 1930s. National Life and Accident Insurance Company.

ment upon arriving in the city. They boarded at one of the girls' homes downtown, secured an unskilled job at a department store or restaurant, and took secretarial courses at night or between shifts. With their new skills they found office jobs, moved into a private room or apartment, and enjoyed whatever surplus income they earned, buying clothes, going to movies, and to Skalowski's or Candyland, the favored ice-cream parlors downtown. Robbie Sanford, on arriving from Nolensville, took a job as a telephone switchboard operator at $9 a week. After three weeks of on-the-job training she received a raise, to $11. Subsequent raises took her wages to $13, then $15 a week. But this was still less than skilled office workers could make, and it was tedious work. Between shifts at the telephone company she took secretarial courses at a secretarial school housed in rooms above the Princess Theater. Soon her sister, Pauline, found a better paying office job at U.S. Tobacco Company and was able to get Robbie a position there. Miss Sanford had to learn to fend off flirtatious advances from her supervisor by playing "so country and dumb," but she had secured the office job she coveted. As a stenographer she was able to start at $18 a week in 1924, and after sixteen years her raises had brought that to $23. Her new affluence allowed her to go "uptown" with Pauline each day for lunch at a restaurant and to enjoy days off at Glendale Park Zoo or at Sulphur Dell, watching the Nashville Volunteers play baseball.[24] Hers was one of hundreds of stories of modest but significant upward mobility assisted by calculated decisions to acquire training, keep a careful eye out for better job opportunities, and remain with one employer whenever periodic raises encouraged long-term loyalty.

Office workers like Robbie Sanford enjoyed wages that were generally above the bare subsistence level to which most other working women were resigned. A careful study by the YWCA in 1929 showed the typical working woman's weekly budget was $14.32, about $10.50 of which went for room and board, clothing, transportation, and other essentials.[25] This meant that many unskilled workers and recently arrived migrants had no discretionary income and often had to subsist on less than the prescribed $10.50 weekly budget for essentials. Many of the girls' homes and the large insurance companies sponsored a variety of free recreational activities, from dances and movies to basketball and weekend picnics.[26] But most office workers were relatively affluent, with money to spare each week for savings, clothing, movies, ice cream, and entertainment. One banker remembers migrant girls arriving in Nashville in flour-sack dresses, men's shoes, and with long, braided hair. With the first week's wages they bought a new dress, the second week produced new shoes, the next makeup, then a new hairdo.[27] When measured against their usually meager standard of living back home in the country, life must have seemed generous in Nashville during the 1920s. The city opened to these rural women an ex-

Figure 12. Women office workers outside National Life and Accident Insurance Company, 1937. National Life and Accident Insurance Company.

citing new world to which they were eager to adapt. Later, one of the Grand Ole Opry's most popular stars, "Cousin Minnie Pearl" of "Grinders Switch," with her fancy store-bought dress and the price tag still dangling from her new hat, came to personify the country girl striving to catch up with modern times, yet remaining unmistakably country in her awkward manners and naiveté.

THE NASHVILLE UNDERWORLD

Some found paths to economic opportunity through the underworld of the city. Nashville's most prominent vice district was on Capitol Hill, surrounding Tennessee's citadel of law. Another vice district, along Sixth Avenue, between Church and Union, came to be known as the Western Front during World War I. It included a cluster of illegal saloons and gambling clubs. Other concentrations of vice were in Black Bottom, south of Broad around Fourth Avenue, and in the Cabbage Hill district north of the Capitol around McKinney Street and Buena Vista Pike. Here Madam Baker, a small woman with a prominent gold tooth and a "small mustache," ran a notorious brothel that served as a "hangout for all crooks and thieves, clip women, jack rollers, sex women and men, and the plotters of vile crimes."[28]

The Capitol Hill area—an outgrowth of a vice center known as Hell's Half Acre when it emerged in the late nineteenth century—offered a variety of commercial vice. Along Cedar Street (now Charlotte Avenue), between Fourth and Fifth avenues, was a cluster of "uptown clubs" catering mostly to a black clientele and owned by a rising element of black entrepreneurs. Among the more prominent was Jim Raines, a ward-level political boss and owner of the Porters and Waiters Club, which offered gambling, illegal liquor, and a place for meeting prostitutes.[29] Also along Cedar Street were the Soldiers Club, Garden Club, Blackhawk Restaurant, Dave's Place, and the Silver Streak ballroom— all uptown clubs for music, dancing, liquor, gambling, and prostitution. This was the heart of "Nashville's Harlem." Further west on Cedar, on the other side of the state capitol, around Twelfth Avenue, were a brothel, headquarters for the Nashville numbers racket, and the "swanky" Hotel Grace built by Bill James, "Kingfish of the Nashville numbers racket." It served as a popular hangout for many of the city's vice lords and "high-class" prostitutes.[30] The numbers racket in Nashville had ties to white organized-crime figures in and beyond the city, but it thrived primarily within the black community. For a small amount of money the most impoverished slum dweller could buy a chance on winning thousands of dollars.[31] Nickels, dimes, and quarters flowed in a steady drain of capital out of the black slums.

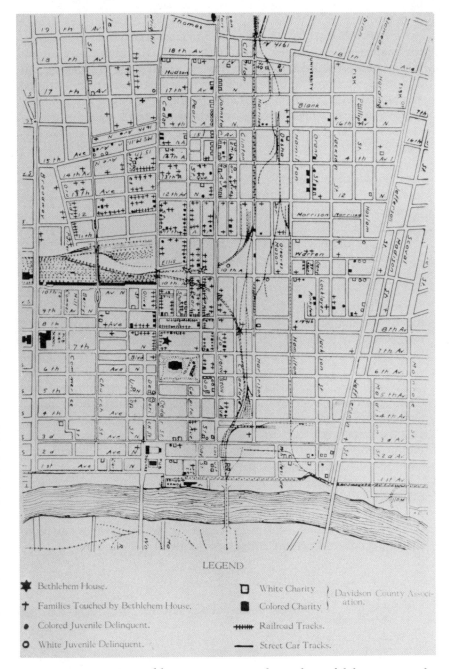

Figure 13. Map: the Bethlehem House area: the ecology of delinquency and dependency as indicated in a map of the center's clientele. *A Social Survey of the Bethlehem House Community, Nashville, Tennessee, December, 1920* ([Nashville, 1920]).

Crawford Street, two blocks north of Cedar and down the hill, was the main red-light district in the city. There, and along Seventh and Fifth avenues toward Jo Johnston Avenue, stood a row of brothels, usually in cheap frame buildings where the women sat at the windows and tapped on them as men walked by.[32] Each brothel was racially segregated, but exchanges were easily arranged when a white or a black customer wanted a woman of the opposite race.[33] Around the Capitol Hill vice district were also a number of "circuses," where lewd sex shows were performed, clubs that catered to male and female homosexuals, dope dens where marijuana, cocaine, and other drugs were available, and several clip joints that used women and gamblers to ply money from unsuspecting customers.

Camilla Caldwell, a social worker in the Capitol Hill area during the 1930s, remembered several young prostitutes among her caseload. Many were country girls who had come to Nashville with few job skills and limited education. They floundered in the legitimate job market and turned to prostitution out of sheer economic expediency. A rural migrant herself, Caldwell sympathized with the prostitutes, and they, in turn, befriended her. Most felt trapped by circumstances and were resigned to their plight. Many, too, were doomed by venereal diseases that ran rampant through the brothels in this period.[34] Most of the brothels were run—if not owned—by women, like Ruth Vance, the "Queen of the Hill," who operated a house near Seventh and Crawford, and Grace Chester, an enormous woman of 235 pounds who ran The Palace at Seventh and Jo Johnston. Ann "Lady" Frank, at Eighth and Jo Johnston, affected elegant manners and used as a prop a long gold cigarette holder mounted on a ring on her finger. "Swamp Lilly" Wilson, a madam on Seventh near Crawford, had a mean dog and horrendous body odor, which kept unfriendly characters at bay. These and other madams kept their girls cloistered except for chaperoned outings to a downtown theater or restaurant.[35] Nashville's underworld of vice mixed closely with the world of virtuous country girls earnestly working their way up in the respectable stores and offices downtown.

THE "UNADJUSTED" POOR

Overlapping the vice districts were the neighborhoods of the poor that ringed the central city and clustered in the low-lying bottoms near the factories and railroads. For the most part the poor in this period were recent rural migrants who had come to the city since the beginning of World War I or a few years earlier. Among black families in the Capitol Hill area around 1940, for example, fewer than 28 percent of the people were born in Nashville, and most had come into the city from the rural environs during the 1910s and 1920s.[36] One 1931 study of blue-collar whites in West Nashville reported that 56 percent had lived in Nashville five years or less and only 9 percent were natives of the city.[37] A similar survey of black families in North Nashville showed that 20 percent were natives of the city, all the rest being rural and small-town migrants who had come in from the country in the 1910s, most of them since 1918.[38] Among poor white families in the Kalb Hollow neighborhood of North Nashville (named for the preponderance of migrants from DeKalb County), about 25 percent were natives of Nashville, and 44 percent had come into Nashville since 1918.[39]

These migrants were poor, according to an underlying assumption of the sociologists, because they had failed to adjust to the city. Poverty, filth, disease, crime, delinquency, divorce, desertion, and numerous other symptoms of disorganization were explained by the inability of these people to alter their habits in order to mesh with the economy and culture of the modern city. Some attributed black poverty to inherent racial traits or the legacy of slavery, but this was a variation on the theme of maladjusted country folk in the city.[40]

The surveys of housing and health conditions among the Nashville poor reveal a level of squalor and misery that contradicted the general prosperity of the 1920s. Except for those on Capitol Hill, most of the poor found cheap rental housing in the low-lying areas of the city, many around Sulphur Dell north of Capitol Hill and west along the railroad corridor, others in Black Bottom south of Broad Street below Fifth Avenue. There was a sprawling slum of blacks and whites in Trimble Bottom in South Nashville and another, known as Crappy Shoot, in East Nashville north of Main Street. All flooded readily when the Cumberland overflowed its banks, and the residents were subject to chronic health hazards from dampness, leaching privies, and contaminated water supplies.[41]

The personal recollections of one family reveal much about the human experience behind all the survey data on Nashville's poor. In 1920 J.B. Williams, his parents, and several brothers and sisters, came into Nashville from Putnam County, where they had lived in makeshift quarters in an abandoned boxcar. They came at first to Kalb Hollow in North Nashville near the Morgan and Hamilton textile mills. Williams's father had worked for the Tennessee Central Railroad, laying the track in the Cumberlands, and he now took a job with the railroad in the city. They were the last of a large kinship group from Putnam County that had preceded them to Nashville. J.B.'s grandparents lived nearby on Eighth Avenue North and later bought a house on Delta in the Cabbage Hill district. An uncle worked for Tennessee Power Company, and four sisters worked as spinners in the Morgan and Hamilton Mills on Eighth Avenue, each for four dollars a week.

By pooling their income the Williams family survived better than many in the city, and their standard of living was a good cut above the boxcar in the Cumberlands. Still, there were no luxuries in their cramped frame house at Eighth and Garfield. The house had no electricity; it was illuminated by a kerosene lamp and heated by a coal-fueled cooking stove. Outside, behind the house, was a toilet, and a hydrant down the street supplied eight or ten families with water; the children were sent with buckets to retrieve it. J.B.'s mother had been reluctant to come to the city and frequently "visited back" with relatives and friends in Putnam County. She was befuddled by the city practice of buying all one's food at the store, but the family rarely lived in one place long enough or had sufficient yard space to raise its own food.

The Williams moved a few blocks in 1924 to a tenant house on Scovel Street. It was one-half of a double shotgun house with four rooms in a row, so the eight children and their parents had little privacy. The next year they lived briefly in West Nashville in another boxcar house while the father laid railroad spurs for the new industries being built there. Then they moved back to North Nashville to a house on Madison Street, just behind the one they had left on Scovel. In 1928 they moved again, to Hudson Street, a low-lying area next to the railroad tracks south of Fisk University. Many of the small frame houses in Mud Flats, or the Bottom, as it was sometimes known, were salvaged from the 1897 Tennessee Centennial Exposition, and many old-timers could still identify the transplanted fortune teller's house.

Mud Flats was a pocket of white families surrounded by black residents during the 1920s and 1930s, when North Nashville became almost solidly black. Nashville's black bourgeoisie of businessmen and professionals lived to the north around Fisk University in an enclave of fine brick homes. But along the railroad tracks north of Cedar Street (now Charlotte Avenue), which served as the border of black Nashville, were mostly very poor blacks. Young J.B. Williams attended the all-white Head School, played at Watkins Park with whites only, and saw movies at the segregated community center there, but he remembered a kind of neighborly sharing between the races in Mud Flats. When his mother was unable to breast feed her newborn baby, a black woman in the neighborhood volunteered to nurse the infant. During the Depression, when many black neighbors had no jobs and were going hungry, Mrs. Williams shared the family's beans and soup. "We didn't know anything about segregation then," J.B. Williams recalled. He was remembering the informal community of interdependence that poor people had brought with them from the country, not the institutional segregation that kept the races apart even in the mixed environment around Mud Flats.[42]

Thousands of families lived at, or well below, the standards this family maintained in North Nashville. Almost all the poor lived in

Figure 14. The homes of the poor, 1920. *A Social Survey of the Bethlehem House Community, Nashville, Tennessee, December, 1920* ([Nashville, 1920]).

frame houses, usually unpainted, with two or three rooms, built cheaply by landlords who apparently made steady profits on small investments with little outlay for improvements or maintenance. The cheapest of these houses rented for $10 to $15 per month in the 1920s and 1930s. A 1930 survey showed that 77 percent of all homes rented by blacks were in this lowest rent bracket, compared with 19 percent of homes rented by whites.[43] Furthermore, the overwhelming majority (71 percent) of black households were renting, compared with 58 percent of whites.[44] Typically, the homes of the poor—black or white—had no indoor plumbing, electricity, natural gas, or furnace. All but a few relied on outdoor toilets, kerosene lamps, coal stoves for cooking and heating, and a hydrant down the street for water.[45] Large families had to crowd into cramped quarters, and many families rented space to boarders to help meet the rent.[46]

Health conditions in this environment were appalling. Added to the environmental problems of unhealthy sanitary facilities, overcrowding, dampness, poor diet, and inadequate heat were the disastrous health practices of rural people unaccustomed to the dangers of crowded city life. Many country folk, to avoid having to purchase the kind of food they had raised for themselves back home, did all they could to maintain some degree of subsistence agriculture amid the squalor of the urban slums. Pigs and chickens ran about the yards—and the houses, in some instances. Vegetable gardens were tended next to outdoor privies. Garbage was strewn about to feed the animals. One astonished surveyor described an indoor chicken coop fashioned out of sticks lashed to the legs of a bed. "In some places five or six [people] live in two rooms, the chickens sleeping in one corner, with very poor ventilation. In some places where the older members of the family used tobacco or snuff, they would spit on the walls; in other places, around the hearth also."[47]

These observations give some clues to why the city's death rates remained high, especially among the poor black population. Nashville's death rates had dropped sharply from the 1870s to the 1890s, when the germ theory of disease was first accepted and a pure water supply and new public health measures curbed the ravages of epidemic diseases. But death rates from the 1890s to the 1920s continued to hover around 18 deaths per 1,000 population. Deaths among whites, at the same time, had declined to about 15 per 1,000, and black death rates also declined but remained approximately 170 percent those of whites.[48] "The higher negro death rate in the city," one social health survey coolly reported in 1930, "may mean a social maladjustment to the urban environment or that the negro is unable to meet urban competition for the right to live."[49] It was not until the 1930s that a concerted effort at improving public health drove death rates down to around 14 per 1,000 for the total population.[50] This trend was also the reward of persistent efforts to help country people adjust to the health perils of urban life.

CHILDREN OF POVERTY

The social scientists and reformers concerned for Nashville's poor directed much of their attention to the children. It was believed that children, with proper education and guidance, could more readily adjust to the urban environment. But the poverty and disorganization in their families and neighborhoods also tended to perpetuate the cycle of poverty. Pressure on the family economy required poor children to forgo education that might have allowed them to escape their parents' plight. Among whites, according to a 1931 public school survey, almost 95 percent of twelve-year-olds were attending school; by age fifteen, only 58 percent, and at seventeen, only 23 percent. Across the city fewer than four hundred white youths were enrolled in the twelfth grade in the city's public high schools.[51] A 1940 survey of Nashville citizens over age twenty-five showed that less than 10 percent of black males had completed high school; less than 24 percent of white males had done so. The female rate of high school completion was only two or three points higher for both races.[52] Black children dropped out earlier by force of economic pressure on the family economy and by the high rate of failure that held back an estimated three of four black students in grades one through six. Over 1,800 black children began the first grade in 1929, but only 52 were in the last year of high school.[53]

Poor children in Nashville entered the working world early in life, usually well before graduating from high school. Their wages, typically less than half what adults could earn, were nonetheless vital to the family economy to which they contributed.[54] Young black males worked as houseboys or sold newspapers and ran errands for a few dollars a week.[55] Their sisters found similar work in domestic service or doing laundry for white families. White boys had more opportunities in industrial work, and white girls with little education or experience could enter textile mills or retail sales.

Whether they were in school or working, many adolescent males from poor families fell into patterns of delinquency and formed neighborhood gangs. The new sociologists were fascinated by delinquency and youth gangs and took great pains to map the characteristics of the neighborhoods and families that produced them. Black delinquency rates were higher, but within both races delinquents came from families broken by divorce, desertion, or death. Their mothers typically worked outside the home, and their families lived in overcrowded rental housing. The families were in disarray, and the youth gang, according to sociological theory, became a kind of substitute family, a "natural group" supplying some form of social organization otherwise thought to be lacking in the slums.

A 1926 study of Henry Emerson, a fourteen-year-old black youth who lived in the Capitol Hill area, described his life in intricate detail.

Henry had repeated fourth grade three times, was often truant, and was distrustful of his teachers. His mother was a maid, and his father, a janitor, had deserted her about the time Henry was born. Another common-law husband had come and gone in Henry's early boyhood and had left behind a baby brother or sister. Both husbands had been kicked out of the house by a hard-working matriarch who had no use for freeloading men. The mother earned $9.50 a week working about 75 hours for wealthy white families in the suburbs.[56] Henry's family lived in a small, disheveled frame cottage surrounded by squalor. His mother, the baby, and Henry shared the same bed in the front room; an elderly black woman who cared for the baby during the day slept in the other room. Henry stayed away from home and from school as much as possible and found his social world in a gang of boys that plotted petty thefts and thrived on the excitement of being chased by police and white victims. Henry worked part-time as an errand boy for a drug store but was an unreliable worker and had trouble holding a job. He dreamed of being a rich banker and surpassing the "poor Niggers" around him but realized that his chances in life were limited.

Henry's world was shared by hundreds of Nashville youths, black and white, with only slight variations. It was a cyclical world in which maladjusted urban migrants would produce delinquent youth who would in turn generate disorganization, delinquency, and dependency within the underclass of the city. The disorganization of the poor seemed to cry out for intervention from social workers and their allies in the helping professions.

THE SETTLEMENT HOUSE MOVEMENT

The sociologists saw in the youth of the poor an opportunity to break this cycle of social pathology, to channel the restless energy of youth into constructive group activities organized and supervised by trained adults. The most important instruments in this cause were the social settlement houses that were organized in the poor neighborhoods of the city in this period.

These settlements were to the southern rural migrant and the urban poor what Jane Addams' Hull House was to the foreign-born immigrant of Chicago. The settlement house idea, transported from London in the 1880s, had become a standard feature of the American city during the progressive era, and by 1910 there were more than four hundred settlements.[57] They were staffed by a new generation of professionally trained social workers—predominantly young women who found in social work a rare opportunity both to fulfill ambition and to serve. They lived in the settlement house and came to know the poor as neighbors. They ran kindergartens, playgrounds, and day-care programs for children of working parents. They offered adult education courses in everything from basic English to home health, family budgeting, sewing, cooking, and Americanization. The settlement house also instigated dozens of clubs within the neighborhoods, part of the general goal to instill social organization in the poor.

These settlement house workers were on the cutting edge of a new theory of scientific charity. They were impatient with emotional alms giving and the misguided charity of the wealthy Lady Bountiful who had dominated community charity organizations in most cities.[58] "It is no longer sufficient to be compassionate for the 'unfortunate,'" Francis McLean informed the Nashville welfare community in 1925. "The old-fashioned motto, 'Help the Poor,' is as archaic as the horse-drawn stages of the last century." The new professional, she advised, ought to be "interested in helping to right such unfortunate conditions existing in the environment or personalities of individuals and families as tend to drag them down into misery or degradation. . . . It's the wisely helping hand which is now demanded."[59]

Nashville's settlement houses were offshoots of religious organizations and remained under the control of particular denominations, as opposed to the typically secular character of northern urban settlements. The Methodists, who had been long involved in the "social gospel" in Nashville and the South since the 1870s, led the way in 1901 when the City Mission Board established the first full-fledged settlement in the South, a former pool hall at Fillmore and Claiborne in South Nashville. Two years later it was named Wesley Community House and, after several moves, it built a new facility on Wharf Avenue in 1913. Described as "one of the most modern settlement plants in the South," it included a full range of recreational and educational programs for the poor.[60] During the progressive era the Methodists organized the Missionary Training School to prepare young women and men to work in the new settlements the church was organizing throughout the South. The Reverend J. E. McCulloch, president of the school, also promoted the Southern Sociological Congress, a new professional association that met in Nashville in 1912.[61]

Another Methodist settlement was inspired by Sallie Hill Sawyer, a black woman who in 1907 approached the Methodists at the Training School and urged them to extend services to the black poor of Nashville. Sawyer was a Fisk graduate, a former schoolteacher, and an active member of Capers Chapel, a black Methodist church. For the next six years she persisted in her pleas to her fellow Methodists, explaining that God "was holding the white people responsible for their darker brothers. . . ."[62] Estelle Haskins, of the Missionary Training School, began kindergarten and recreation programs for blacks in the coming years and finally in 1914 established a separate settlement for blacks at Tenth

Figure 15. The children of Bethlehem House and social workers during a Christmas celebration in 1920. *A Social Survey of the Bethlehem House Community, Nashville, Tennessee, December, 1920* ([Nashville, 1920]).

and Cedar. Mother Sawyer, as she came to be known, served as the housemother until her death in 1918. Bethlehem House (later Bethlehem Community Center) moved to new quarters—the Haskin-Sawyer Building—on Charlotte near Fourteenth in 1923. During the 1920s students of social work from Fisk, Scarritt, and other colleges joined the professional staff in offering programs at the center. They offered kindergarten classes, an employment bureau, a free telephone, sports programs, outings to the country, and a variety of adult courses in sewing, cooking, child care, and job skills. Holidays, such as Christmas and Easter, were celebrated at the center, and special attention was paid to the children. The social workers connected with Bethlehem Center conducted thousands of "friendly visits" to the poor of the neighborhood, encouraging them to participate in the center's programs and offering advice on home sanitation and budgeting.[63]

Centenary Methodist Institute began in 1908 as a settlement for mill workers at Morgan and Hamilton Bag Company's Warioto Cotton Mill. These were the white, predominantly rural migrant workers who lived in Kalb Hollow in North Nashville. The Reverend McCulloch and Maude Cramer, also with the Missionary Training School, asked mill owner Joe Morgan if they could hold religious services inside the mill. He balked but offered instead an empty apartment for their use in one of the company tenements. This became the Methodists' foothold in the mill community, and they set to work furnishing the barren apartment and planning programs for the mill workers. Students from the Training School, all young Methodist women, combed the neighborhood, engaging in friendly visiting with mill families and inviting them to the new settlement. Soon Morgan was sufficiently impressed with the good intentions of these zealous Methodist women that he donated another apartment, then the entire building, for what became known as Warioto Settlement. With their mothers working in the mills, young children were absorbed into a flurry of club activities organized by the settlement workers. Little girls took lessons in making beds, doing dishes, setting tables, and cleaning house. "Always held up before them is a standard of a cheerful, clean, sweet home life." Young men heard lectures from a Nashville businessman on government, preparing them for their future role as voters. Mothers learned about the latest techniques of child care, diet, and disease prevention. "One finds a changed appearance in many homes," one Methodist missionary reported with pride in 1928. "The girls in the housekeepers classes, cooking classes, and health clubs have caught a vision of a better home life."[64] After World War I, the settlement moved to new quarters a few blocks away on Monroe near Seventh, and it was renamed the Centenary Methodist Institute. Its programs for youth proliferated throughout the interwar years, with a growing emphasis on organized sports for young men.[65]

Nashville's Council of Jewish Women sponsored the Bertha Fen-

Figure 16. A group of social science students from Fisk University, 1920. Under the direction of Charles S. Johnson, dozens of social surveys were conducted in the neighborhoods of Nashville's poor blacks. *A Social Survey of the Bethlehem House Community, Nashville, Tennessee, December, 1920* ([Nashville, 1920]).

Figure 17. Girls in a sewing class as Wesley House, part of the social workers' effort to bring order to the lives of the poor and rural migrants in the city. *Missionary Voice* (Apr. 1928): 152, reproduced by Methodist Publishing House.

sterwald Social Center on Capitol Hill. It served the many poor Jews who came to America from Russia and eastern Europe and who wished to avoid the evangelical tone of the Methodist settlements. Though the Fensterwald Center was open to people of all faiths and offered no religious services, about two-thirds of its clientele were Jewish, and most of the rest were foreign-born Europeans. In its early years this settlement was more typical of those in the urban North. It was devoted to the Americanization of foreign immigrants, preparing them for citizenship and teaching them to cope in the American city.[66] As more Jews moved out of the slums and as the Young Men's Hebrew Association and its female complement (counterparts to the YMCA and YWCA) came to serve as the social center for many Nashville Jews, the Fensterwald Center opened its services to the black population that was moving into the Capitol Hill neighborhood. In the 1930s the center was taken over by Fisk University.[67]

There were other settlements in Nashville, seven in all by the late 1930s.[68] They varied their programs over time, and even among the Methodist settlements different priorities were emphasized. But all shared a common mission to organize and socialize the poor, the urban newcomer, and the foreign-born immigrant. All began with a common premise about the breakdown of social organization among the poor, and all promoted similar programs to invest order, cleanliness, and discipline into their lives.

A FUNDAMENTAL SPIRIT

Nashville's newcomers and poor people also found ways of coping with the urban environment through their religion, but in ways that did not always meet with the approval of the social workers. As the Methodists and other religious organizations reached out to the poor and the urban migrants through new institutions, like the settlement house, the poor often turned elsewhere for their spiritual needs, or stayed away from organized religion altogether. The settlements were modern expressions of the social gospel that had emerged in the 1880s in Nashville. Social Christianity, as it was also known, appealed to members of the educated middle class who wished to use the church as an instrument for social reform, not just for individual spiritual comfort. The result was a movement toward a socially active institutional church, and the professionalization of Christian charity and welfare. In cities like Nashville the major Protestant denominations—the Methodists, Baptists, and Presbyterians—had become the domain of the middle class. The downtown churches—McKendree Methodist, First Baptist, and First Presbyterian—were grand urban churches with elaborately designed interiors. By the 1920s these congregations were long-accustomed to an educated clergy, thoughtful sermons, and good-quality choral or instrumental music in their services. These standards of refinement were all the more important to the new suburban churches that followed the exodus of the more affluent parishioners out of the central city.[69]

Country people coming to the city may have belonged to a Methodist, a Baptist, or a Presbyterian church back home, but they often felt uncomfortable in the city churches. In comparison to the small country chapels of their youth, even the churches outside downtown Nashville might have seemed overly large, ornate, and somber. J.B. Williams's kin came from Methodist and Baptist churches in the Cumberlands, where shouting and singing were a normal part of the Sunday service. In Nashville, he recalled, "church folks were not that way." His sisters tried Methodist and Baptist churches in Kalb Hollow, and his mother went to a Church of Christ, but theirs was a restless search for "their kind of church."[70]

Others found spiritual kindred in the dozens of new churches and sects that sprang up in the neighborhoods of the poor, black and white. Some were the product of regional or national schisms in the Methodist and Baptist bodies, others apparently the product of local differences. The pentecostal, holiness, and Church of God movements were usually made up of radical fundamentalists or evangelicals who were in revolt against the liberal theology, high-toned clergy, and stodgy decorum of the established Protestant congregations. They founded churches in storefronts and old shacks in Nashville's poor neighborhoods, and their preachers rose up from the people, with no credentials except their gift for provoking enthusiasm in the congregation.

The federal religious censuses taken in 1926 and 1936 probably undercounted the many small, informal congregations of this sort. But they give some indication of the variety of small Protestant churches, a feature that was barely affected by the Depression of the 1930s (see table 2).

Some of the social surveys of selected Nashville neighborhoods give a better idea of how these small sects were concentrated among the poor. Within the Capitol Hill area, in what was considered "one of the most disorganized sections of the city," one surveyor was surprised to find no fewer than thirty-three religious congregations. Twelve were white, the rest black. Most had church buildings, some substantial brick edifices, others small frame shacks. Seven congregations—all of them black—had no permanent home but met in living rooms or rented space in other churches. Among them were the Third Avenue Mississippi Baptists, Rainbow Mississippi Baptists, Second Rainbow Baptist, Jo Johnston Primitive Baptist, and Bethlehem United Primitive Baptist —each denoting fine differences in doctrine, ritual, or simply in personal leadership. Set amid the teeming vice district of Capitol Hill, these

Figure 18. Two small churches that served the spiritual needs of Nashville's poor and rural migrants: St. John's Baptist Church, "colored," and The Church of God, for whites. *A Social Survey of the Bethlehem House Community, Nashville, Tennessee, December, 1920* ([Nashville, 1920]).

Table 2: Nashville's Religious Affiliations, 1926, 1936

	1926		1936	
	Members	Congregations	Members	Congregations
Baptist				
Southern	9,950	18	12,290	15
Negro (National Convention)	8,724	38	5,597	31
Free Will	276	2	125	1
Primitive	169	2	204	2
Colored Primitive	—		1,331	17
American	—		375	1
General	—		41	1
Methodist				
Methodist Episcopal	1,581	7	1,072	4
Methodist Southern	15,120	23	16,273	19
AME & AME Zion	2,681	12	2,466	15
Colored Methodist	522	4	675	4
Free Methodist	—		11	1
Presbyterian				
(U.S.) Southern	4,894	10	5,014	8
(U.S.A.) Northern	1,103	3	1,270	3
Cumberland	1,329	8	1,454	7
Colored Cumberland	38	1	61	1
Church-Disciples of Christ				
Disciples of Christ	2,673	8	2,317	4
Church of Christ	7,454	36	7,413	28
Episcopal	3,039	6	3,462	6
Other Protestant				
Seventh Day Adventist	355	2	567	4
Brethren	6	1	—	—
Bahai	—	—	15	1
Christian Science	409	3	545	2
Church of God	168	6	234	3
Church of Nazarene	710	4	1,952	10
Church of Living God	54	1	96	1
Congregational & Christian	186	2	365	3
Holiness	18	1	—	—
Mormon	65	1	77	1
Lutheran	695	2	802	4
Pentecostal Assemblies	48	1	—	—
Evangelical & Reformed	175	1	153	1
Salvation Army	13	1	150	1
Spiritualist	—	—	25	1
Theosophical Society	11	1	—	—
Unitarian	50	1	—	—
United Brethren	220	1	—	—
Volunteers	67	1	—	—
Roman Catholic	6,748	12	7,644	9
Greek Orthodox	85	1	170	1
Jewish	4,000	3	4,200	3
Total	73,636	224	78,446	213

SOURCE: Bureau of the Census, *Religious Bodies: 1926* 1 (Washington, D.C., 1930), 476–77; idem, *Religious Bodies: 1936*, 1 (Washington, D.C., 1941), 594–95.

small black and white churches had no shortage of sinners to minister. One black preacher complained of those who thought they could "shout their way to heaven on Sunday after living a life of sin six days in the week." Lillie Bearden, the Vanderbilt sociology student who conducted the survey, earnestly recommended more youth organizations and clubs for the men as a means of bringing social discipline to the neighborhood. But the strength of these churches seemed to rely more on their appeal to the emotions and their concern for the afterlife, not on their capacity for social reform.[71]

A Vanderbilt Divinity School student was appalled by the service he witnessed in one lower-class black church:

> There was little unity in the sermon and the preacher's mind seemed to go from one point to another without any apparent reason. . . . The minister usually starts out in a quiet voice without any emotion and gradually works himself into a fever of emotion. The more he gesticulates and the louder grows his voice the more does he get response from his congregation. . . . "Yes, Yes," "That's right," "Listen to him," . . . "O Lord, Lord," "Jesus, my Jesus." . . . [But the white visitor had to admit:] There is something awe inspiring about these services. One feels that there is an intense spirit of some kind moving in the breasts of the worshippers. . . . There is something extraordinary, undefinable, something primitive and primeval in the worship. . . . They may scream, fling their arms into the air, hurl themselves over benches, leap into the air, shout, dance, prance backward and forward and engage in other strange movements, finally becoming exhausted and falling upon the floor or benches to be revived by other members of the congregation. . . . In these services individuals in the congregation pray long and fervent prayers. The prayers are often sung. The worshipper frequently directs his prayer to Jesus and pours his troubles to Him. These prayers are often very touching and sometimes the prayer becomes a poem — a poem of suffering to a suffering Christ.[72]

In all this religious enthusiasm, the modern clergy lamented, "the large majority of the pastors — at least 90% of them — rarely touch upon the vital problems affecting the lives of the people." Perhaps they admonished their flock not to smoke, gamble, or dance, but there was no sense of the church as an agent for social change.[73] The same tone of impatience was expressed toward the churches serving the white poor in North Nashville: ". . . these people who are unable to see where they are going to get their next meal are turning to the presentation of 'the other world story of religion' for their religion and are swallowing the theory of 'a heaven of eternal bliss' hook, line, and sinker and as they turn their eyes to see beyond the grave and imagine the glories of the other world their trials and troubles of this world sink into oblivion. For a little while they cease to worry about food, clothing, and shelter." It was simply "Escape Religion," according to this account. "There are a few (very few) preachers in North Nashville who have tasted of the Social Gospel and they endeavor to give their church a dose of it but often the people are so bothered by their everyday problems that they prefer to go to hear the sugar coated gospel of otherworldliness and live for an hour in a dream of future satisfaction, a place where everything will be perfect."[74]

The search of Nashville's common folk for a religion of their own often led out of the churches altogether. A Works Progress Administration writer in the 1930s recorded a remarkable scene on the north corner of Lower Broad and First Avenue, across from the City Wharf. Beginning sometime after World War I, on warm Sunday afternoons, this was the site of "free-for-all preachings" where white, black, men, women, fundamentalist, or atheist exhorted whoever was willing to listen. "The audience, for the most part, is made up of people restlessly awaiting their turns to preach. They clutch battered Bibles, which they leaf through and quote from at an instant's notice. Almost without exception they have tried and discarded the standard sects." The crowd would grow, extending up Broad to Second Avenue and across First to the wharf, and preachers competed to gather converts to their fold.

> Often ten or twenty preachers stand on the curb, on packing cases, and in truck beds, all preaching at the same time. . . . Preachers mount boxcars . . . stand on the hoods of cars and perch on the first story window ledges of the produce houses. Some lure listeners by mouthing French harps or strumming banjoes and guitars. Others whoop until a group collects. There is a constant crossfire of heckling between preacher and listeners. Furious men rush up to the preacher and shake fists, Bibles, and canes under his nose. Some ignore the preaching and draw aside to roar Scriptural quotations into each others faces. The preaching continues until about 9 o'clock at night, when the people, satiated and subdued, begin to leave. By 10 o'clock the corner is deserted."[75]

The religious experience of the migrants and the poor was symbolic of their accommodation to urban life. Many joined established churches in the city and, if necessary, adapted to their customs. But others found new modes of religious expression in Holy Roller churches or among street-corner exhorters. Some elements of rural folk culture disappeared, others persisted, and the city seemed able to make room for the elements that survived. If Donald Davidson, or any of the Agrarians, ever came down to the foot of Broad on a warm Sunday afternoon, surely they would have felt heartened (and perhaps a little shocked) by the stubborn tenacity of folk religion thriving there, in the very heart of the city.

The evidence that an urban folk religion was forming among the rural migrants and the poor suggests a whole range of persistent folkways in the city. Instead of breaking down or being discarded in the urban environment, as the social scientists expected, rural values and institutions often became powerful instruments for survival in the city. Thus family and kinship ties were often indispensable to newcomers

Figure 19. Scene from a religious street meeting, c. 1930s. "They clutch battered Bibles, which they leaf through and quote from at an instant's notice." Nashville Room, Ben West Public Library.

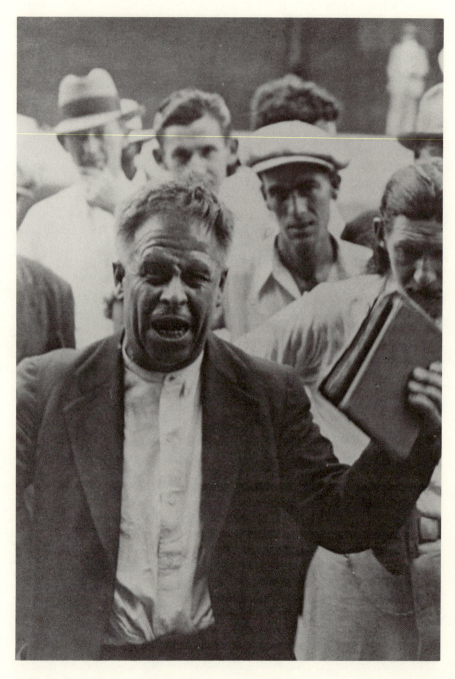

Figure 20. "Some . . . draw aside to roar Scriptural quotations into each others faces." Nashville Room, Ben West Public Library.

in need of housing and jobs. Backyard gardens and chicken coops took the strain off meager family incomes. Country people also brought their music and their musical tastes to the city. The country music that was broadcast from WSM's Grand Ole Opry and other Nashville radio stations, beginning in the 1920s, was often old-time hillbilly music. But it was mixed increasingly with themes of modern life: broken love, cheating spouses, hard drinking, mean bosses, simple religious faith, and reminiscences of the life left behind in the country. The mournful lyrics of country music, like the blues that welled up from the black ghettos at the same time, testify to the often wrenching experience of migration and poverty that white and black southerners endured. For all migrants many old ways had to be abandoned and new skills learned. Some adapted readily, others simply failed.

Helping ease the migrants' passage into the urban world were a multitude of social workers, volunteers, churches, charities, night schools, and settlement houses. Some surveyed the neighborhoods of the poor, peered into their homes and churches, and diagnosed the symptoms of social pathology they found there. They also offered relief, recreation, job training, and practical education in everything from home sanitation and nutritious cooking to typing, stenography, and citizenship. Though occasionally condescending and insensitive in their eagerness to help the poor adjust to the city, these helping professionals and their agencies were indispensible to the welfare of the migrant poor.

The stream of migrants coming from the country to Nashville would continue with World War II and the surge of urbanization that pulled southerners off the farms following the war. For them the choice that Vanderbilt's Agrarians posed between urban modernity and rural tradition was never so simple nor so mutually exclusive. The country folk who came to Nashville did their best to enter the former and hold on to whatever they could of the latter. The city, in turn, seemed to keep one foot in the country.

BOSS HOWSE AND THE REFORMERS

The local political scene was shaped also by the rural migrants, blacks, and poor people who lived in Nashville between the two world wars. They found an able political champion in Hilary Howse, who served as mayor from 1909 to 1915 and again from 1923 to 1938. Howse and his followers among city employees, policemen, ward-level politicos, saloonkeepers, and bootleggers constructed a durable political machine in Nashville. It was a southern version of the Irish political machines that had emerged from the ghettos of the foreign-born in most large northern cities since the 1860s. The Howse machine was based in the neighborhoods where common people, black and white, looked to it for benefits in exchange for their votes. Though a series of registration, ballot, poll-tax, and primary-election "reforms" passed in 1889–93 had disfranchised many Tennessee blacks, the Howse machine rose to power by mobilizing at least some of Nashville's black citizens, paying their poll taxes, and granting favors to win their votes.[1] Howse extended city health services, built new schools and parks, provided free textbooks, gave out free coal and groceries to the poor, and in hundreds of small, symbolic favors—from minor patronage appointments to funeral flowers—he showed the common folk they had an understanding friend in city hall.

Howse's machine also depended on the protection of saloons and bootlegging operations that had been officially banned by the state's prohibition law since 1909 but continued to be demanded by a significant segment of the public. It was the neighborhood saloonkeepers and the like who, in return, would mobilize voters, register them, pay their poll taxes, get them to the polls, and reward them for their loyalty—with a drink perhaps. The Howse machine operated on an understanding that politics was a game involving the practical exchange of favors for votes. The goal was to continue in power and help the common people but not to meddle in their private moral affairs.

Opposing the Howse machine was a group of businessmen and civic reformers, people largely from the white middle class who lived in the wealthy suburban neighborhoods around West End and Belmont avenues, or in East Nashville, around Edgefield and Lockeland Springs. The reformers opposing Howse included a variety of groups, but most shared the goals of what historian George Tindall has labeled "business progressivism." They wanted not just to depose Howse and his cronies, they wanted "good government." This meant restructuring city government to make it more efficient, economical, and honest. They wanted it refashioned in the image of the modern business corporation, with experts from business and the professions in control, people above the parochial politics of neighborhood interests, people capable of rational planning for the entire metropolitan community.[2] They wanted businessmen in control of businesslike government.

In 1913, when Howse was planning to run for a third term as mayor, the reformers mounted a successful campaign to introduce the commission form of government in Nashville. Instead of a mayor and council elected by wards, five commissioners—one to serve as mayor—were elected by the voters of the city at large, a scheme that was intended to favor wealthier, better known candidates over ward-based politicians. Each commissioner would be responsible for particular urban services, and the result would be clean, efficient government run according to business principles.

But Howse's political skill and popular appeal turned the reform of 1913 into a political triumph for the machine. Howse and his allies nearly swept the election and came out controlling four of the five seats on the commission. The reformers were defeated but not about to give up. Under Howse the expansion of city improvements and social services came at the expense of a growing city debt that approached $1 million by 1915. Business leaders and civic reformers mounted pressure for an outside audit of the city's books. Howse finally relented in the spring of 1915 only to announce that some of the key books were missing. Rumors circulated that the books had been burned or dumped into the Cumberland River. The scandals that followed led to a collapse of the Howse regime and the ouster of Mayor Howse himself.[3]

The reformers had at last triumphed over the machine. Now, it seemed, good government would flourish in Nashville. Now the "best people," as they often styled themselves, would control government in the interest of businesslike efficiency, Protestant morality, and rational planning. What followed, however, was an interlude of farcical disarray in city government. It was a period of factional backbiting, wild experimentation with new city charters, and uncontrolled vice, an era that was finally terminated in 1923 by the return of Boss Howse to power.

During the fifteen years that followed, Howse guided Nashville through the flush times of the 1920s and then through the upheaval of the Great Depression and the New Deal. Though reformers rarely acknowledged it, Nashville had reason to appreciate Howse as a professional politician whose machine brought order to civic affairs. (See appendix E for a list of the several mayors discussed in this chapter.)

THE FARCE OF REFORM

Judge Robert Ewing, who was chosen by the city's business leaders to succeed Howse as mayor after his ouster in the 1915 crisis, was described as "a prominent elder statesman in the community." As a member of an old Nashville family with roots in the city's pioneer generation, Ewing's credentials were impeccable. Furthermore, he had experience in municipal office, having been a member of the Board of Public Works in 1891. Ewing promised the reformers who put him in office a "policy of retrenchment and economy that will surprise even the most exacting citizens." He reduced his own salary and watched city expenditures with the diligence of a strict guardian entrusted with a public till that had been so recently pillaged.[4]

But when Ewing's uneventful term was up in 1917, his bid for reelection was defeated in the Democratic primary election. Another businessman-*cum*-politician, William Gupton, now attracted the support of the downtown merchants and manufacturers of Nashville. Gupton, aged forty-seven, was much younger than Ewing and closer to the business community. After arriving in Nashville with his family in 1875, Gupton worked his way up from grocery delivery boy to bookkeeper, shipping clerk, and eventually president of American Steam Feed Company. A good Baptist as well as a successful businessman, Gupton seemed the ideal candidate for good government.[5]

Opposing him was none other than Hilary Howse, who had steadfastly defended his innocence after the 1915 scandal and exonerated himself in the courts. Howse stood on his record as an experienced, professional politician, and he appealed to his constituency in the neighborhoods of the black and white poor. Howse freely admitted he had failed to enforce the prohibition law and implicitly promised he would resume that policy. Howse led in the Democratic primary, with 3,959 votes to Gupton's 2,776, but this was not enough to avoid a runoff in the general election. The *Banner* called on voters to wipe the slate clean: "The old Howse regime was a mixture of lawlessness, graft and flamboyant vulgarity. It ended in disgrace and financial disaster from which the city will for a long time suffer. . . . The kind of advertisement Nashville needs to send out is that it has cleaned house, that the taint of the old gang has been wiped out and destroyed by proper scouring and disinfectants applied by the voters."⁶ Ewing's supporters (1,994 in the primary) now swung their votes to Gupton, bringing his total to 4,976, just 160 more than the votes for Hilary Howse. Howse proved his continuing strength in the inner-city wards, but in suburban East Nashville, in the "silk stocking district" of West End, and elsewhere in the suburban wards, Gupton picked up enough votes to win.⁷

Good government, it seemed, was to stay in the hands of a clean businessman's mayor. Now the reformers sought to throw the remaining Howse loyalists out of county and state government. The Citizens' Democratic ticket in July 1918 appealed to voters by powerful allusions to the Reconstruction era and to the current German enemy. "Nashville Redeemed," one advertisement claimed. After "six years of Howse's misrule" and "with the tremendous spiritual impulse from the declaration of war against the Huns . . . Nashville has been redeemed." "It is no longer a spendthrift and wastrel. . . . It is a safe place for men, women and children. . . . Will the citizens of this new and great Nashville permit the control of it to fall again into the hands of the insatiable Howse?"⁸

Howse graciously retreated from the political arena to tend his retail furniture store and bide his time. Loyal remnants of the old machine remained in the city government, now ironically protected by the civil service reforms introduced by reformers to cleanse government. The machine also continued to hold positions in county government and in the Davidson County delegation to the state General Assembly. But as a cohesive political force the Howse machine had broken down after 1917.

Having raised the moral indignation of the voters against corruption and vice, the advocates of good government soon learned how quickly yesterday's reformers could become tomorrow's rascals. As they found out, prohibition violations and other moral improprieties were easier to condemn than to repress. Statewide prohibition had been enacted in 1909, following a notorious duel in downtown Nashville that ended in the death of newspaper editor Edward Ward Carmack, a martyr to the temperance cause. But Howse rode to power in that year on his promise that prohibition would not be enforced in Nashville. His victory allowed Nashville saloons to continue operations almost without regard for the law. Middle Tennessee's distillers and wholesalers had to shut down operations or move out of state, but there was nothing in the law prohibiting out-of-state shipments to Tennessee. Nashville saloons became "locker clubs," and people bought liquor for home use with impunity. In 1917 the state enacted a "bone-dry" law banning all out-of-state liquor shipments and making it illegal to possess or receive intoxicants. Now the liquor trade went deeper underground and came under the control of a criminal element that made Nashville the headquarters for all of Middle Tennessee. Blockade runners in large cars and trucks loaded with Kentucky whiskey made regular runs from the Kentucky border towns. In and around Nashville a cheaper variety of moonshine, or "white mule," was made in secret stills or concocted with grain alcohol as "bathtub gin." National prohibition came in January 1919, but it was no more enforceable than the state laws had been. Police Chief Alex J. Barthell led a harsh crackdown on bootleggers and other vice operations in 1919, leading to over 16,000 arrests. District Attorney General G. B. Kirkpatrick decried the "reservoirs of liquor" in Nashville and padlocked several of the illegal saloons.[9]

But as legal pressure intensified, bootleg operations became concentrated in the hands of a few powerful men willing to use bribery and guns to protect their profitable enterprise. In Black Bottom and the Woodbine district Harry Lehman, "The Bootleg King," and Sol Cohn operated saloons and controlled a large liquor trade. In the Capitol Hill area Frank Christman, "Boss of the Underworld," operated a "soft-drink" stand on Gay Street and supplied liquor to most of the gambling houses, brothels, and saloons in the area. The Western Front, on Sixth Avenue, and Printers' Alley, between Third and Fourth avenues, were two more clusters of speakeasies, gambling dens, and bootleg operations. There were dozens of other smaller rivals and allies throughout the county, all involved in a loosely organized underworld of bootlegging, narcotics, prostitution, and gambling. With their wealth they were able to buy police protection, hire clever lawyers, and bribe jurors.

The only effective check on their expansion seemed to be the internal warfare and murders that resulted from turf rivalries and mutual suspicions against police informants. In January 1919, Will Winters, a blockade runner, attacked Seth Gibson with a hammer in the streets of the downtown for informing on him. Gibson pulled his pistol and shot Winters dead. In 1922 on Sixth Avenue, the notorious Western Front between Church and Union, Jim Allen acted on a similar suspicion when he shot "Kid Wolfe" (a.k.a. W.L. Aikin). Two years later Frank Christman walked into a diner and, directly in front of a uniformed policeman, shot to death his rival Abbie Arnett. All these cases were dismissed by the Davidson County grand jury, as were most of the cases against bootleggers. It was widely assumed that the jury had been bribed. Judge J.D.B. DeBow, bewailing the lawless atmosphere before a new grand jury in 1926, admitted that "our fair city is being made a charnel house by mobs and assassins."[10] As other underworld kings emerged, their rivalries led to more bloodshed. It was not until May 1939 that state law allowed Davidson County to vote on a local option law allowing the legal sale of liquor (beer was permitted earlier). The vote was an overwhelming endorsement of legalized sales (10,603 to 6,196), and a measure of how weak the public support for prohibition had been.[11] During thirty years of prohibition, from 1909 to

1939, Nashville politics took shape between the high-minded ideals of moral reformers and the lawless vice and violence of the underworld.

The political cost of failing to enforce prohibition rose significantly with the triumph of women's suffrage in 1920. This long-sought victory took on heightened importance in Nashville, for it was in the capital city in August 1920 that women's suffrage lobbyists pushed Tennessee legislators to ratify the Nineteenth Amendment. This gave the amendment the thirty-six states required (the "perfect thirty six" was the suffragists' slogan) for ratification as a constitutional amendment. Much of the lobbying took place during one of the hottest Augusts on record when Governor Albert H. Roberts called a special session of the legislature to consider the amendment. The antisuffrage lobby took the sumptuous Hermitage Hotel as its headquarters. The women fighting for their right to vote, led by Anne Dallas Dudley and Carrie Chapman Catt, had worked hard to build a large majority for suffrage in the Tennessee House of Representatives, but heavy pressure from opponents persuaded many politicians to defect. As the votes lined up evenly on both sides, women suffragists carefully escorted their remaining supporters about the capitol and made certain that none slipped into the hands of antisuffrage lobbyists or out of town to avoid the coming showdown. Up on the eighth floor of the Hermitage Hotel the opposition won supporters by other means, with man-to-man talk over cold bourbon. "Beware, Men of the South, Heed Not the Song of the Suffrage Siren," one antisuffrage handbill warned. Southern womanhood, they argued, did not belong in the "mire of politics." Votes for women, others warned, might encourage blacks to reassert their political rights.

One wavering opponent of suffrage, Representative Harry Burns from Niota, in McMinn County, received a letter from his widowed mother back home in Niota: "Dear Son; Hurrah and vote for suffrage! Don't keep them in doubt. . . . Don't forget to be a good boy and help Mrs. Catt put 'rat' in ratification. [signed] Your Mother." The next day the prosuffrage representatives, with yellow roses in their lapels, were escorted to the house by women who had gathered for a showdown vote on the amendment. The antisuffrage forces, wearing red roses in their lapels, counted on forty-nine supporters against forty-seven for suffrage. But one member, Bank Turner, defected, and two motions to table the bill failed. On the third vote, to approve or reject the bill, Harry Burns, who had voted twice with the antisuffrage forces, now voted for his mother, and for the right of 17 million American women to vote. Rose petals fluttered down from the gallery, and the women sang for joy. In a desperate parliamentary ploy the antisuffrage forces threw Tennessee's ratification into legal question by requiring another vote in three days, then fled to Alabama to prevent a quorum. Governor Roberts signed the bill anyway on August 24, and when Connecticut ratified the amendment shortly after, the issue in Tennessee became moot.

Figure 21. "Southern Chivalry" depicts a Tennessee gentleman giving a demure woman the vote in 1920. Original in *Philadelphia Record*, n.d. Carrie Chapman Catt Papers, TSLA.

Women had the vote, and the formerly masculine world of politics would never be quite the same again.[12]

The advocates of good government, who promised to make the city safe for women and children, now found themselves held to the stricter standards that women voters expected of their elected officials. Mayor Gupton and the city officeholders in general came under careful scrutiny. As the election of 1921 approached, the *Tennessean* began to expose the lackadaisical enforcement of prohibition and focused on a seamy bootlegging and vice district, the Western Front. This area "runs with unbridled license in the heart of the city," the *Tennessean* complained, "thanks to the inactivity and complete acquiescence of Chief Barthell, Mayor Gupton and the police force assigned to that beat."[13]

In the same hyperbolic tone once reserved for denunciations of Boss Howse, the reformers now attacked Mayor Gupton. "Thanks to Mayor Gupton, Chief of Police Barthell and their political machine, your wife, your sister, your children, you, yourself, must pass this place daily if you go up Sixth avenue toward one of our best hotels."[14] From the pulpit of First Presbyterian Church, Dr. James I. Vance joined the chorus of moral outrage, calling "for a spasm of righteous indignation against the beast of evil. . . . Not far from where I am speaking tonight, I am told, vice flourishes and flaunts itself as brazenly as it used to in the old red light district north of the Capitol."[15] Mayor Gupton's proposal to create a segregated and strictly controlled red-light district only encouraged his detractors. "You might as well try to segregate contagious disease as to segregate prostitution," the Reverend Vance exhorted. "Segregation is permission. What the beast needs is not a range in which to roam, but a club."[16]

The repeated failures of municipal reform led many advocates of good government to abandon the entire experiment in commission government begun in 1913. Although the commission form of government with its five citywide executives may have reduced the power of ward-level politicians, it brought unexpected administrative problems. The five separate commissioners, each in charge of different city service departments, tended to operate as five distinct sovereigns with no coordination of government activities. It also was eminently clear that the commission form did not depoliticize city government. Citywide elections depended, no less than ward-level elections, on popular appeal rather than administrative expertise. "Rival political factions," one disappointed observer of Nashville government wrote, "have used the city hall crowd as a means of constant agitation for personal advancement." "The commission form of government is no panacea for factional fights, nor is it a guarantee that a high type of man or an efficiently trained administrator will be elected. . . ."[17]

A movement to reform the city charter and abandon the experiment in commission government began in the summer of 1920. A group of reformers ran on the Citizens' ticket for the Davidson County delegation to the state legislature. Led by Dan McGugin, a popular Vanderbilt football coach, the candidates pledged to end the commission form of government in Nashville and return to the council-mayor system, which in 1913 had been denounced as the bane of good government. In this confused state of affairs it was left to the People's ticket, the old Howse machine's vehicle, to defend the commission form of government as a noble experiment in democracy.

The Citizens' ticket, and the cause of good government—or so it seemed—triumphed again at the polls. But once elected, Senator McGugin, in an unexpected move, composed a new city charter with a city manager as the chief executive. The city manager idea was the latest national fad in the good government movement, having been popularized by its success in Dayton, Ohio, following a devastating flood in 1912. Unlike the elected politician, the city manager was a trained expert in administration, appointed by the city council, with tenure in office to be unaffected by the comings and goings of electoral politics. Elsewhere, usually in small cities, the city manager idea proved irresistible to businessmen and other advocates of good government.[18] But in Nashville, civic leaders, perhaps chastened by their experience with commission government, failed to unite behind this new experiment in government reform. As McGugin's bill worked its way through the legislative chambers, it was amended in so many ways that it became unacceptable to all but a small group surrounding Mayor Gupton. The final bill, approved by the legislature but never by the citizens of Nashville, would have allowed councilmen to be elected from each of fifteen new wards. The bill went so far as to include a list of candidates for council to be voted on at an election on March 31, 1921. If voters approved this slate, Mayor Gupton would act as mayor-manager for six additional months, until September, when the council was to elect a new mayor-manager.[19]

Luke Lea's *Tennessean* adamantly opposed the McGugin charter and denounced it as satisfying neither the democratic spirit of the mayor-council system nor the efficiency of the city manager idea. The voters of Nashville, the *Tennessean* implored, must kill this "municipal Frankenstein."[20] Edward B. Stahlman's *Banner* predictably took the opposite point of view, and the proposed city manager plan became yet another political football to be booted about between the two feuding publishers. Davidson County's other state senator, Finley M. Davis, rejected the McGugin charter as a breach of the platform that he, McGugin, and others stood upon in 1920. The charter found another enemy in the newly organized League of Women Voters, which protested that no women were listed among the fifteen proposed council representatives. Furthermore, the women complained they would not be eligible to vote in the March 31 election because they had not been able to register and pay the poll tax in time. This issue was resolved when Governor Roberts added to the charter bill a provision allowing women to register late. But McGugin did nothing to win female support when he explained that "women would do very well to serve upon humane and hospital commissions" but were unsuited to the manly business of governing the city.[21]

Opponents to McGugin's charter rallied around Felix Zollicoffer Wilson, aged fifty-five, a descendant of the famed Confederate General Zollicoffer, a successful wholesale grocer, and a veteran of the City Council in the pre-Howse era. A slate of candidates (including the first woman candidate for council, Nellie Roche, from the Tenth Ward, encompassing Vanderbilt University) ran against the McGugin charter ticket. They pledged to first elect Wilson as mayor-manager, then scrap the entire McGugin charter and return Nashville to the mayor-council form of government.

On March 31 most of the Wilson slate, which called itself the Citizens' ticket, rode to an easy victory on a wave of moral indignation against Mayor Gupton, Chief Barthell, bootlegging, the notorious Western Front, and the McGugin charter, which was now depicted in the *Tennessean* as a nefarious plot to perpetuate the "Gupton machine." (Nellie Roche lost a hard-fought campaign by only fifty-eight votes. Women were now vitally important in city politics but not yet as officeholders.)[22] On May 5, at their first meeting after the March election, the new council issued charges against Mayor Gupton involving malfeasance, neglect of duty, and "pernicious political activities." They suspended him from office and elected Felix Z. Wilson to take his place immediately. Gupton resigned along with Chief Barthell rather than battle the issue in court.[23]

Mayor Wilson appointed a new police chief, James W. Smith, who personally led a vigorous clean-up campaign, raiding the brothels and gambling houses in the downtown. Nashville, the *Tennessean* announced with satisfaction toward the end of July 1921, was now a "closed town."[24] By January 1922 Chief Smith claimed over 1,000 arrests from enforcing the prohibition laws alone. The next month Gipsy Smith, the famed evangelist, came to Nashville and saved thousands of souls in a protracted revival at the Ryman Auditorium and in tent meetings in working-class neighborhoods. The Methodists and Baptists were inspired to renew their efforts in behalf of Sunday closing laws affecting filling stations and baseball.[25] The *Tennessean* printed every sermon Gipsy Smith delivered in Nashville and applauded the march of moral reform and good government.[26]

By June 1922 Mayor Wilson was prepared to promote a new city charter and return Nashville to the mayor-council plan, as he had promised in the election. In the primary elections for Davidson County's legislative representatives that summer a slate pledged to Wilson's new charter ran successfully against Gupton loyalists who advocated returning to a commission form of government.[27] Wilson's slate was victorious, and plans were laid to introduce a new charter bill when the state legislature convened the coming January. Then, at the end of November 1922, just as Wilson and good government were riding high, a disaffected group within the City Council, apparently hostile to Wilson's moral reforms and perhaps suspicious of his political designs, cajoled a majority of eight councilmen to abruptly vote Wilson out of office. Percy Sharpe, a former magistrate, was elected by the council to fill the job until the enactment of the new charter.[28]

After three charter reforms and three ousted mayors, the new charter approved early in 1923 returned the city to essentially the same style of government it had had before 1913. The mayor would be elected directly by the people, and twenty-five councilmen would be elected by the voters in their wards. Now even the Board of Public Works (composed of the mayor and two other members), along with the city judge and city attorney, would be elected directly by the voters rather than appointed, as before. Even the old ward boundaries were restored with only minor changes.[29]

THE RETURN OF HILARY HOWSE

As the crusaders for good government stood mired in factionalism and splattered with political mud—slung most often by fellow reformers—the irrepressible Hilary Howse, in immaculate costume, returned to the political arena. The irony of his redemption in the city election of 1923 was underscored by his ability to don the sanctimonious garb worn by his reformist foes. Howse had married a "high class Christian woman," Jennie Wheeler, who he claimed had wrought a moral reformation in the former *bon vivant*. Moreover, Howse testified he had been "saved" at one of Gipsy Smith's revivals the previous year. Indeed, he became a deacon in the Vine Street Christian Church and promised, if elected, to enforce prohibition and all the laws of the land. Howse also persisted in clearing his name after the 1915 scandal. He fought the ouster suit all the way to the state Supreme Court, which absolved him of any personal wrongdoing in connection with the city funds. His only sin, he told the voters, was his refusal to enforce the prohibition laws, and now he was a changed man.

Howse walked and talked like an upright reformer, but at the same time he reached out to his old constituency among blacks and working-class whites. He opened his campaign with two speeches to black audiences, promising them a new high school and a friend in city hall.[30] In North Nashville black candidates, W.H. McGavock and Dr. Ernest

Maryland, ran with Howse from the third and fourth wards, respectively. To the recently enfranchised women voters of Nashville, Howse promised more jobs for women in the Police Department and assured them that in his new married and religious state he would keep the community safe from liquor and vice. Howse's former enemy in 1915, publisher Edward B. Stahlman, now endorsed Howse's candidacy in the *Banner*, which was an important confirmation of his claim to respectability in 1923.[31] His opponent in 1923, Felix Z. Wilson, had strong backing from the *Tennessean* but was constantly having to defend against attacks on his record and explain his own embarrassing ouster.[32]

Hilary Howse swept nearly every ward in the election of May 10, 1923, and came away with 62 percent of the total vote, almost 3,000 more than Wilson. Many of Howse's running mates were victorious also, though the two black candidates, McGavock and Maryland, lost, probably because of ballot box tampering. Only the Eighth, Ninth, and Tenth wards, around the silk-stocking district of West End, denied Howse a majority. In all it was a stunning vindication of Howse and the brand of professional politics he personified. Howse embraced some of the reformer's causes and altered his public image in 1923, but this was a measure of his shrewdness as a politician, responding to a new constituency of women and businessmen while continuing to cultivate his old constituency of blacks and working-class whites. Howse went on to win against T. J. McMorrough in 1927 and Felix Z. Wilson again in 1931. Seemingly invincible, he ran unopposed in 1935.[33]

The Howse machine was in reality a coalition of different groups within the community. City and county government employees grew in numbers with the expansion of government in the 1920s and 1930s, giving Howse a loyal core of campaign workers and contributors. City employees were required to donate 1 percent of their salaries to a "welfare fund," which Howse used in a generous mixture of politics and charity to win support among the city's black and white poor. The Howse machine dispensed tons of coal and truckloads of groceries to Nashville's destitute during a period when official channels of welfare were limited, at best. To indignant defenders of good government this was a political slush fund used to bribe voters and pay their poll taxes. To the recipients of Howse's charity it was personal politics at its very best, and they showed their appreciation on election day.

Out in the wards, mobilizing the voters were a constellation of small, neighborhood businessmen (often saloonkeepers, bootleggers, or gamblers) and lower-level city and county officeholders who built small ward-level "machines" through their personal charisma and small favors to constituents. Howse, in turn, earned their support by allowing these saloon owners, gamblers, and bootleggers to operate under cover. He permitted just enough police raids of bootleggers, saloons, and brothels to demonstrate his good intentions to the reformers, but the raids were never sufficiently vigorous to discourage the Nashville underground for long. Tennessee allowed the sale of beer after the nation repealed prohibition in 1933, but liquor was banned under the state prohibition law from 1909 until 1939 when a local option law was passed to permit off-sale liquor and wine. Unintentionally, the prohibitionists had encouraged strong links between the liquor interests and politicians like Howse, who knew how to use his allies to full advantage.[34] Through his control of a large bloc of votes in Nashville, Howse was able to influence who got elected to county office, and the Howse machine reached into state politics as well.[35] Though never as powerful as Boss Ed Crump of Memphis, who dominated Tennessee politics in this era, Howse was a political power to be reckoned with between 1923 and 1938.

THE RISE OF URBAN PLANNING

Howse's political clout did not derive solely from ward heelers, nor from free coal and groceries for the poor. He also made his peace with downtown business leaders, who had come to respect his abilities as a professional politician after 1923—just as Howse had learned to respect their power after his ouster in 1915. Howse was an uneducated man who understood politics in personal terms as a game of exchanging favors and perpetuating his regime. His vision of social change and economic development was shortsighted and subservient to the main object of staying in office. Business progressivism called for long-range social planning, research, rational bureaucratic programs for city improvements, education, and welfare. Howse learned to give these business progressives and planners a role in city government, even if he continued to distrust their aims.

One of the major objectives of business progressivism concerned urban planning, zoning, and traffic control. The age of the automobile brought unprecedented problems in traffic congestion, suburban expansion, rapid neighborhood change, and a host of other difficulties, all exacerbated by rapid population growth.[36] As early as 1917, in the wake of the Howse ouster, the idea for a planning commission was advanced when the Nashville Engineering Association offered its services gratis to the city to prepare new building codes, plan a new water system, and aid in general city planning.[37]

By 1925 the flurry of downtown construction and the pressing problems of traffic control brought business leaders to push for an official city planning commission. Luke Lea and other business spokesmen promoted the idea at a meeting of the Exchange Club in November.[38] The next year the Tennessee legislature, at the behest of the Nashville Chamber of Commerce, passed an amendment to the city charter enabling the council to add a planning commission, and the council complied by authorizing the mayor to appoint such a commission. But Mayor Howse was suspicious of this proposed commission of experts and eminent business leaders, fearing they would hamper his political tactics of granting city contracts to allies. He stalled and refused to appoint anyone to the new commission. The Chamber of Commerce organized a city Planning and Zoning Committee to push for stronger mandatory legislation. In 1929 Lea's *Tennessean* endorsed the idea of a Planning and Zoning Commission in revealing terms: "We have certainly reached the period when a great scheme of city planning should be dominated by the best and most intelligent thought of the community and not be made subservient to any political or factional interest. Nashville has suffered too long from the rule of politics. It now should have a reign of business and of beauty and of appreciation for the present and of the future."[39]

It was not until 1931, however, that Howse finally appointed members to the Planning and Zoning Commission. They included Art J. Dyer of Nashville Bridge Company, chairman, along with three other prominent business leaders; with the Board of Public Works (which included Mayor Howse) they constituted the city Planning and Zoning Commission. By 1932 the commission launched a full-scale study of land-use patterns in the city. Out of this came a comprehensive zoning and building code ordinance, passed by the council in July 1932. Zoning gave businessmen and realtors as well as city planners a powerful tool with which to control the orderly growth of the city, to protect property values, and to reinforce patterns of residential segregation by class and race by imposing restrictions on the number of families per dwelling and the number of boarders allowed with a family.[40] Gerald Gimre, a city planner trained at the University of Illinois, directed the 1932 study and became a major force behind the advance of modern planning in Nashville. He helped push through the state legislature a bill to make the Nashville Planning and Zoning Commission a regional and county planning agency and was instrumental in obtaining federal aid for studies of land use, traffic control, public transportation, housing, and other improvements.[41] The Planning Commission's transportation surveys of 1934 and 1937 placed the whole problem of planning in a historical context and showed how the automobile had disrupted the orderly expansion of a city formerly organized around streetcars. Nashville's transportation problems included notoriously high auto accident rates and badly congested narrow streets in the downtown. The 1934 report recommended a Traffic Commission to formulate a modern traffic code, but this constituted another intrusion on the Howse machine, and it was postponed until 1940.[42] The 1937 report focused on the inadequacy of the streetcar system, in a sorry state of decline because of the advent of the automobile and the migration of the retail shopping center away from the transfer stations near the Public Square.[43]

SUBURBAN GROWTH AND ANNEXATION

One of the greatest obstacles to effective city planning was the rapid expansion of settlement beyond the city limits. This meant that wealthier suburbanites drew away from the city, abandoning their civic responsibility to the city and eroding the city tax base in the process. The solution was to annex the suburbs, to enlarge the tax base, and to make urban services such as water, sewers, schools, and streets more efficient through economies of scale and comprehensive metropolitan planning. Hilary Howse, on the other hand, had a strong political base in the poor neighborhoods of the old central city, and he distrusted the suburbanites who usually voted against him. But here also, Howse learned to compromise. In 1925 a major annexation absorbed the Hillsboro, Belmont, and Sylvan Park neighborhoods on the fast-growing west side of the city. These largely middle-class suburbs were eager to join the city in order to benefit from the services that the city offered in schools, police, water, and streets.[44] Now that the political and financial condition of city government was back on a sound footing and Howse's new public image was more acceptable to reformers, most of these suburbanites saw no reason not to join the city.

Other wealthier suburbs resisted annexation. The Richland district, along West End near present day Bowling Avenue, voted against annexation in 1925 but joined the city in 1929, along with a large area around Lockeland Springs in East Nashville. In Belle Meade, Nashville's richest suburb in the 1920s, 300 voters signed a petition against annexation in 1925, arguing that taxes would increase but services would not immediately improve.[45] Though Belle Meade suffered serious problems in water supply, sewerage, police and fire protection, this wealthy suburb preferred to remain apart from the city and provide its own private services by individual subscription. In 1938 Belle Meade became an incorporated city in its own right, a tactic designed to thwart annexation and prevent additional apartment building through strict zoning. The struggle of Belle Meade's residents to acquire basic services—water, garbage collection, police and fire protection—served as an example to other, less wealthy suburbs of the advantages of annexation.[46]

Despite resistance among wealthier suburbs like Belle Meade the city expanded from 18.2 square miles in 1924 to 26.4 square miles in 1930.[47] Simultaneously the tax base expanded from $130.4 million in 1923 to almost $163 million in 1926. Howse pushed forward eight bond

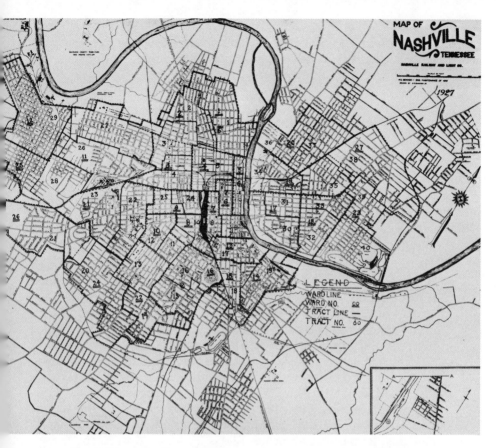

Figure 22. Map: Nashville, 1927. Ward numbers are underlined. Western suburban neighborhoods of Belmont and Hillsboro (Ward 24), Sylvan Park (25), Richland (26), and, on the east side, Lockeland Springs (27) all joined the city in the 1920s, but the automobile allowed settlement to push rapidly beyond the city limits. TSLA.

issues totaling $4.5 million for street improvements, five new high schools, and various other city improvements.[48]

HOWSE'S LAST HURRAH

Howse's success in expanding government services met resistance at every bond referendum and every election. During the 1930s conservative forces renewed their efforts to limit government. The Nashville Tax Relief Association criticized the inflated salaries of public officials. The Taxpayers' League tried, usually without success, to defeat major bond issues.[49] The Taxpayers' ticket opposed Howse's People's ticket at the polls and sought to expose graft and waste in the Howse machine. The *Tennessean*, the voice of reform in Nashville, grudgingly endorsed Howse in 1927 but resumed opposition when Felix Z. Wilson ran against Howse in 1931. Luke Lea's newspaper provided a forum for frequent charges of voter fraud and corruption in the Howse machine. The familiar attacks on the lax enforcement of the liquor laws also reemerged from time to time during Howse's long reign.

The first serious challenge came in November 1929 when Howse fought off another move to oust him from office. Attorney General Richard M. Atkinson brought charges of payroll padding and the misuse of funds against city officials. The newly elected county sheriff, Gus Kiger, exposed the "underworld politics" of the "lawless" Howse machine. Temperance advocates in the Tennessee Anti-Saloon League and the Baptist church rose to the occasion, blasting the sad state of morals in Nashville. Howse dismissed the charges as mere preelection politics, and with support from city attorney and loyal ally Kinnard T. McKonnico, he forced his opponent to withdraw the ouster suit. The calamity on Wall Street helped to distract the business leaders of Nashville from local political reform. When the ouster move failed, Howse, McKonnico, and the "City Hall crowd" danced and sang in the halls, shot off firecrackers, and celebrated another victory over the reformers.[50]

But by the mid-1930s the charges of election fraud, graft, and corruption were mounting steadily, with abundant publicity in the *Tennessean*. Howse, born in 1866, was an old man by this time, and the prospect of his running for a fifth consecutive term at age seventy-two doubtlessly spurred on his enemies after his unopposed victory at the polls in 1935. In that year the County Court investigated charges of corruption and "fee grabbing" in the justice of the peace courts and sparked a campaign to abolish these courts.[51] Later that year, the grand jury conducted a lengthy probe of voter registration in Nashville, which confirmed charges of bribery by machine candidates, usually through paying the poll tax for loyal voters."[52] By 1937 new legislation allowed

Figure 23. Hilary Howse with Huey Long, during the LSU-Vanderbilt football game in 1934. *Tennessean* Library.

the use of voting machines to reduce the possibility of voter fraud, and within a year they were in use across the city.[53] William M. "Billy" Carr, chairman of the Davidson County Election Commission, was forced to resign from public office in the wake of the voting-fraud scandal.[54]

In February 1937 Thomas Cummings, Davidson County representative in the Tennessee legislature, led a more direct assault on the Howse machine by proposing an independent audit commission to inspect the city's books. Though Cummings's bill was defeated by Howse loyalists in the legislature, it brought new public concern to the condition of city hall and reminded many voters of the 1915 scandals that had led to Howse's first downfall.[55] Joe Hatcher, political columnist for the *Tennessean*, wrote that "there's too much smoke not to be considerable fire underneath. . . ."[56] By April, Cummings, representing seven former city employees, called for a probe of the 1-percent payroll deduction for Howse's "welfare fund," which had long been suspected as the source of poll tax payments and small bribes.[57] At the same time Cummings sponsored a bill requiring elected city officials to retire at age seventy, which would have immediately retired Howse, then seventy-one.[58] Within the City Council, John Lechleiter, a dedicated reformer from the West End district, became a thorn in the side of the Howse machine. He was particularly concerned about the city schools and called for probes of political influence in the Board of Education.[59] Another Howse opponent in the council, Elkin Garfinkle, suggested to the Board of Public Works in April 1937 a plan to grant Howse a handsome $5,000 annual pension on retirement to lure him out of office before the next election. The board approved the plan, but the old man proudly refused the offer and swore he would never accept a dollar in retirement pay.[60]

To add to his troubles Howse alienated many stall operators at the new city market house when he raised rents to help cover higher costs. City hall employees also began to grumble about salary discrepancies.[61] The machine was apparently falling into disarray as the scandals erupted one after another. Internal factions jockeyed for position should Howse retire or be defeated in the 1939 election.

The new county courthouse and city hall was nearing completion as the Howse machine was falling apart. Howse, who had ruled the city from his cluttered quarters in the old city hall building, never moved his office to the new modern building; he died quietly on January 2, 1938.[62] Howse had been first elected mayor almost twenty-nine years earlier and was in office all but eight of the intervening years. He died with only one memorial from the city he had served so long. Just before his death the city's "newest and finest high school," in the heart of the silk-stocking district on West End Avenue, was named Hilary Howse High School.[63] Shortly after his death, however, students at the

Figure 24. Mayor Howse's funeral procession, January 1938, in front of the new courthouse and city hall. An unidentified black man pays homage to the mayor. *Tennessean* Library.

school successfully petitioned the Board of Education to change the name to West End High School.[64] Howse's body lay in state in the lobby of the new courthouse as hundreds of citizens passed the bier to pay respects to the man who had ruled Nashville for so long. Outside, as the casket was borne to the hearse, a loyal black admirer bowed to the man who had given his people what little leverage they had in local government. Hilary Howse was a consummate politician, a man of flexible moral principles, willing to close his eyes to petty vice and fraud and glad to exchange favors with his allies. For all these reasons he was unacceptable to those who wanted a businesslike government, and for those same reasons he was indispensable to the city during a period of tumultuous change.

A NEW DEAL FOR NASHVILLE

Nashville's economy had roared through the 1920s, sweeping aside an earlier mood of demoralization and timidity among local business leaders. The outside control of the L&N railroad and the failure to attract and hold local industry was blamed for Nashville's laggard performance before World War I. But the war brought the DuPont powder plant, which was later converted to a rayon plant. Other northern textile, clothing, and shoe manufacturing industries were drawn to Nashville's cheap labor and the Chamber of Commerce's appealing industrial policy.

The city's nascent insurance industry, led by National Life and Accident and Life and Casualty, aggressively expanded into new markets and sponsored new radio stations to promote their product. A new breed of young, competitive bankers made Nashville's "Wall Street of the South" a regional center for banking, brokerage, and bond sales. Leading the pack was young Rogers Caldwell, the "J.P. Morgan of the South," who built Caldwell and Company into a one-half billion dollar financial empire during the 1920s.

Then it suddenly collapsed. The national economy signaled serious trouble in October 1929, when the New York stock market crashed. But it was not until more than a year later, November 14, 1930, that the Depression hit Nashville. Caldwell and Company declared bankruptcy that day, 120 banks throughout the South fell with it, and several local banks had to merge or go under.[1]

When the full force of the national economic crisis was first felt in Nashville the response of business and political leaders was confused. There were repeated efforts to reverse the trend with confident assertions of the coming prosperity. "There's No Depression Here," one full-page advertisement in the *Tennessean* trumpeted in September 1930. With equal confidence Mayor Hilary Howse and the Chamber of Commerce declared Prosperity Week just a month before the collapse of Caldwell and Company.[2] Even as the Depression deepened, voluntary efforts to combat unemployment were preferred by many to government intervention. Businessmen formed a Committee of One Hundred on Unemployment to instill confidence in employers and persuade them to absorb the growing thousands of jobless men and women in the city.[3]

But estimates of unemployment shot up to 25 percent by the end of 1930 despite all the cheery forecasts.[4] After Caldwell's fall the newspapers noted a growing number of suicides among prominent businessmen whose lives were suddenly shattered by financial blows.[5] Signs of massive hunger and poverty appeared by 1931. Armies of transient beggars wandered into the city, some holed up in squatters' shantytowns along the riverbank, others milled around the downtown, looking for work or panhandling. Reports of infant malnutrition and food shortages appeared. Members of the middle class were pawning wedding rings, family heirlooms, even shoes, to buy food and pay the rent.[6] Banks issued scrip for currency, colleges bartered for tuition, and retailers desperately cut prices to draw shell-shocked consumers back to the stores.[7] The normal sources of local voluntary and public relief agencies—Salvation Army, Goodwill, Community Chest, and the County Welfare Commission—were strained beyond capacity by the crowd of new applicants.[8] Relief applicants rose from about 2,600 in 1929 to nearly 10,000 in 1936. Private charitable donations to the relief effort rose slightly at first, then fell as the Depression deepened. Relief would have to come from government, and only the federal government was up to the job.[9]

THE NEW DEAL COMES TO NASHVILLE

For business and political leaders who had come of age in the flush times of World War I and the 1920s and who saw this as the dawn of a new era of sustained, irreversible prosperity, it was difficult to accept the notion that the Depression of the 1930s was an unprecedented crisis requiring entirely new remedies. That the federal government should play an important role in directing economic development was not altogether new to men who during World War I had lobbied for federal projects at Muscle Shoals and Old Hickory and for an army recruitment camp in Belle Meade. But in the 1930s the federal government was to assume a massive and permanent presence in Nashville and the South through a variety of programs, especially the Public Works Administration (PWA), the Works Progress Administration (WPA), and the Tennessee Valley Authority (TVA).

The thrust of federal involvement during the New Deal was particularly strong in the South, which President Roosevelt had identified as "the nation's number one economic problem." Roosevelt was personally fond of the South, but more important, he and his economic planners saw its lack of development as a burden on the entire nation and set out to eradicate poverty in the region. Moreover, Roosevelt, in order to launch his array of federal programs, needed the support of southern politicians, who held senior positions on several key congressional committees.[10] Nashville's strategic political position within the state made the ascendant Democratic regime especially generous in its favors to the city. Nashville and Middle Tennessee acted as a fulcrum in a state weighted with Democrats in the west and Republicans in the east. In 1928 Tennessee Democrats rejected their party's nominee, Al Smith, an Irish-Catholic from New York's Tammany Hall, and the state went for Herbert Hoover. Even Davidson County broke a long string of Democratic landslides in presidential elections and came out for Hoover with over 53 percent of the votes in a heavier than usual turnout. In 1932 Nashville led Middle Tennessee in a massive shift back to the Democratic choice, FDR. The Davidson County vote that year was three to one in favor of Roosevelt.[11]

Strong political links developed between Middle Tennessee and Washington, D.C., as the New Deal evolved. Joseph W. Byrns, Nashville's congressional representative since 1909, served as Speaker of the House before his death in 1936. Cordell Hull, a native of the Cumberland River valley, became U.S. Senator from Tennessee in 1930 and was appointed Secretary of State in 1933. Silliman Evans, Sr., came from Fort Worth, Texas (by way of Washington, D.C., and Baltimore) in 1937 to take over Luke Lea's bankrupt *Tennessean* and turned the paper into a powerful organ for the New Deal.[12] The business community, too, gave its support to FDR. Later, many Nashville business leaders would oppose the New Deal for its prolabor policies and its incursions into slum clearance, public housing, and electric power with TVA, but in the dark days of 1932 and 1933 the commercial civic elite of the city rallied strongly behind FDR.

In the summer of 1933 the National Recovery Administration (NRA) held meetings with employers to gain support for a code of fair practices. The NRA code required employers to pledge to maintain uniform wages and prices within each line of business and to rehire laid-off workers. The Chamber of Commerce, led by its Committee of One Hundred on Unemployment, spearheaded the drive to enlist employers in the NRA. It held daily meetings to explain the new code and sent out seventy-five speakers to spread the word. By August 6, 70 percent of Nashville employers had signed the agreement. One thousand workers went door-to-door, seeking pledges from 50,000 consumers that they would buy only from NRA businesses, marked by the sign of the blue eagle in the store window.[13] There were suburban women who worried

Figure 25. House Speaker Joseph W. Byrns of Nashville, *right with hand on hat,* escorts President Franklin Roosevelt, Eleanor Roosevelt, and Governor Hill McAlister during the president's visit to Nashville in November 1934. *Tennessean* Library.

that the NRA code would apply to domestic servants, and several employers could not agree on the standards for wage and price controls. But most Nashville businessmen responded with alacrity, displaying the NRA blue eagle as a proud symbol of the spirit of patriotism and cooperation that FDR instilled in America at this time. There were glib prophecies that payrolls would grow, purchasing would soar, and the Depression would rapidly recede. "The system seems so simple," the *Tennessean* buoyantly exclaimed, "it is a wonder that mankind has lived through all the depressions of history without a single nation ever daring to undertake giving it a trial before."[14]

FEDERAL RELIEF AND PUBLIC BUILDING PROJECTS

These expectations led to disappointment, the Depression dragged on, and FDR moved to more drastic measures. Nashville's business community did not object strenuously in 1935 when FDR went beyond regulating employers in the private sector to make the federal government a major employer. The WPA was established under Harry Hopkins in 1935 to attack with federal construction and service projects the persistent problem of unemployment. Nashville became state WPA headquarters, and Colonel Harry S. Berry, an old army friend and political ally of Luke Lea, was appointed state WPA administrator. Nashville became one of the country's leading recipients of WPA funds, and it was through this program that the New Deal left its most impressive marks on the city.[15]

At first local politicians feared that the intrusion of WPA funds would undermine their system of patronage. When Berry won a $236,000 road project for Davidson County, the county highway commission simply refused it, fearing the project would require federal regulation of contracts and hiring of the unemployed, which would upset politically favored road contractors. Though new county roads were desperately needed by farmers trucking produce to Nashville, the county government preferred to channel the money into an enormous malaria-control project. This employed four hundred men, pumped thousands of dollars into the local economy, but was a wasted endeavor, given that malaria had long since ceased to be a serious threat in Davidson County.[16]

Soon the WPA learned to work within the existing political structure rather than reform it, and local politicians learned that the flow of federal dollars could bolster rather than erode their political power. All the dollars that poured into the Nashville area were not spent with careful forethought; there was no time for that, and the primary goal was simply to get people working again. Moreover, the relatively low cost in wages and materials during the 1930s made the WPA projects a bargain despite the margin of waste.

WPA workers were mobilized in 1937 during a devastating flood that left 5,000 homeless in Nashville. They restored Fort Negley, a neglected remnant of the city's Civil War history. The city government also used WPA funds to pave and expand Nashville's dilapidated street system. What began as a modest $1.5-million paving program rapidly escalated into a massive $8.3-million project, which would have added 5,000 men to the city payrolls. This project was trimmed considerably (to about $2.5 million) before completion, but it was a major improvement in a city that had long since outgrown its street system.[17]

The municipal airport was another long-sought goal of the city's business leaders that the New Deal finally brought to fruition. As early as 1930 the Chamber of Commerce recognized the importance of a modern airport to Nashville's future among southern cities. Just as railroads had incited vigorous competition among the region's cities before World War I, the air age opened up a new round of rivalry. The first landing strip, Hampton Field (in the area of present-day Hampton Avenue), served the city until 1921 when residential expansion and larger airplanes made it obsolete. Blackwood Field, built for the state National Guard, served the city from 1921 to 1928, when McConnell Field (now McCabe Park Golf Course) was built; it remained in use until 1939.[18] The growing interest in air passenger service and Nashville's claim on federal airmail service to the South required a "Class A" airport on the outskirts of town. In 1930 the Chamber of Commerce unsuccessfully urged the people of Nashville to approve an airport bond issue.[19] The chamber set up a special Aviation Committee, which began a second push for a new airport the next year, this time with federal dollars from a Reconstruction Finance Corporation loan to be repaid with airport revenues.[20] With the arrival of WPA, Nashville business leaders now saw their opportunity to finance the airport. The city purchased a site in October 1935, and construction began the following November.[21] By the end of 1937 the new airport was finished; American Airlines landed the first plane. Rumors of boondoggles among contractors and politicians marred the opening celebration. The original cost estimate of $385,000 had vaulted to $1.2 million by this time. But Berry pointed to the rapid construction of the facility, and a city that had waited so long for a new airport seemed in no mood to question the fine points.[22] In 1939 the airport was named Berry Field to honor the man who had exerted his power as Tennessee's WPA administrator to bear favorably on Nashville's future.[23]

Nashville's public parks were equally indebted to the federal funds that poured through the WPA. The park system begun in 1902 had suffered from the neglect of a tax-shy citizenry. Nearly $55,000, allotted to construct Elmington Park on West End Avenue in 1936, was surrep-

Figure 26. WPA workers removing abandoned streetcar rails on Church Street, part of a massive program to improve and resurface the city's streets. *Tennessean* Library.

Figure 27. American Airlines carries the U.S. mail into Nashville's new airport, Berry Field, 1940. Tennessee Department of Conservation Photograph Collection, TSLA.

titiously diverted into the construction of walls, sidewalks, and other improvements in parks throughout the city. The most significant WPA contributions to the city's park system were the improvements of Percy Warner Park and Edwin Warner Park. The former was a vast, hilly area of 868 acres donated to the city by Luke Lea during his heyday in 1927 and named to honor his father-in-law. Located at the terminus of the Belle Meade Boulevard trolley line, the park drew weekend visitors and helped make the streetcar line profitable while it enhanced the development of Belle Meade. Lea's generosity was compounded by the addition of Edwin Warner Park in 1930. But all this land remained an undeveloped, rugged range of old farms and forest before the WPA poured $215,000 into park improvements in 1936. A work force of 300 men cut miles of new roads curving through the park. They erected retaining walls, picnic grounds, and a handsome entrance gate at the end of Belle Meade Boulevard. Then in 1938, in a remarkable display of generosity to Nashville's horsey set, another $45,000 in WPA funds was added to construct a steeplechase course and $12,000 for a riding academy inside the park. A congressional investigation later that year used this project as a devastating example of corruption in the WPA. Here the sport of kings, in a park almost fifteen miles from the city, accessible only by auto, and by custom closed to black citizens, was being underwritten by the taxpayers—and at twice the cost necessary, according to one estimate. The investigation also revealed that almost $2,500 was spent on a granite monument, near the main gate of the park, that memorialized Colonel Berry and his World War I regiment, the 115th Field Artillery.[24] Critics took delight in quoting William I. DuPont, Jr., the "internationally known . . . sportsman," who admired the steeplechase as "the finest course in America and one that compares favorably with famous plants in foreign lands." It was revealed in the investigation that Mr. DuPont "had a hand in designing" the steeplechase "at the insistence of local horsemen and members of the city park commission."[25] Those patricians who grumbled that federal relief was corrupting the poor now had reason to wonder if it had not done the same to the rich.

These and other scandals marred the reputation of the WPA and gave fuel to critics of the New Deal. But the Warner parks—steeplechase and all—were a magnificent legacy to the people of Nashville, one that would be used by more of its citizens in the affluent times following World War II, when widespread automobile ownership and desegregation eventually opened the parks to the enjoyment of all people.

Federal dollars also helped rebuild Nashville's school system during the New Deal. Before the federal works projects of the 1930s the condition of local schools made a mockery of the city's claim as the Athens of the South. The 1931 Bachman Report, a survey of the city's public schools directed by Frank Bachman of Peabody College, scandalized the Board of Education. It showed that Nashville, compared with

Figure 28. Horseback riders on the bridle paths of Percy Warner Park overlooking Belle Meade Boulevard. This WPA project benefited the poor who built it and the wealthy who enjoyed the bridle paths, steeplechase, and other amenities of a park next to the western suburbs. WPA Photograph, in *Tennessean* Library.

Figure 29. Hilary Howse High School in the final stages of completion, 1938, renamed West End High School after Mayor Howse's death. *Tennessean* Library.

seventeen other southern cities, ranked sixteenth in per pupil expenditures, seventeenth in per pupil value of school property, eleventh (among fourteen cities) in instructional cost per pupil, and last in teachers' salaries per pupil.

A few new suburban schools for whites met minimal standards in space, lighting, and amenities, but the overall condition of the school plant was grim, especially the black schools. The Bachman Report compiled masses of statistics to demonstrate the poor condition of school buildings, but it was the photographs of dark classrooms with old fashioned benches, coal stoves, wooden latrines, and inadequate playgrounds that told the story best.[26] With millions of federal relief dollars available through the PWA, beginning in 1933, Nashville took advantage of the opportunity to build several new schools. East High School, West End High School, and the new Pearl High School for blacks were erected with PWA funds in the 1930s, as were several junior high and elementary schools.[27]

As the new school buildings went up, a valiant group of school reformers fought hard to improve conditions in the old schools, upgrade teachers' salaries, raise school taxes, and take the schools out of politics. Led by George Cate, Sr., on the Board of Education, Mrs. Delbert Mann of the Parent Teachers Association (in 1938 the first woman to be appointed to the Board of Education), John H. Lechleiter on the City Council, and aided by Silliman Evans, Sr., and his *Tennessean*, school reform made slow, uphill progress before World War II. In 1936 Nashville stood dead last in per student school expenditures among all American cities of 100,000 or more population. There was no place to go but up for the public schools of the Athens of the South.[28]

The federal public works programs of the New Deal also brought new life to construction downtown. Indeed, before the PWA and WPA, commercial construction downtown had come to a halt with the Depression. The PWA program allowed construction of the Tennessee Supreme Court Building, State Office Building, a new post office on Broadway, and remodeling of the state capitol. The new Supreme Court and State Office buildings displaced many of the last remaining mansions on Capitol Hill and anticipated the urban renewal project launched on that site in 1949.[29]

The Public Square was also radically changed with the destruction of the old city hall, courthouse, and market house and the construction of the Davidson County Public Building and Court House, finished in late 1937. When plans for the demolition of the old courthouse were first announced, as early as 1930, defenders of this landmark, led by the Centennial Club, the Daughters of the American Revolution, and the Young Women's Christian Association, insisted that it had been designed by William Strickland, the famous architect of the state capitol and the First Presbyterian Church. When this claim was disproved

Figure 30. The new Davidson County Public Building and Court House after its completion in 1937. *World Outlook* (Nov. 1939).

(Strickland's son, Francis, was the architect), demolition proceeded. The *Tennessean* kept up a constant refrain that the new building must follow classical architectural style. The winning design, by Emmons Woolwine of Nashville, was a remarkable blend of neoclassical and art-deco styles. Inside the courthouse WPA artist Dean Cornwell produced several fine murals, but some defenders of the public morals objected to nudes in the courthouse lobby. That, Cornwell wryly answered, was a curious complaint in the Athens of the South.[30] The courthouse and the new market house on the north side, along with the new state government buildings and the new post office, were monuments to the enlarged role of government during the New Deal and the growing dependence of local and state government on Washington. The federal Customs House on Broadway bulged with bureaucrats during the New Deal and new office space had to be rented downtown.[31]

PUBLIC HOUSING AND THE LIMITS OF REFORM

The most controversial buildings that the New Deal sponsored in Nashville were two public housing projects, Cheatham Place for whites and Andrew Jackson Court for blacks, both completed early in 1938 with $4 million in PWA funds. Nashville's slums had been a serious threat to health and a public eyesore since the depression of the 1890s. Now, as the Great Depression hit Nashville, a disturbing number of the poor began to colonize the riverbanks in crude shantytowns. "Some of the families have been there as long as three years," the *Tennessean* noted of a group of five families near the Jefferson Street Bridge in June 1935. "Their houses are made of scrap sheet iron, pieces of tin, wood, and cardboard."[32]

A year earlier the city had proposed a $2-million housing project, and in the summer of 1935 work began on the Andrew Jackson Court for blacks near Fisk University and adjacent to a prosperous neighborhood of middle-class blacks. By March 1936 a white housing project, Cheatham Place, in North Nashville in the Kalb Hollow neighborhood, broke ground.[33] Public housing was a bold new venture in American reform, and in the heady days of the New Deal it seemed to be a logical solution to the slums that blighted the cities. The *Tennessean* heralded the Cheatham Place project with enthusiasm as a "new and clean little town within Nashville [which is] bustling toward completion to house people who formerly existed in dilapidated and unsanitary slums. . . . The spot will resemble a cozy English village . . . with green lawns, flower and vegetable gardens, parks, paved sidewalks and an air of freshness and healthfulness. . . . juvenile delinquency, crime, vice, immorality, disease and all social evils will be greatly reduced." The new public housing project, many hoped, would serve as a yardstick against which to measure housing quality and fair rentals in privately owned housing.[34] Sociologist Charles S. Johnson, of Fisk, spoke eloquently of the public housing program as "a rare opportunity to introduce enlightened social planning and guidance into work with a group long handicapped by low income, [and] poor physical surroundings. . . ."[35]

Nashville's landlords and realtors were less enthusiastic about this experiment in public housing. When plans were announced to expand public housing with a $5-million federal grant, local realtors exerted enormous pressure on the mayor and City Council to limit competition with the private housing market. City officials tried to assuage realtors with promises that public housing would accommodate only the lowest wage earners, those unable to afford private housing.[36] At a spirited public hearing in the fall of 1938 the realtors and landlords vented their grievances openly before the City Council. A latent concern for the plight of the slum dwellers surfaced among some realtors, who urged the city to force slum landlords to clean up existing housing for the poor and obviate the need for federal intervention. "Let's clean up our slums as Christians would do it," one realtor implored. "Let's try to inculcate in these poor people, who live in our slums the desire to live in better surroundings. . . . Let's lift them up spiritually to higher levels first, then they'll take care of their own housing." The realtors were delighted to find an ally in Ira T. Brown, a black landlord who, amid jeering from fellow blacks, stood and denounced public housing: "you can take us Negroes out of the slums, but you can't take slum ways of living out of some classes of us Negroes."[37]

The opposition of realtors and landlords to public housing only proved the point that housing reformers were arguing. "If low cost housing competes with privately owned slums," a U.S. Housing Authority representative explained, "the government doesn't mind." Also, as labor leader Harry Nelson pointed out, the $5-million housing project would provide desperately needed jobs to over 1,200 workers and would pour over $1 million in wages into the local economy.[38]

The City Council went forward with the housing program, but large concessions were made to the opposition by appointing three of their sympathizers to the five-member Nashville Housing Authority Board.[39] The new board now escalated the program to request $12 million in U.S. Housing Authority funds. The purpose of public housing, at the same time, was redefined as a mechanism for controlling property values. A "belt" of public housing projects, with individual homes and yards rather than row-house apartments, would ring the existing slums of the central city and serve as "a barrier to protect the better residential sections" in the suburbs.[40]

Labor unions and blacks in Nashville protested the composition of the Nashville Housing Authority Board to no avail until U.S. Sena-

Figure 31. Cheatham Place, in the Kalb Hollow district of North Nashville, the first public housing project in Nashville for whites, completed along with Andrew Jackson Court for blacks in 1938. Metropolitan Development and Housing Agency.

tor Kenneth D. McKellar, a strong supporter of the New Deal, intervened. McKellar pointed out that three members of the Nashville board lived outside the city and that one other member had openly opposed FDR in 1932 and 1936. McKellar effectively blocked the federal housing grant to Nashville until the board resigned and five politically agreeable members were appointed in their place. Gerald Gimre, who had served as state director of the U.S. Housing Authority, was named executive director of the reconstituted Nashville Housing Authority Board.[41] McKellar's intervention ensured that Nashville's public housing program would remain in the hands of New Deal loyalists. But the countervailing forces of local politics and social attitudes guaranteed that public housing would go forward within safe channels that threatened only limited competition with private housing. This agreement allowed existing slums to fester and perpetuated—even accentuated—the residential segregation of blacks and whites in Nashville.[42]

WHEN NASHVILLE LABOR STIRRED

The New Deal changed relations between Nashville's employers and labor as much as it changed the city's streets, buildings, parks, airfields, and housing. Before the New Deal, labor in Tennessee had suffered a long history of losing battles against employers, who were often aided by the state.

Before and during World War I the strength of skilled craft unions grew steadily under the umbrella organization of the American Federation of Labor (AF of L) and its state affiliate, the Tennessee Federation of Labor (TF of L), founded in 1896. During the war, labor was strengthened by the National War Labor Board, which sanctioned labor's right to organize and discouraged interruptions of war-related industries by supporting higher wages. In Nashville the DuPont powder plant drew workers away from local employers by offering no more than three dollars a day. Nashville's labor leaders contributed significantly to the union movement in Tennessee. William Birthright, a Nashville barber, became president of the Tennessee Federation of Labor in the 1920s. David Hanley, president of the Nashville Trades and Labor Council, was an active lobbyist for prolabor legislation at the state capitol. Gerald Foley, a plumber, became president of the TF of L in 1939 after twenty years as a labor activist in Nashville.[43]

After the war, employers in Nashville and across the country concentrated on reversing the small gains that labor had made and set out to crush the union movement. The Russian revolution in 1917 and the heightened fear of socialism at home set off a vicious Red Scare in 1919, which played into the hands of antiunion forces. As businessmen dropped wages at the end of the wartime boom, labor mounted a series of strikes in 1919 and 1920. In Nashville in the summer of 1919, one thousand textile workers went out on strike for higher wages, Model Laundry workers were locked out after a strike, and streetcar operators with the Nashville Railway and Light Company struck for recognition of their union.[44] Antilabor forces in Nashville's business community used the Red Scare to whip up popular opposition to the labor movement, and labor leaders were reduced to disavowing socialism and doing their best to wrap the union movement in the flag of patriotism.[45]

During the 1920s the surge in the American economy emphasized new, large-scale, assembly-line manufacturing of consumer goods. These industries typically recruited new laborers outside the old crafts, which now declined in power. In Nashville several new factories producing such items as textiles, shoes, and clothing migrated from the North to avoid unions and socialist influence, which employers identified with the foreign immigrant workers and the intellectuals of the North. These factory owners were attracted to Nashville, as they were to other parts of the South, by industrial promoters in the Chamber of Commerce who boasted of the city's docile, cheap work force, made up—it was invariably pointed out—of "native American stock" and free of "Bolshevik ideas." "It is Nashville's proud boast," a *Tennessean* editorial announced in 1926, "that more than 98 per cent of its population is native born."[46]

During the 1920s Nashville businessmen joined a national movement to advance the "American plan" of "open shops." They assaulted the labor movement as "un-American" and "Bolshevist." John Edgerton, a Gallatin textile manufacturer, became president of the National Association of Manufacturers and served as a national as well as local leader in the campaign against organized labor. Gus Dyer, a Vanderbilt economics professor and an articulate ally of Edgerton, became a popular luncheon speaker at businessmen's clubs, where he attacked the labor movement as a threat to the entire American way of life.[47]

The TF of L tried to counter the antiunion assault of business with a political action committee and a concerted lobby effort.[48] By the end of the 1920s, however, the union movement had failed to arrest the decline in membership and political power. Nothing demonstrated the powerlessness of the labor movement in Tennessee better than the Elizabethton strike of 1929. A spontaneous walkout by young women rayon workers in the East Tennessee town escalated into a militant strike that ended only when Governor Henry Horton called out the National Guard. The Guard teargassed the women strikers and provided an armed guard for scab workers.[49] It was a demoralizing low point in a decade of decline for Tennessee labor.

During the Depression it was the adversaries of labor who were now demoralized. The New Deal soon intervened on behalf of labor and put it on a whole new footing. The National Industrial Recovery

Act, passed in 1933, included Section 7(a) guaranteeing labor's right to organize and bargain collectively through a representative of the workers' choosing. In 1935 the National Labor Relations Act, or Wagner Act (after its sponsor, Senator Robert Wagner of New York), reconfirmed this doctrine and gave it teeth—the National Labor Relations Board (NLRB) was to supervise collective bargaining elections. Employers tried to evade these laws, often by setting up management-controlled company unions. By 1937, however, the courts had ruled on several questions in favor of the unions. In 1938 Congress approved the Fair Labor Standards Act to ensure minimum wages (forty cents per hour) and maximum hours (forty per week) and prohibit child labor whenever interstate commerce was involved.

Buoyed by the support of federal legislation, organized labor in Nashville grew in membership and surged in political prowess and public favor. But Nashville's business community stood tough before the new wind blowing in favor of unions. They worked hard through the Chamber of Commerce to oppose the NRA and the Wagner Act. They supported various sedition acts to tighten immigration laws and suppress communist infiltration. They organized the Southern States Industrial Council in 1933 to thwart the union drive. John Edgerton of Gallatin, the council's leader, defended the South's low wages as a reflection of the "notorious inefficiency" of southern labor and argued vociferously against minimum wage laws. Low southern wages, Edgerton argued, would "preserve labor's racial purity, that is foreign labor will not be attracted to the Southland."[50] Antagonism between workers and management intensified in the 1930s as each side pressed for advantage. Nashville labor organizer Matt Lynch, while organizing hosiery workers in Rockwood, Tennessee, was even kidnapped, apparently by henchmen of the factory owners.[51]

In September 1934 the AF of L's United Textile Workers met a crushing defeat at the end of a twenty-two day general strike. It was, one historian of Tennessee labor wrote, "Elizabethton multiplied several times." Conflict between capital and labor intensified when the Congress of Industrial Organizations (CIO), led by John L. Lewis, split off from the craft-dominated AF of L to organize industrial workers. Their most stunning success came in the organization of textile workers. The CIO's Textile Workers Organizing Committee renewed the campaign to organize southern textile factories. They were determined to end the southern wage discrimination that allowed northern plant owners to undermine northern unions by threatening to move south.[52] The CIO drive in 1937 concentrated in the large cities of the South and made Nashville one of its prime targets. The union paid hundreds of organizers to distribute pamphlets, talk to workers, and hold meetings to draw unskilled factory workers into the movement. In Nashville the CIO made important gains, winning about ten unions and 7,000 members to its cause by 1938. It focused primarily on the publishing, meatpacking, and textile factories.[53] In Nashville the TF of L began its own membership drive in the face of CIO competition and boldly announced a goal of 16,000 new members.[54]

To counter the growth of labor militancy, Nashville's moderate business leaders, in alliance with concerned clergymen, organized the Citizens Council for Industrial Peace to bridge the widening gulf between labor and management. The council attempted to set up a board to arbitrate local labor disputes. The Nashville Trades and Labor Council president T.O. Denham supported the plan but twitted the businessmen: "Labor would respectfully insist that if industry would observe and carry out the laws enacted by the representatives of all the people, as it expects labor to do, there would be no conflict and hence no necessity for a 'peace' council."[55] Another group of businessmen organized Associated Industries, which became part of the Chamber of Commerce in May 1937. It was dedicated to preserving "the harmonious relations between employers and employees which have contributed greatly to the growth and prosperity of this community...."[56] Other, more conservative business leaders rallied behind the Southern States Industrial Council and the Tennessee Manufacturers Association to attack the very legitimacy of the union movement.[57]

The tensions came to an explosive head in April 1937 when the CIO-affiliated Amalgamated Clothing Workers moved to organize the Washington Manufacturing Company workers at three Nashville plants. Elaine Wright, the Amalgamated representative in charge of the drive, passed out handbills at all three plants and held a mass meeting at the Maxwell House Hotel on April 24.[58] The company, an old Nashville firm, took a tough stand and threatened to fire any employees who joined the union, but a growing number of defiant workers joined Amalgamated Clothing Workers. On May 1, by tradition a day of celebration for labor, the company shut down all three plants and locked out 650 employees rather than deal with the union. The factories were still shut down when the NLRB began hearings in the summer of 1937. Washington Manufacturing Company claimed that it had closed down solely because of financial difficulties, but the NLRB charged that the company was guilty of a "deliberate lock out ... designed to crush its employees' effort to organize."[59] The company refused to reopen and, with support from the Chamber of Commerce, attacked the dictatorial ways of the NLRB.[60] The shutdown, they retorted, "was a severe blow to Nashville business ... a deterent to progress, harmful to the city's reputation as a manufacturing center, and damaging to business in many lines."[61] Congressman Clare E. Hoffman warned the Chamber of Commerce in August 1937 of the "turmoil, industrial strife and violence that has followed Communistic agitators in the industrial areas of the North and East...."[62]

Labor used the lockout to blast the business leadership of the city. In August 1937 the *Labor Advocate* denounced the "Vicious Inner Circle of the Nashville Chamber of Commerce," along with John Edgerton and "Disgustus" Dyer, for their efforts to "Landonize" Nashville (Alf Landon, FDR's Republican opponent in 1936, wished to repeal the New Deal) with their "labor-hating" and "Roosevelt-hating" defense of the Washington Manufacturing Company lockout.[63] The lockout coincided with a wave of strikes in other factories. About 1,100 employees at Werthan Bag Company and Ingram Company, both textile plants, walked out in June. Meatpackers at Neuhoff Packing and at Swift and Company went out on strike later that month.[64] Several other, smaller strikes in the long summer of 1937 escalated the antagonism between labor and management. Ultimately the NLRB hearing exposed the Washington Manufacturing Company's illegal efforts to crush the union and forced it to reinstate its workers. It was a victory for labor and for the industrial workers in the CIO in particular. But it was a victory that would never have been won without the powerful arm of the federal government.

Many businessmen would continue to oppose the rise of organized labor, but the significance of the Wagner Act and the authority of the NLRB were now beyond dispute. Though union membership in Nashville remained a minority of the work force, the city's labor leaders enjoyed a political leverage within the Democratic party unknown before the New Deal. If they were not yet on a par with business leaders, they nonetheless had come a long way from the demoralizing days of the 1920s.

THE TENNESSEE VALLEY AUTHORITY

If Nashville's business leaders were generally hostile to federal intervention on behalf of labor as a group, for the most part they were eager to have the government supply cheap electric power to the region, even though TVA was the New Deal's boldest challenge to the principle of private enterprise. When Dwight Eisenhower, the first Republican president since Hoover, attacked the TVA as a symbol of "creeping socialism," he spoke for a large number of conservative Americans. But TVA is better understood as an extension of modern capitalism, a deliberate effort at regional economic development directed by the federal government and justified as both a stimulus for private investment in the region and a model for central economic planning. TVA was only the most extreme among a multitude of New Deal programs designed, not to push America down the road to socialism, but to save capitalism by reforming it and shoring it up where it was weak.

This particular experiment in centralized planning for regional development began haltingly long before the economic crisis of the 1930s. By the time of World War I many farsighted economic leaders were concerned about the uneven development of the national economy. Industrial growth was overly concentrated in the Northeast and Great Lakes regions, and many factories in these regions, particularly those in textiles, shoes, and other old industries, were becoming obsolete. Many textile, clothing, and shoe factories migrated south in the 1920s. The shift toward industrial production of consumer goods required industrialists and government planners to encourage higher wage industries and diversified agriculture in the South.[65]

The first step in the direction of government-sponsored regional development came much earlier, with President Wilson's National Defense Act of 1916, which authorized the construction of Wilson Dam at Muscle Shoals and the construction of a nitrate plant to produce gunpowder and, later, nitrous fertilizers. The project, begun under the emergency of war, became the subject of a long debate over the proper role of government at Muscle Shoals. In 1921 Henry Ford offered to take over the Muscle Shoals development with a long-term lease and turn the area into a "Southern Detroit." But his offer died as Congress debated the merits of government versus private enterprise. Senator George Norris of Nebraska and Kenneth D. McKellar of Memphis, Tennessee, championed the idea of government ownership and together nursed two bills through Congress in 1928 and 1929, only to be vetoed by Republican presidents Coolidge and Hoover. In the campaign of 1932 FDR announced his backing of the Norris-McKellar plan for the Tennessee Valley, and as president-elect he visited Muscle Shoals. On this tour Roosevelt gave hints of grander plans for the valley, with Muscle Shoals now one part of a comprehensive scheme to transform the valley. It would be, FDR speculated, "an opportunity to accomplish a great purpose . . . an example of planning . . . tying in industry and agriculture and flood prevention . . . into a unified whole over a distance of a thousand miles . . . for millions yet unborn. . . ."[66] By April 1933, a bit over a month after he took office, Roosevelt asked Congress to create the Tennessee Valley Authority, "a corporation clothed with the power of government but possessed of the flexibility and initiative of a private enterprise."[67] Within ten days of this message to Congress the Nashville Chamber of Commerce, which had actively promoted the 1916 powder plant at Muscle Shoals, began to organize city, county, and state government officials, along with Chamber of Commerce delegates, from the entire Tennessee Valley region to form the Tennessee Valley Association. Its purpose was to smooth the path for this grand experiment in central planning.[68] By October the association met and elected as its president William R. Manier, Jr., an officer in the Nashville Chamber of Commerce. The association promised to "cooperate in every way possible with the TVA," and Dr. Arthur E. Morgan, TVA chairman, thanked the association for having "ironed out the conflicts of interest which have beset it since its [TVA's] foundation last May."⁶⁹

A "great wave of enthusiasm" for the TVA swept over most of Nashville and the whole valley in the spring of 1933, but there were other interests less enthusiastic about the entry of the federal government into the business of electric power production. The privately owned power companies operating in Tennessee understood fully what FDR and Norris meant when they said TVA would serve as a "yardstick" against which to measure the appropriate services and prices of private power companies. It meant they would be driven from the field by government-subsidized competition, and they fought TVA in the courts and in the marketplace to the bitter end.

In the Aswander case the stockholders of the Alabama Power Company brought suit in August 1933 to prohibit TVA from producing surplus electric power at Wilson Dam and to challenge its constitutional legitimacy. The power companies won a temporary victory in federal district court, but in 1936 the U.S. Supreme Court ruled in TVA's favor on the first question, leaving the whole issue of constitutional legitimacy unresolved. In May 1936 Tennessee Electric Power Company (TEPCO), which had absorbed Nashville Electric Railway and Light Company in 1930, along with eighteen other power companies, joined forces in a new legal attack on TVA. They charged the federal government with "coercion and fraud" in forcing municipalities and counties to buy TVA power under the threat of withholding federal relief funds. TVA, they further charged, had gone beyond its constitutional bounds in building dams for navigation and flood control to become not just a yardstick for private power companies but an aggressive competitor with private enterprise in the production of electric power. The U.S. Supreme Court ruled on the TEPCO case in 1938, giving TVA free rein to "develop its service area" as it chose.⁷⁰

The power companies, failing in their legal attacks on TVA, tried to fight in the marketplace. TEPCO dropped its rates 37 percent beginning in the fall of 1933 to limit the advance of cheap TVA power. TEPCO also began extending power lines into sparsely settled rural areas, which they formerly ignored because of low-profit potential. Rural cooperatives, like the Middle Tennessee Electric Membership Corporation, organized to lure TVA service into their area, were suddenly invaded by "spite lines" brought in by TEPCO to thwart TVA.⁷¹ In the end TEPCO and the other private companies could not compete for long with the cheap hydroelectric power offered by TVA, nor could they rival the federal leverage inherent in PWA and WPA grants. Recognizing their legal and economic defeat, private power companies withdrew from the fight. Wendell Willkie, president of Commonwealth and Southern, parent company of TEPCO, offered to sell outright to TVA all company properties in the region. TEPCO agreed to sell out all but its transit system in Nashville and Chattanooga for $78.6 million. At Mayor Thomas Cummings's urging the Nashville City Council agreed to chip in $14.2 million for control of the Nashville power system, which was reorganized under an autonomous, nonpartisan Electric Power Board, filled with the leading businessmen of Nashville. Because of a prolonged political and legal battle Nashville was the last Tennessee city to get TVA power. TEPCO appealed futilely to businessmen in Nashville to defend free enterprise in the face of government encroachment. At the end of its losing battle the company bought a full page in the daily newspapers, showing a mock book, *The History of TEPCO,* alongside such classics as Pollard's *The Lost Cause,* and Wise's *The End of an Era,* and other immortal works of Tennessee and southern history. "And so," its last page read, "private ownership and initiative withdrew in favor of Government. The Company—pioneer citizen and taxpayer—which for more than half a century served the people of the State of Tennessee—was liquidated."[72]

But the citizens to whom such appeals were being made were excitedly celebrating the long overdue arrival of government-subsidized power in Nashville. On August 19, 1939, a large crowd gathered at Memorial Plaza downtown to hear speeches and brass bands. Patricia Ann Cummings, the mayor's daughter, flipped a switch that set aglow a large sign with the letters "TVA" mounted on top of the state capitol. The *Tennessean* trumpeted the coming of TVA and deservedly took credit for having successfully brought TVA to Nashville.[73] In an editorial cartoon the powerful hand of TVA was shown ringing the doorbell to the city.[74]

Cheap, abundant electric power quickly wrought a miracle in Nashville's economy and its standard of living. From a little over 52,000 customers consuming 257.5 million kilowatt hours of electricity in 1939, the Nashville Electric Service expanded to 200,000 customers by 1949. Prices dropped from 2.64 cents per kilowatt hour to 1.99 cents within ten and one-half months of TVA's takeover.[75] With the advent of cheap TVA power the pall of coal smoke that hung over the city began to abate. Families at all but the lowest level of income could now afford electric service in their homes.[76]

The coming of TVA was only one of several important changes the New Deal brought to Nashville. Though the economic crisis of the 1930s was a severe blow to the local economy and a devastating experience for thousands of Nashville families, the federal government's response to it laid down a new foundation that has shaped Nashville and the South's social and economic development ever since. With the coming of World War II a new generation of political and business leaders would build upon that foundation a more prosperous economic structure and a more open and just social structure. Influencing the construction of both was a strong, but not always comfortable, partnership between the federal government and the city, an alliance forged in the hard times of the Great Depression.

Figure 32. In these cartoons by Tom Little in the *Tennessean*, TVA is depicted as a powerful savior for Nashville and the entire Tennessee Valley region. *Tennessean*, Aug. 20, 1939.

Figure 33. The celebration of TVA's arrival in Nashville in August 1939 featured enormous electrified letters attached to the columns of the state capitol building. *Tennessean* Library.

INTO THE SUNBELT

Once again, war swept Nashville into the currents of profound historical change. Before World War II the leaden hand of the Great Depression still slowed economic recovery. The war launched Nashville and the South into an unprecedented era of sustained growth. In 1940 Nashville, with 167,402 people inside its borders, stood fiftieth in size among American cities. When the population of Davidson County and contiguous suburban counties was included, beginning in 1950, the Nashville Standard Metropolitan Statistical Area (SMSA) claimed 321,758 and was fifty-fifth in size. Three decades later the population in the Nashville SMSA shot up to 850,505, and Nashville climbed eleven notches to forty-fourth place. Urban development across the South boomed with the new economic trends of postwar America.[1] What had been the "nation's number one economic problem" in the 1930s had become by the 1970s the Sunbelt, a prosperous region of new-line industries and healthy cities.[2]

Though many predicted a relapse into economic depression after the war, America as a whole enjoyed remarkable vitality throughout the late 1940s and, with few interruptions, the next two decades. Pundits began talking about the new "post-industrial economy," an advanced stage of development that could meet the basic necessities of food, shelter, and clothing with but a fraction of the nation's productive capacity. The rest could be devoted to consumer goods and services. The modern worker would be rewarded with higher wages, fewer hours, and a planned retirement. The most vital sectors in this new economic order would be in services such as finance and insurance, tourism, entertainment, health, education, military defense, and government administration. In all these capacities, Nashville's economy—which was slow to join the age of "smokestack" industries—was ideally positioned to

108

take advantage of the new currents of development in America. (For a statistical overview of the occupational shifts attending the emergence of Nashville's service economy, see appendix C.)

In addition to its established strength in the coming growth sectors, Nashville had by the 1940s a number of distinct advantages as a site for new enterprises. TVA brought cheap, abundant electric power, with rates frequently 40 percent or more below those of private utility companies elsewhere. By 1946 a natural gas pipeline from the Southwest further enhanced the city's supply of cheap energy.[3] New breakthroughs in transportation also strengthened Nashville's trading capacity. During the 1940s the Army Corps of Engineers began a series of dams on the Cumberland River, finally opening it to year-round navigation and reducing the risk of floods for factories and warehouses near the river. In 1945 the Interstate Commerce Commission broke the long and powerful grip of northern-owned railroads on the South by ruling that southern freight rates were discriminatory and must be revised. This, at long last, allowed Nashville shippers and manufacturers to compete on a more even basis with their northern competitors. The construction of the Municipal Airport, Berry Field, in 1937 and its expansion in subsequent years gave the city a Class A airport. Served primarily by American and Eastern airlines, the airport handled a growing volume of airfreight and passenger traffic.[4] The federal highway system constructed in the 1950s and 1960s brought Interstates 65, 24, and 40 through Nashville and reinforced its role as a key intersection for traffic entering the South from the Midwest and the West.

As Nashville and other Sunbelt cities thrived in the postwar era, the South, once the pitied home of poverty from which the poor escaped to northern opportunity, by the 1970s had become a land of promise. This was underscored by the decay of older cities in the Northeast and the Midwest, and the decline of their old smokestack industries. Out of cities like Detroit and Cleveland job-hungry workers began migrating south, reversing a trend that had drained the South ever since World War I. The publicity of postwar prosperity obscured the festering poverty of the region and the community, particularly among the lower-class black population, but those problems were no longer the peculiar burden of the South.

The currents of change that reshaped the economy, in turn, pushed Nashville toward new forms of metropolitan government, new patterns of race relations, and in many subtle ways altered the frame of mind through which its citizens viewed the world. Among Nashville's business and political leaders, and the public at large, some responded to these changes with great zest while others dug in their heels to preserve the community's traditions.

THE INNER CITADEL AT WAR

In many ways the war accelerated trends already at work in Nashville. The New Deal, for example, brought the federal government into intimate connection with the local economy and the political machinery. The war effort was, in effect, a massive extension of the New Deal's multifaceted program to stimulate economic recovery. Millions of dollars in military payrolls and defense contracts took up where WPA and PWA left off.

The first sign of the war boom came to Nashville as early as the fall of 1939, when Aviation Manufacturing Corporation of California (later AVCO) announced plans to locate a large airplane manufacturing plant, to be named Vultee Aircraft, adjacent to Nashville's airport. Rumors of the new airplane industry had been rife in Nashville for over two years. The City Council and Mayor Thomas Cummings worked diligently, along with county officials and the Defense Committee of the Chamber of Commerce, to lure the new plant to Nashville. The city provided a large tract of land near the airport. New county schools were funded for the workers' children, water mains and sewer pipes laid, new housing units constructed, and a four-lane highway replaced the former country lane that was Murfreesboro Road.[5]

As the war in Europe expanded, large defense contracts poured into the Vultee plant to produce the Vultee Vengeance bombers. When the plant opened in May 1941 it cost $9 million and would employ 7,000 workers. It was, Mayor Cummings and Councilman John Lechleiter announced with no exaggeration, "the biggest industrial advance made in Nashville in a decade." The *Tennessean* saw the Vultee plant as the pioneer showing other large industries the way south. The proximity of raw materials (particularly aluminum for modern aircraft in Alcoa, Tennessee), the availability of inexpensive TVA electric power, and a large supply of relatively cheap labor in the area ("native-born American workers . . . devoted to the ideals of Americanism," the Chamber of Commerce reminded prospective employers) — all these made Nashville a promising site for the war industries boom.[6]

By the spring of 1941, still several months before the attack on Pearl Harbor, the city's boosters were euphoric about Nashville's potential for war industries. "Nashville in Splendid Position to Take Lead in Industrial Expansion of 'Inner Citadel,'" a headline for a lengthy article in the *Tennessean* touted.[7] (The slogan "In the Inner Citadel of the Nation" appeared on the newspaper's front page every day during the war.) Admitting that Nashville "has been a slow growing and conservative town," the reporter went on to say the city had built a large pool of capital safely invested in insurance companies, banks, conservative bonds, just waiting to be tapped through private ventures or government

Figure 34. The dedication of the Vultee Aircraft plant in May 1941. The crowd surrounds one of the "Vultee Vengeance" bombers. *Tennessean* Library.

Figure 35. The Vultee Aircraft plant in 1947. Later named Avco Corporation, this company remained a strong addition to the city's industrial sector after the war. Tennessee Department of Conservation Photographic Collection, TSLA.

bond sales for the coming industrial boom. Following the Vultee plant came other wartime enterprises, many of them established firms lured by hefty defense contracts into converting to war industries. Nashville Bridge Company, with its success during World War I fresh in mind, quickly adapted to produce navy submarine chasers, mine sweepers, and other small ships. Tennessee Enamel Company made shell and torpedo parts, Kerrigan Iron Works made pontoons, Allen Manufacturing made stoves for the army and navy, Phillips and Buttorff made pontoons, DuPont made parachutes, Werthan Bag made sandbags, General Shoe made military footwear, and all the major textile firms—Washington Manufacturing, Southern Manufacturing, and O'Bryan Brothers—converted to the production of uniforms. Tennessee Aircraft joined Vultee in the production of military planes, and plans to bring in a Goodyear tire plant were scuttled at the end of the war, when it was no longer needed.[8]

Two major military installations in the city helped the construction industry during a time when business was extremely slow. Thayer General Hospital, constructed off White Bridge Road in West Nashville, cost $3.5 million. It served 13,000 wounded soldiers and later was converted to a Veterans Administration Hospital and relocated near Vanderbilt University. The Army Air Classification Center on Thompson Lane cost about $5 million to build. It classified thousands of recruits in the flying services, was later converted to a convalescent hospital for wounded air force soldiers and, finally, served as a demobilization center at the end of the war.[9]

Every aspect of Nashville's economy was touched by the war effort, not always favorably by any means. The federal Office of Production Management (OPM) coordinated the defense industries and worked with the local Defense Contracts Service of Nashville, organized in May 1941. "The present situation," an OPM representative told Nashville businessmen immediately after the attack on Pearl Harbor, "calls for a complete dislocation of our economic system."[10] The signs of this dislocation came soon enough. Precious resources like steel, brass, rubber, and dozens of other materials were channeled into war-related industries, often leaving other manufacturers with no supplies. Young people scoured the city, collecting scrap metal and old rubber to donate to the cause. To conserve electric power for war industries Nashville went on daylight savings time. (When the governor issued a mandate for the state to follow suit, the *Tennessean* congratulated Tennessee for adjusting to "Nashville time.") Consumer goods, from coffee and sugar to gasoline, were carefully rationed, and a thriving black market offered more for those willing to pay the price. Victory gardens sprang up in backyards across the city, and more than one thousand acres were under cultivation in Percy and Edwin Warner parks for extra vegetables.

Offices and schools collected typewriters and shipped them to the military. All construction projects not essential to the war effort came to an abrupt halt. The draft, instituted in July 1941, immediately processed young men into the army after Pearl Harbor was attacked on December 7.[11] Women streamed into the Vultee plant and other war industries to take their places. "Rosie the Riveter" became a popular symbol of feminine valor during the war and a precedent for women reentering the work force in later years. The impact of Vultee and other war industries on Nashville would multiply as the dollars from the defense contracts rippled through the local economy. "The Athens of the South," the *Tennessean* predicted, ". . . is changing in a dozen ways."[12]

The war brought far more than a dozen changes. The summer of 1941 saw the beginnings of Camp Campbell, an army training camp near Clarksville. Already Camp Forrest in Tullahoma had brought thousands of GIs to the Nashville area. The establishment of Smyrna Air Field (later renamed Sewart Air Force Base in honor of Allan J. Sewart, a Nashvillian who died at Pearl Harbor) in 1941–42, added a third military installation to the area surrounding Nashville.[13] The open, hilly land and mild climate of Middle Tennessee also made it an ideal location for army maneuvers, which brought some 600,000 soldiers to the environs of Nashville in 1943–44.

Soldiers from the nearby bases and maneuvers camps streamed into Nashville on weekends and during leaves. Within the first year of the war alone, the city drew over 1 million soldiers, and during maneuvers they made an estimated 2.4 million visits to servicemen's lounges in Nashville. Most of these soldiers were raw recruits who came from all parts of the South, the Midwest, and the Northeast. However temporary the recruitment camps and war maneuvers might be, Nashville's civic boosters felt confident that the role of Nashville as host to the soldiers would serve as a "wonderful advertisement" for the area and that many would return after the war. Local volunteers struggled to organize "wholesome entertainment" and provide clean makeshift sleeping quarters for the visiting soldiers. The First Presbyterian Church converted its basement to a dormitory. The YMCA, the YWCA, and the Young Men's and Young Women's Hebrew Association offered lounges for visiting soldiers. The newspapers and voluntary associations pleaded with local citizens to open their homes to the deluge of servicemen. But the pressure of visitors on a limited supply of housing proved too much, and the GIs spilled out into the parks and streets, where they slept in the open. When manufacturer Joe Werthan saw young soldiers exposed to the cold one night in December 1942, he hastily converted two old mansions on Elliston Place into the Werthan Service Men's Center, a free dormitory that served thousands of soldiers and became a proud symbol of Nashville's effort to meet the nation's hardship with hospitality.[14]

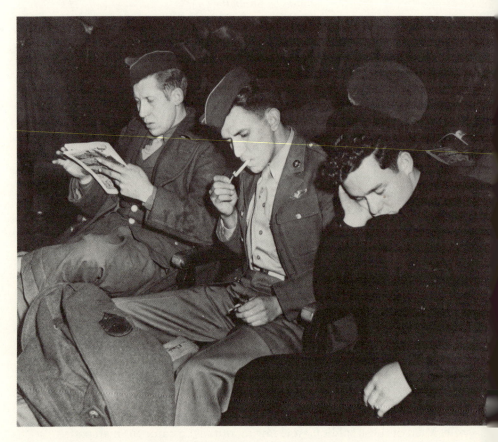

Figure 36. Two soldiers and a tired sailor—among the thousands who poured into Nashville while on leave—wait in Union Station before returning to duty, January 1944. *Tennessean* Library.

For every earnest effort to provide decent quarters and "wholesome recreation" for the visiting soldiers, there were dozens of honky-tonk saloons and hundreds of prostitutes (responding to their own wartime boom) offering cheap thrills and companionship to young soldiers who were away from home and willing to be tempted by the wicked city. The old red-light district around Capitol Hill swarmed with prostitutes and their military clients. Much of this business flowed out of the brothels and into the streets, where veteran hookers were joined by a new class of young, amateur floozies eager to profit from the deluge of lonely young males in Nashville. It was the prostitutes, for the most part, who were responsible for an epidemic of venereal disease that broke out in the city during the war. Despite the best efforts of Dr. John Lentz, Davidson County's health officer, syphilis and gonorrhea spread wildly through the vice industry during the war.[15]

PLANNING FOR A NEW NASHVILLE

The war accelerated and enlarged the thrust of the New Deal years not only through government stimulation of the local economy but also through its compelling force to bring business and government together in a cooperative effort to plan the city's physical, economic, and social development. The excitement of the wartime boom, and the knowledge that it must someday end, moved a few civic leaders as early as 1943 to advocate an official, organized process of planning for the postwar reconversion of the economy.

Beginning about this time there was a growing tension, more visible in later years, between those who saw the city on the verge of great possibilities and were impatient for progress and those who, out of conservative reaction or inertia, resisted change. The former element, often inspired by Silliman Evans, Sr., of the *Tennessean*, were usually New Deal liberals who believed that government was the proper benefactor of citizens. They believed that with enough farsighted planning and enough government spending, a community—a whole society—could be positively improved. On the editorial page of every issue the *"Tennessean* Firsts" set the agenda for liberal reform: for the Cumberland-Tennessee region, inclusion of the Cumberland River in the TVA; for Tennessee, killing of the poll tax, legislation of a merit system in state government; for Davidson County, the consolidation of county health services and school systems, and permanent voter registration; for Nashville, an extension of Lafayette Street, smoke abatement, a sewage disposal plant, and a municipal auditorium. The list changed year by year as each goal was met and new objectives emerged.[16]

Figure 37. V-J Day, August 1945, a frenzied public celebration of the end of war with Japan. *Tennessean* Library.

Figure 38. Mayor Thomas Cummings, left, and Silliman Evans, Sr., publisher of the *Tennessean*, tour the new Newspaper Printing Corporation, April 1941. *Tennessean* Library.

Figure 39. James G. "Jimmy" Stahlman, publisher of the *Banner,* and his wife, July 1947. *Tennessean* Library.

Countering this confident vision of progress through planning were powerful forces of conservatism. They included an assortment of old-line politicians who were by instinct wary of reform, along with small businessmen and manufacturers who operated within the local economy, feared the uncertainty of new ventures, and loathed the tax burdens of public projects. They were joined by tax-shy suburbanites who were indifferent to the plight of the central city. The *Banner*, because of its long-standing feud with the *Tennessean* and because of the strongly conservative political leanings of its owner, James G. "Jimmy" Stahlman, served as the organ for those elements who questioned the New Deal liberal faith and the planners' vision for Nashville's future.

The war, in the liberals' view, presented Nashville with another opportunity for a federal windfall. The *Tennessean* blasted the City Council and Luther Luton (a former lieutenant of Hilary Howse and now the powerful Fire and Public Works commissioner) for dithering over the organization of a postwar planning agency. "Nashville's officials are completely apathetic in the face of civic demand that somehow, someway Nashville must take advantage of the next big wave of federal works expenditures." More progressive cities are not content to say, as Nashville has, "we've got a few old plans left that never were used under the old PWA and WPA programs."[17]

The Chamber of Commerce took the initiative and set up a Postwar Planning Committee, headed by Phillip Davidson of Vanderbilt University. But this committee disbanded in May 1944 after months of study, and its report sat idle with the chamber's Board of Governors. "For this community to delay longer . . . is stupid and unthinkable," the *Tennessean* complained. It must get on with the serious task of "planning for a greater Nashville" and the "postwar building of a permanently prosperous and growing urban area."[18]

The *Tennessean* also chided the chamber for its qualified endorsement of the U.S. Chamber's statement against federal government involvement in electric power service. "After years of watching opportunities for development of the Cumberland River slip by," the local chamber has endorsed a policy that would cancel "the advantages handed Nashville's leading businessmen and industrialists by the TVA program, [and] . . . disastrously crush the greatest wave of prosperity these local business men [sic] have ever enjoyed." This was "convincing proof of a truly magnificent ability to look without seeing, which many in the community long have suspected." When the chamber opposed municipal ownership of the new natural gas service from the Southwest, the *Tennessean* again lambasted the "head-in-the-sand attitude of the same Chamber of Commerce [which] has discouraged every effort to provide Nashville with natural gas in the past twenty years" and reminded citizens that the chamber had even opposed public ownership of TVA electric power in Nashville.[19]

Whether it was the *Tennessean*'s prodding or simply the exhilaration of the wartime boom and the postwar promise of Nashville, the chamber shifted course about 1945 and played an active role in promoting a series of projects that were vital to the economic future of the city. By 1945 the chamber was advocating flood-control dams on the Cumberland, which went forward eventually under the auspices of the Army Corps of Engineers rather than TVA. The chamber also advocated city government reform, with more power concentrated in the mayor's office. It pursued long-standing goals of traffic reform, parking, and street improvement and promoted the Church Street improvement project, the extension of Lafayette, and the widening and improvement of Broadway–West End in the mid-1940s. The chamber also pushed hard for the municipal auditorium, and it urged the city to extend sewers to the outlying suburbs. In 1949 the chamber stood solidly behind the federal programs for slum clearance and urban renewal that focused on the Capitol Hill Redevelopment Project.[20]

The business leaders in the chamber continued their traditional role in advocating "good government" and serving as watchdog over new bond issues and tax assessments. But increasingly the emphasis was upon the *expansion* of government, the consolidation of county and city health services and school systems, and eventually the merger of the two governments altogether. "Good government" had become redefined to mean efficient, comprehensive, centralized power to advance the general welfare of the community, not just a tightfisted reaction against new bonds and taxes. Not all Nashville business leaders embraced the New Deal liberal faith, not consciously at least, but the progress of postwar economic planning operated on the unspoken premise that government was the indispensable helpmate to a healthy economic and social environment in the service of "greater Nashville."

A general civic reawakening began to take place in the mid-1940s, an outgrowth of the urge to plan the postwar city. It engaged not only downtown business leaders in the Chamber of Commerce but university professors and a new generation of planners and politicians, many of them young veterans returning from war to claim a place in the city's leadership. A sure signal of the new spirit was a tendency toward criticism of Nashville's old ways in government and a tone of impatience with its social and environmental problems. Generally, it was the projects that attracted federal funds, like urban renewal, or the problems that brought external legal pressure, as did desegregation, that achieved the most success in the postwar years. Those problems depending purely on local initiative for their solution, like county-city government reform and improved urban services, were postponed more easily.

DOWNTOWN RENEWAL

The new partnership between the city and federal government that was forged during the New Deal appealed to businessmen most in the areas affecting urban development rather than social services. Perhaps the goal closest to the hearts of Nashville's business leaders was the revitalization of the downtown. In this task conservative businessmen, who by instinct suspected government, found their strongest ally in the federal government, which embarked on a massive publicly funded program of urban renewal beginning in the late 1940s. Like many medium and large cities in the age of the automobile, Nashville's central business district (CBD) suffered from the steady accretion of residents, along with retail, wholesale, and manufacturing businesses from the city center to the periphery. Beginning in the late nineteenth century, as the business district and government offices expanded, the mansions on former streets of fashion along the edges of the CBD were broken up into rooming houses and became surrounded by ravaged slums and vice districts. Their growth further accelerated the exodus of middle-class families. On the north and west slopes of Capitol Hill, which was too steep to accommodate the expansion of large business and government buildings, a sprawling slum of ramshackle frame houses and outdoor privies, interspersed with brothels and gambling dens, became the twentieth-century legacy of Hell's Half-Acre.

Around the Public Square and elsewhere in the CBD, old office buildings and stores, many of them built before World War I, were often unsuited to the needs of modern business. They stood idle or were rented by marginal businesses because investment in new construction or rehabilitation in the CBD seemed risky, especially in the wake of the Great Depression. On the outer edges of the CBD, particularly on the downhill slope between Church and lower Broad, a growing number of these older buildings were giving way to parking lots to accommodate what one observer called "the lemming-like hordes of private cars which make their way into the CBD at eight and out at five." The heart of Nashville, he continued, was being "strangled with relentless rings of chromium-plated civic cancer cells."[21] Some advocated a revival of rapid transit as a remedy to the auto-glutted downtown, but most retailers feared that if they did not welcome the automobile with more parking space and better thoroughfares, the rising suburban shopping centers surely would. Already, by the 1950s, the migration of retail stores to the suburbs was well under way.[22] This migration followed and accelerated the drift of upper-income families to the periphery of the metropolis.

Nashville's CBD was anchored by institutions and activities that could not easily follow the suburban trend. The state capitol and the proliferating number of state office buildings were clustered downtown.

Figure 40. The downtown and Capitol Hill sometime in the early 1930s. Note the old mansions facing the Capitol on Park and Seventh avenues, and the small shacks below Seventh. Vanderbilt University Photographic Archives.

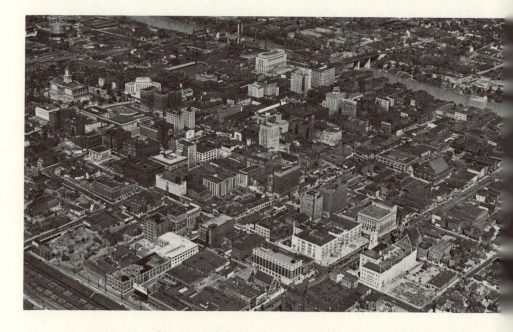

Figure 41. Another view of the downtown from the southwest, c. 1940. The New Deal brought the Supreme Court Building and State Office Building to the left and right of the Capitol, respectively, and the new courthouse farther to the right. Otherwise, the skyline barely changed in the 1930s. Tennessee Department of Conservation Photographic Collection, TSLA.

Figure 42. Some of the shacks on the west side of Capitol Hill during the Capitol Hill Redevelopment Project, 1954. The State Library and Archives and Supreme Court buildings had displaced the old mansions on Seventh Avenue by this time. *Tennessean* Library.

Figure 43. Looking south from Crawford Street, the heart of the Capitol Hill vice district. The smoke from furnaces and factories that burned soft coal darkened the sky downtown. This picture was taken in the middle of a winter day, 1940. *Tennessean* Library.

Figure 44. Commuter traffic along Broadway, 1947. Though buses supplied public transportation after the demise of the trolley cars in 1940, the downtown became clogged with automobile traffic. *Tennessean* Library.

The county courthouse, along with other local government offices, also served as a permanent magnet not only for city and county employees but also for lawyers and others whose livelihood was linked to government. Cultural institutions, like the War Memorial Building, the State Museum, and the downtown Carnegie Library, were also rooted in the CBD and drew patrons into the city. Banks, insurance companies, stockbrokers, and others involved in financial activities also required daily face-to-face interaction and therefore continued to favor centralization downtown. A few downtown hotels, the Hermitage, Maxwell House, Andrew Jackson, and Noel among them, served the needs of visiting businessmen and government officials. Nashville's downtown, in short, was not to be surrendered lightly to the decay of slums or the strangulation of the automobile. Too much was at stake, too much permanently committed to the downtown, to allow it to slide much further.

The Federal Housing Act of 1949 came, after the interruption of World War II, as a continuation and expansion of the New Deal program of public housing and slum clearance. The idea was to clear central city slums, turn the valuable land to commercial use, and relocate the poor in new public housing projects. Urban renewal, as it came to be called, was linked also to a program of inner-city loop thoroughfares and parking lots to help alleviate the automobile congestion downtown. Urban renewal stimulated a massive reconstruction of the American city to accommodate the age of the automobile.

The program optimistically joined the planners' notion of what was best for the poor with the business interests' notion of what was best for the downtown. Though many conservative businessmen feared the intrusion of the federal government into local planning and construction, urban renewal became a bonanza for downtown business interests. The poor, on the other hand, found that the urban renewal program was much more efficient at tearing down their homes and replacing them with parking lots or high-rise office buildings than it was in providing new housing. Most of the neighborhoods targeted for urban renewal projects were heavily black, and critics accused urban renewal of being simply a disguised program of "Negro removal."[23] Slum clearance and federal housing projects reinforced a pattern of residential segregation in Nashville, but that pattern was already in place before the 1940s.

Nashville was first in line for the new round of federal grants. As early as October 1945, Nashville's Planning commissioners, led by Gerald Gimre, executive director and secretary of the Nashville Housing Authority, and Charles Hawkins, director of the city Planning Commission, began to make plans for the anticipated federal projects. It was rumored that cities with a comprehensive plan already in place would receive favorable treatment. Hawkins laid the groundwork with a new land-use study. In 1949, after a long delay due to political infighting in Congress, the Housing Act was passed, and the first grant application submitted was Nashville's Capitol Hill Redevelopment Project.[24]

The project received a loan of $8.3 million from the federal government to purchase seventy-two acres of land on the steep western and northern slopes of Capitol Hill, a neighborhood described by the developers as "one of wretched dwellings, dingy alleys, and crumbling pavements." About 427 families and 279 single residents, most of them poor blacks, lived on the hill. New housing projects got under way to house many of the homeless. Some—including all the single residents—did not qualify for public housing, but the Nashville Housing Authority promised to do all it could "to accomplish the relocation program with the minimum disruption of family life and site clearance schedules."[25] Once the residents were removed, the land was cleared. James Robertson Parkway, a semicircular, six-lane thoroughfare, routed traffic behind the CBD and across the Cumberland by way of the new Victory Memorial Bridge. Just below the state capitol the land was terraced for parking lots to serve the growing legion of state office workers. Much of the steep land was planted with grass and trees. More than half the land was sold to private developers for motels, an apartment building, office buildings, and some industrial plants. The city also planned its long-awaited municipal auditorium for the site, though this part of the project ran into stiff opposition from black businessmen and professionals whose offices along Charlotte and Fourth were threatened. It would be more than a decade before the auditorium was finally completed.[26]

At the same time, the capitol grounds were relandscaped and improved under the auspices of state officials. The State Library and Archives Building was erected, along with a new state office building, the Cordell Hull Building. Along Park Street old structures were torn down to provide a clear vista of the east side of the capitol, which architect William Strickland had designed originally as the front, facing the river.[27]

The Capitol Hill Redevelopment Project was a milestone in the city's postwar reawakening. It was an economic and aesthetic success in its own right. It turned a seedy slum into an inner-city greenbelt of lawn and trees, a convenient parkway, and new buildings whose owners paid several times the property tax collected from the former tenants. The project also launched a series of new public and private efforts to revitalize the CBD, to clear additional substandard housing, build several more public housing projects, and construct a massive system of expressway loops. There was also an intangible but genuine renewal of civic pride and commitment among downtown businessmen. Gerald Gimre and Chester D. Campbell announced in 1961, "Capitol Hill was just the start of Nashville's renaissance."[28] Forces emerging within the private sector joined with the rising power of government planners

Figure 45. Capitol Hill and the downtown, 1969. The slums were cleared for parking lots and the James Robertson Parkway (*bottom*) to alleviate the pressure of the automobile on the downtown. Tennessee Department of Conservation Photographic Collection, TSLA.

Figure 46. Another view of Nashville's changing skyline, c. 1977. The Downtown Urban Renewal Project created a near-solid row of new skyscrapers from the National Life building (*right*) to the First American Center (*left*). New construction on the James K. Polk State Office Building and on Commerce Union Center's Radisson Hotel is evident in this scene. *Tennessean* Library.

on the local and federal levels. A partnership, not always comfortable, nor always conscious, had been consolidated between the federal government and the city.[29]

The response of private business to urban renewal in the CBD was remarkably slow at first. There were signs of new life from the private sector in the late 1950s, but it was not until the 1960s that the Nashville skyline began to take on a radically new profile. The Downtown Urban Renewal Project rebuilt the heart of the downtown between Union, Deaderick, the courthouse, and Eighth Avenue. Old buildings put up in the robust era of the 1870s and 1880s, along with many from the flush times of the 1920s (the Nichols Building, which housed Caldwell and Company, and the Andrew Jackson Hotel, for examples), were hauled down one after another to make way for a new stand of gleaming steel-and-glass skyscrapers. The most dramatic changes took place along Union Street, the Wall Street of the South, where Nashville's bankers and insurance magnates constructed mammoth new office buildings to house their enlarged financial empires.

THE INSURANCE GIANTS

After World War II, Nashville's insurance industry became a dominant force in the city's economic life. Several new insurance companies, Cherokee and Cherokee Life, American Educational Life, Hermitage Health and Life, Cumberland Life, and State Insurance Company of Tennessee, made Nashville their headquarters in the 1940s and 1950s. "Nashville," financier Sam Fleming remarked in 1963, "is more like Hartford Connecticut than any other city I know. It is hard to meet very many people here before you run into someone connected with an insurance company." Together with the "Big Two"—National Life and Accident, and Life and Casualty—the city's eight insurance companies in 1963 claimed over $2 billion in assets and invested untold millions in local real estate, construction, mortgages, and stocks and bonds purchased through local brokers.[30] The future of Nashville's downtown and the vitality of the whole urban economy rested heavily on the insurance industry.

Within the private sector Life and Casualty Insurance Company (L&C) boldly led the way in the downtown revival, and without federal assistance from urban renewal. On the corner of Church and Fourth, L&C broke ground in 1956 for a new thirty-story building. Completed the next year, the L&C Tower stood like a lonely sentinel high above the squat profile of the old downtown for nearly a decade before a flurry of new skyscrapers nearly hid the L&C Tower from view. L&C met its fiftieth anniversary in 1953 having reached its goal, set twenty-five years earlier, of $1 billion of insurance in force.[31] The company continued a strategy of expanding sales of ordinary life insurance, mostly to middle-income whites, and it rose with the tide of prosperity that came to the postwar South.[32]

Even as it grew into a corporation of national scope, L&C retained the soul of a family enterprise. In 1950 the founder and president, Andrew M. Burton, retired to his estate, Seven Hills, on Hillsboro Pike, and he died in 1966. Paul Mountcastle, a former company director from Knoxville, took over as president for two years and then became chairman of the board. With the election of Guilford Dudley, Jr., as the new president in 1952, the second generation of the L&C family had arrived in power. The son of one of the original founders, Dudley nonetheless worked assiduously to earn his promotions within the company.[33] Under Dudley, L&C followed its earlier pioneering role in radio with the purchase in 1954 of WLAC-TV, a CBS affiliate. By 1961 L&C passed $2 billion insurance in force, and Dudley promised to double that again within a decade.[34]

L&C's success attracted the attention of outside investors. In 1959 Texas oilman Clint W. Murchison bought 24 percent of the stock, worth $40 million, mostly from Dudley, Mountcastle, and P. M. Estes, Jr., another son of a company founder. In 1968 Murchison's American General Group of Houston, Texas, bought controlling interest in L&C. The name was preserved, and many members of the old firm continued, but L&C, a Cinderella company that had been built by local entrepreneurial talent sixty-five years earlier, was now an appendage of a distant conglomerate.[35]

National Life also surged with the South's postwar prosperity. From less than $707 million of insurance in force in 1939 the company claimed over $2.3 billion in 1949 and $9.1 billion by 1967. At its seventy-fifth anniversary in 1977 National Life had nearly $4 billion in assets, up from $72.6 million in 1939. This once small industrial insurance company stood fifth among the life insurance companies in the nation in 1963 (and nineteenth in 1978). The company continued its policy of expanding ordinary life insurance but never abandoned its old foundations in industrial insurance, small weekly policies sold traditionally to poor blacks. The television program "Sixty Minutes" in 1979 did an exposé of industrial insurance and showed National Life in the worst possible light. But by this time industrial insurance formed only a small part of a large, diversified conglomerate.[36]

In 1968 National Life reorganized as the NLT Corporation, a holding company originally tied to Third National Bank, until federal regulations forced the bank to withdraw. By the 1970s NLT included extensive real estate holdings in shopping malls and apartment complexes, WSM radio, WSM-TV, a massive theme park called Opryland, a computer processing service, and major investments in mortgage bonds.[37] Beginning in 1978 NLT became the target of several takeover bids by American General (the Texas company that had swallowed L&C a decade earlier) and Ashland Oil, another cash-rich firm looking for diversified acquisition. The officers of NLT stoutly resisted the merger attempts, and there were many in Nashville rooting for NLT's continued independence, regardless of how sweet a financial deal these outside corporations might offer stockholders. Most of the key officers were the sons, grandsons, and sons-in-law of the company founders. They had gone to Vanderbilt, worked their way up in the company hierarchy, and kept many of the traditions of this essentially family-based firm. An inside report by American General criticized the inbred quality of NLT's management, but here was a company that offered testimony to the resilience of family capitalism in an age of giant corporations.[38]

The expansion of National Life after World War II required more space at the home office, but—unlike L&C—National Life held off on any major new construction until the late 1960s. The company's decision to stay and build in the downtown provides a case study in the new relationships between business and government on the local and federal levels. National Life's six-story headquarters, built in 1923–24 on Sixth and Union, had two wings added in ensuing years. A new eleven-story addition was completed in 1942. In the late 1940s the company revised its premiums, added new employee benefits, and introduced an intensive training program for agents and staff managers, all of which required more space at the home office. From about 700 employees in 1945, the home office increased to nearly 1,500 over the next twelve years. Bulging at the seams, the company took over the former Young Men's Hebrew Association building in 1948. Nine years later the company expanded again, into the Memorial Hotel building at Seventh and Charlotte, and bought property along Eighth Avenue between Union and Charlotte for future expansion.[39]

While the L&C Tower was rising across the central business district, it looked as though National Life was preparing for a new home office to meet its present and future needs. But the company hesitated and, for a time, even threatened to leave Nashville. At issue was the heavy personalty tax levied by Davidson County and the city of Nashville. A state law of 1907 gave counties the sole authority to assess property and levy taxes on insurance companies with headquarters in the county. Davidson County and Nashville took advantage of this law to extract revenue from its two home-owned insurance companies. The tax burden had grown as National Life's assets in property and stock increased. President Edwin W. Craig denounced the tax as a serious disadvantage to the company's competitive position. In 1956 Craig pushed the point by purchasing farmland in Williamson County and making public his threat to leave Nashville. The county and city tax assessors eased up on National Life the next year, and the company immediately invested

$700,000 in renovating the Memorial Hotel. The Capitol Hill Redevelopment Project also allowed National Life to purchase a large plot for $500,000, which it used temporarily for an employee parking lot. But National Life cautiously postponed any commitment to a new building and kept its options open on sites in both Williamson and Cheatham counties.

In 1965 the personalty tax on National Life rose again, this time to $12.5 million per year, up 25 percent from the previous year, which demonstrated just how vulnerable Nashville's insurance companies were to the whims of tax assessors and politicians. Mayor Beverly Briley brought National Life executives together with tax officials and worked out a plan to limit tax increases to $500,000 each year. At the same time Briley and the county worked out a brilliant plan to encourage National Life and other insurance companies to embark on new construction downtown. The assessed cost of any new construction was to be written off as a credit against the personalty tax so that every dollar spent on new construction was a dollar saved in taxes. "We are staying in downtown Nashville," National Life president G. Daniel Brooks announced that October. "This is where we started, and where we want to stay."[40]

Construction of the National Life Center began late in 1966, and the building was dedicated in 1970. Rising thirty-one stories above a subterranean block (one story more than the L&C Tower), it dominated the skyline of the downtown. The National Life Center became a symbol of the downtown revival that ensued rapidly in the next few years. It acted as a powerful catalyst for the Downtown Urban Renewal Project, which revamped the entire strip of land between Union and Demonbruen from the National Life Center to the Courthouse Square.

THE BANKS AND DOWNTOWN RENEWAL

Nashville's banks emerged from the Depression fewer in number but stronger than ever. The crisis of the 1930s had produced a more centralized and more carefully regulated banking system across the country. The city's second generation of young, aggressive bankers who came of age in the 1920s, Rogers Caldwell, Ed Potter, Jr., Paul Davis, and Frank Farris, continued—with the exception of Caldwell—to guide their banks into the postwar era. But those strong individuals who ran their banks as extensions of their own aggressive personalities gradually gave way in the 1960s to a third generation of Nashville bankers. This group of financiers may have comprised a like number of bright, ambitious individuals, but they operated in a banking world more constrained by federal regulations and by the corporate hierarchy of large bank holding companies. This generation of bankers was also less exclusively involved in their own banks and more devoted to cooperative efforts in developing the city's economy.

Since James E. Caldwell's mammoth Fourth and First was absorbed into the American National during the collapse of 1930, there had been no single dominant bank in the city. The major three—American National, Third National, and Commerce Union—were close enough in size to become fiercely competitive after 1940. This was manifest in a vigorous campaign to solicit customers as borrowers and depositors. Many older bankers considered it unseemly for banks to "ask for business," but Third National's young president, Frank M. Farris, broke that tradition in the 1930s, and the other major banks followed suit.[41] As competition for depositors and borrowers escalated, banks opened more branches near suburban shopping centers, offered cheaper checking service and loan rates, higher interest on deposits, and projected a new style of "friendly banking" to make the customer feel welcome instead of intimidated in the banks' offices. By the 1970s newcomers to Nashville were astonished by the efforts of effervescent bank representatives who called long distance, picked them up at the airport, and even lavished gifts on them—all to curry favor with potential customers.

The competition among the Nashville banks was played out more dramatically in concrete, steel, and glass along the new Wall Street of the South that revived in the 1960s and 1970s. Third National, the youngest of the "Big Three," set the standards with a magnificent twenty-story building completed in 1968. The bank outgrew its old quarters at Fourth and Church (which subsequently became home for J.C. Bradford and Company) and moved diagonally across the intersection to the site of the old Maxwell House Hotel, a venerable landmark destroyed by fire on Christmas night 1961. L&C owned the site and decided, instead of selling it to Third National, to finance the construction of a large office building, give a long-term lease to the bank on the lower floors, and rent out the other offices. This investment bolstered L&C's commitment to the downtown, already evident in the L&C Tower. By this time the resolution of the personalty tax issue and the new tax incentives for insurance companies to invest in downtown construction made it all the more attractive for L&C to enter this venture. In June 1965 plans were laid for a $10-million, twenty-story office complex with Third National being the main tenant. The upper floors were leased to numerous stock and insurance brokers, as well as other financial service agencies, thus extending the Union Street financial axis down Fourth Avenue. On the top floor the Nashville City Club, a downtown lunch club founded in 1957 and formerly housed in the Maxwell House, gave the building added importance to the revival of the downtown.

The Third National Bank building, as it came to be known, was applauded by business leaders and by Mayor Briley as a significant act of faith in the downtown. It was the first major new construction since the L&C Tower in 1957. Sam M. Fleming, president of the Third National Bank, announced at the ground-breaking ceremonies: "possibly this will be a forerunner to things greater than has [sic] been in the past, and will help change the image of the Athens of the South." Mayor Briley also commented on the historical significance of the building: "We are now creating part of the history of the new South, and it is fitting that it is on the site of the famous old Maxwell House where great things have been done and so much history has been made."[42]

When the building opened in April 1968 it was acclaimed as an aesthetic triumph. It was Nashville's first truly modern high-rise to use setbacks and landscaping. It had bronze anodized aluminum and tinted glass walls with a gold solar screen. Inside, a spectacular lobby had waterfalls and pools, with freestanding escalators rising to a thoroughly modern banking room where tellers and loan officers worked in one open space.[43]

The new building was a fitting home for an aggressive young bank that had been a fast-rising pioneer in Nashville. The bank, established in 1927, entered the Depression burdened with fewer loans outstanding, and it suffered fewer defaults during the hard times. Frank Farris, the young founder and president, saw his advantage in the 1930s and pushed hard to expand. In 1935 the bank decided to raise more capital by offering more common stock, an improbable strategy for most banks in the Depression years. The demand for Third National stock was so great, however, that current shareholders had to be asked to waive their purchase rights in order to allow other eager investors to buy shares in the bank.[44]

When Farris died in 1950, the presidency passed to Sam M. Fleming, who had been with the bank since 1931. Fleming, like so many in the Nashville financial community, was born to banking. His father and uncle ran a bank in Franklin, and at age eight Sam became a part-time runner for the bank. He entered Vanderbilt at age sixteen, did a stint with the New York Trust Company after graduation, and returned to Nashville in the depths of the Depression. During the hard times of the 1930s it was Fleming who led Third National's aggressive campaign to draw clients away from the older banks.[45] After he rose to the presidency, Third National launched a second stage of expansion involving two bold mergers and a vigorous effort to attract depositors to the new branch offices and their conveniences.

The first merger in 1964 involved the bank in a landmark antitrust case. Nashville Trust, formerly part of the James E. Caldwell empire, had been rescued during the Depression by Horace G. Hill, Sr., the grocery-store magnate, along with Robert and John Cheek, descendants of the founder of the Maxwell House coffee empire. Hill invested $1 million of his own capital to help stabilize Nashville Trust; he reorganized it, saved the depositors investments, and restored public confidence in an institution that had served many of the city's old monied families since its founding in 1889. Having retrieved the Trust from the brink of ruin, Hill chose a strictly conservative course aimed more at preserving capital than at the growth of bank assets. In 1936 Hill passed the management of Nashville Trust to Charles Nelson, grandson of the founder, and Nelson continued the same conservative strategy for ten years before his death. The next president, Warner McNeilly, an old employee of the Trust and a true "gentleman banker," considered it "intrinsically wrong if the bank had to ask someone to do business with them." It was not until 1956, when W. S. Hackworth became president, that Nashville Trust tried to compete with the Big Three banks in Nashville. Hackworth changed the name to Nashville Bank and Trust, opened the first branch office in 1959, erected a large parking facility behind the downtown office to cater to the automobile-age public, and actively sought new business. Within three years Nashville Bank and Trust's business doubled, and profits tripled.[46]

The once stodgy old trust company now became an eager, if much smaller, competitor of the giants of Nashville's banking world. In 1964 a group of National Life executives, headed by William C. Weaver, formed a syndicate and purchased controlling interest in Nashville Bank and Trust from H.G. Hill Company. Their plans were to further modernize the bank, expand branch offices, attract new bank officers with higher salaries, and build it into a serious competitor. With the sale, however, many depositors withdrew funds, and former clients who were tied to the bank through their business connections with the H.G. Hill Company no longer felt obligated to keep accounts there. As deposits declined from nearly $46 million to under $40 million, Weaver's group found they did not have the capital necessary to modernize the bank, and Third National offered to buy their stock.[47] Third National saw the merger as an opportunity to close the gap between it and First American, the leading Nashville bank.[48]

The U.S. Comptroller of the Currency approved the merger on the logic that Nashville Bank and Trust, "a declining and leaderless" state bank, offered no serious competition to any of the three major banks in its present state. An investigation by the federal district court upheld this decision, but the merger also required the approval of the Justice Department, which ruled against it. As a result, in 1968 Third National was ordered to divest itself of Nashville Bank and Trust, though it was allowed to keep the trust department. Nashville Bank and Trust once again had survived merger with one of its giant rivals and returned to set its own course as the city's second-oldest bank.[49]

Precisely as Third National was losing Nashville Bank and Trust, it joined National Life and Accident in another novel merger that provoked federal intervention. The alliance between these two institutions went back to the founding of Third National in 1927 when Cornelius A. Craig protested James E. Caldwell's willingness to finance his son Rogers Caldwell's ventures in competing insurance companies. Now the stocks of National Life and Third National were merged to form a holding company, NLT Corporation. It would have been one of the largest financial institutions in the South, but federal regulations against one-bank holding companies tightened, and Third National was forced to leave NLT in 1970. The ties between these two companies continued, however, for Sam Fleming served simultaneously as president of NLT and of Third National.[50]

In 1971 Third National formed its own holding company, Third National Corporation, which brought in seven other Tennessee banks and included a cluster of subsidiary agencies. The move toward bank holding companies, which all the Nashville banks followed in the 1970s, allowed vast expansion without technical violation of Tennessee's 1925 law against intercounty branch banking. In 1977 the bank began its second half-century with close to $1 billion in deposits and $1.4 billion in assets, which placed it 122nd among all U.S. banks.[51]

American National Bank, the oldest and largest of Nashville's banks, maintained its supremacy after the Depression. P. D. Houston and Paul Davis pulled the bank, and the newly merged Fourth and First Bank, through the 1930s with reassuring strength. When rural correspondent banks were threatened by a run of panicked depositors, Houston and Davis filled suitcases with cash, took them to the country bank, and piled the money behind the teller's cage to sooth anxious depositors. It was the strength of this correspondent bank business that was the key to American National Bank's continued expansion after the Depression.[52]

By 1940 American National had total resources of over $77 million and was in excellent position to thrive on the war boom and postwar prosperity that came to the region. In 1950 the name was changed to First American, a distinction that derived from the 1930 merger with Fourth and First.[53] Parkes Armistead followed Paul Davis as president in 1948, then came P. D. Houston, Jr., in 1951. In 1960 Andrew Benedict took over as president. At forty-six, Benedict was the youngest man ever to serve as president of the bank and one of several new financial leaders to take charge on the Wall Street of the South in the 1960s.[54] Under Benedict and his successors, T. Scott Fillebrown (who served as president from 1969 to 1976), Kenneth Roberts (1976–79), and Owen G. Shell (1979–), First American maintained its position as the largest Nashville bank despite constant challenges from local rivals. By 1964 the bank was ranked 102nd in deposits among all U.S. banks. In answer to Third National's plans to form NLT, First American formed its own holding company, First Amtenn, in 1968 and in 1971 began acquiring several affiliate banks in Tennessee, Georgia, and Florida.[55]

First American also contributed to the downtown revival when it built a twenty-eight-story office tower and an adjoining bank building in the block bordered by Union, Deaderick, Third, and Fourth avenues. This was part of the Downtown Urban Renewal Project that transformed the whole center strip from the courthouse to the National Life Center. First American Center, completed in 1974, was constructed around the old Caldwell bank, built in 1921, and when it was finally razed in 1973 the event marked the passing of an era on the Wall Street of the South. The powerful individual financiers of Caldwell's day had given way to giant corporations, vast holding companies, and gleaming skyscrapers. The First American Center provided open public space with planters, fountains, and a plaza for noon-hour entertainment during summers. It became a busy public place and went a long way toward restoring the human, as well as the architectural, vitality of the downtown.[56]

Commerce Union Bank was soon to match the towers of its rivals with Commerce Place, a striking pair of triangular structures with banks and offices in one tower and the Raddison Hotel in the other. Ed Potter, Jr., had steered his young bank through the troubled waters of the Great Depression with great skill, and he retained a reputation for innovative banking, which always kept his two larger competitors on their toes. In 1938, for example, Potter introduced small installment loans on consumer items. In 1948 he upset the whole banking community by raising the interest rates offered on savings from 1 to 2 percent.[57]

It was Potter, also, who recharged the downtown retail sector by bringing Fred Harvey to town and bankrolling his department store. When Lebeck Brothers Department Store, an old favorite of Church Street shoppers, went bankrupt in the Depression, Commerce Union was awarded a long-term lease on the property as part of the settlement. It looked like a white elephant to many, but in 1942 Ed Potter met Fred Harvey, an imaginative retailer formerly with Marshall Fields in Chicago. Potter agreed to finance Harvey's store and asked him to pay rent on the basis of sales. He also gave Harvey an enormous line of credit to help turn the store around. It was Potter's idea to set the Harvey family up in the former mansion of P.D. Houston on Belle Meade Boulevard and clip the hedges low so that all could see that Harvey was well set and in Nashville to stay. Harvey underlined the point by painting his name in big letters on the mailbox.[58]

Harvey's Department Store became the most exciting new force in the Nashville retail district. Harvey challenged the older department stores, Cain-Sloan and Castner Knott, with a barrage of new merchandising gimmicks—bright colors, carousel horses (from the defunct Glendale Park), monkeys in cages, popcorn, escalators (the first in Nashville, with signs warning riders they must wear shoes!), and a flurry of novel advertisements and sales proclaiming "Harvey's Has It!" and "It's Fun to Shop at Harvey's." Sales climbed from barely one-half million dollars in 1946 to almost $9 million by 1950 and to over $11 million by 1954, surpassing Cain-Sloan. The resentment of the older and more staid retailers was manifest in a bitter drawn-out legal suit from 1951 to 1954 between Cain-Sloan and Harvey's over legal rights to the property where the old Lebeck building stood on Church Street. But in the end Fred Harvey's flashy style set the standards for retailing in the postwar era, and most of the other department stores followed the trends he established. Harvey's success was also a tribute to Ed Potter and his commitment to revitalize the downtown.[59]

By 1940 Commerce Union needed more office space and moved from its old quarters in the Stahlman Building to the Nichols Building, former home of Caldwell and Company, on Union and Fourth Avenue. Next door the Equitable Securities Building was purchased and remodeled for Commerce Union offices. After the war Potter saw the ways in which the automobile was rendering the old style of banking obsolete. He converted the old streetcar transfer station near the bank's downtown office into a three-level parking garage. Then in 1948 Potter began building branch banks in Nashville, the first at Seventeenth and Church, surrounded by ample parking space.[60]

Commerce Union remained very much "Mr. Potter's bank" through the 1950s. He and his family owned one-quarter of the stock, and all departments, personnel, loans, and policies of the bank remained under the supervision of the founder. Some criticized it as a "one-man bank," but when Potter fell ill in 1960 he retired from the presidency and let William F. Earthman, Jr., a rising young executive in the bank, take his place. In 1962 the Broadway National Bank, an affiliate of Commerce Union since the crash of 1930, was merged and made into a branch office.[61] At the end of 1971 Commerce Union followed the trend of the times and organized the Tennessee Valley Bancorp, a holding company that began its first acquisition two years later and soon controlled eleven affiliated banks. Though Commerce Union remained third in total assets among the Nashville Big Three, its holding company moved past the First Amtenn and Third National Corporation with a phenomenal growth rate in the 1970s. By 1977 Tennessee Valley Bancorp had over $1.6 billion in assets, First Amtenn claimed $1.5 billion, and Third National Corporation had $1.4 billion.[62] Commerce Union's assets included Noel-Palmer Mortgage Company, a major force in Nashville's suburban expansion, and two insurance companies, as well as the affiliated banks.

By 1980 Tennessee Valley Bancorp, now housed in its new skyscraper in Commerce Place, claimed $1.9 billion in assets. The new Commerce Union president, Edward Nelson, great-grandson of banker Charles Nelson, was a reminder of the strong currents of tradition that ran through the Wall Street of the South and a spokesman for the modern style of banking that had taken hold in recent years.[63]

Nashville's major banks entered the age of computerization, automatic tellers, and vast holding companies with remarkable competitive vigor. Together, these banks, along with the insurance companies, had gone far in accumulating and supplying the capital needs of Nashville's burgeoning economy in the post-1940 era. It was the banks and insurance companies, too, that guaranteed the successful revival of the downtown.

The skyscrapers that transformed the Nashville skyline in the postwar era were the most visible symbols of the city's robust economy. The prosperity that had eluded Nashville for so long before World War II came with the large shifts in regional economic development, the intervention of federal programs, and the willingness of local businessmen to capitalize on the new opportunities offered to Nashville in this period.

Nashville's financial service sector also expanded through enterprises that emerged as major firms in the postwar era. Equitable Securities Corporation, founded by Brownlee O. Currey and four college friends from Vanderbilt in 1930, helped fill the vacuum created in the South by the fall of Caldwell and Company. Like Caldwell, Currey specialized in marketing southern municipal bonds and industrial stocks. Currey, the son of a prominent Nashville insurance man, started his career as a bookkeeper with James E. Caldwell's Fourth and First National Bank while still an undergraduate at Vanderbilt in 1921. He followed Rogers Caldwell by moving beyond marketing bonds and securities to become an investor in new issues. In 1935 Equitable opened its New York City office and began investing heavily in publishing companies. It bought the *Southern Agriculturalist*, a popular farm journal, and seven other periodicals. The company also moved into urban transit systems, first in Knoxville and then in nine other cities. During the gas shortages of World War II bus transportation soared, and Equitable's profits did also. Riding the tide of postwar economic resurgence, Equitable Securities by 1966 had become the second largest firm of its kind in the country, with a net worth of nearly $60 million. Currey had died in 1952, and the company was led by Ralph Owen, one of the founding partners. In 1967 Equitable acquired controlling interest in American Express Company of New York and merged with it the following year, raising the company assets to $114 million. Equitable Securities was reorganized as a subsidiary of American Express, but it had long since grown beyond the local and regional company that began in 1930. As a successor to the ill-fated Caldwell and Company, Equitable Securities was an impressive reminder of the financial talent that grew out of the Wall Street of the South.[64]

J. C. Bradford and Company, a leading regional stock brokerage firm, also sprang out of the chaotic climate on Union Street in the 1930s. James Cowdon Bradford was another Nashville native and Vanderbilt student who started young and fast in the 1920s. Starting in the insurance business, Bradford became involved with the Piggly Wiggly grocery store expansion, then moved into banking. Bradford was already a wealthy young man in 1927 when he and Walter Robinson bought the securities firm of Joe Palmer and launched into the risky world of the stock market. Most every brokerage firm in Nashville failed during the Depression, but J.C. Bradford and Co. held on by drawing on Bradford's personal capital of $500,000. Bradford came to specialize in financing industrial revenue bonds, a business that expanded with the shift of industry to the South. Like his predecessor, Caldwell and Company, Bradford also came to specialize in southern municipal bonds, along with regional stock sales. By 1943 the company opened its first branch bank in Knoxville, and by the late 1970s it had thirty-eight branches across the country, most of them in the Southeast. This, too, was a family firm, and after 1981, when the founder died at eighty-four, his son James C. Bradford, Jr., carried on.[65]

The insurance, bank, and securities sectors of Nashville's economy were already in position to benefit from the post-Depression boom in the region. There were also many new ventures, products of the entrepreneurial talent that Nashville's business community either nurtured or attracted. Perhaps the most notable example of Nashville's new enterprise was the hospital management companies that emerged in the late 1960s. Nashville had become a regionally important center in health care, medical research, and education since the 1920s, after the medical schools of Vanderbilt and Meharry had been singled out in the Flexner Report as the most promising schools in the state for concentrated development—northern foundation money followed.[66] In the post–World War II economy the health industry across America expanded because of a combination of new medical treatments, a growing population of aging and affluent consumers, the expansion of private group health insurance, and new federal health insurance programs. Health care expenditures as a percentage of the gross national product went from 6 percent in 1966 to over 10 percent by the early 1980s, and almost half of those expenditures were in hospital care.[67]

The rise of Nashville's hospital management companies was due in part to the same partnership of federal subsidies and private enterprise that had shaped so many aspects of the local economy, from urban renewal to education. The federal government played a major role in the expansion of the health industry after World War II. The Hill-Burton Act of 1946 had supplied federal funds to construct new hospitals in areas designated as underserved. The Veterans Administration built and operated its own hospitals in growing numbers after the war. The National Institutes of Health channeled federal funds into medical research, often at university medical schools.[68] Most American hospitals remained in the hands of cities and counties, churches, or medical schools, and they were run on a nonprofit basis. Except for the few large cities and churches that operated multiple hospitals, most American hospitals were run independently.

One of the major incentives for the entry of profit-seeking companies into the hospital industry was the introduction of Medicaid and Medicare during President Lyndon Johnson's promotion of the Great Society in 1965. By the early 1980s about 35 percent of hospital costs were met by these federal insurance programs. At the same time, nonprofit insurance companies, Blue Cross and Blue Shield, and commercial health insurance companies had expanded their coverage through corporate group insurance programs. As a result of expanded federal and private insurance, only about 10 percent of hospital costs were now borne by individual patients.[69] With the guarantees of federal and private insurance coverage, private hospital management companies entered a field formerly dominated by nonprofit organizations. Their plan was to serve the expanding demand for hospital care at a profit by applying the most efficient management techniques, especially the economies of scale that came from centralized administration of a chain of hospitals. These companies would raise private capital, through loans and corporate sale of their stock, for new hospitals and the expansion of existing hospitals.

Hospital Corporation of America (HCA), founded in 1968, was the brainchild of Thomas F. Frist, Sr.; his son, Thomas Frist, Jr. (both were Nashville physicians); and Jack Massey, who had built a personal fortune in Kentucky Fried Chicken. Thomas Frist, Sr., organized Park View Hospital near Centennial Park in 1956. During the mid-1960s he and the other physicians at Park View decided to sell the hospital to a management team that would operate the hospital and raise the capital necessary to expand it. Frist found there was no such company prepared to take over the management of a hospital, so he and his son consulted with their friend Jack Massey, and the three decided to set up their own management company. Park View Hospital became the flagship for the HCA empire. Massey transferred his entrepreneurial skills from fast-food franchising to the new concept of a chain of hospitals. HCA, the second company of its kind in America, soon became the national leader.[70]

The same year HCA began operations, two other Nashville doctors—Irwin Eskind and Herbert Schulman—joined forces with businessmen Baron Coleman and Richard Eskind to form Hospital Affiliates International (HAI). General Care Corporation was the third Nashville company to enter the field, also in 1968. This company remained a relatively small operation; only eight hospitals were under its management by 1979. HCA and HAI, on the other hand, quickly expanded into the nation's leading hospital management companies. Each raised capital on the stock market and rapidly extended operations, buying up old hospitals, building new ones, and managing others on contract. By 1979 HCA owned or managed 140 hospitals with over 20,000 beds. HAI claimed about the same number of hospitals and 18,000 beds. Together, these companies received annual revenues of $2 billion.[71] Most of the hospitals these companies operated were in the Sunbelt, many in the new suburbs. A large population of Medicare recipients in states like Florida, a generally prosperous economy, and a liberal regulatory environment that allowed rising costs to be passed on to insurors without government interference made the Sunbelt suburbs attractive. In Nashville, for example, HCA hospitals included Donelson, Hendersonville, Southern Hills, Edgefield, and West Side, in addition to Park View.

As the industry matured in the late 1970s, mergers and acquisitions were inevitable. HCA took over General Care Corporation and in 1981 merged with its rival, HAI. With close to 50,000 hospital beds and 354 hospitals owned or managed, HCA became the largest company in the field, leading a national trend toward health care for profit in which more than a third of all hospital beds were under the control of investor-owned hospitals by the early 1980s.[72] HCA was also expanding overseas, and the potential for future expansion seemed endless. "Private enterprise ... in the health care field may well be the ultimate bulwark against socialized medicine in America," Jack Massey predicted in 1972. But HCA is better understood as an example of entrepreneurial drive from the private sector joining government-sponsored social programs in the mixed economy that had become so vital to the economic health of Nashville and the South since the 1930s.

In several instances, it was a mixture of private enterprise and federal government aid that since the 1930s had transformed Nashville's whole economic foundation. The emergencies of the Great Depression and World War II vastly increased the federal impact on the local scene. But through urban renewal, public housing, interstate highways, military spending, and a multitude of other programs, the federal government continued in the postwar years a vitally important role in pulling Nashville and the South out of the shadows of regional poverty and underdevelopment and into the Sunbelt. Civic leaders and businessmen, for the most part, embraced the federal-city partnership with an optimistic faith in the power of rational government planning to overcome what were once seen as insurmountable obstacles to economic progress. By the 1970s the most visible monuments to that faith were the gleaming new skyscrapers that had transformed the Nashville skyline.

MUSIC CITY, ATHENS, AND THE PROTESTANT VATICAN

Outside the city center the diversity of Nashville's economy was demonstrated in three more novel sectors: the music industry, higher education, and religious publishing, education, and administration. Each was established well before World War II, and each benefited enormously from the new economic and social currents that swept through America, and especially the South after the war. Postindustrial society and the economic resurgence of the Sunbelt required a more educated work force with more skills and professional training. At the same time it provided the affluence and government support to make college education possible for large numbers of people. The venerable Athens of the South rose to the occasion.

The rise of music and religion as important parts of the local economy and the public image seemed, on the other hand, to emerge from a powerful undertow of traditional values in a city and a region awash in change. During and after World War II the South was coming in from the countryside in greater numbers than ever before. Southerners left behind their farms and small towns and adapted many of their rural ways to the new demands of the city. Country music and evangelical religion represented elements of the rural culture that southerners brought with them to the cities. Of course, both were transformed into modern, urban phenomena by new media and new audiences. Nashville served as an ideal place to translate those rural traditions to suit the needs of the modern South.

MUSIC CITY, U.S.A.

Nashville's music industry emerged as a major force in the city's economy and public image after World War II. In these years a multifaceted, integrated music industry emerged as radio entertainment led to recording, which in turn spawned music publishing, licensing agencies, television production, a musical theme park, and a booming tourist industry.

Though originally a spin-off of Nashville's insurance companies, the entrepreneurial talent and capital behind the music industry came entirely from outside the established business elite of Nashville and mostly from the rural areas outside the city. Nashville's early embarrassment at having the Athens of the South image besmirched by hillbilly music slowly disappeared when the profits and popularity brought by the music industry became apparent.

By the 1970s it was clear that Nashville's music industry was not confined to country music in any particular form but included pop, rock, gospel, and a variety of musical styles within each genre. Indeed, one of the confusing features of the music industry was the blurring of boundaries separating different music styles, artists, and audiences. The phenomenon of the crossover, which, for example, allowed a country song or artist to make a hit on the pop music charts, brought tremendous new profits to country music performers and encouraged them to appeal to the broadest audience possible. In turn, pop and rock singers found loyal fans and abundant radio outlets in country music as they began crossing over and adopting country music styles.

Many purists in country music—fans and performers alike—denounced the corruption of the tradition and threatened to ostracize the renegades. A 1974 protest against Country Music Association awards to such doubtful country music artists as Olivia Newton John and Charlie Rich was joined by many of Nashville's established country stars. Two of the protesters, however, were Dolly Parton and Barbara Mandrell, who soon made their own departures into pop musical styles and Hollywood productions. It was nearly impossible to draw boundaries around a musical movement that was finding wider popular acceptance and greater profits.[1]

The blurring of boundaries that set apart country music and its performers was nothing new to the 1970s. The music had been evolving as long as professional artists and those who managed them tried to make a living by catering to the broadest possible spectrum of public taste. That evolution accelerated in the 1920s when radio station WSM gained clear channel access to a huge audience across the nation and began modifying the Appalachian sound of old time folk music, introduced cowboy and western swing, and generally offered a variety of styles for its more diverse audience.[2]

Roy Acuff, the "King of Country Music," is today regarded as the standard-bearer for an older and purer tradition of country music, but he, too, was an innovator and popularizer who, more than any other performer, shifted the direction that country music took in the post-

Figure 47. WSM's Grand Ole Opry radio show, broadcast live from the Dixie Tabernacle in East Nashville from 1937 to 1939 before it moved to War Memorial Auditorium and then to Ryman Auditorium in 1941. This show was the seedbed of Nashville's flourishing music industry. Nashville Room, Ben West Public Library.

1940 era. Acuff came from East Tennessee in 1938 to join the Grand Ole Opry after an ill-starred career in baseball. Acuff's full-voiced singing and his hit songs, "The Great Speckled Bird" and "Wabash Cannonball" won tremendous following among Opry fans. His role in a minor Hollywood movie, "The Grand Ole Opry," in 1939 also helped establish his national reputation.[3]

It was World War II that allowed Acuff and other country music artists to tap a mass national market. The war pulled millions of northerners into the South and brought millions of southern boys, with their radios, guitars, and harmonicas, into contact with nonsoutherners who, often for the first time, heard and learned to enjoy southern hillbilly music. The Camel Caravan (sponsored by Camel cigarettes) brought Opry stars to military bases across the nation for live shows during the war. When the Japanese attempted to rattle American Marines on Okinawa, they could think of no greater string of insults than: "To hell with President Roosevelt! To hell with Babe Ruth! To hell with Roy Acuff!" So great was Acuff's popularity after World War II, the Republican party nominated him for governor of Tennessee in 1948. The campaign, which featured Acuff's music, did less to further Republican prospects in Tennessee than it did to enhance Roy Acuff's burgeoning musical popularity in the 1940s.[4]

In the years following the war, country music more often appealed to the millions of southerners and other rural folk who were streaming into the cities of the South and all parts of the nation. The lyrics often lamented the hard times in the city, the strain on family ties, trouble with the boss, hard drinking, loneliness, unrequited love, and sweet memories of life back home. The popular honky-tonk style evoked a sense of urban sinfulness. Country music came to be the white working-class counterpart to the black blues that came wailing out of the ghettos of Memphis, New Orleans, and northern cities. For all the differences in style and lyrics, country music and black blues shared common ground as a southern musical response to the pains of transforming rural folk into an urban working class.[5]

No artist captured this new meaning of country music better than Hank Williams, a young singer and songwriter from Alabama, who joined the Opry in the late 1940s and teamed up with songwriter Fred Rose. Williams picked up much of his musical style from an old black street singer and brought a pained blues tone to lyrics that stressed the heartbreak of contemporary personal life. "Cold, Cold Heart," "Lovesick Blues," "Your Cheatin' Heart," and "I Can't Help It If I'm Still in Love with You" were just some of the hits that launched Williams as a popular star. Unlike Acuff or other stars of the Opry, who stressed their rustic, wholesome qualities, Williams led a tragic life, very much in the public eye and filled with drinking and marital problems. He was fired from the Opry in 1952 after a drunken fall off the stage. He died only

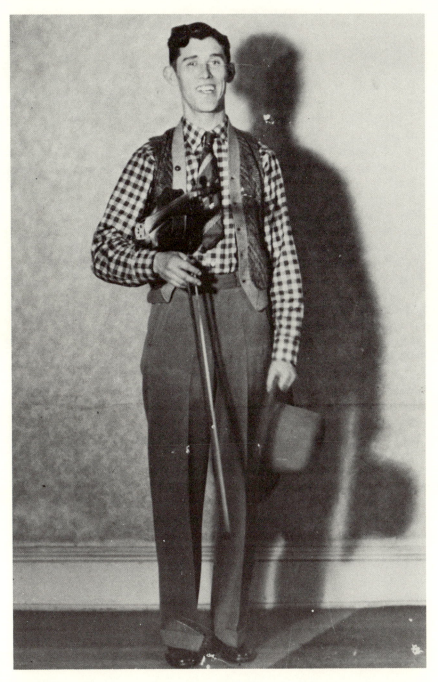

Figure 48. Roy Acuff, c. 1940, one of the first nationally popular stars of the Grand Ole Opry in the 1940s and a pioneer in the Nashville music industry. Country Music Foundation Library.

Figure 49. Stars of the Grand Ole Opry toured by bus throughout the South and Midwest to meet their radio fans in person. Here, Kitty Wells (*center*) and a troop of country music groups pose before Ernest Tubb's tour bus, 1958. Country Music Foundation Library.

six months later, on New Year's Day in 1953, at the age of twenty-nine. In the back seat of a Cadillac driven by his chauffeur, Hank Williams suffered a sudden heart attack caused by a lethal dose of drugs that a quack had given him for a back ailment. Hank Williams became a cult figure among a large, diverse audience who found in his jaded life and his musical lamentations something that touched their experience.[6]

Williams's phenomenal success with pop and country hits encouraged others to cross over. Eddy Arnold, a country boy from Henderson, Tennessee, who learned to play on a Sears mail-order guitar, began his career in the 1940s as the "Tennessee Plowboy." His manager, Colonel Tom Parker (later manager of Elvis Presley), encouraged Arnold to change his image, don a tuxedo and black tie, and croon softly. Arnold appeared in nightclubs, on television specials with pop singers, and even performed in Carnegie Hall.[7] When Patti Page, an aspiring pop singer, recorded a country tune on the flip side of one of her singles in 1950, the music industry was astonished to see it become a major hit. "The Tennessee Waltz" within six months sold over 5 million records. "More than any other single country song of the time," historian Charles Wolfe writes, "'The Tennessee Waltz' anticipated the way in which country music was to become a major American cultural force."[8]

As the audience for Nashville's "uptown country" was being broadened in the 1940s and 1950s, the Nashville music industry was creating an elaborate infrastructure linking performers, studios, songwriters, publishers, licensing agents, and booking agents. One component of this industry encouraged the growth of others in rapid fashion. Before the 1950s New York and Los Angeles dominated the studio recording of pop songs, and most country music had to be recorded in these locations. After World War II the recording industry rose in a tide of affluence that allowed more people to buy phonographs and records, first 78rpm singles, later long-playing albums. Just as New York's popular Tin Pan Alley songs were being challenged by the "Nashville sound," Nashville began a rival recording industry in the 1950s.

About 1945 three radio engineers with WSM—Aaron Shelton, George Reynolds, and Carl Jenkins—organized Castle Studio downtown in the old Tulane Hotel at Church and Eighth Avenue. WSM discouraged this moonlighting venture, and Castle Studio closed a few years later, but this example showed major recording companies the logic of bringing the studios to the performers, many of whom were tied to the Opry and to regional bus tours out of Nashville. Producers also found that the southern country musicians and singers performed more naturally in the relaxed atmosphere of Nashville studios than they did in New York studios. Decca Records sent Paul Cohen to produce several records in 1945. RCA Victor set up a studio at Fourth Avenue and Union in 1946. Capitol Records came in 1950 and Mercury Records in 1952.

Figure 50. Hank Williams, c. 1950. Country Music Foundation Library.

These big labels coming from New York became important in the Nashville music industry, but it was a local entrepreneur who deserves credit for founding Nashville's "Music Row." Owen Bradley, from Westmoreland, Tennessee, was a musician and musical director at WSM in the late 1940s when he linked up with Decca's Paul Cohen and learned about the new technology of record making. In 1952 Bradley bought an old house on Sixteenth Avenue South, in a rundown neighborhood not far from Vanderbilt University. He set up a studio in the basement, then in 1955 installed a three-track stereo console in a quonset hut that had been built next to the house. The Quonset Hut, draped with burlap, somehow had ideal acoustics, and Bradley proved an unusually skilled A&R man (Artists and Repertoire, meaning producer). He had a relaxed, engaging personal style, knew how to put together appealing arrangements, and was usually open to musical innovation.

Bradley's Quonset Hut became the magnet for a string of new recording studios and publishing companies in converted houses and new high-rise buildings that came to be known as Music Row. Inevitably the big-label companies from New York and Los Angeles followed Bradley, and in 1962 Columbia Records bought Bradley out. Columbia carefully built their new corporate offices around the Quonset Hut, which remained in use as a studio, its legendary magic undisturbed.[9]

Bradley's contract with Columbia guaranteed that he would not set up a competing studio in Davidson County. But recording was in Bradley's blood, and in 1965 he bought property in Wilson County and set up a studio in an equally unlikely site, an old barn. Bradley's Barn became enormously popular with country, pop, and rock musicians, who flocked to Nashville to enjoy the relaxed atmosphere, the superb studio musicians, and the magic sound attributed to the barn. The celebrated Nashville sound that Bradley helped invent had as much to do with the relaxed atmosphere in the studio and the improvisational skill of the studio musicians, as it did with any technical quality of the music itself.[10]

Chet Atkins, another East Tennessee native, came into Nashville in the 1940s as a backup guitar player and began doing session work in the studios in the 1950s. He persuaded RCA Victor to set up a studio in Nashville and in 1957 became chief of the company's local operations. Atkins became a major recording star in his own right, with dozens of albums featuring his versatile guitar instrumentals in country, pop, even classical styles. Atkins, like Bradley, was open to musical innovation within the country and western genre, and he welcomed all kinds of music to the RCA studios on Music Row. When a young singer from Memphis who sang a mixture of black rhythm and blues and white "rockabilly" music joined RCA, Atkins welcomed him. Elvis Presley shocked Music Row in the 1950s with his long hair and eye

Figure 51. Owen Bradley (*seated*) with Warner Mack, Paul Cohen (*left*), and other unidentified persons. Country Music Foundation Library.

shadow, but Atkins showed that Nashville was just as capable of producing hit songs in rock music as it was in country and western.[11]

While the studios were creating a national reputation for the Nashville sound, another integral link in the music industry—the songwriters and publishers—came to Music Row. With the advent of the radio and phonograph, the market for sheet music had declined precipitously, but music publishers were still essential to protect copyrights and ensure that royalties flowed to the correct authors and songwriters. Before the 1940s this part of the music industry was dominated by the Tin Pan Alley songwriters of New York City who had moved into country music as early as the 1920s and 1930s.[12] Fred Rose came to Nashville in 1933 with a background in Tin Pan Alley and Chicago as a pop song writer and piano player. In the late 1930s Rose also developed contacts in the emergent Los Angeles music industry, where former Nashville country singers and film actors Gene Autry and Tex Ritter had moved. Rose might have stayed in Hollywood, but he had married a homesick Nashville girl and returned with her to Tennessee about 1942. In that year Roy Acuff approached Rose with the idea of forming their own music publishing company to cater to the nascent Nashville music industry. Rose and Acuff had met earlier at a recording session. When Acuff needed another song to fill out a new album Rose volunteered, stepped out of the studio, and returned in a matter of minutes with a finished number. Acuff, a rising star, was suspicious of New York publishers who wanted to buy his songs; he wanted his own publishing company to protect copyrights. Rose saw an opportunity to nurture new talent and fill a void left by the New York publishers, who spurned country music for the most part. In 1945 Rose brought his son Wesley, a former businessman in Chicago, into the firm to manage all the business affairs, while he turned to songwriting and recruitment of talent.[13]

In Acuff-Rose Publishing Company northern business acumen and popular music joined the informal style of country music in a new way. Into a world of cutthroat competition and ruthless "song sharks," who bilked artists out of songs, fees, and royalties, Fred Rose brought a rare standard of honest dealing and fatherly support for budding writers and performers. Immediately Nashville's musicians and writers came to trust Rose and sought his aid as a writer, an editor, and a promoter. It was Rose who helped Hank Williams turn his unpolished songs into popular hits. Acuff-Rose's most important hit in its early years was "The Tennessee Waltz," which helped launch the young company and pointed the way toward musical innovation and crossover music. Before Fred Rose's death in 1954 the company had become an important element in the Nashville music industry and continued as such under the direction of Wesley Rose.[14]

Other publishers followed Acuff-Rose. Two Austrian brothers, Julian and Jean Aberbach, established Hill and Range Songs, Inc., in 1945, which later formed part of the Aberbach Group. Jim Denny, formerly with WSM, founded Cedarwood Publishing Company in 1953. Jack Stapp, also with WSM, founded Tree Publishing Company the next year and rose to fame in the 1960s as publisher of Roger Miller's series of country-pop hit songs. By 1975 about 244 publishing houses had been formed in Nashville, many of them small operations based solely on the hopes of one or two songwriters who had suitcases full of songs and heads full of dreams.[15]

The rise of the recording and publishing industries in Nashville coincided with the establishment of Broadcast Music, Incorporated (BMI), a licensing agent that logs radio shows and collects royalties for affiliated publishers, artists, and songwriters. Before 1940 the American Society of Composers, Authors, and Publishers (ASCAP), organized in 1914 and based in New York City, had rights on nearly all the established composers of popular tunes. ASCAP ignored country music. Only the Selected Editions of Standard American Catalogues (SESAC), founded in 1931, offered even minor competition to ASCAP. With its near-monopoly secure, in 1940 ASCAP tried to raise its royalty fee for radio performance rights. Radio broadcasters rebelled and formed BMI to offer competition to ASCAP. Country music publishers found a new outlet at BMI, and at fees far below those of ASCAP. BMI also welcomed the new rock music of the 1950s and generally opened up the whole music industry in America. In 1939 there were about 1,000 songwriters and 137 music publishers across the country. By 1965 those numbers had skyrocketed to 19,000 writers and 8,000 publishers.[16]

In 1955 BMI appointed Frances Williams Preston head of its Nashville operations. She ran BMI out of her home for three years before opening an office in the new L&C Tower in 1958. In 1964 the growth of BMI in Nashville was signified by a striking new office on Music Row. Preston by this time had become a singular presence on the row. She discovered and nurtured new talent and helped open Nashville's country music to the new currents of innovation and commercial appeal that came in the 1960s.[17] In 1948 it was estimated that 90 percent of the nation's songs were licensed by ASCAP. By 1958 BMI licensed 57 percent of the songs licensed in America, and in 1965 that rose to 80 percent.[18]

It was not long (1962) before ASCAP established its own office on Music Row, a signal that it had come to recognize the commercial importance of the Nashville sound. At the cocktail party ASCAP held for the Nashville music people that year, one observer noted that "many country-music people were gloating over the long belated recognition by the 'good music' group, enjoying every snack and drink from the hand that had once stung the hillbilly."[19] By early 1963 *Broadcasting*, a trade magazine, reported that one-half of all American recordings issued from Nashville. By that time it was estimated that Nashville was the home for 1,100 musicians, 350 songwriters, 110 publishing houses, and 15

Figure 52. Francis Preston of Broadcast Music, Incorporated, with Roy Horton, c. 1967. Country Music Foundation Library.

Figure 53. A display at the DJs' convention, Municipal Auditorium, promoting Nashville's music industry and the new Country Music Foundation's Hall of Fame and Museum, 1966. Country Music Foundation Library.

recording studios. Altogether, the Nashville music industry brought in about $40 million each year, and the music business was just beginning to grow.[20]

By the mid-1960s the business leaders and Chamber of Commerce downtown were beginning to take notice of the happenings out on Music Row and to recognize its potential for Nashville's economy. Leaders of the music industry also began to take their business more seriously. The Country Music Association (CMA), a trade group formed in 1958, brought together all elements of the country music industry—from disc jockeys to performers and publishers—in a cooperative effort to promote country music. In the early 1960s the CMA organized the Country Music Foundation and began raising funds for a Country Music Hall of Fame. The city donated property for the Hall of Fame, and the state of Tennessee contributed $25,000 to the construction fund. Some of the city's leading businessmen took an active part in raising the rest of the $750,000 for the Hall of Fame. Banker Andrew Benedict, chairman of the fund-raising committee, said, "Nashville is known the world over principally for her country music fame. The shining star of this industry has risen with local men and women who have gone out as our representatives. The goodwill they have achieved for Nashville is without estimate."[21]

When the Hall of Fame opened in 1967, Governor Buford Ellington, Representative Richard Fulton, and Mayor Beverly Briley all turned out to pay tribute to Music Row.[22] The Hall of Fame, a modern interpretation of a country barn, housed a museum and a library and archives devoted to the serious study of a musical tradition that had for too long been the object of snobbish scorn. Like the music itself, the Hall of Fame museum learned to cater to all popular tastes. Elvis Presley's gold Cadillac shared the museum with Hank Snow's rhinestone cowboy jacket and Uncle Dave Macon's banjo. It became a central attraction for tourists, and by the 1970s the hawkers of souvenirs and tourist shows were leaving Lower Broad to form a new cluster around the Hall of Fame. At the same time the museum and library, sponsored by the Country Music Foundation, helped "lend dignity and acceptance to country music."[23]

The tourist industry that built around Nashville's country music attractions inspired new ventures beyond Music Row. In 1972 NLT (National Life and Accident Insurance Company's parent company), which had been ambivalent toward its connection with the Opry in years past, opened Opryland. This was a $66-million complex with a 217-acre theme park, a 614-room Opryland Hotel, and a new Grand Ole Opry auditorium. The new Opry was rigged for the latest technology in television production, which, through Opryland Productions, was fast becoming another important spin-off of the music business.[24]

When the Opry's last show in the old Ryman Auditorium, its home since 1941, came in 1974, there were tears in the beer at Tootsie's Orchid Lounge nearby, and a tone of regret from Roy Acuff, Minnie Pearl, and their millions of Opry fans.[25] The very success and popular acceptance that country music had been striving for now forced it out of its raffish home downtown, away from the honky-tonk bars and peep shows, off to a clean, modern suburban showcase, where the modern country music fan would feel more at home. Many stars and fans longed for the old Opry house and decried the surrender to commercialization. But Opryland was only the most recent step of a series that had made country music a commercial success. In many ways it was a perfect representation of what Nashville's music industry had become. The musical shows at the theme park offered slick renditions of everything from bluegrass and country to jazz and minstrel styles, all packaged to appeal to every tourist's taste.

The Hall of Fame and Opryland became new focal points for a booming tourist industry that by the 1970s was drawing people from every corner of America, along with a growing stream from Canada and abroad.[26] Millions of fans flocked to Nashville to attend the Opry, see the Hall of Fame, buy souvenirs, see the small bar-shows on Lower Broad, and gape at the homes of the stars from tour-bus windows. In 1977 it was estimated that over 7 million tourists spent $170 million in the Nashville area. About 84,000 conventioneers spent another $12 million in 1978. By the early 1980s plans for a convention center at the Opryland Hotel and another adjacent to Ryman Auditorium promised to build on the tourist industry and make Nashville host to major conventions throughout the year.[27] Tourism, an appealing "clean industry" that brought millions of moderately affluent consumers through the city with little strain on tax-supported services, became a major focus of Chamber of Commerce campaigns in the 1970s. The slogan "Music City, U.S.A.," now gained favor over "Athens of the South," and advertisements in national magazines lured tourists to Nashville with Dolly Parton's striking profile, an image that threatened to displace the Parthenon as Nashville's icon. The city received greater notoriety when Robert Altman produced the movie *Nashville* in 1975. Some in the music industry felt that Altman did not flatter Music Row or the community, but the movie was a hit, and it did bring national attention to what Altman called America's "new Hollywood."

Most Nashvillians by this time were well beyond the early phase of embarrassment or apology for the music that had brought such wealth and fame to their city. This acceptance was reflected also in the growing visibility of music stars and producers within the city's social elite. The early parvenues of country music often displayed their success in what some considered garish clothes, custom-decorated automobiles, guitar-shaped swimming pools, and other such extravagances. Shunned for the most part by the established, monied families of Belle Meade, many of the *nouveaux riches* from Music Row laid out their own grand mansions along Franklin Road or in Hendersonville.

One indicator of the emergence of a Music City social elite was the publicity their charities received. Charity often serves as an important means for the wealthy to visibly establish their status and confirm their value to society. Vanderbilt University, the Nashville Symphony, the Hermitage, and Cheekwood Botanical Gardens have been among the favorite beneficiaries of Nashville's old money. By the 1970s Music City's elite began identifying their own worthwhile causes. Minnie Pearl lent her personal support to the Tennessee State Museum. Hank Snow organized a foundation in behalf of abused children. Tom T. Hall, bard of the pick-up set, affected the style of an old regulation southern planter and played host to numerous well-publicized benefits for his favorite charities, the Humane Society and Democratic politicians. President Jimmy Carter's family were among the celebrated guests at the Halls' home, Fox Hollow.

The Music City parvenues were also being recognized by—and even accepted into—the established business elite and social set of Nashville by the late 1970s. Wesley Rose, the wealthy chief of Acuff-Rose Publishing Company, was appointed to the Board of Directors of First American National Bank and the Board of the Nashville Symphony Association. Frances Preston of BMI became the first woman to serve on the Chamber of Commerce Board of Directors.[28] They were the first of several Music City entrepreneurs to enter the city's most prestigious board rooms. Music Row executives and producers, like Frances Preston, Buddy Killen of Tree International, and several others, were also being invited to the Swan Ball at Cheekwood, the annual charity-cum-society extravaganza of Nashville's social set. More telling of the fact that Music Row had truly arrived in Nashville was the entertainment by Barbara Mandrell and Loretta Lynn, respectively, at the 1981 and 1982 Swan Balls. While Loretta Lynn, the coal miner's daughter from Butcher Hollow, sang her hits, Swan Ball guests stood on chairs and clapped to the down-home music that had made Nashville famous in ways the old Nashville elite would never have predicted just a few years earlier.[29] The scene was symbolic of how far the country music industry had come since its beginnings in 1925 when the Grand Ole Opry started. It was also a sign of how far Nashville had come in recognizing one of its most valuable assets.

BOOM, BUST, AND MERGER IN ATHENS

The rise of Music City crowded, but did not displace, Nashville's historical role as an educational center in the South. Indeed, this tradition fitted nicely with the new thrust of the postindustrial economy, which required more people with college education and advanced degrees. Education became another major component of the city's service economy, along with finance, insurance, entertainment, and tourism. Like the downtown renewal that benefited the financial sector, the expansion of higher education depended increasingly on federal government funds. Table 3 outlines the aggregate growth of the new Athens of the South after World War II.

The growth trends in higher education after 1940 were far more volatile than those in finance and insurance, however. World War II and the GI bill drew swarms of former soldiers onto the campuses with government financial support. During the 1950s the Cold War with Russia and the successful launch of Sputnik, the Russian satellite, in 1957 jolted Americans out of their complacency with regard to education and scientific training in particular. Millions of federal dollars flowed into college programs in the sciences, engineering, and mathematics in a massive effort to "catch up" with the Russians. Many of these funds overflowed into general campus improvements: new libraries, dormitories, and classrooms, as well as laboratories and graduate fellowships. Some of Nashville's colleges, particularly Vanderbilt, Peabody, and Meharry, which were more oriented toward research and professional training, benefited from the new partnership with government. Most of the city's colleges and universities enjoyed an unprecedented period of growth in students, buildings, and programs before the 1970s. The flood of postwar students was sustained as the baby boom generation came of college age in the early 1960s.

The national effort to tear down the barriers of segregation and overcome the disadvantages that blacks suffered also helped stimulate the expansion of the city's black colleges, Fisk, Meharry, and especially Tennessee State University (formerly Tennessee A&I) beginning in the 1950s. Here again, the federal government played a decisive role in allocating funds for student aid, construction, and general support. The boom in higher education ended suddenly in the early 1970s. The national economic disruption caused by the Vietnam War and the energy

Table 3: Nashville's Higher Education Industry, 1950, 1960, 1970

Value of endowment (*millions*)	1950	1960	1970
Colleges and universities	10	13	14
Students	11,103	14,587	21,673
Nonresident students	7,342	10,242	13,625
Value of properties (*millions*)	$37.8	$67.4	$194.1
Value of endowment (*millions*)	$46.0	$73.9	$166.2

SOURCE: Nashville Area Chamber of Commerce, *Statistical Record*, 1950, 1960, 1970.

crisis, the student disruptions brought on by protests against the war and against black inequality, and the demographic decline of college-age population after the baby boom generation were among the chief causes of what became a painful series of financial difficulties, especially for small private colleges. This depression in higher education affected colleges just as economic depressions usually affect business firms; some folded, others retrenched or merged with stronger institutions, and the result was consolidation, with the already large and strong institutions becoming more dominant by the end of the depression.

Vanderbilt University Vanderbilt continued as a leading university in the South, with growing aspirations for national prominence in the postwar years. Chancellor James Kirkland's forty-four-year reign ended in 1938. Kirkland had taken Vanderbilt from a struggling, obscure Methodist college to a regionally powerful university with a first-class medical school, all built upon strong support from northern foundations, a well-organized alumni association, and strong links to the Nashville business elite.

Kirkland's successor, Oliver Cromwell Carmichael, was to serve the shortest term of any Vanderbilt chancellor, from 1938 to 1946, years of adversity for the best of colleges. A native of Alabama, a Rhodes scholar, and a member of Herbert Hoover's Belgium Relief Commission during World War I, Carnichael brought to his career in academic administration worldly experience and superb intellectual credentials. Undaunted by the hard times of the 1930s, he launched an expansion program in 1939, nurtured a beneficial connection with Frederick W. Vanderbilt, the commodore's grandson, and together with Andrew Benedict, Sr., as university comptroller, built the endowment to over $30 million before he retired. When he resigned in 1946 to take the presidency of his alma mater, the University of Alabama, Carmichael left Vanderbilt in excellent condition to benefit from the postwar expansion in higher education.[30]

His successor, B. Harvie Branscomb, was former dean of the Divinity School at Duke University. Vanderbilt's Board of Trust was skeptical about bringing a Methodist theologian to head a university that had gone through a wrenching battle to sever its ties to the Methodist church. But Branscomb led Vanderbilt through a dynamic period of physical expansion and new academic leadership in the region. Branscomb saw Vanderbilt's domain as the only noteworthy private university south of the University of Chicago and north of Tulane. He aggressively pursued money from the Ford and Rockefeller foundations and used federal funds to help build new dormitories after the war. When Branscomb arranged for Commodore Vanderbilt's statue to be placed on the new entranceway in front of Kirkland Hall, Dean Madison Sarratt quipped that he "faced it north toward the Ford Foundation."[31] Concerned that the campus had become hemmed in by the city that had grown up around it since the 1920s, Branscomb toyed with the idea of leaving the Medical Center where it was and building a new campus ten or fifteen miles outside Nashville. Instead, he launched a major building program, filling in the empty corners of the existing campus with thirty-six new buildings. He also began purchasing small plots of adjacent land in preparation for future growth.

Vanderbilt had achieved a respected academic reputation in the South, but Branscomb felt that it had grown complacent. New state universities with low tuitions drew away many southern students in the Depression years. By 1946 half the student body was from the Nashville area, nearly two-thirds from Tennessee. Seventeen new dormitories and an aggressive recruitment campaign increased out-of-state students to 58 percent by 1963.[32] Branscomb tried to deemphasize the dominant role of fraternity life and resist the Southeast Conference trend toward professionalization of intercollegiate sports. He pushed graduate education, faculty research, and tried to create a more stimulating intellectual atmosphere in the undergraduate colleges.

Branscomb also pushed gently to bring new, younger members to the Board of Trust and strengthen ties to men of great wealth outside the Nashville area. He skillfully rekindled interest in the university among members of the Vanderbilt family who, with the exception of Frederick W. Vanderbilt, had lost touch with the campus their ancestor had established in 1873. As a result Harold Stirling Vanderbilt, a railroad executive like his grandfather, not only gave large sums of money to the university, he became a fast friend of Branscomb and an active member and president of the Board of Trust.[33]

Through Vanderbilt's vast network of alumni and its prominent Board of Trust members, the university was extraordinarily well connected to the sources of political power and wealth both in and outside Nashville. When plans were in the works to rebuild the Veterans Hospital on White Bridge Road, instead of relocating it next to Vanderbilt Hospital as planned earlier, Harold S. Vanderbilt used his influence with friends in the Eisenhower administration to oust the administrator for Veterans Affairs and replace him with someone who agreed that the hospital should be placed next to Vanderbilt.[34] When urban renewal came, Vanderbilt benefited from the University Center Project, but it displaced dozens of middle-income families living in perfectly sound housing between the campus and Blakemore Avenue in order to give the campus more room to grow. These and other displays of power brought expressions of public outrage from people who resented Vanderbilt as an elite, overprivileged institution, insensitive to the community around it and oblivious to the social issues at stake in the South and the nation.[35]

When the university did venture to respond to the changing society around it, however, disgruntled alumni were equally vociferous in their resistance to change. A case in point was the desegregation issue. Eager to retain the support of northern foundations, Branscomb complied with their wishes that Vanderbilt desegregate. "The university," Chancellor Branscomb admitted, "was not so much taking the lead in this area as being carried along by events."[36] Branscomb's early effort to desegregate the Law School in 1949 was defeated by the Board of Trust, but in 1953 the Divinity School opened its doors to Vanderbilt's first black student.[37] The Law School followed in 1956, and the publicity outraged many alumni, who organized a renegade alumni association. Branscomb and the Board of Trust placed Vanderbilt in opposition to desegregation of downtown lunch counters, in effect, when they expelled James Lawson for leading the sit-in demonstrations in 1960.[38] It was not until 1962, against the expressed wishes of a majority of the student body, that Vanderbilt accepted desegregation in the undergraduate colleges.[39]

Branscomb's successor in 1963, Alexander Heard, was another controversial appointment. A graduate of the University of North Carolina and Columbia University, Heard had served in government during the New Deal and was considered a liberal Democrat at a time when Democrats of any stripe were rare on the Vanderbilt Board of Trust. Those worried by Branscomb's moderate leanings on the race question had reason to fear that the new chancellor would further upset Vanderbilt's conservative traditions.[40]

As the winds of civil rights and antiwar protest began buffeting college compuses across the nation in the late 1960s, Vanderbilt remained remarkably serene. The fraternities and sororities continued to absorb the attention of most Vanderbilt undergraduates, and women students readily admitted that Vanderbilt's high ratio of men to women was one of its principal attractions. A small, short-lived chapter of the radical Students for a Democratic Society folded as early as the spring of 1965, and one of the few demonstrations on campus was staged by students *in support* of the American war effort in Vietnam.[41]

It was precisely this placid, conservative ambience at Vanderbilt that made many alumni so sensitive to anything that might challenge it. When students invited black-power advocate Stokely Carmichael to speak at the Impact series in the spring of 1967 a howl of protest arose, mostly from Nashville-area alumni who tried to pressure Heard into banning Carmichael from campus (see chapter 8). James G. Stahlman, a major benefactor and trustee of Vanderbilt, issued a series of strident editorials in his newspaper, the *Banner*, blaming Heard for the whole affair. "Nothing that could be said by way of public apology . . . can remove the stench of the Stokely Carmichael visit to Vanderbilt University," the *Banner* snorted, adding pointedly that "the ultimate responsibility lies at the door of the chancellor. . . ."[42] The *Tennessean*

Figure 54. Vanderbilt students in 1959 protesting Chancellor Branscomb's effort to deemphasize fraternities on campus. *Tennessean* Library.

answered Stahlman and the Vanderbilt old guard with its own strong language: "Vanderbilt can easily survive the arrogance of Stokely Carmichael. But it cannot survive the ignorance of those who will love the school only if they can remember it as it was in the past."[43] The Carmichael affair had blown into a major crisis and became an implicit challenge to Heard and to his future at Vanderbilt. Heard stood firm against attacks from Stahlman, angry alumni, the American Legion, and even a resolution by the state senate. He staunchly defended the principle that the university was an "open forum" where invited speakers aired their views, however unpopular or disagreeable.

After the Carmichael affair the Vanderbilt community and the press became more supportive, and Heard moved more certainly toward the goals he had set for the university. When he arrived, Heard launched a major planning study, and the massive report that resulted from it became the blueprint for the coming years. He expanded the administration, overhauled several departments, added foreign campus affiliates, expanded foreign area studies programs, and pushed hard to upgrade graduate education and faculty research. Under Heard, Vanderbilt continued to draw more students from outside Tennessee and a growing percentage from the Midwest and the Northeast. There were some older alumni who were disturbed by a subtle but undeniable tendency to deemphasize Vanderbilt's southern affinity, but that was the price of pursuing national stature.[44]

Heard embarked on an ambitious fund-raising campaign for $55 million in 1966. The campaign drew $11 million from the Ford Foundation, matched by another $11 million from Harold S. Vanderbilt, and the drive was successfully completed by 1970. Some of these funds launched a new Graduate School of Management, which strengthened ties between the university and the business community.[45] The University Center urban renewal project went forward soon after this fund drive was complete, and a large residential neighborhood south of the Medical Center to Blakemore Avenue was slated for clearance to make way for the expansion of Vanderbilt.

The financial stringency that hit higher education in the 1970s restrained the university from expanding as rapidly as it had planned, but the hard times that struck other campuses were never serious at Vanderbilt. During Heard's final years at Vanderbilt he devoted nearly all his time to fund raising, and the board created a new office of president, filled by Emmett Fields in 1977, to take over daily administrative duties. A centennial fund drive, begun in 1975, set its target at $150 million and was actually oversubscribed by more than $40 million. Heard retired in 1982 to head a study of presidential politics.[46]

Peabody College   George Peabody College for Teachers had enjoyed many of the same growth trends as its larger neighbor, Vanderbilt, in the postwar era. The baby boom created a surge in demand for schoolteachers and administrators of teachers colleges. Peabody's graduates were highly sought in both these areas. New federal programs to aid "culturally deprived" and handicapped students also buoyed programs in special education in the 1960s. A growing number of foreign students, many sponsored by the American government, flocked to Peabody for training as educators.[47]

President Bruce R. Payne's death in 1937 ended twenty-six years of Peabody's golden era of expansion. Sidney C. Garrison pulled the college through the rougher years of the late 1930s and World War II before he died in 1945. Henry A. Hill, a nationally recognized public school administrator, took the helm after 1945 and steered Peabody along its traditional track as a teacher training school. He brought in prominent faculty, reorganized the curriculum and faculty into four "educational task forces," and took full advantage of the postwar boom in education.

By the late 1950s, however, the fundamental problems of Peabody's future were revealed clearly. Peabody had grown since World War I with the proliferation of state teachers colleges throughout the South and the nation, colleges that Peabody graduates filled as professors and administrators. "Peabody," historian Jack Allen explained, "had effectively bred its own competition." The competition, moreover, offered low tuition to future teachers, whose earning power did not seem to justify the more costly investment in a Peabody degree. Furthermore, Peabody's ability to raise funds from alumni was inherently limited by the low-salaried professions for which it trained its students.[48]

As GI-bill students declined in the late 1950s and as Peabody's financial picture darkened, President Hill urged expansion of nonteaching undergraduate programs. When Hill retired in 1961, Peabody and Vanderbilt University officials met to study the possibility of "closer cooperation," which some interpreted to mean eventual merger (a prospect that had been in the wings since 1909, when Peabody made plans to move its campus adjacent to Vanderbilt). Opinion at Peabody was divided on this issue, but the Peabody Board of Trust voted overwhelmingly to remain autonomous.[49]

In the ensuing years, under the leadership of President Felix C. Robb, Peabody ventured away from its role in teacher training to add a new research dimension in special education. With aid from the Kennedy Foundation, federal grants, and endowment funds, the John Fitzgerald Kennedy Center for Research in Education and Human Development opened in 1965. The Kennedy Center, directed by psychologist Nicholas Hobbs, gave Peabody national stature as a research institution.[50]

There were renewed efforts to diversify undergraduate programs beyond teacher training, as well as a major endowment drive, but these campaigns did not succeed. By 1973 the Board of Trust, chaired by Horace G. Hill, Jr., decided to pull back and redirect Peabody to its original purpose—training teachers. President John M. Claunch, who had succeeded Robb in 1967, retired in 1973, and a new, young president, John Dunworth, was appointed to revitalize the ailing institution. Dunworth, following a faculty committee report he commissioned in 1974, performed radical surgery on Peabody. He eliminated three departments, totally reorganized the others, jettisoned the Demonstration School, and cut out a whole layer of administrators. He launched new fund-raising campaigns, but the endowment failed to grow. At only $12 million in 1967, the endowment was inadequate, but twelve years later amid the ravages of inflation, which virtually cut the purchasing power of those dollars in half, the endowment stood still at $12 million.

Peabody, nonetheless, was free of debt, and it boasted a valuable and attractive campus. Now was the moment, the Board of Trust decided, to bargain for a merger. The obvious partner for such a prospect was Vanderbilt, but because of its own preoccupation with fund raising (and its past experience with failed mergers) Vanderbilt remained aloof. Peabody's Board of Trust announced alternative plans to merge with Tennessee State University, the predominantly black school in North Nashville, or to pull out of Nashville altogether and take its endowment to Washington and Lee University in Virginia. Vanderbilt administrators, apparently realizing Peabody's intentions, entered into serious negotiations, and the merger soon was announced. Peabody would become a school within the university, devoted primarily to research in human development and special education. The merger was painful for Peabody's faculty, trustees, students, and alumni, but the alternative of continued decline and eventual financial crisis made the move more palatable.[51]

Fisk University   Nashville's two renowned private black schools, Fisk University, Meharry Medical College, along with Tennessee State University, shared to some degree the flush times of the postwar era and the hard times of the 1970s. In addition, they were affected by the civil rights movement and desegregation, which, on the one hand, enhanced black political power and drew federal aid to black schools. On the other hand, the opening of formerly white schools to blacks eroded the monopoly that segregation had created for black schools. For some, black colleges were seen as vestiges of an obsolete order of race relations. For others, they were part of a proud historical tradition that had its own enduring justification.

During the early 1940s Fisk floundered after President Thomas Jones took leave from his duties to head a Quaker pacifist organization during the war. He finally resigned entirely in 1945 and was succeeded in 1947 by Charles S. Johnson, a sociologist of national reputation, who became Fisk's first black president.[52] Johnson demonstrated that a black administrator was at no serious disadvantage in shaking funds from

Figure 55. Charles S. Johnson, president of Fisk 1947–1956, and a nationally prominent sociologist of race relations. Fisk University Library.

northern foundations or in nurturing alliances with the white Nashville business elite. At the same time, Johnson utilized his position to advocate improved race relations and better treatment of Nashville's black community. The Fisk Race Relations Institute grew into a respected research agency and served as host to annual conferences that provided a widely noticed forum for leaders of both races to address the changing course of postwar race relations.[53]

When Charles S. Johnson died in 1956, Fisk found a new leader in Steven J. Wright. President Wright brought Fisk through the tumultuous years of Nashville's desegregation, in which Fisk students took a leading role.[54] In 1966 Fisk celebrated its centennial with understandable pride. The endowment stood at about $11 million, up from $2.4 million in 1940, and plans were laid for a $17.8-million centennial fund drive.[55] But later that same year, Wright went on to a job with the United Negro College Fund and was replaced in 1968 by James R. Lawson, an accomplished physicist and former acting president.[56] Lawson faced a series of problems that set in by the late 1960s. Desegregation confronted Fisk with new competition from predominantly white state schools charging lower tuition. The Fisk student body had become two-thirds female, as more black males went to formerly white schools. The militancy of the civil rights movement also erupted in protests against Fisk administrators in the late 1960s.[57] Faced with these problems, the centennial fund drive went forward slowly, and outside grants were harder than ever to extract. By the mid-1970s Fisk faced severe cutbacks in personnel and salaries; summer school was canceled, tuition hiked, and debts increased with local banks in order to meet operating expenses. The endowment withered from over $11 million to less than $4 million, with half of that encumbered as collateral on building loans. Lawson quit under the pressure in 1975 and later took a post with the federal government. Morale on the Fisk campus plummeted.[58]

The hoped-for revival of Fisk began in October, 1977, with the installation of Walter Leonard as the next president. A former administrator at Harvard University, with experience at three black schools, Leonard brought to Fisk prestigious credentials and a familiarity with both the traditions and the new problems confronting black colleges. He used his visible position to push the city into cleaning up the neighborhood around Fisk and building a new viaduct across the L&N tracks (Jubilee Memorial Bridge) connecting Fisk, Meharry, and North Nashville to the West End area. Leonard attracted federal funds to help restore Fisk's historic Jubilee Hall and Fisk Chapel. Most important, he embarked on a sorely needed fund drive for nearly $11 million and worked to revitalize the confidence of alumni and community donors in the future of Fisk. But as Fisk entered the 1980s that future seemed as uncertain as it had ever been since its early struggles to survive, more than a century earlier.[59]

Meharry Medical College Next door to Fisk another venerable black school, Meharry Medical College, thrived in the postwar years, felt pinched in the 1970s, and suffered throughout as a small black institution fighting for its rights against the powerful medical school of Vanderbilt University. Issues of race inevitably entered every contest between these two medical schools, but conflicting philosophies of medical education were at odds as much as race per se. Meharry continued to see its mission in training black doctors, dentists, and nurses to serve black patients in a system of segregated health facilities. Meharry emphasized training medical professionals to treat the common ailments that afflicted the black poor, not advanced research and esoteric specialities. After World War II the nationally prominent medical schools, like Vanderbilt, became increasingly devoted to advanced research, highly specialized training, and rarefied medical and surgical treatments.

Foundation support for Meharry continued to flow but at a slower, more uncertain rate in the 1940s. Abraham Flexner of the Rockefeller General Education Board (GEB) led a largely successful $6-million fund drive, completed in 1944. It was clear, however, that Meharry had to find more constant and reliable sources of support. For a time, Meharry administrators considered a merger with Fisk, but the faculty preferred to remain autonomous.[60] Edward L. Turner, Meharry president from 1938 to 1944, had been highly successful in attracting Rockefeller funds, and he helped recruit a new echelon of black deans and other administrators to prepare Meharry for a transition from white to black leadership in the future. President M. Don Clawson, who succeeded president Turner in 1944, urged southern states to follow Tennessee's example by utilizing Meharry as a regional center for the education of black doctors. This would satisfy recent U.S. Supreme Court decisions that required equal opportunities in professional education for blacks. That same year several southern states established the Southern Regional Education Compact, which guaranteed a steady flow of state-supported black medical students to Meharry. For a time it appeared Meharry's very control of the school would also pass to this interstate organization, but alumni successfully opposed this move.[61]

In 1948 Meharry pushed for more reliable support from the city government, which was to pay Meharry for taking care of indigent patients at Hubbard Hospital. The city's General Hospital had just signed an exclusive contract with Vanderbilt Medical School to provide care for indigent patients, an essential component of Vanderbilt's medical training. Hubbard also received thousands of indigent patients, but the city argued that many were rural blacks (who came to Hubbard because no hospitals in their communities admitted blacks) and were not the responsibility of the city. To Meharry's request for $225,000 to cover the costs of indigent care, the city offered only $100,000. Meharry threatened to close Hubbard Hospital altogether, which would have placed unbearable pressure on General Hospital. After lengthy negotiations, Meharry and the City Hospital Board agreed in 1949 to shift indigent black patients from General Hospital to Hubbard (and some also to Vanderbilt Hospital).[62] This was an issue that would erupt again in the tense relations between Meharry, the city, and Vanderbilt.

It was segregation of health care that, ironically, rescued Meharry and Hubbard Hospital. Having ensured the survival of Meharry for the time, President Clawson stepped down in 1950, and in 1952 Meharry elected its first black president, Harold D. West. It was West who led Meharry through the difficult years of desegregation. As white schools began opening doors to blacks, Meharry felt morally obligated to begin accepting whites. But the demand for spaces in medical schools increased; by 1964 Meharry was receiving two applications from whites for every one from blacks. Furthermore, many whites had stronger educational records, and Meharry was faced with the rare and ironic dilemma of choosing to maintain its traditional role in training black doctors or opening the school to the best qualified, regardless of color. The whole process of desegregation in many ways forced Meharry into an uneasy period of self-examination and public scrutiny.[63]

When Lloyd C. Elam took over as president in 1968, Meharry once again raised the issue of merger with Fisk, and there were even rumors of merger with Vanderbilt, but Meharry remained autonomous. Elam replaced many of the Nashville area members of the Meharry Board of Trust in order to construct a nationally based board, a prerequisite to a major $50-million, seven-year expansion plan to construct new and renovate existing facilities and to add new programs in the health professions.[64]

Meharry passed its centennial year in 1976 with major new additions to its campus but in shaky financial circumstances. Hubbard Hospital, a modern hospital constructed largely with HEW (the federal Department of Health, Education, and Welfare) funds, opened in 1977, but too many of the beds remained empty, and Meharry had to default on the $29-million construction loan. Simultaneously, the old problem of city support for indigent care at Hubbard erupted again as a public issue. Federal distress funds from HEW were injected repeatedly, but the chronic problem of insufficient income continued to plague Meharry. In 1978 Meharry received $15.9 million in federal funds but still ran serious deficits. A federal report in 1979 described the financial condition as "precarious," with eleven dollars in debt for every one dollar in assets, and blamed, in part, internal management problems for the deficits. At the present rate, the report concluded, Meharry would run a $30-million deficit over the next five years.[65] Major fund-raising drives to increase the endowment and pay off massive debts began in 1979.

Amid all the red ink Meharry's most valuable asset remained the proud tradition of more than a century. It was small comfort to an institution that had arisen out of cruel necessity in an age of segregation that the South's progress toward desegregation after World War II challenged its very reason for being.

Tennessee State University   Tennessee Agricultural and Industrial State College (its name from 1935 to 1951) had remained under the leadership of William J. Hale for thirty-two years when he left the presidency in 1943 under a cloud of financial scandal. The legal progress in civil rights gave Tennessee A&I greater leverage in its long struggle for recognition from state educational authorities. In 1942 graduate training at the master's level was permitted in certain fields. In 1951 university status was conferred by the state Board of Education, and the faculty was reorganized into five schools. By 1958 the Southern Association of College and Secondary Schools gave Tennessee A&I State University accreditation. The same year the state Board of Education recognized the university as a full-fledged land-grant university, a status shared by the University of Tennessee.

During these years, as the educational opportunities for blacks began to open, Tennessee A&I served a rapidly escalating number of students, many of them seeking certification as teachers. By 1966 enrollments, which stood at 669 in 1943, peaked at 5,614, then subsided slightly when admission standards for out-of-state students were tightened in reaction to fears that out-of-state students were responsible for the militant civil rights protests. When Andrew Torrence took over as president from Walter S. Davis in 1968, Tennessee A&I appeared to have established itself as a respectable, multipurpose academic and vocational institution with steady, if unequal, support from the state. The change of name to Tennessee State University (TSU) in 1969 signified its academic aspirations. The postwar boom in enrollment had been matched with a sizable flow of funds for new buildings and campus expansion.[66]

Not least among TSU's achievements in these years were the numerous triumphs in athletics, which won international acclaim. One of Nashville's WPA projects in the late 1930s had been an athletic field and stadium for Tennessee A&I. It was on this track in the 1950s and 1960s that coach Ed Temple built his Tigerbelles into a powerful women's track team through ingenious recruiting and hard-nosed training. His leading stars were runners Wilma Rudolph, who won three gold medals at the 1960 Olympics in Rome, and Wyomia Tyus, who won a gold medal at both the 1964 and 1968 Olympic Games. In all, Temple's Tigerbelles brought back twenty medals from the Olympics, twenty-six from the Pan American games, and numerous national prizes. During the late 1950s the Tennessee A&I basketball team won a streak of league championships. By the 1960s the university was also fielding a powerful football team that dominated nearly all opponents.[67] Indeed, with Vanderbilt falling into the shadows of the Southeast Conference teams, it was TSU that gave Nashville its only genuine claim to athletic prowess in these years.

As TSU was consolidating its gains in academic and athletic status, another state institution had emerged as a new force in Nashville higher education. In 1947 the University of Tennessee began offering extension courses, mostly in the evening, in various locations in Nashville, with admission only to whites initially. Ten years later the University of Tennessee Extension Center was serving over 2,000 students and took over a building downtown at 810 Broadway. By 1968 this facility was overflowing with close to 4,000 students, and plans were laid to build a new $5-million facility at Tenth and Charlotte. By 1970 the new classrooms opened, and the Extension Center was renamed the University of Tennessee at Nashville (UTN). At the same time it was accredited by the Southern Association of Colleges and Secondary Schools as a four-year degree-granting college. Though the UTN student body had been desegregated years ago, it remained predominantly (about 85 percent) white, mostly working adults who attended part-time in the evenings.[68] The emergence of UTN and the flow of state funds into its expansion program were inevitably seen as an effort to reinforce a "dual system" of segregated education. That UTN was a night school with a distinct clientele of part-time adult students was less important to TSU than its identity as a branch of a predominantly white, and historically favored, university expanding in TSU's domain, just as TSU was achieving its hard-won status as a genuine state university.

In 1968 a group of Tennessee A&I faculty, led by Rita Sanders, a Vanderbilt law student and part-time history instructor at A&I, and George Barrett, a white civil rights and labor lawyer, filed a suit to block construction of the new University of Tennessee facility downtown. Their argument in *Sanders* vs. *Ellington* was that this new campus would ensure the perpetuation of a dual system of state-supported education. U.S. District Court judge Frank Gray, Jr., denied the injunction against construction of the new facility, but he ordered the state to formulate a plan to desegregate both institutions. *Sanders* vs. *Ellington* (which later evolved into *Geier* vs. *Blanton*, as married names and governors changed) became an important test case in the desegregation of higher education in the South. A civil rights group outside TSU, Citizens for Justice in Higher Education, hired attorney Avon Williams, Jr., to pursue the case in the courts. The case wore on until 1977 when Judge Gray, impatient with the stalled efforts of the state to voluntarily desegregate, ruled that a "radical solution" was necessary and that the two institutions must merge. He decided also that TSU, the older of the two, would be the dominant party in the merger. There were appeals by the University of Tennessee, but the merger went through on July 1, 1979 (the same day Peabody merged with Vanderbilt, as it happened), and UTN became TSU, Downtown Campus.[69]

Having won the battle in the courts, Frederick S. Humphries, president of TSU since 1974, was now faced with the more challenging task of absorbing a predominantly white student body, faculty, and administration into a historically black institution. Enrollment, projected at 10,000 after the merger, sagged to about 8,400 the first semester. State funding, based on enrollment, was almost cut back, but TSU was granted a two-year period of grace to adjust to postmerger conditions. More stressful perhaps was the ambiguous future of a state university designed originally to serve a segregated society, now forced to reach beyond its black constituency, to bring in more white students, to open the faculty and administration to whites as well. If desegregation helped TSU more than its neighbors, Fisk and Meharry, it was not without its cost, for victory over the dual system of education also pointed to the eventual demise of TSU's tradition as a black school.[70]

In places the foundations of the Athens of the South looked weak, if not beyond repair, but elsewhere it was stronger than ever. Nashville's economy and national image no longer depended on higher education as it had earlier, and the Athens motto was invoked only on rare occasions once Music City took center stage. Still, the city's several colleges continued to influence Nashville's quality of life as well as its payrolls.

THE PROTESTANT VATICAN

Nashville's role as a regional center of higher education was supplemented in new ways after World War II with the dramatic expansion of religious institutions in the city. The "Protestant Vatican," as it came to be known, included several church-sponsored colleges that trained thousands of missionaries and ministers, religious publishing houses that became a major industry in Nashville, and administrative offices for several large denominations. When James W. Carty, Jr., described Nashville as a world religious center in a book by that title in 1958, he hardly overstated the case, for millions of religious periodicals and hundreds of missionaries were emanating from Nashville to Africa, Latin America, and Asia—wherever evangelical Protestantism spread.[71]

Nashville's expansion as a religious center was a product of a strong revival that swept across America after World War II. It was generated in part by America's Cold War with Russia, which pulled many churches and evangelists into a conflict of patriotic Christianity that affirmed the "American way of life" against "godless communism." In the emerging nations of Africa, Latin America, and Asia, where American interests faced revolutionary challenge, Christian missionaries enlisted in a crusade to build a Christian bulwark in the Third World.[72] At home, church membership soared along with the new affluence and family-centered culture of postwar suburban life. By 1960 almost 70 percent of Americans claimed membership in a church, up from 49 percent in 1940. Annual expenditures on church construction went from $26 million in 1945 to over $1 billion by 1960, most of it to accommodate the new suburbanites, who found in religion a confirmation of the wholesome family life they sought in suburbia.[73]

Within this national surge of religious feeling after the war, the South as a region became more than ever a bastion of traditional Protestant belief and practice. Indeed, the southern Bible Belt remained one of the enduring distinctions of the South, a counterforce to the trend toward interregional homogenization caused by economic development and the reform of race relations. Dominated by Baptists, Methodists (who claimed, respectively, one-half and one-quarter of all southern Protestants), and Presbyterians, the South retained a strikingly conservative understanding of Christian doctrine and values. In comparison with Protestants outside the South, surveys in the 1950s and 1960s demonstrated that southerners of all denominations attended church more regularly, listened more often to religious radio and television programs, believed in the literal truth of the Bible, and tended to measure private and public morality against strict standards of Protestantism. Even when researchers controlled such variables as education, income, and urban-rural residence, southerners were revealed to be more intensely religious than their counterparts outside the South.[74]

Nashville after World War II became the "buckle of the Bible Belt." Its reputation as a religious center rested partly on the community's high concentration of churches, which by 1958 included 637 congregations among 56 denominations. It had more churches (one for every 256 people) than any other city its size.[75] The religious zeal of Nashville was also evident in the Billy Graham crusade of 1954, which brought 650,000 people to Vanderbilt's Dudley Field during the month-long revival. It was the largest turnout Graham had seen during any of his crusades.[76] But the city's regional and national importance in Protestant America was due more to the religious educational, administrative, and publishing services that made Nashville their headquarters.

Though much of the evangelism of the modern era took place over the television and radio airwaves, the revival of religion in the post-World War II era depended on the massive production of published materials—tracts, songbooks, Bibles, and periodicals. Here, Nashville's historic role as a publishing center for the Southern Methodists, Cumberland Presbyterians, National Baptists, and other small denominations set the precedent for new and expanded operations. The city's central location within the southern Bible Belt and its good rail and expressway connections also made it an ideal distribution point for religious publishers. By 1976 the religious publishing business in Nashville claimed over $100 million in annual sales. It employed over 10,000 people with a payroll over $68 million by the early 1980s.[77]

The United Methodist Publishing House, established in 1854 after the Methodists split over the slavery issue, expanded rapidly in the post–World War II era. By 1958 it was putting out 4 million books each year and thirty-four periodicals with a total circulation of 91 million.[78] Nashville also became the "Methodist Hollywood," producing films, recordings, television, and radio programs for parishioners. Abingdon Press, under the auspices of the Methodist Publishing House, printed a variety of books catering not only to church leaders but to a lay audience interested in, for example, the problems of modern marriage and teen-age child raising.[79] The Southern Baptist Sunday School Board by 1958 was publishing 73 million copies of seventy-nine different periodicals and 14 million tracts for distribution throughout the world. Broadman Press, established by the Baptists in 1934, was publishing between sixty and seventy-five book titles each year, including inspirational, advice, juvenile literature, and songbooks, along with audiovisual materials.[80] The Thomas Nelson Company, founded in 1798 in England, was acquired by Sam Moore, who transferred the company to Nashville from New York City in 1969. Within seven years its annual sales of Bibles and evangelical literature rose from $2 million to $16 million. The relocation in Nashville gave the company closer access to the Bible Belt, lower transportation costs, and relatively cheap labor.[81]

Other, smaller denominations established publishing operations in Nashville by the 1970s. The Southern Publishing Association of the Seventh Day Adventists, the African Methodist Episcopal Sunday School Union, and the National Baptist Convention of America had presses in Nashville. The National Baptist Convention, USA, Inc., the largest black Baptist denomination, founded its press under the direction of Richard Henry Boyd in 1896. Through its Sunday School Publishing Board, established in 1915, this church put out periodicals with a circulation of 3.6 million by 1958.[82] These smaller religious presses clustered in Nashville to take advantage of the location, cheap labor and transportation, and the cumulative advantages that the city's publishing industry had acquired because of ready access to paper and printing supplies and to a pool of skilled technical labor. The expansion in Nashville of Ingram Book Company, the largest wholesale trade bookseller in the nation by the 1970s, reinforced the city's advantages as a center for secular and religious publishing.

Education was another major service of the Protestant Vatican. Nashville's several church-sponsored colleges flourished, along with the expansion of evangelical religion after World War II, but the harsh financial realities of the 1970s buffeted some of the small religiously affiliated schools. Scarritt College for Christian Workers was brought to Nashville in 1923 by the Methodists to train missionaries and teach techniques of religious music and drama. During the late 1950s, as the Methodist's world missionary program expanded, Scarritt produced over 40 percent of the church's missionary force.[83] By the 1970s, though it enjoyed continued support from the Methodist church, Scarritt suffered from a thin endowment and a declining market for missionaries and church social workers. A new president, J. Richard Palmer, came from a successful fund drive at Berea College to rescue Scarritt in 1973. Palmer enlarged the faculty, attracted more students, began an ambitious $16.7-million fund drive, and expanded programs in continuing education and women's studies. But four years later Palmer resigned, frustrated by internal dissension and the relentless search for gifts just to cover operating expenses.[84] Scarritt cut back its undergraduate programs and survived largely by renting space to visiting organizations and continuing its widely noted program in religious music.

David Lipscomb College, founded by the Church of Christ in 1891, celebrated its seventy-fifth anniversary in 1966 with good reason for optimism. It had developed a full range of affiliated elementary and secondary schools. Under the leadership of President Athens Clay Pullias since 1946, Lipscomb had achieved a respectable level of visibility in the local area, and it enjoyed financial stability. Its major benefactor, Life and Casualty Insurance Company president Andrew M. Burton, granted $3.5 million and large bequests of valuable land. It was on Burton's prescient advice after World War II that Lipscomb embarked on a major expansion program in time to meet the flood of government-sponsored veterans. But the doldrums of the 1970s caught up with Lipscomb too, and President Pullias stepped down in 1977 in part because of mounting financial pressure.[85]

Trevecca Nazarene College was founded in 1901 to train missionaries for the small sect whose name the school bears. It was nearly ruined by the 1930s Depression, was accredited as a four-year college in 1941, and rapidly expanded its new campus (since 1935) off Murfreesboro Road. By 1976 it celebrated its seventy-fifth anniversary, still short on endowment and operating revenue but serving a unique role in educating students and preparing missionaries for the First Church of the Nazarene.[86]

Belmont College, connected to the Southern Baptist church since 1951 when it superseded Ward-Belmont School for girls, met the financial problems of small church-related colleges in unexpected ways in the 1970s. Under President Herbert C. Gabhart, it opened a series of innovative vocational programs, including ones in "business music" and recording, which found a ready market down the road in Music City. By 1976 Belmont boasted almost 1,700 students.[87]

There were several other small religious colleges that found a place in Nashville's educational complex after World War II. Free Will Baptist College joined Nashville's cluster of small church-related schools in 1942 and built its campus amid the old mansions of the Richland–West End neighborhood.[88] Aquinas Junior College, founded in 1961 by the Catholic church, built next to the new St. Cecilia Academy campus on Harding Road. The American Baptist Theological Seminary, founded in 1924 to train black ministers and supported jointly by the National Baptist Convention, USA, and the Southern Baptist Convention, continued to serve a small, racially integrated student body on its campus on Whites Creek Road. It was out of this school's student body that John Lewis and other civil rights activists emerged in the 1960s.[89]

Vanderbilt Divinity School emerged amid the religious resurgence of the 1950s as one of the leading interdenominational theological schools in the nation. Following the university's break with the Methodists in 1914, the school struggled to gain students and endowment. During the 1920s and 1930s it found a role in training a new cadre of social activist ministers whose activities on behalf of labor and blacks made Vanderbilt Divinity School one of the centers of southern radicalism in this period. After World War II the school emphasized scholarly training in its Ph.D. programs, and it attracted theologians of international reputation to its faculty. Vanderbilt Divinity School was active in the ecumenical movement of the 1950s and continued a more liberal posture on social as well as theological issues. The school's commitment to the black civil rights movement led to its pioneering role in desegregating Vanderbilt's student body in 1953 and to a crisis over the expulsion of James Lawson in 1960. When the dean and many of the faculty resigned to protest Lawson's treatment, the school declined in stature and recovered only slowly. Still, Vanderbilt Divinity School remained locally the strongest scholarly component of the Nashville's Protestant Vatican.[90]

As American churches expanded at home and overseas after World War II, new administrative offices emerged along with Nashville's church-sponsored colleges and publishing houses. Following the 1939 unification of the southern Methodists with the northern church, Nashville became a headquarters city for the United Methodist Church in the South. The Methodist Board of Education, near Scarritt College, was responsible for planning religious literature, administering the church's services to Methodist colleges and student organizations, and overseeing the Methodist's world evangelical movement. One of the board's offices, the Upper Room, which contains a major tourist attraction, a carved wooden replica of Da Vinci's *Last Supper*, also produced a devotional book published in twenty-nine different languages and distributed to 10 million readers by the late 1950s.[91]

The Southern Baptist Convention, once the most fiercely congregational of the major Protestant denominations, rose to the challenge of modern evangelism with new, centralized organizations in this period. Nashville became a major administrative center for the church. The Executive Committee, the chief administrative body of the denomination, brought its offices to Nashville. The Education Commission, responsible for serving the Southern Baptist's fifty-one colleges and the Baptist Sunday School Board, made Nashville headquarters for its publishing and educational services to the church. Also located in Nashville were the Southern Baptist Foundation and the Southern Baptist Education, Christian Life and Historical Commission. The Free Will Baptists expanded their much smaller following through their Foreign Missions Board, which settled in Nashville. The Presbyterian Church in the U.S. matched the Baptists and Methodists by establishing their own Board of World Missions headquarters in a large new building on Twenty-first Avenue in 1957. This board placed hundreds of missionaries around the world and supervised the evangelization and philanthropic aid extended to 40 million people.[92]

The religious sentiment that emanated from Nashville via publications, films, and worldwide missions, was in many ways a response of traditional values to the changes sweeping the city, the region, and the world. The religious zeal of the Cold War era inspired ecumenical cooperation and even formal mergers among denominations. Nashville's Catholic and Jewish communities grew alongside the evangelical Protestants without significant discord after World War II. The religious faith that permeated the city may have been one of the most pervasive adhesives amid the vast changes in Nashville's economy, politics, and race relations in the decades following 1940. Its power to heal social divisions would be tested fully in the civil rights upheavals of the late 1950s and 1960s. In the meantime the churches, colleges, publishing houses, and administrative headquarters of the Protestant Vatican cast Nashville's national reputation in a new light. Religion, along with higher education and country music, was more than just a sturdy pillar in the city's postwar economy; all three influenced the tone of the community and coined the distinctive image of Nashville among American cities.

INTEGRATING THE GOVERNMENT

With the boom in the local economy during the war and the unprecedented affluence of consumers in the postwar era, Nashville's population growth exploded outward. By 1960 the county population outside the city boundaries exceeded that of the central city. The automobile became commonplace among middle-class and blue-collar families by the 1950s, and the two-car family was on the rise. With their increased freedom of mobility, suburban commuters could now live nearly anywhere on an expanding grid of county highways and interstate expressways that radiated from the central city. By applying techniques of mass production to housing, suburban developers were able to throw up thousands of inexpensive tract houses on cheap land in the country. Buyers took advantage of low-interest, long-term mortgages, often underwritten by federal programs like the Federal Housing Authority (FHA) or the Veterans Administration (VA). The federal-city alliance that rebuilt the downtown also guided suburban growth.

People came to the suburbs for new, affordable houses and for wholesome living in a semirural setting that had a special appeal to southerners, so many of whom had grown up in rural surroundings. They also came to the suburbs as a refuge from the city. They escaped the pall of coal smoke that hung over the city in winter. They escaped the decaying neighborhoods, the crime and disease that concentrated in the city. Many white suburbanites also left the city out of an unspoken fear of blacks, an effort to maintain social distance by creating more physical distance between the races at a time when the legal barriers of racial segregation were beginning to crumble.

The fundamental political problem of the post-Depression era was how to fashion a government that could provide adequate services and plan for the future development of a metropolitan community that was unified economically but artificially divided by political boundaries. This was the task of a new generation that took its place in the city's leadership after World War II. They were young men and women whose background, college education, or military service helped them to see and understand the broader horizons of the metropolitan community and the modern South. They saw themselves as standard-bearers for a progressive Nashville, eager to make up for lost time, impatient with petty politics, and devoted to an idealistic faith that human progress was possible if rational, informed citizens and leaders played their proper roles.

MAYOR CUMMINGS AND THE FRUSTRATIONS OF REFORM

After the death of Hilary Howse in January 1938 reformers continued to rail against the "machine," repeating their old promises to throw the rascals out and bring good government to Nashville. But the Howse machine was never a monolithic organization, and in Howse's declining years the city hall crowd became a chaotic jumble of small cliques and shifting personal alliances. The county government continued to be dominated by an old guard, including William T. "Bill" Jones, an old ally of Hilary Howse who headed the Davidson County Democratic Executive Committee, and county judge Litton Hickman, who had been in power since 1918. During the 1940s the county machine also became riddled with factionalism and torn by recurrent scandal. The disorder of the old city-county machines did not help the reformers, who were themselves fragmented by divisions over personalities and by city-suburban conflict. The result was a long period of frustration for reformers, who eventually came to see the consolidation of city and county government and the centralization of power in the hands of a progressive mayor as prerequisites to any further reforms.

Mayor Thomas Cummings was a businessman's mayor with strong backing from the Chamber of Commerce, which had always been at odds with the Howse machine. But unlike previous champions of business efficiency and good government, Cummings was no political dilettante. He was a gregarious man who loved politics and all the backslapping camaraderie that goes with politics. Nor was he the type of effete reformer who wilted in the heat of political battle. Cummings knew how to fight, and he was presented with plenty of opportunities to do so in the faction-ridden world of Nashville politics during close to fourteen years in the mayor's office between 1938 and 1951. (See Appendix E for a list of the mayors dicussed below.)

Like Howse, and so many of the Nashville population, Cummings was a country boy, born in 1891 in the small farming village of New, a few miles outside McMinnville, Tennessee. He came to McMinnville with his parents to attend high school and later opened a grocery store with his younger brother. When he sold the store a few years later, Cummings had enough money to pay his way through law school. In 1912 he joined another brother in Nashville, where he entered Vanderbilt University Law School. After he graduated in 1915 Cummings took a job in the law office of William C. Cherry, one of his former professors at Vanderbilt and a prominent judge. Cummings became an active and popular lawyer in Nashville and ran successfully for state senator in 1927 against the Howse machine. In 1937 he returned to the state senate and acted as a leading opponent of the city-county machine during Howse's declining years. Cummings also became an important ally of Governor Gordon Browning, a vigorous opponent of Boss Ed Crump's Memphis machine.

Cummings, with his background in law and politics and his high visibility as an opponent of the Howse machine, was the ideal candidate around whom reformers could rally. Cummings won the special election in February 1938 to fill Howse's unexpired term. Cummings faced a field of five candidates, including former mayor Felix Z. Wilson and anti-Howse councilman John Lechleiter. John Keefe, assistant city attorney under Howse, bit into the Cummings majority in five of twenty-seven wards, mostly in the heavily black neighborhoods of North and South Nashville, and in the working-class districts of West Nashville, but Cummings took 52 percent of a record voter turnout.[1]

Cummings's victory was decisive, but the old city hall crowd that had built a coalition around Hilary Howse was not to be dispatched so easily. Between his victory in February and the next mayoral election in May 1939, Cummings had time to break apart major components of the Howse organization. Hoisting the banner of business efficiency and good government, he appointed committees of businessmen to audit several city departments. Cummings was skilled at using the communications media to win public favor for his reforms. The City Council chambers became packed with spectators; Cummings promised more seats in the gallery and installed a public-address system to ensure that everyone could hear the deliberations.[2] He cultivated the support of Silliman Evans, Sr., and the *Tennessean* reporters in frequent late-night visits to the pressroom.[3] Cummings also followed FDR's technique of reaching citizens by evening radio speeches explaining his clean-up campaign in city hall.

Cummings directed the harsh glare of publicity into every dark and long-ignored corner of the Howse regime. Delinquent taxes, amounting to over $3 million, were due the city from numerous political favorites of the old city hall crowd.[4] J. Washington Moore, the city attorney, was summarily suspended and forced to resign after the mayor charged him with misconduct and negligence in connection with the tax scandals.⁵ Cummings's mentor, Judge William C. Cherry, took over as city attorney and used his office to help the mayor root out other members of the old Howse machine. City purchasing agent Verner Tolmie became the object of a long investigation before the Civil Service Commission. It dragged on for twelve days and became an ideal opportunity for the *Tennessean* to expose the gamut of corruption under the Howse regime.⁶ As the investigation progressed, the discovery of the funds generated by the 1-percent city payroll deduction for the Municipal Government Emergency Committee—amounting to over $100,000 —implicated dozens of machine loyalists who, it was revealed, used this welfare money as a slush fund to pay poll taxes and other political campaign expenses.⁷ Tolmie was found guilty and fired, and Cummings promised he would quickly move in on other department heads whose names had come up in the Tolmie trial.⁸ In the ensuing weeks several officials resigned before Cummings's probe could expose their involvement. Others were fired by Cummings or granted early retirement.⁹

The new mayor launched a flurry of constructive reforms at the same time he worked at the destruction of the old regime. Within a few months after taking office Cummings and his bloc of supporters in the City Council proposed a $2.5-million school building program, airport expansion, a massive street-paving program, revision of the city legal code, tax reform, a city property inventory, new public housing, enforcement of whiskey laws, retrenchment in the city payroll, and smoke abatement—all lauded on the front page of the *Tennessean*.¹⁰ By the fall of 1938 Cummings was cautiously pushing the city toward the adoption of TVA electric power, though the final agreement between TVA and TEPCO was delayed until after the May election.¹¹ With growing enthusiasm for Cummings's dramatic reform movement, Silliman Evans's *Tennessean* announced a "Reveille in Sleepy Hollow."¹²

Cummings's opponents scrambled to put together a new coalition before the 1939 city election, but they had no charismatic candidate nor any public agenda that could rally the old constituency that Howse once commanded with ease. Pro-Cummings candidates swept four of six legislative seats in the Davidson County delegation in August 1938.¹³ The names of various candidates emerged in the months preceding the May city election, but the remnants of the Howse machine appeared too battered to put together a slate. Former mayor Felix Z. Wilson was the only one to finally run against Cummings in May, and since Wilson had long been identified as an "anti-machine" candidate, he offered no serious opposition to Cummings. Mayor Cummings swept the election two-to-one, along with many of his supporters on the council and Dr. John W. Bauman on the Board of Public Works.¹⁴ Several councilmen who had served twelve to eighteen years were turned out of office as Cummings supporters took their place. In all, thirteen incumbents on the council were defeated, and fourteen new men joined the council.[15]

Having won an overwhelming mandate from Nashville's newly aroused voters, Cummings's burst of reform failed to sustain itself. Within a year of the election the enthusiasm of the *Tennessean* cooled, and it began carping at Cummings for his sometimes heavy-handed blows against political opponents and his lack of forceful leadership on the major issues before the city. The election, one *Tennessean* editorial reminded Cummings, was a mandate for progressive leadership, an "end to drifting," a call to catch up after years of neglect and economic depression.[16]

Though Mayor Cummings's achievements were many, his long term in office was a period of repeated frustrations for those who wished to see a progressive government in Nashville. The fault was by no means all Cummings's, but his tendency to step on sensitive political toes often exacerbated factionalism and, in the end, spoiled his chances to build and lead a sustained coalition for progress in Nashville. The mayor also faced continued opposition from entrenched remnants of the old machine. On the Board of Public Works former Howse supporter Luther Luton used his position as fire commissioner and his amiable personality to win a loyal following among city employees. Luton became a major opponent and managed to block a number of items on the mayor's political agenda.[17] In the county political arena Judge Litton Hickman also identified Cummings as an adversary. Bill Jones, the unofficial head of the county machine and regarded as an ally of Memphis Boss Ed Crump, was another persistent opponent of Cummings and the reform movement in general.[18]

Cummings's momentum slowed almost immediately as his opponents closed ranks. Luther Luton openly broke with Cummings in 1940 to support a Davidson County legislative ticket opposed to the slate Cummings endorsed. Cummings's allies won only two of the nine legislative seats, giving his enemies a strong position in state government from which to attack the mayor.[19] In the state legislative elections of 1942 anti-Cummings forces continued to build their power base outside city government rather than oppose the mayor directly on his own turf. Led by Bill Jones, the People's ticket won a smashing victory over the Democratic ticket endorsed by Cummings. At the same time Jones's followers took over the Democratic Party Executive Committee, which played a powerful role in controlling nominations.[20]

From their stronghold at the state and county levels, Cummings's enemies found an ideal opportunity to thwart their adversary in a movement to reform the city charter. Ironically, this reform was initiated by Cummings's supporters in the City Council. They sponsored an efficiency survey of Nashville's government by the Public Administration Service (PAS), a consulting team based at the University of Chicago, in cooperation with the Civic Affairs Forum, a local group of business and professional men dedicated to good government.[21] The PAS report criticized the unwieldy size of Nashville's government and recommended consolidation of the existing twenty-seven wards into seven, with one councilman elected from each ward and two at-large representatives elected by voters in all wards. In addition, the PAS report criticized the dispersion of administrative authority in the mayor, the Board of Public Works, and thirty-five assorted commissions and boards. The PAS remedy was to abandon the Board of Public Works, reorganize the nearly three dozen separate administrative units into eight departments with clearly defined jurisdictions, and vest in the mayor the authority to appoint and dismiss all department heads.[22]

Cummings's adversaries understood the implications of the PAS reforms all too well, for these changes would not only strengthen the mayor's constitutional power enormously but also end Luther Luton's base of power on the Board of Public Works. At the same time the anti-Cummings delegation in the state legislature recognized the public mandate for charter reform. They moved ahead with a revised charter, which followed the PAS recommendations for ward and administrative department consolidation but retained the Board of Public Works under a new name, the Board of Administration. This board, consisting of the mayor and two commissioners (one for fire and public works, another for water and health), would now be elected directly by the people rather than appointed by the mayor or the council. Furthermore, each commissioner would now enjoy autonomous control over specific departments. This provision would only further fracture the city's executive authority and was roundly condemned by the PAS consultants and local reformers as a step backward for Nashville. "Nashville," the PAS commented on this latest charter reform, "has bartered efficiency for a system of checks and balances which divides authority, destroys responsibility, and substantially defeats any probability of effective city administration."[23]

Nonetheless, the 1943 charter passed both houses of the legislature and became law prior to the 1943 city elections, which witnessed a mad scramble of incumbent councilmen to find constituencies in each of the seven new wards.[24] Anti-Cummings forces picked a young assistant district attorney named Ben West to head their ticket, with Luther Luton and Sam Jenkins running for the new Board of Administration. Cummings and his ally Dr. John W. Bauman, incumbent water commissioner, were joined by George Cate, an attorney and a former Board of Education head, who was widely respected as a progressive reformer. The voters, apparently confused by the recent charter reforms coming down from the state legislature and by the ward boundary changes, gave a poor turnout on election day, and their vote was indecisive. Cummings and Bauman narrowly defeated West and Jenkins, respectively; George Cate lost to the popular Luther Luton.[25] Most of the nine men elected to council ran independent of either mayoral ticket, so neither Cummings nor Luton could count on a solid majority in the coming years. The PAS team was dismissed by the new council the following summer, before it had completed its report, and it looked as though Nashville would continue to drift, now with a "three-headed" executive and continued jealousy between city and county political factions.[26]

No sooner was the new charter in place and the PAS sent home than a group of prominent downtown businessmen working within the Chamber of Commerce began reformulating the city's structure of government. Thomas Cummings agreed to resign as mayor and allow county attorney Horace Osment to take his place, on the condition that his opponents would support charter amendments allowing a strong mayor.[27] The Davidson County delegation in the state legislature at the same time was promoting a bill to amend the new city charter by adding two commissioners to the three-man Board of Administration, an apparent attempt to pack the board in favor of Luton and the anti-Cummings forces.[28] The *Tennessean* blasted the Chamber of Commerce group, many of whom, it was pointed out, lived in Belle Meade and other suburbs outside the city. Mayor Cummings was also taken to task by the *Tennessean* for cutting deals behind closed doors with no regard for public opinion. The Chamber of Commerce movement for charter reform quickly folded as a result, and the anti-Cummings legislative delegation now went ahead with its charter amendments. The three-headed executive of Nashville government became a "five-headed" monster. Nashville's city government had become not only an obstacle to progress locally but also a source of embarrassment in the national press.[29]

It was in this demoralized atmosphere that John E. Windrow, head of the Peabody Demonstration School, offered an incisive critique of the sad state of civic affairs in a speech before the Kiwanis Club in July 1945. Wryly titled "The Athens of the South," Windrow's speech ticked off a whole list of Nashville's problems—from smoke pollution and political corruption to venereal disease, tuberculosis, racial intolerance, juvenile delinquency, and slum housing. In treating each affliction he demonstrated how it affected the entire community and how it required a cooperative response from civic-minded people in the universities (which he singled out for their lack of community concern), the churches, business, as well as from government officials. For all its claims to intellectual achievement and cultural refinement, the Athens of the South was wallowing in a plethora of social and environmental problems. Worse than all these problems combined, in Windrow's view, was the syndrome of apathy and helplessness that seemed to render the community incapable of mounting any effective attack on them. It was not enough to blame the politicians, he insisted: "The fault, Dear Brutus, lies not in our politicians or in our stars but in us. 'We the People.'"[30] Windrow's speech was reprinted in the *Tennessean*, published in pamphlet form, and distributed widely among civic leaders.

Windrow's critical blast at the city and the ensuing publicity led to the organization of the Citizens Protective Committee (CPC) in the fall of 1945.[31] The CPC, a broad-based citizens group chaired by businessman Walter Stokes, Jr., became the vehicle for local government reform. The CPC attempted to form a nonpartisan coalition for reform that could surmount the hopeless factionalism and distrust of local politics and serve as an impartial advocate for progressive, efficient government. By June of 1946, after months of study and debate, the CPC released a preliminary draft of their model charter for public consideration. The main features included an expansion of the City Council to twenty-two members (three from each of the seven new wards and one elected at large to serve as council president and vice mayor), the abolition of the five-member Board of Administration, and the centralization of executive authority in the hands of the mayor. Having crafted their model charter in the serene climate of nonpartisan deliberations among disinterested citizens, Walter Stokes and the CPC now chose to take it into the rough-and-tumble world of politics. The CPC selected a slate for the Davidson County legislative delegation before the primary election of August 1946. An opposing slate of World War II veterans led by Beverly Briley, a young attorney, ran as the "GI Joe" ticket. Stokes and *Tennessean* publisher Silliman Evans had a bitter falling-out during the campaign, and Evans, who took credit for inspiring the CPC and its charter reforms, now swung the influence of his paper behind Briley and the veterans' ticket. At the same time, Evans denounced Stokes and the CPC for moving beyond nonpartisan reform, into the political arena.[32] The CPC ticket won, and early in 1947 the new Davidson County delegation began to push the CPC charter through the legislature.[33] The 1947 charter was passed with no major changes in the version drafted by the CPC.

Now the stakes were higher than ever, for the new mayor would be a strong executive with unprecedented power over the administrative departments of city government. The 1947 city election witnessed a curious realignment of political friends and foes that had even veteran political observers like *Tennessean* columnist Joe Hatcher scratching their heads. Bill Jones's county machine fell apart before the election. Some, like Luther Luton, Attorney General J. Carlton Loser, attorney Jack Norman, and others, joined Walter Stokes and the CPC in backing Weldon White, an attorney, for mayor. Jones refused to endorse White and remained aloof from the mayoral election. Elkin Garfinkle, sheriff Garner Robinson, chief deputy Jake Sheridan, and city commissioner Seth Mays split with the county machine and led a faction in support of Cummings. Ben West, a political enemy of Cummings, now joined the Cummings ticket as a candidate for vice mayor.[34]

In what was described by Joe Hatcher as one of the bitterest campaigns in memory, Cummings won reelection with strong support in North, South, and West Nashville, losing heavily to White only in the West End, where the CPC following was strong.[35] With a new charter providing for a single, strong mayor and promising signs of realignment in the county and city political organizations, the 1947 election portended a new day for city and county cooperation.[36] By September 1948, Bill Jones's twenty-year reign as county kingmaker was in rapid decline when a coalition of Cummings, Elkin Garfinkle, and Jake Sheridan ousted Jones as chairman of the Democratic Executive Committee. Within two years county judge Litton Hickman ended his thirty-two year career when Beverly Briley, running on a strong reform platform with special attention to the sorry condition of the county's public schools, defeated him.

That this breakup of the county political machine and the charter reform of city government coincided with the fall of Boss Crump, the rise of Estes Kefauver, and the resurgence of Governor Gordon Browning on the state level seemed to underscore the possibilities for a new political agenda in the late 1940s and early 1950s.[37] Cummings, in his last term as mayor, witnessed the demise of the old city-county machine, but he was not able to capitalize on the public demand for reform that had thrust him into office back in 1938. Cummings deserves credit for a number of major achievements, including the coming of TVA in 1939 and the completion of the natural gas pipeline in 1946. These helped lay the base for several new industries that Cummings worked hard to attract to the city. The Vultee Aircraft factory (later named AVCO) and, after the war, Aladdin Industries were the major credits in industrial growth during the Cummings years. He was also quick to respond to the urban renewal program in 1949 and went to Washington after its passage to place Nashville's application at the head of the list. Cummings pushed persistently for the Municipal Auditorium and for the expansion of Berry Field into a modern airport. He also led the move to develop Lafayette Street, once in the midst of a dilapidated neighborhood, into a major retail shopping strip. Many of these projects were not completed before Cummings was defeated in the mayoral election of 1951. The Cummings years, however, remain more notable for the many frustrated plans for major reforms, suburban annexations, and civic improvements. These goals were postponed by political factionalism and fundamental flaws in the structure of city and county governments that Cummings was unable to surmount.[38]

Figure 56. Beverly Briley, newly elected county judge, with retiring judge Litton Hickman, 1950. *Tennessean* Library.

Figure 57. Mayor Thomas Cummings stumping for reelection at 46th Avenue North and Charlotte Avenue in 1951. *Tennessean* Library.

Figure 58. Mayor Cummings, after almost fourteen years in office, turns over the office keys to newly elected Mayor Ben West, 1951. *Tennessean* Library.

MAYOR BEN WEST AND THE COMING OF METRO

Ben West defeated Cummings in the city election of 1951 by a scant fifty-five votes, hardly a decisive mandate for change in Nashville's leadership. Yet the coming twelve years of West's reign witnessed a breakthrough in the obstructive politics of factionalism, hamstrung leadership, and city-county opposition.

Born in Columbia, Tennessee, in 1911 West came with his parents during the Depression to the blue-collar neighborhood of Flat Rock in the Woodbine district, near the L&N's Radnor Yard, where his father worked. He attended Central High School, Cumberland Law School, and later Vanderbilt University. West worked his way through school with odd jobs, including several years as a copyboy and reporter for the *Banner* (a relationship that was repaid by that paper's loyal support of West throughout his career). On graduating from Vanderbilt in 1934, West worked as an assistant district attorney and built a reputation as a skilled criminal prosecutor. He left the district attorney's office in 1943 to run for mayor, narrowly losing to Cummings. In 1947 West withdrew from another race against Cummings and White, then ran successfully for vice-mayor and council president in a strange campaign that paired him with his foe, Thomas Cummings. In 1949 West was elected state senator, an office he held simultaneously with his job as vice-mayor of Nashville.[39]

In the state senate West steered an important amendment through the legislature, allowing election of Nashville city councilmen from small, single-member districts. This system gave blacks an advantage in their neighborhoods, and it helped cement a strong alliance between West and his black constituency.[40]

West's link to the Cummings administration did nothing to mollify his political enmity toward the mayor. Indeed, he used his position as vice-mayor to build political alliances against Cummings and to arouse popular opposition to the mayor.[41] West's occasionally vitriolic attacks did not bode well for a city already wracked by petty personal factionalism. The *Tennessean* had long ago pegged West as a minion of the county machine, and his victory in 1951 was interpreted as a serious setback for the cause of reform in Nashville. Yet once in office West grew into the job. He became a skilled statesman in local politics and a respected national spokesman for urban America. It was West who championed the cause of the cities in the battle for legislative reapportionment in the case of *Baker* vs. *Carr*, which in the U.S. Supreme Court decision of 1962 confirmed the principle of one-man, one-vote and strengthened urban representation in government. Tennessee's legislature had not been reapportioned since 1901. "Moore County's 9,000 cows and 5,000 sheep have more representation in the state legislature than Davidson County's 380,000 people," West often complained.[42] His national stature grew, and West was elected president of the American Municipal League in 1957.

West's achievements during twelve years in office were many, the most notable being the Capitol Hill Redevelopment Project. The central importance of the West years, however, was the culmination of the long campaign to consolidate city and county governments. Ironically, it was an achievement that West opposed at the very end but one that he had advanced irrevocably during his three terms in office. The triumph of metropolitan government in Nashville was also the product of the increased cooperation between government and the academic community, which provided consultants and a disinterested perspective on problems that for too long had been understood in purely political and personal terms.

The call for metropolitan consolidation had been sounded as early as 1915, when a study sponsored by the city commission recommended massive annexation and a single city and county government. But suburban opposition stifled this plan. Later, in 1940 County Court member Seth Wall revived the idea. The issue was quickly dropped, but the problems that inspired it multiplied in the coming years.[43] During the long reign of Hilary Howse the expansion of the city's boundaries was limited because of the mutual distrust between Howse and wealthy suburbanites. Small parcels on the West End and the Lockeland Springs neighborhood of East Nashville were added in annexations of 1925, 1927, and 1929. But since 1929 no significant change had been made in the city's boundaries.[44] Annexation required state legislative approval, which, in turn, required support from the Davidson County legislative delegation. Rural interests dominated Tennessee's legislature, and as the suburban population outside Nashville grew, the county delegation increasingly reflected the suburban indifference and hostility to the needs of the city.

The suburban population residing outside the city limits, but dependent on the city for its livelihood, had grown steadily with the rise of the automobile since the 1920s. This growth was restrained by the hard times of the 1930s and World War II, but after the war the suburban population exploded. Population within the city boundaries grew slowly in the 1940s, then declined in the 1950s for a net gain of only 2 percent over the two decades. At the same time the county population outside the city limits in 1960 had grown 155 percent exceeding the central city population by nearly 58,000. (See appendix A for complete city and county population figures.)

The stagnant city population hid metropolitan Nashville's healthy expansion from public view, but more was involved than mere booster pride. One major set of problems involved the shoddy quality of services available to suburbanites, which presented a threat to their safety and a serious obstacle to future growth. The suburban explosion oc-

Figure 59. Suburban tract housing sprang up rapidly after World War II to satisfy the demands of the prosperous, mobile white middle class. This unidentified aerial view was taken in 1960. *Tennessean* Library.

Figure 60. Prospective suburban home owners swarmed out to the Hillbrook subdivision on a hot July day in 1961 to look over display models. *Tennessean* Library.

curred with little planning, and tax-shy suburbanites seemed all too willing to forgo urban amenities, at least until some kind of calamity hit them.

One of the first prerequisites for suburban expansion was water service, and Nashville was blessed with an abundant water supply from the Cumberland River. The city, instead of using its control of pure water to force suburbs to annex, as some officials suggested, allowed private suburban water companies to purchase city water. In the late 1930s several new suburban utility districts took over the job of distributing city water to suburban residents. The First Suburban Utility District, serving the Radnor and Flat Rock neighborhoods, began in 1937, followed by counterparts in Madison and Belle Meade in 1938, and the Old Hickory Utility District in 1951. Both the Radnor and Belle Meade companies bought city water at wholesale prices from the city and distributed it to suburban customers. Thousands of other suburbanites bought water directly from the city, though at rates significantly higher than those for city residents. Thus, Nashville actually encouraged the expansion of suburban communities outside its boundaries by generously supplying water to the suburbs and eliminated one of the crucial incentives for joining the city.[45]

It was much easier to bring in fresh water than it was to dispose of sewage, however. Nashville's blessing of abundant water was balanced by the curse of a solid Ordovician limestone base under a thin layer of soil. Laying sewer pipes in this land required slow, expensive blasting and digging. The solution was septic tanks buried in suburban yards and surrounded by large lots, often an acre or more, to allow for the leaching of sewage. So, the sewer problem, instead of restraining suburban expansion, encouraged rapid dispersion of low-density development. This pattern of settlement, in turn, made it difficult to provide efficient services such as electric street lighting, garbage collection, water lines, and even police and fire protection. The septic tanks were not always adequate to the job, and when rainwater drenched the surrounding soil, the sewage percolated to the surface. The foul smell that resulted not only betrayed the suburban dream of wholesome rural air, it posed a serious threat to public health. County health officer Dr. John J. Lentz issued repeated warnings about the sewage and garbage problems in the suburbs and pleaded with government officials for an integrated city-county disposal plan for both. "Urban Nashville," a *Tennessean* editorial warned in 1949, "is sitting on a bacterial time bomb. By the grace of God, the explosion of disease and epidemic has not yet taken place. . . . But there is not time to lose." Less than half the people of Davidson County were served by sewers in that year, the rest relied on septic tanks and crude outhouses. At least ten percent of the septic tanks discharged sewage to the surface on a regular basis, thus polluting the water supply. An estimated eight percent of the ground water was unsafe to drink as a result. This was a public health disaster just waiting to explode. "It is beyond all reason that Nashville's disease bomb should be permitted to tick on until the worst happens," the *Tennessean* implored. But the call for "deactivation" went unheeded, and the bomb ticked on for another decade and more.[46]

The story of inadequate services was the same throughout the suburbs with regard to garbage collection, street lighting, and fire and police protection. Fire protection in many suburbs was provided by private companies who served only residents subscribing to their service. The homes of nonsubscribers could burn to the ground next door to one of these private fire companies, and nothing would be done. Even when the fire company did answer the call, they were hampered by the small water mains in the suburbs, which rarely provided sufficient water pressure. Most of the fire companies carried their own water and used high-pressure fog nozzles, which worked well enough on small blazes but failed tragically whenever a fire got beyond the capacity of this meager equipment to control.[47]

Police service was hardly better. The county sheriff was technically responsible for law enforcement outside the city. Since 1946 the sheriff had been aided by a small county highway patrol, but there was too much territory to cover for a force that stood at only sixty men in 1952. Several suburban communities relied on private subscription police patrols, similar to the fire companies. Belle Meade hired a county sheriff's deputy in the 1930s to help crack a ring of thieves who were operating in collusion with house servants. A small patrol was added, and the city of Belle Meade took it over sometime after 1938. Inglewood and Madison set up their own private police and fire company in 1940, and subscribers paid a mere ten dollars a year for the service. In Goodlettsville one resident moonlighted after work each evening as a one-man police force.[48] These makeshift police patrols gave an illusion of security, but the problem of crime and vice (bootlegging and gambling, in particular) — once thought to be the special curse of the inner city — became growing problems in the suburbs after World War II. The inadequacy of the system was underlined when police were called upon to take action against one of their own subscribers.[49]

In every way the system was costly, inefficient, and potentially dangerous to the health and safety of the entire community. The shoddy, incomplete services available to suburban Nashville were detrimental not simply to the residents but to the corporate vitality of the whole metropolitan community. The lack of reliable urban services on the periphery of the city, for example, was a major obstacle to bringing in new industry to Nashville. In every instance it was clear that the services could be provided more efficiently and rapidly by a combined effort of a single city and county agency. It was not enough, however, to educate county residents in the various advantages of consolidation, for most saw matters in narrow, private terms. They paid significantly lower taxes than their counterparts in the cities, at a cost in safety and health that rarely affected the individual's pocketbook.

Another aspect of the suburban problem was more potential than real. This was the spectre of political balkanization, the multiplication of small, independent satellite cities surrounding Nashville, each with vested interests opposed to the consolidation of a single metropolitan government. Before 1950 Belle Meade was the sole incorporated city in the county outside Nashville. It incorporated in 1938, in part to enforce "snob zoning" ordinances against apartment buildings but also to better resist annexation by Nashville. This wealthy suburb of luxurious mansions was joined in 1950 by Berry Hill, a predominantly lower-middle-class and blue-collar community of small tract homes south of Franklin Pike. Berry Hill, with a little over 1,000 residents, voted, after heated public debate, to incorporate as a city, with the avowed purpose of avoiding annexation and keeping taxes low.[50] By 1952 Oak Hill, a wealthy suburb of about 3,000 people south of Berry Hill on Franklin Pike, also voted to incorporate as an independent city, a controversial decision that attracted much attention in the newspapers.[51] (See map p. 196.)

As other young suburbs developed a community identity, they organized civic clubs and improvement associations that began to act as forums for discussions about suburban community needs. These groups could easily become the launchpads for a host of satellite cities—Belle Meade, Berry Hill, Oak Hill. Once in place, this ring of independent suburbs would make the political integration of metropolitan Nashville all but impossible. By the early 1950s community groups in the Hillsboro–Green Hills neighborhood were considering incorporation.[52] By 1960 Goodlettsville and Dupontonia (later Lakewood), two remote suburbs northeast of the city, and Forest Hills, between Belle Meade and Oak Hill, had become incorporated cities. It was precisely this fear of an irretrievable trend toward suburban "isolationism" that spurred the politicians, planners, and academicians of Nashville to push the community toward metropolitan integration in the early 1950s. Unlike old cities of the Northeast, which were long ago hemmed in by independent suburbs, Nashville had a last opportunity to solve one of the most intractable problems of modern urban life. "One of the greatest tragedies ... of metropolitan areas," Vanderbilt professor Daniel Grant observed around 1955, is that "most of the work being done on these problems is curative rather than preventative." Nashville stood "on the brink of metropolitan disintegration" and if the trend toward more suburban incorporation should be allowed to continue even for a few more years, Grant warned, "all hope of checking in their early stages the diseases of metropolitanism ... will have been lost."[53]

The PAS report of 1943 had recommended consolidation of county

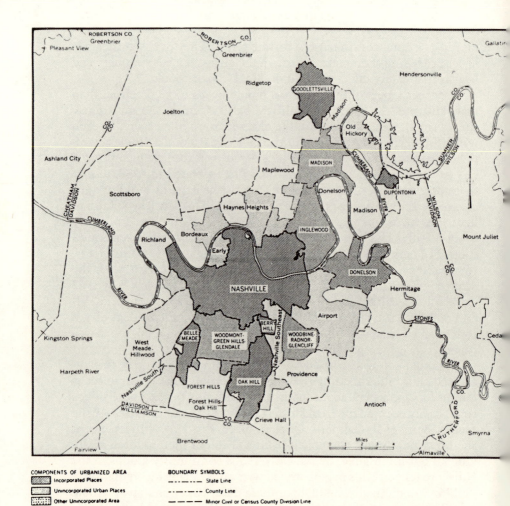

Figure 61. Map: Nashville and suburban communities, 1960. Bureau of the Census, *Census of Population: 1960*, 1, *Characteristics of the Population*, pt. 44, Tennessee (Washington, D.C., 1961) 23.

and city services and major annexation of suburbs, but its sensible program of reform was dismissed, in part because it came from outsiders —academic consultants whose objectivity was not sufficiently balanced by an appreciation of the local political scene. The impulse for reform would have to come from within and from planners and politicians in the city and county governments, in league with representatives of business, labor, blacks, women, and academics. Reform would also require the unusual cooperation of both daily newspapers if it was to acquire the necessary public support. After the charter reform of 1947 a group of local politicians and political reporters from the *Tennessean* and the *Banner* began to meet informally to discuss the problems of integrating city and county services.[54] During his 1950 campaign for county judge, Beverly Briley urged a new study of county government. The Tennessee Taxpayers Association, a respected nonpartisan force for good government, produced such a study in the fall of 1951, and it strongly advocated consolidation of city and county government.[55] Earlier that year the Davidson County delegation successfully proposed the creation of a Community Services Commission (CSC) to produce a thorough study of the need for consolidated government. It was this comprehensive study, made public in June 1952, that laid the groundwork for the move to metropolitan government that culminated a decade later. The CSC employed a professional staff of political scientists directed by Lee S. Greene, from the University of Tennessee, Knoxville, along with Daniel R. Grant from Vanderbilt, who acted as assistant director. The commission itself represented a cross-section of the community.[56] Their report, *A Future for Nashville*, was a highly readable survey that made the history and problems of government services understandable to any educated citizen. The CSC rejected city-county consolidation only because of state constitutional obstacles, but it recommended major annexations that would absorb 90,000 people and sixty-nine square miles into a single metropolitan government. The CSC also recommended outright consolidation of city and county public schools, hospitals, public health and welfare service, all of which were to fall under county responsibility. There were other important recommendations, including home rule for Tennessee cities and counties, which would allow charter changes and consolidation, for example, without state legislation. It also noted the need for redistricting to give urban areas representation on the County Court proportional to their population.[57]

The CSC report was heralded with unprecedented unanimity by community leaders and both the *Banner* and *Tennessean*, a notable departure from their ritual of antagonism on nearly every public issue. Parts of the report were implemented when city public health services and the city juvenile court were transferred to county control, and there was partial integration of other services in the ensuing years. The proposal for a referendum on annexation required the backing of the

Davidson County legislative delegation, which by Tennessee's "local bill" system could approve such annexations merely by their own unanimous agreement. Most of the politicians who ran for legislative office immediately after the CSC report were equivocal in their endorsement of its recommendations, and the election gave no clear mandate for or against Nashville's expansion. When the annexation issue came up in the 1953 General Assembly, Davidson County's two senators, Carl R. Hardin and H. Frank Taylor, opposed it, and the issue died, along with the move to redistrict the county.[58] The CSC disbanded later that year, and once again, it seemed, the good intentions and well-documented recommendations of the reformers had been foiled by the jealousies of local politicians. It failed also because no local organization outside politics had stepped forward to carry the banner for reform.[59]

The possibilities for metropolitan integration were quickly given new life in the spring and summer of 1953, when the state had a limited constitutional convention that added amendments enabling the city and county governments, or the service departments thereof, to consolidate, provided only that a popular vote gave concurrent majorities in city and county to such mergers.[60] Other legal obstacles to consolidation and local home rule were removed by the constitutional amendments that were ratified by popular vote later in 1953. Two years later the legislature gave Tennessee cities the authority to annex by ordinance alone, with a provision for state court review of the "reasonableness" of annexation, if appealed. No longer was state legislation required for annexation, and local governments now had an important component of home rule.[61]

The legal path to a metropolitan Nashville was now reasonably clear of constitutional obstructions, but it would require an active leadership, a clear strategy, and a sustained effort to pull the community down that path. That leadership and strategy came primarily from a group of planners and academics organized in 1953 as the Advanced Planning and Research Division, a creation of the city and county planning commissions. It included Irving Hand, a professional planner with a degree from MIT who served as director; Robert Horton, a young political scientist from Vanderbilt who acted as director of research; and Daniel R. Grant, a Vanderbilt political science professor who was consultant to the division. In the summer of 1955 the planning commissions of the city and county jointly authorized the Advanced Planning and Research Division to embark on a number of long-range studies dealing with the integration of city and county services. Hand, Horton, and Grant, together with Charles W. Hawkins, director of the joint city and county planning commissions and a veteran of Nashville planning since the 1930s, met informally for lengthy discussions about the goals and strategy of metropolitan integration. These discussions, one observer later stated, were "among the most crucial ever held in Nashville and Davidson County."[62] These men combined the passion of the professional planner and the political scientist for rational government with a savvy about the often irrational nature of local politics and personalities. They agreed to avoid, if at all possible, such piecemeal solutions as special sewer districts and the like and push instead toward complete consolidation.

They recognized the political problems that remained in the path of metropolitan government. Most critical was the inherent conflict between the heads of county and city government. Mayor West preferred that the city annex settled adjacent areas, a process that would be controlled by the city for the city's benefit. In a speech before the Rotary Club in June 1955, Judge Briley, on the other hand, had become the first politician in this period to publicly endorse a single consolidated government for Nashville and Davidson County. The careers of both politicians would ride on these alternatives. To risk alienating either of these powerful political figures was to doom both goals. The strategy devised by Hand, Horton, Grant, and Hawkins was to promote annexation as a short-run first step, with consolidation as the long-term goal. Both politicians, they surmised, would support such a movement, each hoping that his preference would ultimately be the only one practicable.[63]

By the fall of 1956 the Advanced Planning and Research Division had prepared a public report issued under the auspices of the joint city and county planning commissions as *A Plan of Metropolitan Government for Nashville and Davidson County*. It was this report that eventually became the basis for the Metropolitan charter approved in 1962. The 1956 report briefly reviewed the now familiar litany of problems inherent in the existing system of city and county government: poor suburban services, the incapacity of county government to provide urban services, the division of loyalties among political leaders between city and county, and the dissipation of citizen control over local government. It pointed to the dangers of permanent fragmentation in the older cities of the North and emphasized the rare opportunity presented to Nashville to avoid this fate. The report laid out the conventional alternatives: suburban annexation by the city, city-county consolidation, or special countywide service districts for sewers and water, for example, along with other solutions to the "metropolitan problem." The major thrust of the report was to reject "piecemeal or halfway measures" in favor of a comprehensive new plan for metropolitan government.

The report moved the debate beyond the stalemate of annexation versus consolidation to a third, compromise position. The key feature of this plan was a system of dual service districts, each with distinct tax rates but supervised by a single metropolitan government with a mayor and twenty-one council members. The General Services District would receive the basic county services of schools, sheriff's patrol, roads, and so on; the Urban Services District would provide more complete urban services at higher tax rates to any area of the county "that requires urban services." The boundaries of this higher taxed Urban Services District would expand in stages as the water and sewer systems became capable of serving new areas. This was, in effect, a method of annexation by city fiat, but without subjecting all county residents to higher taxes until they were about to receive full urban services. The time lag between the expansion of the Urban Service District and the actual implementation of full urban services would become a serious point of contention under Metropolitan government in the 1960s, but the plan had the virtue of avoiding that conflict, in theory at least. The 1956 plan also shrewdly allowed for the continued existence of independent incorporated cities within the county until they elected to join the metropolitan government. This provision effectively defused the issue of forced consolidation in the six incorporated satellite cities.

Earlier plans had died on the vine for want of a clear agenda for action. The 1956 plan included a clear, realistic timetable identifying each of the several legal steps that would have to be taken before the plan could become a reality. The first step was to secure an act enabling Tennessee's major cities to form single metropolitan governments. County judge Beverly Briley played an important role by gaining support for the plan among the Davidson County legislative delegation, and then among the representatives of Tennessee's three other metropolitan counties. As president of the Tennessee County Services Association, Briley enjoyed considerable support among rural legislators as well.[64] By early 1957 the act was approved, and the next step was to appoint a charter commission. The City Council showed overwhelming support for the plan, but the County Court was split, with magistrate Ewing Clouse of Berry Hill leading the opposition. Thirty voted in favor of the charter commission and only eighteen against, but this was an early sign of county opposition to metropolitan government.[65]

The charter commission appointed by Judge Briley and Mayor West in 1957 was a masterful representation of most all the community's local interest groups. Judge Briley appointed Carmack Cochran—a lawyer, president of Nashville Transit Company, and head of the Chamber of Commerce—who became chairman of the charter commission. Briley's other appointments included K. Harlan Dodson, Jr., an attorney who as senator had led the fight for enabling legislation; Victor S. Johnson, president of Aladdin Industries; Dr. George S. Meadors, a respected black pharmacist and community leader; and Edward D. Hicks, Jr., a wholesale seed dealer. Mayor West appointed Rebecca Thomas, a well-known woman attorney; Robert N. Chenault, principal of Warner Elementary School in East Nashville; Cecil Branstetter, a young attorney with strong support from labor; Z. Alexander Looby, a prominent black

Figure 62. The first metropolitan charter commission in 1958. *Clockwise from bottom:* E.C. "Bud" Yokley (Executive Director), with back to camera, Dolly Butler, secretary, K. Harlan Dodson, Jr., Z. Alexander Looby, Victor S. Johnson, Irving Hand, Carmack Cochran (Chairman), Rebecca Thomas, Edward D. Hicks, Jr., Cecil Branstetter, Thomas E. McGrath, Robert N. Chenault, Robert Horton. Dr. George S. Meadors is missing. *Tennessean* Library.

attorney and city council member; and Thomas E. McGrath, a labor union official who worked for the L&N.[66]

After a series of public hearings and lengthy deliberations the charter commission adopted the 1956 plan in its essential outlines: two service districts with distinct tax rates and a single government headed by a mayor with a twenty-one-member council, fifteen to be elected by district and six elected at large.[67] The plan won widespread endorsement from community leaders. The Chamber of Commerce had been actively behind metropolitan government for many years. The League of Women Voters, an influential force for mobilizing voters, also showed enthusiasm for the proposed charter. The Nashville Trades and Labor Council approved the charter on behalf of labor, as did the Tennessee Taxpayers Association and the Tennessee Municipal League. Even the *Tennessean* and the *Banner* dropped their usual bickering to support the new plan for metropolitan government. The major political leaders, including Judge Briley and Mayor West, along with about half of the City Council and County Court members endorsed the charter. College professors and various civic leaders joined what appeared to be a chorus of approval for this enlightened, long-overdue reform.[68]

Eminent people from a variety of organizations formed a Citizens Committee for Metro before the popular referendum on the charter in July 1958. They sponsored speakers and radio and television discussions, and they distributed literature and copies of the proposed charter. But for the most part the community leaders who promoted Metro spoke to people like themselves—educated, above average income, white, middle-class citizens who were generally sympathetic toward the proposed reform. At the same time both newspapers were bombarding the public with stories, cartoons, and editorials extolling the virtues of the new charter as a solution to metropolitan ills. Until quite late in the campaign no serious opposition to the charter materialized, and for this reason the pro-Metro forces never mounted an effective grassroots campaign to reach the ordinary citizen.

The opposition to Metro took form in the Committee to Save Davidson County Government. It included an assortment of vested interests, suburban fire and police companies, old-line county politicians, suburban merchants, and county bootleggers and gamblers, all of whom felt threatened in different ways by the changes metropolitan government would bring.[69] There were a number of wealthy suburbanites who contributed heavily to the anti-Metro campaign. Several private fire and police companies contributed $500 each, and many county gamblers and bootleggers were reported to have donated to the campaign chest to stop Metro.[70] Ed Potter of Commerce Union Bank was the chief financial backer of the anti-Metro campaign. Potter was a conservative dedicated to fighting big government, and he may have feared that metropolitan government would bring fiscal reform and the end of the days when county and city revenues were left idle in local banks.[71] While the reformers were addressing civic clubs, holding panel discussions on radio and television, and distributing educational literature in support of Metro, their opposition lay silent. Then, a week before the referendum on June 17, 1958, the anti-Metro forces mounted a propaganda blitz that can only be described as a scare campaign. Full-page newspaper advertisements, radio jingles, and door-to-door appeals, aimed primarily at county voters, warned that Metro meant higher taxes and the dictatorial concentration of power in the hands of big government.[72]

During the 1950s the postwar reaction to totalitarianism and the general climate of paranoia during the Cold War with Communist Russia turned what seemed quite innocuous reforms into insidious conspiracies fraught with implications for the subversion of American democracy. The anti-Metro campaign exploited this visceral American reaction by appealing to vague fears of big government as a threat to locally rooted democracy. The reformers promoted Metro as a general benefit to the economic development and political efficiency of the whole metropolitan population; The opposition appealed to fierce local pride and particular interests.

The eleventh-hour campaign by the opposition turned the apparent victory of reform into an upset defeat. A relatively large turnout (almost 44 percent of registered voters) in the county went against the new charter almost three to two, with strong opposition in the northern and eastern suburbs of Donelson, Madison, and Inglewood, along with the rural districts. The incorporated western and southern suburbs of Belle Meade and Oak Hill, along with Hillwood, were the only areas outside Nashville to support the charter. Within the city a majority of three to two supported Metro, but the turnout was remarkably light (only 22 percent of registered voters) due to the low-key campaign by pro-Metro forces. Support was strongest among the wealthier residents of the West End (Ward Four) and the blue-collar neighborhood of Woodbine (Ward Three). There was substantial opposition in many of the poorer wards, particularly among black voters, who understood that their growing voting strength within the existing city would be diluted within a metropolitan government.[73]

Academicians who analyzed the 1958 vote concluded that the wealthy, educated, and politically involved residents of the city and the county favored Metro, but the reformers had not done enough to convince the poor and working-class voters of the desirability of this change.[74] One observer, political scientist Daniel Elazar, saw it as a contest between "cosmopolitans," who identified Metro with the good of greater Nashville against "locals," who tended to reject Metro because it might hurt their more narrowly defined neighborhood interests. Some criticized the "ignorance" and "apathy" of voters who refused to see the logic of reform. Others blamed the "ultraconservatives" who scared the tractable populace into a rejection of the bogeyman "big government."[75] Most interpretations of the 1958 vote served to justify defeat by discrediting the opponents of Metro, but they did little to explain the failure of its proponents to mobilize the electorate in their favor. In truth, too many reformers were out of touch with the ordinary citizens that the new charter was intended to benefit.

In the wake of unexpected defeat in 1958, the earlier tone of consensus among city and county politicians and between the two daily newspapers quickly disintegrated. City and county officials scrambled to enact piecemeal reforms, and one party's solution became the other's headache. The *Tennessean*, and its publisher Silliman Evans, Jr., refused to abandon the dream of metropolitan consolidation and pushed relentlessly for a second referendum. Mayor Ben West and his supporters at the *Banner* proceeded on the premise that consolidation was now a dead issue and the only alternative was to annex the suburbs by city ordinance and raise taxes from county residents by whatever means necessary in order to support new and existing services supplied by the city. West, who had preferred this path from the outset, created a strenuous reaction in the suburbs against forcible annexation and against the "green-sticker" wheel tax he imposed on all users of city streets. This backlash cost West his political future, and it led Davidson County back to Metro.

For the city the critical problem was the growing strain on services brought by the increased suburban population combined with a stagnant tax base. The 1960 census showed a net loss of population, the first in the city's history (see appendix A).[76] Furthermore, within this shrinking population was a growing percentage of poor, elderly, and black city residents. It was a population that required growing expenditures for social services, such as police, health, and welfare, while its per capita taxable property and sales tax revenues were not rising accordingly. Also, the expansion of government, education, and religious institutions within the city meant that a growing percentage of land — close to 40 percent by 1958 — was exempt from taxes altogether.[77] The interstate highway and urban renewal projects of the 1950s also eradicated, or at least temporarily disrupted, taxable property the city needed to support its budget. Although per capita tax revenues increased by slightly more than three times between 1938 and 1960, per capita expenditures multiplied by nearly six times in the same period (see appendix D). Mayor West had to expand the tax base through annexation and devise new taxes to make suburbanites pay for the city services they used.

State law now permitted annexation by simple city ordinance, so long as the courts, on appeal, approved of its "reasonableness." Within a month of the Metro referendum the City Council voted to annex three industrial areas adjacent to the city — one in West Nashville, including the new Ford Glass Plant; another in North Nashville, around Bush Lake (now Metro Center); and a third to the east, on Elm Hill and Murfreesboro pikes. These areas, the city argued, were already receiving city services, and as there were few residents, a referendum was not essential. At the same time Mayor West assured suburbanites that they would have to approve by referendum any major annexation of residential areas. This annexation of about seven square miles gave the city a valuable addition to its tax base without the political risk of alienating large numbers of residents. In December 1958 a group of fifty-three businessmen challenged this annexation, just before it was to be final, and the issue was tied up in the courts for more than two years.[78]

Mayor West and the City Council now took another tack in their search for additional tax revenues. In August 1959 the council created a wheel tax of ten dollars per year on all vehicles using the streets of Nashville at least thirty days or more during the year. The green-sticker law taxed commuting suburbanites for the city service most obviously benefiting them, but it was bound to be unpopular. It taxed people who lived outside, as well as inside, the jurisdiction of the city and raised cries of "taxation without representation." Many drivers refused on principle to pay this tax, and it was a law that, by its nature, was difficult to enforce. Those who complied voluntarily with the new law vehemently criticized the city for not making everyone comply. The city responded with a tough police crackdown in which the offending automobile owners were arrested, taken before Judge Andrew Doyle, and fined fifty dollars. The *Tennessean* hammered relentlessly at West in a series of green-sticker atrocity stories, but the publicity served to warn Nashville drivers, and they quickly lined up to pay the wheel tax. The tax was enforced, but the green sticker became a symbol of bitter distrust toward Ben West.[79]

New efforts to revive Metro came from the County Court, which proposed a new commission and referendum in February 1960 and again in May.[80] The City Council rejected the proposal both times. Instead, the city revealed plans to annex by ordinance four large residential areas, including over forty-two square miles and about 82,000 people.[81] This included the Early school district in North Nashville, a large stretch from Cockrill Bend and Richland to Green Hills, the Radnor-Woodbine-Airport area south and west of the central city, and a small section in East Nashville known as the Joywood-Rosebank-Dalewood neighborhoods. Councilman Aubrey D. Gillem, Mayor West's floor leader in the council, and councilman Charles Bramwell pushed the annexation ordinance rapidly through three readings in April 1960. Mayor West, who had earlier promised no residential annexation without a popular referendum, had to veto the ordinance, but the council overrode his veto. West lived up to his promise technically, yet it seemed clear, at least to West's critics at the *Tennessean*, that he had given the go-ahead to the council, a majority of which always followed West, to pass the ordinance and then override his obligatory veto.[82]

The annexation was immediately appealed, and it was not until March 1961 that it, along with the 1958 annexation, was upheld by the state supreme court.[83] Having joined the city and been subjected to city taxes, the former suburbanites enjoyed few of the amenities of city services. Roads were in bad repair, and improvement projects planned by the county were immediately abandoned with annexation. The county, after all, had just been deprived of an enormous portion of its tax base and was in no position to offer help to the city. The city could not even supply bus service to schools as the county had done. Water and sewer lines were years in the future for most of the newly annexed neighborhoods. The suddenness of the annexation move, and the prolonged legal battle that followed it, allowed none of the necessary advance preparation. The lack of immediate benefits and the abrupt loss of important county services made residents in the newly annexed areas bitterly opposed to West and more receptive than before to the idea of metropolitan consolidation.[84]

Ben West was in political hot water. The green-sticker tax and the annexation controversy severely alienated county voters. They spoke at the polls in April 1960 in a landslide defeat of West's candidate for sheriff, Thomas Cartwright, and in favor of the *Tennessean*'s candidate, Leslie E. Jett, who made the revival of Metro a major campaign issue. At the same time, county judge Beverly Briley's allies gained strength on the County Court, and the rift between the two men and their opposing policies of annexation versus metropolitan consolidation was becoming clearly defined. The *Tennessean*, a steady advocate of Metro, vilified West and denounced his annexation scheme as a dastardly betrayal of popular government. The debate over annexation versus consolidation had become a contest of pro- and anti-West forces. The *Tennessean*, and the proponents of Metro, were able to shrewdly redirect popular sentiment in the county *against* West and *against* the city's preemptive annexation into a movement in *favor* of metropolitan consolidation, with Judge Briley as their champion. West had committed his forces to annexation, and he understood the movement to revive Metro as a deliberate effort to end his political career. Politics and personal factionalism, formerly the annoying obstacle to government reform, now became a key ingredient to the success of metropolitan consolidation, in ways the reformers would never have anticipated.[85]

West and his majority in the City Council had proved a solid roadblock to County Court proposals for the revival of a metropolitan charter commission in February and May of 1960. Furthermore, West's strategy of annexation remained in legal question until March 1961. Proponents of Metro in the Davidson County legislative delegation now tried an end run by introducing an amendment to the 1957 enabling act that would allow the creation of a metropolitan charter commission by private legislative act as well as by joint resolution of County Court and City Council. The strategy worked. The legislature approved the amendment in March 1961, and the next Davidson County delegation, elected in August 1960 with enthusiastic support from the *Tennessean*, went to the legislature pledged to sponsor such an act. Though there was some disagreement and one dissenting vote among the delegation, the legislature took the unprecedented step of approving the private act creating a new charter commission for Nashville and Davidson County.[86] This act had to be approved by separate majorities in the city and the county outside Nashville. The referendum on August 17, 1961, was preceded by far less publicity than the 1958 referendum, and the turnout was light. Pro-Metro forces put together a citizens' organization to mobilize voters behind their cause, holding public meetings throughout the county; the opposition did little more than pass out literature. The private act creating the commission was approved by a surprising landslide within the city (11,096 to 3,730) and a strong majority outside Nashville (7,324 to 3,848), with much of the newfound support for Metro coming from the voters in recently annexed suburbs and adjacent suburban communities who now saw the choice as one between Metro and annexation.[87] The charter that was ultimately approved by Nashville voters in 1962 was, in its fundamental points, the same charter rejected in 1958. The charter commission was essentially the same one that drew up the 1958 charter. Eight members of the 1958 commission were named in the referendum approved in 1961. Another, Edward Hicks, had died in the interim, and Tom McGrath excused himself from duty, since he was now one of the state senators who had passed the private act naming the commission members. In their places Judge Briley appointed Charles Warfield, a young lawyer active in the Metro revival; Mayor West appointed Joe E. Torrence, his city finance director and close political ally.[88]

The charter commission held some seventy-five lengthy meetings, countless subcommittee meetings, and numerous public hearings over the course of six months. Every phrase and comma of the 1958 charter was discussed, but the outcome was a document virtually the same as the one devised in 1958. There was heated controversy over schools, involving the rejected proposal to elect school board members and an approved amendment allowing appeal to public referendum if the school budget were cut by the council.[89] In the end the most significant change was the enlargement of the council from twenty-one to forty-one members, with thirty-five to be elected by district, five elected at large, and a presiding vice-mayor, also to be elected at large. This was a compromise to make the charter politically palatable to as many neighborhoods as possible. Voters in the new wards were chagrined that they were underrepresented on the existing council. Black politicians and commu-

Figure 63. The second charter commission, 1962. *Clockwise:* Rebecca Thomas, *seated center*, Edwin F. Hunt (legal counsel), K. Harlan Dodson (*seated in chair behind*), Cecil Branstetter, Z. Alexander Looby, Charles Warfield, Robert N. Chenault, Dr. George S. Meadors, Joe E. Torrence, Carmack Cochran. *Seated at table behind:* Donald Jackson, of Tennessee Taxpayers' Association, and Robert Horton. Victor S. Johnson is missing. *Tennessean* Library.

nity leaders, in particular, were vitally concerned that their voting strength and representation on the council would be reduced by consolidation with the white suburbs. Councilman Robert Lillard spoke for many blacks when he vigorously opposed the Metro charter and filed a lawsuit questioning the constitutionality of the charter commission.[90] To assure blacks of continued, even increased, representation, councilmanic districts were carefully drawn to almost guarantee blacks six seats on the new council. Further provisions required adjustment of district boundaries according to population changes reported in the federal census each decade.[91]

There were other minor changes in the 1962 charter, but in its substantive measures, it was a replica of the 1958 version. The charter commission felt that the 1958 referendum was less a rejection of the charter than a complacent endorsement of the status quo. With Mayor West's green-sticker tax and preemptive annexations, the status quo had changed radically. The commission wanted to present the same alternative to voters rather than confuse the issue by introducing too many new and unfamiliar changes.[92]

If the commission and its charter were the same as in 1958, there were few similarities in the campaign, its organization, and political style. Pro-Metro reformers in 1958 saw their task as educating concerned citizens and winning endorsements from leading civic organizations. These were people who disdained factional infighting and personal politics, and they saw Metro as an antidote to these ills. The strategy was to placate factions and forge a broad consensus in support of Metro. This high-minded appeal to reason was successful to a degree, but it produced a lackluster campaign and no hard core of citizen support. When the opposition attacked with a barrage of nearly hysterical propaganda in the last week of the campaign, county voters, driven by baser fears of illogical conspiracies, stampeded to the polls to defeat the reformers. The lessons of 1958 and the political events of the intervening years led reformers to devise a very different strategy in 1962. Instead of taking the high road of consensus and community education, the reformers of 1962 deliberately set out to politicize and personalize the campaign for Metro. They played on suburban distrust of the central city and exploited suburban enmity toward Ben West in particular.

Silliman Evans, Jr., publisher of the *Tennessean* and persistent champion of metropolitan consolidation, played a key role in plotting the strategy and organizing the second Metro campaign before his untimely death in July 1961. Prior to the August 1961 referendum on the charter commission, Evans and James H. Roberson, an insurance man who had been active with Evans in supporting a pro-Metro county delegation in the August 1960 primary, met to discuss the 1958 failure and work out a winning strategy for the coming battle.[93] Evans helped set up and finance the Citizens Committee for Better Government (CCBG), which

Roberson coordinated. This became a steering committee and umbrella organization for a coalition of pro-Metro organizations. After directing the successful campaign to approve the Metro Charter Commission in August 1961, the CCBG went on to forge a broad-based political organization drawing on neighborhood leaders, salesmen, service station owners, and the like. This formed the core of a small volunteer army of some 5,000 canvassers organized within a hierarchy that went down to precinct and block captains.[94] The CCBG made special efforts to involve women in the campaign. They organized a women's division under Mrs. J.D. Sanders of Madison, and they forged alliances among women's organizations. By early 1962 the CCBG had the energetic support of the League of Women Voters, long dedicated to metropolitan consolidation, the Council of Jewish Women, three Business and Professional Women's clubs, and the Education Council, a predominantly female teachers' organization.[95] George Cate, Jr., who shared his father's reputation as a champion of educational reform, became general chairman of the CCBG. The Metro campaign became strongly identified with better public schools, an issue with special appeal to women as mothers and teachers.[96]

Through the CCBG and its allied organizations, pro-Metro forces reached out to inform every voter about the new charter. They went door-to-door with fact sheets, sponsored neighborhood coffees with invited speakers, and held public meetings across the county. Instead of seeking the endorsement of prominent individuals and civic organizations, the strategy was to make direct contact with the voters. The CCBG made special efforts to align black voters in favor of Metro by enlisting Vivian Henderson, a Fisk University professor; Lurelia Freeman, a Tennessee A&I professor; Avon Williams, a civil rights lawyer; C.M. Hays, president of the National Association for the Advancement of Colored People (NAACP); and Z. Alexander Looby, a respected lawyer, councilman, and member of the charter commission. These people and others spoke to neighborhood gatherings about the benefits Metro would bring to all Nashville's citizens and did their best to counter the fears of diluted strength among blacks as a voting bloc.[97]

As the CCBG made its direct appeals to the citizens through its impressively organized coalition, the *Tennessean* led an aggressive campaign to discredit Mayor West and arouse disgust at his recent moves to tax and annex the suburbs. A steady stream of *Tennessean* news articles and editorials deliberately cast Ben West as "the devil" and made his political past and future a central issue in the referendum. The strategy was to excite people to vote against an unpopular individual rather than solely for an abstract reform. The strategy worked well, not just because of West's recent unpopular actions involving the wheel tax and annexation but because he had been in office since 1951 and was an easy target for a campaign aimed at arousing dissatisfaction with the status quo. The *Tennessean* depicted West as an obstacle to Nashville's progress, an agent of urban corruption and enemy of the suburbanite. It was unfair to a man who had championed urban renewal and the revitalization of the downtown. It was unfair to a mayor who had spoken so forcefully in behalf of the nation's cities. It was also unfair to a man who had benefited all the nation's cities by his dogged support of the landmark U.S. Supreme Court case *Baker* vs. *Carr*. The *Tennessean's* image of West as a political reprobate was unfair, but it was shrewd politics, and politics was a game that West knew how to play skillfully.

The mayor fought back with his own brand of organization and propaganda. West recognized that Metro could be defeated in either the city or the county and decided to concentrate his efforts where his political organization was strongest, in the old central city. West held a series of closed meetings with city employees and political supporters on the council to discuss strategy and enlist support to defeat Metro. He appealed to their personal loyalty to him instead of debating the merits of Metro. This was an attack on Ben West and therefore on his political allies in city government. In the police and fire departments West could draw on hundreds of willing supporters to influence voters and get them to the polls. West's use of city employees in the campaign quickly became another example of machine politics in the *Tennessean's* attack on the mayor. Like his opponents, West recognized the vital role of women as campaign workers and as voters. He enlisted the wives of policemen and firemen to help distribute campaign literature and convince neighbors to vote against Metro. The *Banner* and its political reporter Dick Battle, always loyal supporters of West, did their part in defending the mayor's record and discrediting the Metro movement as little more than vicious political factionalism masquerading as reform. Metro government, its opponents argued, was untested, probably unconstitutional, and a false panacea for imagined ills.[98] Joining West's battle against Metro were an odd assortment of right-wing extremists, including Thomas J. Anderson of the John Birch Society, white racist agitator John Kasper, and others who linked Metro to the attack on states' rights in the current desegregation struggle or to a Communist dictatorship abroad.[99] For Ben West, a liberal defender of black civil rights, it was a sorry example of the adage that politics makes strange bedfellows.

Amid the barrage of campaign literature, speeches, newspaper stories, and cartoons, the voters in each section of the city and the county voted on a set of particular issues distinct to their location. Voters in the old central city were choosing whether or not to continue with their mayor of the past eleven years. Those in the recently annexed suburbs chose between remaining underrepresented and poorly served citizens within the existing city government or becoming first-class citizens in a new metropolitan government committed to providing the needed services within the Urban Services District. Among these voters especially, Ben West's political future was a powerful issue, and there were few defenders of the mayor who, they believed, had betrayed his promise not to annex them without their approval. Outside the city limits, county voters looked at the choice of remaining subject to annexation, with no guarantee of improved services, or becoming subject to another form of annexation in the Urban Services District within a year. These voters also now faced a choice between taxation without representation through the green-sticker tax and other such measures as might be passed in the future or becoming subject to the general services tax but having an opportunity to elect representatives to council. Those chioces were often clouded by the rhetoric of both sides in the campaign, but they were the essential choices that voters weighed as they went to the polls on June 28, 1962.[100]

The results showed a reversal of the 1958 referendum. In the county a relatively strong turnout (44 percent of registered voters) turned in a solid majority of almost 56 percent in favor of Metro, with especially strong support in the Eighth District (71 percent in favor), which included West Meade; the Third District (69 percent in favor), which included Donelson; and the Sixth District (68 percent in favor), which included Oak Hill and Crieve Hall. Support was weakest in the more remote areas, such as Goodlettsville and the rural fringe of the county.[101]

Within the old wards of the central city Ben West's political organization delivered an impressive 55 percent vote against Metro, but the turnout was comparatively light (34 percent). The anti-Metro vote was strongest in the poor white and black neighborhoods of Ward Two. There, recently elected councilman Gene "Little Evil" Jacobs worked tirelessly to link Metro with Communist dictatorships. "RUSSIA HAS ONE GOVERNMENT," "CASTRO HAS METRO," his placards exclaimed. In Ward One in North Nashville, West's political allies, led by Henry "Good Jelly" Jones, pulled black voters into the anti-Metro camp.[102] Only Ward Four, on the West End, and Ward Three, in the Belmont neighborhood, carried majorities for Metro. The majority against Metro in the old city was buried in an avalanche for Metro in the newly annexed wards. There, a heavy turnout (over 45 percent) voted 72 percent in favor of Metro and pushed the city's total vote to a resounding majority of 57 percent in favor of the new charter.

West's successful battle for the long-overdue expansion of his city led ultimately to his political demise. He read the vote for Metro as a personal defeat and refused to run for mayor of the new government the following November. He was also convinced the first term as mayor under the new charter would be political suicide. For his valiant and politically risky crusade to revitalize his city through bold annexations and unpopular taxes, West became an unlikely symbol of urban cor-

Figure 64. The anti-Metro campaign in 1962 linked itself to popular fears of communism and big government. Councilman Gene "Little Evil" Jacobs led the campaign with placards like these. *Tennessean* Library.

Figure 65. Henry "Good Jelly" Jones, one of Mayor Ben West's black allies, joined the anti-Metro campaign by carrying carloads of voters to the polls in the charter election of 1962. *Tennessean* Library.

ruption and chicanery, against which righteous suburbanites rose up in anger—this time to swallow the city rather than repel it. In this unlikely role as "devil," Ben West left Nashville one of his most important —if unintended—accomplishments.

METRO AND THE GREAT SOCIETY

The legal challenge to the constitutionality of the new metropolitan government, brought in the suit by suburban officials Lewis Frazier of Forest Hills and Sam Davis Bell of Belle Meade, and by Robert Lillard, the black city councilman, was denied by the chancery court and then the Tennessee Supreme Court in October 1962.[103] With West out of the running in the first Metro election, held in November 1962, it was an easy victory for Judge Beverly Briley to become the first mayor of Metropolitan Nashville and Davidson County. The new government would go into effect the following spring, and it was for Briley and the officials of the old city and county governments to plan for the transition.

Briley was born in Nashville in 1914 and grew up in East Nashville.[104] He was graduated from Central High School, attended Vanderbilt, and studied law at Cumberland Law School in Lebanon. When he began practicing law in 1932 he was the youngest Tennessean ever admitted to the bar. During World War II, Briley served in the navy and returned with a generation of veterans brimming with ambition for themselves and their community. His first political campaign in 1946, on the "GI Joe" ticket, was, he admitted later, a campaign to boost his law practice after his return from the war.[105] But Briley was a natural politician, and he soon became a principal figure in the destruction of the old county machine that had been in place for over thirty years. He became the favorite of the *Tennessean,* whose strong backing was instrumental to his rise to power. Following his victory over Judge Litton Hickman in 1950, he fought a hostile County Court to revamp the county's fiscal policies, expand the schools, and rebuild the road system. Briley brought to the task long experience and expertise as a tax lawyer. He made Davidson County the first in the state to adopt a public works department, which, with Briley's prodding, built the first county sewage treatment plant. As a founder of the Tennessee County Services Association he assumed leadership in the state among county officials. On the national level Briley won notice as president of the National Association of County Officials in 1962. Since 1955 Briley had been a leading voice for metropolitan consolidation, and he built a political career as the "father of Metro." After the charter victory, Briley confidently predicted the consolidation of the five surrounding counties and promoted Nashville as a model of progressive urban government.

On April 1, 1963, Metropolitan Nashville–Davidson County superseded the old city and county governments. A city of 73 square miles and approximately 171,000 people suddenly became a new entity of 508 square miles and over 400,000 people.[106] The approval of Metro, Daniel Grant observed, "set off a chain reaction of civic enthusiasm." Nashville won a place in the national spotlight as a pioneer (along with Miami–Dade County) in metropolitan reorganization. Many heralded Metro as the cure-all for the ills descending on urban America during the 1960s. So much blame had been fixed on the old city-suburban divisions, many were convinced that the coming of metropolitan government meant a whole new era of economic growth, downtown revitalization, and general improvement in the quality of urban life. For the generation of World War II veterans and others who came of political age in the 1950s, Metro's triumph confirmed their faith in the value of cooperation among politicians, business leaders, professional planners, and academics.

Metro enlivened a surge of popular interest in Nashville's future progress. Mayor Briley shrewdly built upon the grass-roots organization constructed to pass the new charter. He brought dozens of men and women into the process of policy making during the transition and first several years of Metro. He appointed study groups to examine issues ranging from juvenile delinquency to the environment, sewers, water, and transportation. The mayor added citizen advisory groups to city departments, boards, and commissions to help define the role of government units under Metro. Consultants from Nashville's business, academic, and medical communities also were enlisted in the service of Metro during the 1960s. Robert Horton estimated that seven hundred to eight hundred private citizens became involved in some capacity with the new metropolitan government in these formative years. The promise of Metro, Daniel Grant observed, "stimulated a kind of civic revolution of rising expectations."[107]

Those expectations were not met entirely, but the consolidation of city and county governments proceeded without disruption, and the promised sewers and other urban services gradually penetrated the suburban frontier. The more densely settled and contiguous suburbs annexed into the Urban Services District of the new metropolitan government saw dramatic improvements over the course of the first decade. The painfully slow and expensive process of constructing sewers and water mains gradually extended into Nashville's dispersed suburban neighborhoods. Sewers were the most pressing problem facing the new government. The task was first to catch up with the suburban frontier that decades earlier had moved beyond the sewer lines and then to keep up with the expansion of new neighborhoods. The Metro charter required the city to construct sewers within two years of annexing areas into the more highly taxed Urban Services District. But the increased tax base that came from these annexations never covered the high initial cost of building new sewers. Early in 1965, after extensive study, the Metro sewer program was overhauled, with future financing to come from increased water and sewer bills for consumers and from revenue bonds. The plan involved $120 million over eight years to lay sewers to every home and business inside the 54-square mile Urban Services District.[108] Within eight years under Metro the city laid 400 miles of new sewers and added another 674 miles during the 1970s. New water mains, police and fire service, and garbage collection came into the suburbs at the same time.[109] There were some gains in the efficiency of providing these services through a consolidated government, and though tax rates increased in 1971 (from $5.30 to $6.00 per $100 of assessed valuation) and water and sewer rates went up, the quality and extent of urban services improved commensurately, in the view of most citizens. Even as the Metro budget climbed from $60 million to $243 million between 1962 and 1975, Briley was reelected in 1966 and again in 1971. Metro may have meant higher taxes, but Nashvillians apparently were more impressed with the improvement in services after decades of primitive suburban government.[110]

Whatever advantages Metro offered to the efficient delivery of urban services, the most important results of the consolidation were a coherent governmental structure for long-term planning and an effective strategy for drawing federal support to the city. The explosion of downtown building and the rapid construction of new freeways around the downtown were the most visible evidence of post-1963 vitality. Surely some of this construction would have come without Metro, but consolidation allowed local government to articulate a clear and consistent plan for urban development. Downtown business leaders saw in Briley and in the new government allies that favored their interests in revitalizing the city center, and they welcomed the end of city-county squabbling. When the National Life and Accident Insurance Company threatened to leave Davidson County to avoid the heavy tax burden placed on insurance company assets, Briley and the Metro tax assessor were able to act decisively to alleviate the tax load, keep the company downtown, and encourage it to build new offices (see chapter five). Under the old system of buck-passing and city-county rivalry this could never have been handled so expeditiously.[111]

The benefits of metropolitan consolidation were even more apparent in the city's relations with the federal government. Under Briley, and continuing under Mayor Richard Fulton, Nashville developed an effective team of planners and politicians who kept alert to new federal programs and lobbied in Washington, D.C., for grants that flowed with increasing velocity to the nation's cities during the 1960s. Fortuitously, metropolitan consolidation came just before President Lyndon Johnson launched the Great Society. On a scale that dwarfed FDR's New Deal, Johnson carried out a "war on poverty" and attacked the "urban crisis" with such programs as "model cities," designed to revitalize inner-city neighborhoods. Metro pursued an aggressive course in response to these federal programs. Briley's office set up the Policy Analysis and Program Analysis units to concentrate on the acquisition and monitoring of federal grants. These units tapped the intellectual resources of Nashville's universities, medical facilities, and business community and brought local experts into league with city and state government in a variety of federally sponsored projects. The Urban Observatory, set up in the late 1960s, became a grant sponsor for projects that linked Metro to academic consultants at Vanderbilt, Tennessee State, and Fisk universities. By the early 1970s, Robert Horton recalled, Metro was involved in over 170 federal grants at one time, and the city ranked well above larger rivals in federal funds received.[112]

In Washington, Congressman Richard Fulton, elected to the first of seven terms in 1962, represented Metropolitan Nashville's interests effectively through his key positions on congressional committees. Fulton was a young, liberal Democrat who quickly established contacts with the party leaders during the Kennedy and Johnson years. He was among the few southern congressman to back such legislation as the voting rights, fair housing, and fair employment acts, and he earned the support of blacks and poor people back in Nashville. As a member of the House Ways and Means Committee, beginning in his second term, and chair of its Subcommittee on Public Assistance, Fulton had his finger on the pulse of the Great Society.

Congressman Fulton formed one strong link in a chain between Washington and the mayor's office during the 1960s. Nashville, Horton recalled, "learned to play all the angles" in federal grantsmanship. Because metropolitan consolidation raised the average household income of Nashville above the eligibility limits for federal poverty grants, the city pushed the government to fund "pockets of poverty" that qualified for support.[113] Nashville enjoyed an edge over rivals because its consolidated government ensured a coherent governmental structure and monitoring system for carrying out federal programs. Nashville's planners and politicians, Horton said, "learned how to speak the language" that the federal granting agencies used, and they worked diligently to curry favor with Washington.[114]

The dependence of local government on federal assistance was in no way the invention of the new metropolitan government, but the consolidation of city and county government and the heightened faith in government-sponsored planning that accompanied the advent of Metro strengthened the federal-city partnership during the 1960s as never before. Even when the political winds shifted with the election of Richard Nixon as president in 1968, Nashville maintained strong leverage in Washington. When Mayor Briley, a Democrat, endorsed Nixon over George McGovern in 1972, Nashville's grant seekers found the doors of Republican agency chiefs opened to them again.[115]

Metropolitan government and federal funds were no panacea, however, and a long tradition of political factionalism was not about to be swept away by a new charter. During Briley's first term he enjoyed a political honeymoon and was able to implement the merger of city and county governments with unexpected ease. Ben West, who had anticipated that the first years under Metro would be fraught with political dangers that would undo his rival Briley, returned to challenge the incumbent in 1966, but Briley won handily.[116] So did thirty of the forty-one incumbent councilmen, and after 1966 they became a more independent political force, often opposed to the mayor. When the council defeated Briley's proposed budget in 1967, the lines of opposition hardened, and Briley lost much of the political mastery he had enjoyed earlier. He did nothing to help smooth relations with council members when he referred to them as "forty jealous whores" (he excused the vice-mayor) in a much-publicized speech following the 1967 budget debacle. Nor did his repeated attempts to reduce the size of the council improve matters. Briley's battle with alcoholism also interfered with his capability as mayor, beginning in his second term and on occasion quite seriously in his third term. The mayor also alienated many fellow Democrats by his conservative positions and by his defection in the presidential election of 1972. Earlier, during his 1971 reelection campaign against antibusing candidate Casey Jenkins, Briley eked out a victory in a runoff by shifting to the right, denouncing busing, and complaining that it was a federal mandate he was forced to obey.[117]

When Briley retired in 1975 at the end of his third term, Richard Fulton returned from fourteen years in Washington to run for mayor with Briley's blessings. Fulton, born in East Nashville in 1927, had been part of the generation who came of age politically in the 1950s, eager to move the city and the South forward. Fulton was a navy veteran who had attended the University of Tennessee in Knoxville and gone into partnership with his older brother, Lyle, in a small variety store in East Nashville. Lyle, a popular, young politician on the rise, won the Democratic nomination in the state senatorial primary in 1954, but he died of cancer before the general election. Governor Frank Clement, Mayor Ben West, and others urged Dick Fulton to run in his brother's place. Fulton won the general election, but at age twenty-seven he was too young to be seated. Full of ambition, he ran for U.S. Congress two years later and again in 1960 but lost both times. In 1962, in a wave of support for John F. Kennedy and a young generation of Democrats, Fulton defeated incumbent J. Carlton Loser in a tough election for Nashville's

Figure 66. Congressman Richard Fulton visiting the slums of Capitol Hill during a conference on housing in November, 1967. David K. Wilson (*left*), president of the Chamber of Commerce; Daniel Grant, a Vanderbilt political science professor; and Inman Otey (*right background*), a civil rights activist, are also shown. *Tennessean* Library.

congressional seat.[118] In Washington, Fulton immediately joined the liberal Democratic coalition that formed behind presidents Kennedy and Johnson. He voted for civil rights legislation that was controversial among white southerners and was an active supporter of Johnson's Great Society programs. The benefits these programs brought to Nashville helped offset concerns about his liberal record, and Fulton built a loyal constituency that reelected him time and again, even when the Republican tide came in with Nixon in 1968 and 1972. He could have continued in Washington but stepped down in the middle of his seventh term to return to Nashville.[119]

Traditionally, politicians have sought local and state offices as progressive stepping-stones leading away from city politics. For the first time in the city's history a seasoned politician came in the opposite direction—from Washington to the mayor's office. Given the growing importance of the federal-city partnership, Fulton's knowledge of Washington would prove a valuable asset. Some suspected that the new mayor wanted to use his office only as a step to the governor's mansion. After his bid for the gubernatorial nomination failed against Jake Butcher in 1978, Fulton ran successfully against Dan Powers for a second term as mayor, and he settled into the job with new conviction.[120]

Fulton's experience in drawing federal funds to Nashville was tested in the more austere climate of the Ford, Carter, and Reagan presidencies. But Nashville's combination of consolidated government, academic and medical facilities, and the momentum of past experience in federal grantsmanship continued to draw federal funds to the city. In 1978 alone, the total federal outlays that went to the city, universities, hospitals, and other area programs and agencies amounted to more than $927 million.[121] Fulton managed to continue the expansion of the city's water, sewer, and fire services to the suburbs. He redirected Briley's program of downtown revitalization toward the neglected retail districts along Church Street and Lower Broad, and the warehouse district along Second Avenue. The decline of the retail shopping district downtown had accelerated with the opening of new suburban shopping malls in the 1950s. Fulton transformed Church Street with new sidewalks, a serpentine streetway, brick pavement, modern lighting, and planters that enlivened the area and inspired many retailers to stay downtown. The mayor's wife, Sandra Fulton, made the beautification of the waterfront a pet project, and the first stage of a Riverfront Park at the foot of Lower Broad opened in the summer of 1983. Fulton also pushed hard for a downtown convention center adjacent to the venerable Ryman Auditorium at Sixth and Broad. Together with the Riverfront Park and the rehabilitation of the warehouse district on Second Avenue, the convention center aimed at stimulating a revival of the long-neglected strip of historic commercial architecture along Lower Broad. The massive glass-and-steel skyscrapers that the banks, insurance companies, and state government had erected under urban renewal were now balanced by a concern for refurbishing the older parts of downtown, where buildings were rehabilitated and occupied by small firms beginning in the late 1970s (see chapter nine).

Fulton served as president of the National Conference of Mayors in 1982 and brought national visibility to him and to the city he represented. The mayor's election to a third term in 1983 carried on a tradition of continuity and strong executive leadership that the city had enjoyed since the day Hilary Howse returned to power in 1923. In the intervening sixty years Nashville had been served by only five mayors, all of whom served at least three terms.

Mayors Briley and Fulton, and the professional planners and city officials who served with them, may not have delivered Nashville into the metropolitan utopia that some reformers had envisioned before 1963. But the arrival of metropolitan government obliterated the demoralizing quagmire of factionalism and petty politics that seemed to obstruct any progress toward reform. Metro's triumph instilled in citizens a new confidence that they could plan the future.

INTEGRATING THE PEOPLE

As Nashville politicians and citizens were struggling to integrate city and county governments to promote what they envisioned as a more rational, progressive *political* community, black leaders and students, in league with white liberals and moderates, were breaking apart the walls that had separated the races to realize their vision of a more rational, humane *social* community. If local politics inspired metropolitan integration, it was national events that forced desegregation of the races. The growing political prowess of blacks within the Democratic New Deal coalition, the struggle against fascist racism in World War II, and America's world role as defender of the free world against Communism in the 1950s — all combined to make Jim Crow an unwelcome embarrassment for enlightened whites and an intolerable insult for a new generation of blacks who came of age in postwar America. The prosperity that descended on the South after the war gave blacks new economic leverage, especially among the downtown merchants whose white customers were flocking to suburban shopping malls. As racial tensions flared, hard-headed business leaders also became eager to avoid unfavorable publicity, which would only discourage the flow of industry and capital into the region.

The forces of change in race relations moved like waves, first across the South, then across the rest of the nation before the 1960s were over. The response of local citizens varied with the quality of leadership, the character of the local economy, and the historical traditions that characterized each community within the South. In this respect Nashville was far more than just a passive recipient of national trends. It became a testing ground for the civil rights movement, a place where the enemies and the defenders of Jim Crow fell short of complete victory but where the community found a middle path. Nashville's historic role as a border city proved important. Just as Nashville had stood on the northern edge of the Confederacy, was the first city to fall to the federal invasion, and became a center for education and economic change after the war, so Nashville became an important force in what became known as the Second Reconstruction.

"Something happened in Nashville that did not happen any other place in America," recalled John Lewis, a veteran of the civil rights movement, on the twenty-fifth anniversary of the Nashville sit-ins. Those sit-in protests began in Greensboro, North Carolina, one of his fellow activists, Reverend C. Tindell Vivian, added, "but the *movement* began here in Nashville." That movement was a planned, sustained, highly organized campaign to change social relations through non-violent protest. Whether or not that movement actually began in Nashville, this was the first major city in the South to experience widespread desegregation of public facilities. Out of the Nashville movement came a cadre of skilled leaders for the civil rights struggle. Had non-violent protest led to racial strife and bloodshed in Nashville the history of the South might have been very different. As it was, "the Nashville way" proved that desegregation could take place peacefully and that blacks could move the world once they decided to stop cooperating with a system designed to oppress them. "We were not the light," Reverend Vivian recalled, "but we were witness to the light."[1]

If all its citizens had been willing to accept the new racial order, the Nashville story would hold little regional or national significance. There were many who fought the tide of desegregation, some out of mean-spirited bigotry, others out of a historically rooted resentment toward federal intervention in southern affairs. Some fought the Second Reconstruction in the courts, others in grass-roots citizens' organizations, and still others with epithets, spit, rocks, anonymous telephone threats, and dynamite in the dark of night. The violence of white resistance in Nashville paled in comparison with that in Little Rock, Birmingham, Selma, and other parts of the Deep South, but it was real enough.

Whatever one makes of white resistance in Nashville, however, the overwhelming fact was that it failed. Segregationists failed to mobilize a massive resistance movement of the kind that flourished in Virginia. The protests and bombings by white racists failed to ignite a sustained campaign of violence against blacks or integrationists. When the smoke cleared from the dynamite blasts and the jeers at the lunch counters died down, it was apparent that Nashville was simply not receptive to the kind of race-baiting and hatred that erupted elsewhere in the South — and soon enough in the North.

One of the least tangible forces for moderation, but an immeasurably important one, was Nashville's historical self-image as a refined, progressive New South city, a regional center of education and religion

—the Athens of the South. If Atlanta was the city "too busy to hate," Nashville might claim it was "too genteel to hate." Few were more aware of the city's traditions of tolerance than segregationists frustrated by their failures in Nashville. One denounced Nashville as "the very citadel of carpetbag liberalism." Another argued that "more leftwing and integration propaganda emanates from this city than any other city in the South." "Nashville," one despondent segregationist summarized, "is the worst city in the world."[2]

Beneath the image were conditions that allowed a more amiable adjustment of race relations in Nashville. Local black leadership was strong. When the civil rights struggle began, black Nashville had a cadre of articulate and experienced leaders—lawyers, clergy, and educators—ready to help steer their people through dangerous times.[3] Even when younger college students, often coming from outside the community, took over the movement with more militant tactics of sit-ins, boycotts, and pickets, representatives of the local black establishment, notably lawyer Z. Alexander Looby and clergyman Kelly Miller Smith, maintained important influence.

Among Nashville's several black colleges and religious institutions, Fisk University played a special role in national as well as local spheres as a forum for discussion and criticism between the races. Since 1944, when Charles S. Johnson began the Fisk Race Relations Institute, the annual conferences came to serve as an important occasion to inventory both progress and setbacks in the changing order of southern race relations.[4] Fisk attracted a nationally respected biracial faculty who provided an important voice for the cause of interracial reconciliation. Since the 1920s Fisk's strong academic reputation had attracted bright young students from the North as well as all parts of the South. Meharry Medical College, American Baptist Theological Seminary, and Tennessee Agricultural and Industrial State College (later TSU) also attracted to Nashville a large group of students from across the South and from the North. Northern blacks especially brought to Nashville a sense of irreverence for the established customs of racial accommodation by which their elders in Nashville's black community had lived for generations. But in Nashville, unlike some other cities, members of the established black community stood behind the students, most of whom were not from the community. Even as the movement turned more militant in the late 1960s, there was no open breach between the young activists and the Nashville black community.[5]

In the political arena too, black Nashville had long enjoyed a certain leverage within the Howse machine (1900–15, 1923–38) and later within Ben West's coalition (1952–63). Howse's black followers received favors, but blacks exacted more substantial concessions from the West regime in exchange for their political support. The political power of blacks enlarged in these years in part because their numbers grew within restricted city boundaries while whites moved to the suburban fringe. In 1940 blacks constituted 28 percent of the city's population; by 1960 they claimed 43 percent (see appendix A).

Voting power also grew as restrictions on suffrage were repealed and white politicians began cultivating black support. The *Tennessean*, under publisher Silliman Evans, Sr., and editor Jennings Perry, led a crusade against the poll tax, beginning in 1938. This tax, introduced back in 1890 to reduce black Republican strength, acted as a double-edged sword. It discouraged voting, particularly among the poor, whether black or white, and drove election turnouts below 30 percent of voting-age citizens by the 1940s. At the same time, the poll tax also gave political machines, like Crump's in Memphis and Howse's in Nashville, the power to control votes by paying the poll tax for their supporters. As the crusade against Crump and the poll tax gained ground in the 1940s, black voters in Nashville and across Tennessee organized registration drives and began to assert their political power. In 1947 Nashville blacks organized the "Solid Bloc" to mobilize the dormant political power of blacks in the community. The drive to arouse black voters continued in the City-County Democratic Civic League in the elections of 1948 and 1950.[6] Though it was not until 1951 that the Tennessee state poll tax was rendered ineffective and not until 1953 that it was officially repealed, Davidson County no longer required voters to match the state's one-dollar poll tax as of 1941.[7] In city elections the poll tax requirement was dropped for the special election in 1938 and in the elections of 1939 and 1943. It was reintroduced in the charter election of 1947 but no longer in force after that election. Davidson County passed a permanent registration law in 1945 that allowed voters to register at any time. Voting machines were gradually introduced to reduce the chances of election fraud. New laws restricted campaign activities in and around polling places. Finally, a series of registration drives slowly mobilized Nashville voters during the 1940s. The numbers of registered voters in the county climbed rapidly, from a little over 45,000 in 1939 to nearly 79,000 in 1948 and almost 149,000 four years later. Voter turnouts in city elections also rose slowly, from over 18,000 in 1943 to over 32,000 in 1955. Much of this voter mobilization was concentrated in the newly awakened black wards. In the Fifth Ward of North Nashville, for example, registration jumped from under 7,000 in October 1948 to over 16,000 four years later.[8]

In Nashville the clearest sign of the black political awakening was the city election of 1951, when two blacks, Z. Alexander Looby and Robert Lillard, both won seats on the City Council.[9] Not since 1911, when the Howse machine helped elect Solomon Parker Harris to the council, had blacks been elected to that body.[10] The principal reason for this breakthrough, in addition to the sheer growth in black voting strength, was the 1949 charter amendment that allowed the election of councilmen by the voters in each of twenty-one single-member coun-

Figure 67. A banner across Church Street in 1942 urges citizens to "Pay Your Poll Tax Now." "In dictator nations you vote Ja, Si, or else. In America yes or no as you choose." *Tennessean* Library.

Figure 68. The poll tax and registration laws were an obstacle to black voters in the city election of 1947. Here, District Attorney J. Carlton Loser (*standing, with glasses*), an ally of mayoral candidate Weldon White, challenges the eligibility of a black woman, as a poll watcher for Ben West, candidate for vice-mayor on Thomas Cummings's ticket, looks on. *Tennessean* Library.

Figure 69. The City-County Democratic Civic League led the drive to register black voters in behalf of Governor Gordon Browning and the City-County legislative candidates in 1950. *From left:* William Powell, Willie Mai Davis, James Archie (*standing*), Portice Paytes, Mildred Keeble (*standing*), Maxine Gilliam, Mrs. Tommie Williams, Irma Leftwich, Nathan Paytes (*standing*), Risie Lee Tease, Helen Alexander, Sallie Welch, Miss Theodore Ford. *Tennessean* Library.

cilmanic districts. Now, black majorities within certain districts could elect their own representatives rather than be swallowed up in the white majority that prevailed in each of the seven large wards. It was Ben West, as senator from Davidson County, who pushed through the private legislative act amending the city charter. Black voters, in return, were essential to West's narrow victory in the mayoral election of 1951.[11] Lillard and Looby were far more than token concessions to black political power. Both became forces to be reckoned with in local politics, and Looby especially commanded great respect among whites as well as blacks.

Looby had come to the United States from the British West Indies in 1914, as a boy of fifteen. He was graduated from Howard University in 1922, studied law at Columbia University and New York University, and came to teach economic law at Fisk in 1926. Looby was admitted to the bar in 1929 and began a promising legal career. Most black lawyers, he later recalled, were shuffling Uncle-Tom types who sprinkled their addresses to white judges and lawyers with "Yassuh's." Looby spoke the King's English with genuine eloquence, and his background in the West Indies and New York did not prepare him for any self-effacing pose of deference toward whites. One day in a Memphis juvenile court Looby sat in the front row. When a white man tapped him on the shoulder and told him that "niggers sit in back," Looby cooly answered, "Let them sit there then."[12] It was in 1946, after the race riots in Columbia, Tennessee, that Looby, with Thurgood Marshall, of the NAACP, won national attention as the defenders of twenty-five blacks who were brought to trial for attempted murder. The two attorneys won acquittal for all defendants, and Looby became known as Mr. Civil Rights. After his 1951 city election victory Looby was a major figure in the local political scene. He served on both charter commissions and was a crucial element to the success of metropolitan consolidation.

Ben West came to power as mayor in 1951, the same year Looby and Lillard came to the council. He had the support of black Nashville behind him. As vice-mayor under Cummings, West had addressed the Fisk Race Relations Institute in the summer of 1949, a risky but politically adroit gesture on West's part. There he urged blacks to become more active in politics and he pointed to the gains they had already made.[13] He also took credit for the charter amendment of 1949 that opened the City Council to blacks. As mayor he made a number of concessions to his black supporters. During the 1950s West saw that more blacks were hired by the police and fire departments and that the restaurant at the Municipal Airport and the city golf courses were integrated. West appointed Coyness Ennix, a black lawyer, to the Board of Education and helped end Jim Crow restrictions on the city bus system. These moves were forced by federal court mandates, but West turned these to political advantage.[14]

Nashville's passage through the rough waters of desegregation was aided by strong leadership from whites at the national, state, and local levels. With the demise of the Shelby County Crump machine in the late 1940s, Senators Estes Kefauver and Albert Gore, Representative Percy Priest, along with Governors Gordon Browning and Frank G. Clement, emerged as representatives of a new breed of liberal or moderate southern politician. Though often cautious about endorsing integration, these were leaders who rejected entirely the kind of racist appeals that men like George Wallace in Alabama, Orville Faubus in Arkansas, or Ross Barnett in Mississippi exploited. In 1954 Kefauver, Gore, and Priest refused to sign the Southern Manifesto, which pledged to fight for segregation.[15] Nor did racial demagoguery ever take firm hold in local politics. Ben West was elected mayor in 1951, 1955, and 1959 with considerable support from the politically awakened black voters of Nashville. West's close alliance with Nashville blacks might have become a target for segregationist attacks, but no viable candidate successfully exploited white racial fears against him to advance a political career.[16]

The logical vehicle for such a campaign would have been the *Banner*, which reacted vociferously to desegregation. Publisher James G. Stahlman's scathing editorials and cartoonist James Knox's acerbic pen provided strong opposition to the desegregation movement, to be sure. But Stahlman and the *Banner* had been supporters of Mayor West and remained loyal to him despite the obvious conflict over the race question. It was the rival *Tennessean*, under the leadership of Silliman Evans, Jr., from 1955 until his death in 1961, that opposed West. But the *Tennessean* remained a steadfast, if cautious, defender of desegregation. Evans was considered less liberal than both his father and the *Tennessean*'s editor, Coleman Harwell. But when Evans died in 1961, his younger brother, Amon Carter Evans, took over as publisher and brought in a new editor, John Siegenthaler, who took a liberal stance on civil rights. Siegenthaler had worked for Attorney General Robert Kennedy and had suffered a fractured skull at the hands of white antagonists during the summer of 1961 when he served as federal mediator during the Freedom Riders' bus trips into Alabama. The antagonism between the two newspapers, and the cross-alliance between Mayor West and the conservative *Banner*, helped to militate against a closed-minded posture of defiance in Nashville and against the kind of political opportunists who in other parts of the South rode to power on segregationist sentiment.[17]

There were other general conditions and individual leaders that allowed Nashville to face the racial crisis of the 1950s and 1960s with a fair chance of success. But to point out these ameliorating factors tells little about the humiliation and injustice of the everyday experience of segregation, which brought on the crisis in the first place. By the 1950s the races in Nashville had never been more segregated. Neighborhood racial patterns were now shaped by public housing, urban renewal, city zoning policies, and by an unwritten code among the city's realtors and home mortgage lenders. As whites moved to the suburban fringe, there was an increasing tendency toward the residential concentration of blacks inside the city.

The growing percentage of blacks within the city between 1940 (28 percent) and 1960 (43 percent) was due in part to a rapid exodus of whites to the suburbs. In 1940, 120,084 whites lived within the city's boundaries; by 1960 that number had declined to 98,085. At the same time the number of whites in the county outside the city limits grew from 80,386 to 224,826, and they made up no less than 98 percent of the county population outside Nashville (see appendix A). Within the city, racial boundaries became at once more sharply defined and more volatile as black residential frontiers intruded into white neighborhoods. In 1940 a virtually solid black area north of Charlotte Avenue stretched from the black business district on Capitol Hill westward to the Tennessee A&I campus, with Jefferson Street as its main artery. In South Nashville, the neighborhoods along Eighth and Twelfth avenues and the old Trimble Bottom district around Lafayette and Fourth Avenue formed two other generally poorer black neighborhoods. In Northeast Nashville another black district sprawled north from the old Crappy Shoot quarters above Main Street near the river.[18] New public housing projects and urban renewal plans reinforced these patterns of racial concentration. However, by 1960 these neighborhoods, especially North Nashville, had expanded tremendously to accommodate the enlarged black population.[19] This meant blacks' "invading" white neighborhoods or taking over formerly mixed neighborhoods. Fearing a loss of property values or the less tangible uncertainties of racial mixing, whites withdrew as blacks advanced. The proportion of Nashville whites living in census tracts with a designated number of blacks dropped from over half in 1940 to less than a third in 1960.[20]

It would be misleading to suggest that residential segregation was simply a measure of black degradation. On the contrary, the expansion of black neighborhoods and the white exodus that accelerated that expansion were accompanied by a growing percentage of black homeownership, which rose from less than one-quarter in 1940 to over one-third by 1960.[21] In the Bordeaux area, north of the Cumberland River, a wealthy neighborhood of black professionals came to be known as the Gold Coast. This was but one measure of a general trend of gradual upward mobility among blacks in the relatively prosperous economic environment of postwar Nashville.[22] At the same time those whites left behind in the central city were declining in status as a group during the 1950s.[23]

The job market was no less segregated, with blacks dominating the

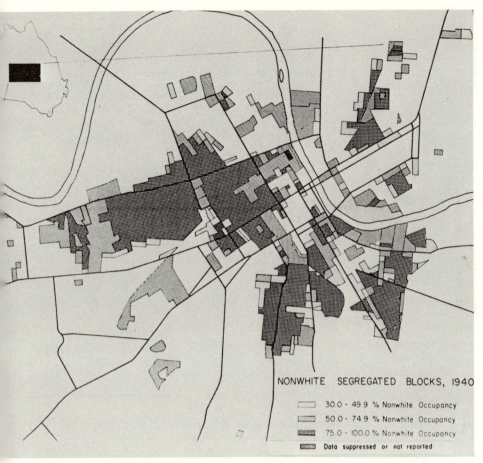

Figure 70. Map: Nashville Residential Segregation, 1940. The area north of Charlotte Avenue was now predominantly black, and smaller concentrations of blacks were evident in areas of South and East Nashville. Metropolitan Planning Commission, *A Study of Nonwhite Residential Distribution in Nashville, Tennessee in 1940, 1950, 1960, and 1970* (Nashville, 1975).

Figure 71. Black poverty persisted amid the prosperity reflected in Nashville's imposing skyline in 1962. *Tennessean* Library.

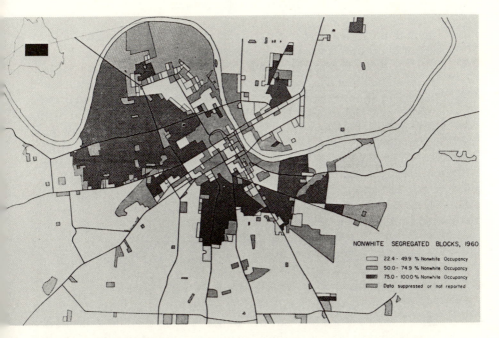

Figure 72. Map: Nashville Residential Segregation, 1960. *A Study of Nonwhite Residential Distribution in Nashville, Tennessee in 1940, 1950, 1960, and 1970* (Nashville, 1975).

menial, unskilled, and low-wage occupations. Vivian Henderson, professor of economics at Fisk, surveyed the job prospects of black Nashville in 1960. Though he found a relatively prosperous class of black professionals and white-collar workers, the rest were stuck in unskilled work and shut off from any genuine upward mobility. Though some 12,000 new industrial jobs had been created recently by such plants as Ford Glass Company and Gates Rubber, fewer than 4 percent of them went to blacks. In the retail and wholesale sector there were "virtually no Negro salesmen." The same pattern held true in public utilities, government employment, and telecommunications. The banks, insurance companies, and department stores downtown hired blacks only as porters and janitors, even though they welcomed them as customers. Nashville's black businessmen and professionals, whose offices were clustered along Charlotte Avenue downtown, before urban renewal displaced them, catered to a segregated clientele. The limited opportunities for black professionals and businessmen meant that many had to leave Nashville, usually for the North.[24]

Blacks were excluded from most white-owned restaurants and taverns. Except for one black-owned movie theater, the Bijou, blacks had to enter movie houses by the alley entrance and sit in a Jim Crow balcony. They were welcome to buy clothing and furnishings in downtown department stores but were not allowed to sit at the lunch counters. City-owned parks, swimming pools, and golf courses excluded black citizens, and blacks were assigned their own Jim Crow parks well within established black neighborhoods.[25]

Everywhere that blacks were allowed access to public facilities, they were constantly reminded of the inferior status that segregation was designed to impress upon them. On city buses they were required to sit in the back seats. At Union Station they sat in separate waiting rooms, used separate toilets, and boarded separate railroad cars. In public places, like Ryman Auditorium, they sat in a special Jim Crow section on the side of the balcony. Even in the city hall and county courthouse they were required to use separate bathroom facilities in the basement. Blacks who violated the etiquette of racial segregation were subject to a ready stream of intimidating abuse, even when they were not subject to legal prosecution. In turn, well-intentioned whites who betrayed the code by inviting blacks to social affairs or otherwise treating them as equals were subject to harsh forms of censure.[26]

DESEGREGATING THE SCHOOLS

It was segregation in the public schools that became the first and most critical issue in the civil rights movement. Separate schools had traditionally ensured that blacks would receive a second-rate education with underpaid black teachers, overcrowded substandard school buildings, and lax academic standards perpetuated by an educational system designed to prepare most black children for their assigned roles as servants and menial workers. The desegregation of the schools was more than a point of racial honor for blacks; it was the door to opportunity that had to be opened for the advancement of the race.

The story of Nashville's school desegregation battle can only be sketched here.[27] In May 1954 the U.S. Supreme Court ruled in *Brown vs. Board of Education of Topeka Kansas* that "separate educational facilities are inherently unequal" and therefore are a violation of rights guaranteed under the Fourteenth Amendment. In May 1955 the Court issued an ambiguous order that all public schools must proceed toward desegregation "with all deliberate speed." The Nashville Board of Education, like most institutions faced with major turns in policy, appointed a committee to study the issue and muddled along with the existing segregated system. But in September 1955 an East Nashville black youth, Robert Kelley, faced the prospect of commuting across the river to Pearl High School, though he lived only a few blocks from the all-white East High School. His father, Alfred Z. Kelley, a barber with a keen sense of the social justice promised in the *Brown* decision (and an occupation that was independent of white patronage), filed a class action suit in behalf of Nashville black school children. *Robert W. Kelley, et al. vs. Board of Education of Nashville* demanded open admission to the city's public schools without regard to race. Representing the plaintiffs were Z. Alexander Looby and his young law partner, Avon Williams, Jr. Another year passed before federal district judge William E. Miller heard the case and ordered the Board of Education to prepare a plan for desegregation no later than January 1957.

The Board of Education now began to deliberate in earnest, and what evolved came to be known as the Nashville Plan. This plan, as it eventually took form, allowed one grade per year to be desegregated, beginning with the first grade in September 1957. Linked to this gradualist program was a policy permitting transfer of students upon written request from parents whenever a white or black student was zoned to a school in which a different race predominated. A third component of the board's plan was a radical gerrymandering of the school zones, which left only 115 of the 1,400 Negro first-graders eligible to enter formerly all-white schools in the fall of 1957. The parents of ninety-six of these black school children, responding to anonymous telephone threats and a long history of intimidation, took advantage of the transfer provision to pull their children out of their assigned schools before the term began. Nineteen black children and their parents were now left with the frightening challenge of integrating Nashville's public schools in the coming September.[28]

Figure 73. Z. Alexander Looby (right) and his law partner, Avon Williams, Jr., reviewing the federal hearings on desegregation of Nashville public schools in 1958. *Tennessean* Library.

Critics of the Nashville Plan had every right to denounce the evasive tactics of the city's officials, which were clearly designed to avoid substantial integration without technically defying the Supreme Court ruling. The Nashville Plan undeniably was a deliberate program of gradual and token desegregation formulated by people who had no enthusiasm for integration. But much like Lincoln's famous Emancipation Proclamation, which, practically speaking, freed no slaves, the Nashville Plan was important not for the numbers it integrated but for the principles it implicitly endorsed. The Court had spoken, segregation must end, and Nashville's leaders chose a course of compliance. That course was agonizingly slow, piecemeal, and often insincere, in the eyes of integrationists, but it was a fundamentally different course from the bold defiance of other parts of the South where less responsible leaders led citizens into a futile battle against the inevitable.

The gradual and limited features of the Nashville Plan did little to dissuade those who opposed any degree of court interference. In June 1955 a group of Vanderbilt professors and downtown businessmen organized the Tennessee Federation for Constitutional Government to challenge the legal and moral justifications for federal intervention in southern race relations. It was led by Donald Davidson, professor of English at Vanderbilt. Davidson remained a thoroughly unreconstructed former member of the Fugitives and Agrarians who had opposed industrialization, TVA, and—according to one admiring observer—"the whole tendency of things in this country since 1865." The federation waged an above-board, responsible campaign of lobbying, legal challenges, and public education in defense of states' rights. It was an approach that appealed primarily to a handful of educated, middle-class segregationists in Nashville. This group organized more than a dozen other chapters, mostly in West Tennessee, but remained weak in its grass-roots organization. The federation had no taste for the violence and race hatred promoted by the Ku Klux Klan and other segregationists groups, and it served as a counterweight to the fanaticism of those organizations.[29]

While the federation's lawyer, Nashville attorney Sims Crownover, challenged the constitutional premises of desegregation, other whites organized the Parents School Preference Committee in the summer of 1957. They passed around petitions and otherwise exerted enormous pressure on the Board of Education to abandon the desegregation plan and to set up a three-school system providing the choice of segregated white and black schools or an integrated school. This alternative was also enacted as law by the state legislature. When federal judge Miller declared this ploy unconstitutional, and when other legal pleas failed, the only recourse for the diehard segregationist was extralegal protest, school boycott, or violence in the streets.

There were always a number of whites in Nashville who, out of prejudice or fear, responded to the call of racial animosity. But their hostility had to be aroused and focused by an effective popular leader, and none had emerged within Nashville. Not only was it an outsider who provided this leadership but (as the local press never tired of pointing out to a nation standing in judgment of Nashville) he was also a northerner. Frederick John Kasper, a native of Camden, New Jersey, was educated at Columbia University in New York City and became a devotee of the doctrines of Ezra Pound, the famous poet who had embraced fascism late in life. Pound befriended Kasper, who visited him in a mental hospital in Washington, D.C., where the poet had been imprisoned. Kasper ran a bookstore specializing in anti-Semitic literature in Greenwich Village and later in the Georgetown section of Washington, D.C. When the desegregation issue erupted, Kasper shifted his interests and organized the Seaboard White Citizens' Council and, later, a similar council in Tennessee. Kasper defended his movement as the white counterpart to the NAACP, the civil rights group that had been so instrumental in the legal battle for desegregation. He roved about the South, organizing White Citizens' Councils, staging rallies, handing out literature, and arousing discontented whites to confront the integrationists with violence if necessary. Whereas other segregationists generally preferred to argue their case in terms of states' rights, Kasper minced no words defending white supremacy and attacking the "race mongrelizers."

Kasper arrived in Nashville in June 1957 after stirring up a violent confrontation in Clinton, Tennessee, an affray that ended only when National Guard troops and tanks arrived to quell the disorder in the little town. In Nashville, Kasper joined the Reverend Fred Stroud, a native of Illinois who had been minister at the Second Presbyterian Church in Nashville before being dismissed in 1936. Stroud now ran his own "Bible Presbyterian Church." Stroud and John McCurrio, a native of Ohio and self-styled evangelist who lived without employment in Nashville, lent a tone of Christian zeal to the white segregationist stand.[30] Kasper and Stroud shrewdly posed as defenders of the peace and protectors of the family. It was the integrationists, they argued, who were pushing the decent citizens of white Nashville to defend their way of life with violence. "Keep the niggers out of white schools.... Save Your Kids!" One handbill pleaded, "Prevent Race Riots, Murder, Dynamiting, and Hanging."[31]

The Ku Klux Klan, dormant since the 1920s when it had swept through the South and other parts of America as a nativist and antiblack movement, revived for a third time in the 1950s to oppose school desegregation.[32] The Klan sent representatives to Nashville to stir white resistance. They drove about in menacing cars plastered with Klan stickers. Apparently jealous of Kasper, a northern interloper on southern turf, the Klan disavowed him, banished him from their meetings, and urged him to "go back to New Jersey."[33] Davidson's Federation for Constitutional Government disapproved of Kasper and the Klan alike, and asked federation sympathizers to follow peaceful means of legislative reform and legal appeal. The division among segregationists contributed to their ineffectiveness in Nashville. The federation won a small following and was able to get some 6,000 signatures on its petition to the Nashville Board of Education. But the rallies sponsored by Kasper and the Klan were notable for their poor turnouts. Mayor Ben West also helped dampen enthusiasm by promising to uphold the Supreme Court ruling and by disallowing a Kasper rally in Centennial Park in early August 1957.[34] The segregationists did not find the necessary support to sustain their movement, either from local politicians or grass-roots organizations.

The frustrations of militant segregationists in building support in Nashville did not prohibit a few from spreading fear among the black community. Kasper promised that each family of the black children registered to enter white schools would be "visited" by one of his band. Some parents received terrifying telephone threats: "We'll beat your little girl to death and string her up by her toes. Then we'll burn your home."[35] The parents of twelve of the nineteen black students registered to attend white schools bravely showed up at six elementary schools on the morning of September 9 with their first-graders. Police were there to escort the black students past small but mean crowds of jeering white parents and teenagers who shouted racial epithets and threatened violence against the six-year-old children who were entering the white schools. Kasper, Stroud, and Klan members showed up to encourage the segregationists and to urge white parents to boycott the integrated schools. A crowd of whites hurled sticks and stones at some black parents. One furious black mother faced them boldly, whipped out a paring knife, and challenged her startled attackers to "come and jump me now."[36] But white segregationists preferred to carry out their violence in less direct confrontations.

That evening a large crowd of angry whites, estimated at five hundred people, armed with bricks and bottles, converged on Fehr School, one of the integrated elementary schools in the Kalb Hollow neighborhood of North Nashville. A quick show of force by police dispersed the crowd without further incident. Then, shortly after midnight an enormous explosion roared across the city. An entire wing of Hattie Cotton School, one of the integrated schools in East Nashville, was demolished by a dynamite blast. A car, plastered with Klan stickers and filled with weapons and wire matching that used to detonate the bomb, was found near the scene.[37]

The air of calm that had prevailed among city officials up to that point was suddenly shattered, and the city was "seized by a degree of panic." School attendance dropped sharply the following morning. Mayor

Figure 74. Caldwell School on September 9, 1957. Alfred Z. Kelley, the plaintiff in the desegregation suit, is seen wearing a hat *(left)*. *Tennessean* Library.

Figure 75. Whites look on as blacks enter a formerly all-white school September 9, 1957. The sign reads "Keep our White Schools White." *Tennessean* Library.

Figure 76. A young boy ponders the destruction of Hattie Cotton School, September 10, 1957, the morning after the bombing. *Tennessean* Library.

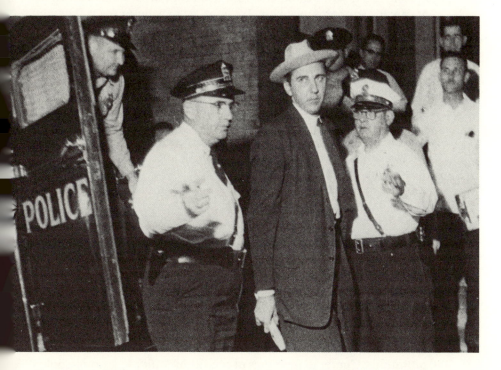

Figure 77. John Kasper under arrest, September 10, 1957. *Tennessean* Library.

West ordered a police crackdown. Barricades went up on every street surrounding the integrated schools. Thirty-nine arrests were made on Tuesday, September 10, including thirteen blacks, several of whom were caught carrying shotguns and pistols. John Kasper was arrested by city police, thrown in jail, and required to put up $2,000 as bond, and then arrested and jailed again for illegal parking outside the courthouse. He paid another $500 bond on this charge and walked free, only to be awakened twelve hours later and arrested by a county constable on a charge of inciting to riot. Kasper stayed in the county jail, unable to raise more bail money among supporters in Nashville.[38] On September 16, Judge Miller issued an injunction forbidding Kasper, Stroud, and eight other militant segregationists from interfering in any way with the Nashville schools. Two days later Kasper met bail and left Nashville. He returned in August 1958 to lead another protest against Nashville's school desegregation, but a rally held outside the city limits attracted only thirty adults, and Kasper left Nashville, discouraged by the poor showing. He returned in November to stand trial and was sentenced to six months in the fully integrated county workhouse and a $500 fine.[39] At one of the hearings city judge Andrew Doyle spoke for many Nashvillians when he told Kasper, "If any blood is shed on the streets of Nashville it will be you and your kind that are responsible. We do not care for your presence here. We hope we may never see you or your likes again."[40]

Kasper and the violent opponents of desegregation had performed an unexpected service for the cause of integration. They pushed the community to the brink of chaos, and their use of violence helped galvanize the hitherto soft, equivocal support for school desegregation into a strong defense of Nashville's integrity as a community. Whatever the Board of Education, mayor, police, and citizens at large felt about integration per se, the issue now had become one of law and order. Nashville was not going to be another Clinton, Tennessee, with army tanks and soldiers necessary to keep the peace. There were scattered incidents of harassment in the days that followed the Hattie Cotton bombing, but calm and public order were the rule.

Violence found another victim in March 1958 when a second dynamite explosion shook the Jewish Community Center on West End Avenue. Following the blast a telephone threat to Rabbi William Silverman warned that other Jewish institutions would be bombed, along with any other "nigger-loving place or nigger-loving person in Nashville." Rabbi Silverman and other Nashville Jews had befriended the black community and openly supported integration. As victims of racial arrogance themselves, many Jews felt that they had no moral choice but to defend the black civil rights movement. They opened the Jewish Community Center to meetings of the Community Relations Conference, a liberal interracial group devoted to improving conditions for blacks. The Reverend Will Campbell, who came to Nashville in 1956 as southern representative for the National Council of Churches, recalled that the Center and the Unitarian Church were the only places where such biracial groups could meet in Nashville at that time. Even then, participants were exposed to threats and tire slashings.[41] The link between the civil rights movement and the Jewish community, of course, played into the hands of the Ku Klux Klan and their sympathizers, who had traditionally joined Negrophobia and anti-Semitism. The anonymous telephone threat also promised to "shoot down Judge Miller in cold blood," making it clear that the attack was also against school desegregation.[42] But this bombing was, in retrospect, the last desperate act of violence against school desegregation; it was a measure of the frustration that segregationists met in their attempts to build a grass-roots resistance movement in Nashville.

The low school attendance of September 1957, initially attributed to a white segregationist boycott, returned to normal within a month, once the threat of violence in the schools vanished and the inevitability of integration became clear. Nine black children remained in integrated classrooms during the fall of 1957. The Board of Education submitted, and Judge Miller approved, the full "grade-a-year plan" early in 1958. But Z. Alexander Looby and Avon Williams, Jr., joined initially by NAACP lawyer Thurgood Marshall, were dissatisfied with the plan, particularly its liberal transfer provisions, and they appealed the case to the federal Sixth Circuit Court of Appeals in Cincinnati. Losing that round, they appealed to the U.S. Supreme Court in 1959 but failed to get the requisite votes for a hearing. Justice Hugo Black of Alabama defected from the liberal ranks to vote with the majority against reviewing the case. The Nashville Plan had become law and was quickly imitated by dozens of southern communities.[43]

The number of blacks in Nashville's formerly all-white schools grew from a handful in 1957 to 189 by 1960 and to 728 by 1963. This was hardly a massive or sudden integration of the races, but it was quiet testimony to the faith that black parents had in Mayor West's guarantee of their safety and to the acceptance by much of white Nashville of the new order of race relations in the schools.[44]

DESEGREGATION BEYOND THE CLASSROOM, 1960–1967

Just as school desegregation became an established fact, by about 1960, the movement suddenly broadened to become a more general civil rights protest. As the scope of this movement shifted, so did its leadership and tactics. It was increasingly a movement led by black college students, whose youth and determination drove them to use more direct means of protest and civil disobedience, much of it inspired by the example of Martin Luther King, Jr., and the teachings of Mohandas K. Gandhi, the famous Indian prophet of nonviolent social change. The NAACP, with its alliance of established black community leaders and its strategy of legal appeals, was soon overshadowed by the dramatic tactics of the student protest movement. The students enlisted in newer organizations, like the Congress of Racial Equality (CORE) and later the Student Nonviolent Coordinating Committee (SNCC). CORE established one of its first southern chapters in Nashville as early as 1956, with the help of Anna Holden, a white woman connected with Fisk.[45] But the most important organization in the events of 1960 was the Nashville Christian Leadership Conference (NCLC), which had been established in 1958 as a branch of the Southern Christian Leadership Conference (SCLC), organized by King the previous year. The new chapter found as its principal leader the Reverend Kelly Miller Smith, pastor of Nashville's black First Baptist Church. The NCLC came to provide an important bridge between a restless group of young students devoted to new techniques of Christian nonviolent protest and the older black establishment who followed the NAACP path of legal challenges to segregation or were inclined to accommodate segregation. Smith, aged thirty-nine in 1960, was himself a vital link between the two groups.[46] The NCLC met at Smith's church and at Clark Memorial Methodist Church and began to lay the groundwork for the Nashville assault on Jim Crow.

Among the young blacks who met with Smith in 1958 were James M. Lawson, Jr., John Lewis, and Diane Nash. Lawson was a young minister who had spent time in India and was steeped in the teachings of Gandhi. He came to Nashville with the Fellowship of Reconciliation, a Christian pacifist organization, and enrolled in Vanderbilt's Divinity School in 1958. Beginning in March 1958, Lawson, in cooperation with Glenn Smiley of the Fellowship of Reconciliation and CORE's Anna Holden, offered workshops in the techniques of nonviolent protest. More workshops were held in February 1959, in the basement of Kelly Miller Smith's First Baptist Church.[47] At thirty-two, Lawson had the experience that could propel him to a leadership role in the early stage of the movement. John Lewis was a student at the American Baptist Theological Seminary in Nashville. He had grown up in a small Alabama town and discovered in Nashville his "first opportunity to do something about racial injustice in the South." He came to Lawson's workshops and soon became one of the principal student leaders. Diane Nash, a student at Fisk, had grown up in the relatively open environment of Chicago. When she came to Fisk she was appalled at the degradation that Jim Crow forced on blacks in Nashville and joined Smith and the others to set things right.[48]

Early in 1959 the NCLC agreed to begin the assault by protesting whites-only lunch counters in the department stores and five-and-dime stores downtown.[49] Here were the most glaring examples of the hypocrisy of segregation, for blacks were perfectly free to spend money elsewhere in these stores. In November and December 1959 Smith, Lawson, Lewis, and other students and ministers tested the lunch counters of Harvey's and Cain-Sloan by purchasing items in the stores and then sitting down at the counters. As they expected, they were refused service, and they left. Both stores rejected efforts to negotiate.

At the same time, Lawson's workshops on nonviolent protest were resumed in preparation for the first demonstrations. Then, early the following year, outside events launched the Nashville movement ahead of schedule. On February 1, 1960, at the Woolworth's lunch counter in Greensboro, North Carolina, another group of black protesters won national attention by staging a sit-in. After being denied service they refused to leave the lunch counter. Douglas Moore, a Methodist minister involved in the North Carolina demonstrations, called his friend James Lawson on February 10 to ask for a demonstration of sympathy from the students in Tennessee.[50] Within days the Nashville sit-ins were under way. On Saturday, February 13, a blanket of snow eight inches thick covered the city. On that day about 124 students from Fisk, American Baptist Theological Seminary, and Tennessee A&I converged on the downtown. They rallied in the Arcade and then at about 12:40 p.m., toward the end of the lunch hour, in groups of two and three they entered three five-and-dime stores along Fifth Avenue: Kress's, Woolworth's, and McClellan's. They purchased items in the stores and then sat down at the lunch counters. The store owners closed the counters, and the students left after two hours of quiet protest. They were back on Thursday, February 18, now with 200 or more students, sitting in at the three lunch counters and the one at Grant's. They struck the stores at noon as a busy week-day lunch hour began. The counters closed. They came again, 350 strong, on Saturday, February 20 and sat down at the same lunch counters beginning at 11:45 p.m. Walgreen's, a new target, was struck at 1:30, and quickly brought out a prepared sign: "Closed in the Interest of Public Safety." Police cleared Walgreen's after hecklers taunted Carol Ann Anderson, a white protester attending Fisk.[51]

Similar sit-in demonstrations broke out across the South, leaving the *Banner* to denounce the "organized effort projected from outside sources."[52] On the next Saturday, February 27, 400 students resumed the sit-ins, which now spread to Cain-Sloan's lunch counter. They marched in silently under careful instructions not to respond in any way to insult or attack. When refused service they sat patiently while white onlookers harassed them. The police had refused protection of the sit-in protesters inside the stores, with the excuse that it would disrupt trade to have police enter businesses. At McClellan's, one demonstrator, Paul LaPrad, was pulled from his seat and pummeled by whites while reporters and photographers looked on. Now the police entered but only to arrest LaPrad for "disorderly conduct." At the store manager's request, police then arrested all the demonstrators and cleared the store. But as police loaded one group of protesters into the paddy wagon, other students streamed into the store to take their places. In the basement of Kelly Miller Smith's First Baptist Church hundreds of more protesters waited to be summoned by runners watching the arrests from the streets. Police asked the protesters at the counters to leave voluntarily, but they would not budge. As the afternoon wore on and the arrest toll mounted, a crowd of angry white hecklers converged on the downtown, and police withdrew, leaving the demonstrators at the mercy of their antagonists.[53] David Halberstam, a young reporter for the *Tennessean*, described the scene in Woolworth's: "For more than an hour the hate kept building up.... First it was the usual name calling, then spitting, then cuffing; now bolder punching, banging their heads against the counter, hitting them, stuffing cigarette butts down the back of their collars. The slow build-up of hate was somehow worse than the actual violence."[54]

At the end of the day, 81 demonstrators had been arrested and booked on charges of disorderly conduct, with bail set at $100. They refused to pay the bond and, in effect, continued their protest within the city jail. The black community, through Looby, offered to pay the bail, but the protesters refused again. Bail was finally reduced to $5; still they refused to pay it and stayed in jail until they were released without bail under the custody of their schools on the promise that they would return for trials the following Monday.[55] These young people had few of the constraints of jobs, family, and community ties that tempered the commitment of older blacks, and they were impatient with the tedious process of legal appeals, favored by their elders. They also brought to the movement the zeal of Christian martyrs, and all efforts to discipline them by arrest, jail, or extralegal violence simply played into the hands of protesters, whose aim was to expose to world view the hypocrisy of their oppressors.

School officials were no more successful than the police and the courts in discouraging these student activists. On the Monday following the arrests James Lawson, representing the student protesters, met with the mayor and a group of black ministers. He was quoted in the *Banner* as saying that he would continue to advise students "to violate the law" and that the law was merely a "gimmick" to oppress his race.[56] The *Banner* editorials denounced Lawson as a "ramrod of strife directed from outside" who was "out-Kaspering Kasper" and compared him with "flannel-mouth agitators" and "the paid agents of strife-breeding organizations." The editorials pressured Vanderbilt to take disciplinary action. Lawson had "forfeited his privilege to further education at Vanderbilt," a *Banner* editorial argued. "The sooner both Nashville and Vanderbilt

Figure 78. A sit-in at the Walgreen's lunch counter, February 20, 1960. *Tennessean* Library.

Figure 79. James M. Lawson, Jr., addresses a crowd at Gordon Memorial Methodist Church, March 1960, to discuss the student sit-in demonstrations with Nashville's black citizens. Kelly Miller Smith and John Lewis are to Lawson's right. *Tennessean* Library.

are rid of the presence and the baneful influence and tactics of Mr. Lawson, the better."[57] The Board of Trust's Executive Committee, which included James G. Stahlman, publisher of the *Banner*, pushed for Lawson's expulsion. Lawson was asked to withdraw voluntarily. He refused, arguing that the *Banner* had deliberately misquoted him. Chancellor Harvie Branscomb then expelled him, and won approval from the *Banner* and the Vanderbilt student newspaper.[58] But Lawson's expulsion only led to campus demonstrations, a national outpouring of support for Lawson, protest resignations from ten of the sixteen Divinity School faculty, and national embarrassment for the university because of its clumsy effort to repress Lawson and the civil rights movement.[59]

On Monday, February 29—the same day Lawson met with the mayor and the ministers—the trials of the arrested students began. A crowd of 2,000 to 3,000 sympathizers, mostly black students, gathered around the courthouse, prayed, stood vigil and sang the hymns and spirituals that would become the anthems of the southern civil rights movement. Inside, a group of twelve black lawyers defended the students, most of whom were found guilty and fined $50. They refused to pay and were sentenced to the county workhouse for thirty-three and one-third days. They again refused bail money from the nearly $50,000 that had been raised within the Nashville black community.[60] As the jail swelled with more protesters, the crowd remained outside the courthouse. On Wednesday, March 2, 350 more students staged sit-ins, this time including the lunch counters at Harvey's and the Greyhound and Trailway bus terminals. More were arrested, now on tougher charges of "conspiracy to obstruct trade and commerce." This was a state offense, intended to be more intimidating. Simultaneously, those arrested on February 27 were now rearrested in jail and charged with the same offense.[61]

Mayor West, torn between his loyal black political supporters and the rabid reaction of his sponsoring newspaper, the *Banner*, referred the problem to a biracial committee, which he appointed on Thursday, March 3, to study the issue and make recommendations. The committee arranged a temporary "truce" early in March.[62] In the meantime Greyhound Bus Company agreed to conform to anticipated federal regulations as an interstate carrier and serve blacks at the lunch counter in its terminal. Four black students tested the agreement and dined at the Greyhound terminal, but they were badly beaten afterward by whites. A stream of telephone threats came in to Greyhound officials from segregationists, and the next day two bomb detonators were found in the terminal.[63] The truce was also broken briefly when sit-ins resumed on Friday, March 25. This coincided with a visit from CBS reporters and camera crews, who were in Nashville to film a documentary on the sit-ins. Governor Buford Ellington and the *Banner* accused CBS of staging the demonstration, and the furor nearly wrecked the truce.[64]

By early April the mayor's biracial committee, chaired by Vanderbilt's popular dean of students, Madison Sarratt, issued a full report recommending partial trial integration. It was a plan reminiscent of the school preference law: three sections at the lunch counters — one for whites, another for blacks, and a third to be integrated.[65] The student protesters had no intention of accepting "token integration"; and they explained that "a restricted area involves the same stigma of which we are earnestly seeking to rid the community...."[66]

New pressures were brought to bear on downtown merchants when the Reverend Smith and Professor Vivian Henderson of Fisk organized a boycott of all downtown merchants just before Easter. This "economic withdrawal," as Henderson dubbed it, deprived store owners of untold amounts of business during an important shopping holiday.[67] Blacks, Henderson estimated, spent over $50 million a year in Nashville, and he urged them to use their economic power: "No fashions for Easter."[68] Black women mobilized the boycott in a powerful display of solidarity with the student protesters.

The sit-ins resumed after Easter on April 12, this time with pickets outside each store. Several demonstrators were beaten by whites that day, and racial tensions heightened across the city again.[69] Then at five-thirty on the morning of April 19 a bomb hurled from a passing car exploded outside Z. Alexander Looby's house, causing massive damage but somehow leaving the venerable black leader physically unscathed. That afternoon a crowd of at least three thousand marched from Fisk to the courthouse to protest the bombing and racial injustice in general. They marched in complete silence, three abreast, in a procession that stretched ten blocks and became one of the most impressive moments in the Nashville civil rights movement. "The line seems to be endless," one observer said as it proceeded up Capitol Hill.[70]

Mayor West met the protesters on the courthouse steps. He urged interracial tolerance and promised a $10,000 reward for information leading to the arrest of the Looby bomber.[71] The Reverend C. Tindell Vivian read a prepared statement condemning the mayor for having "refused to speak out" against segregation, particularly the biracial committee's proposal to continue a modified form of segregation. The mayor defended his record, but Vivian and Diane Nash pressed him hard to make a personal, moral stand on desegregation. "I appeal to all citizens to end discrimination...," West pleaded. "Then, mayor," Nash came back, "do you recommend that the lunch counters be desegregated?" "Yes," the mayor finally responded. The crowd applauded, then dispersed in an orderly, silent march that took them back to Fisk. The *Tennessean* committed the mayor irrevocably with front-page headlines "INTEGRATE COUNTERS — MAYOR."[72] This was the turning point.

The next day, April 20, 1960, Martin Luther King, Jr., came to Nashville and addressed a crowd of four thousand at Fisk University. King

Figure 80. A silent march of students and black Nashville citizens on April 19, 1960, to protest the bombing of Z. Alexander Looby's home. *Tennessean* Library.

praised the strong discipline of the Nashville movement and urged his audience to carry on the struggle.[73] Under pressure from the boycott, six stores, led by Cain-Sloan and Harvey's, relented and on May 10 allowed blacks to be served.[74] As the protesters strengthened their resolve, downtown merchants met behind the scenes to confront their dilemma. Most of the store owners were what *Time* dubbed "pocketbook integrationists."[75] They had no strong commitment to segregation, but neither did they wish to lead the process of social change. Once they understood the depth of feeling and the tenacity of the civil rights movement, most realized that there was no choice but to desegregate. "It's inevitable," Fred Harvey, Sr., instructed his store's treasurer, Greenfield Pitts, in a telegram, ". . . go ahead."[76] The disruption, the boycott, and the inability of the mayor's biracial committee to achieve compromise made it economically untenable to continue much longer without a settlement. Segregationists denounced the "profit-hungry merchants [who] capitulated to Negro 'sit-down' agitators," but most Nashville businessmen apparently felt no strong attachment to the Jim Crow customs they now rejected.[77] If segregation was necessary to conduct business with the white majority, they concurred with Jim Crow. If desegregation was necessary to resume operations—and if it could be introduced without alienating white customers—then pragmatic businessmen concurred with that also. Department store owners could defend their freedom to serve whom they pleased, but they had no moral ground on which to stand in defense of discrimination against blacks at lunch counters when blacks were accepted as customers in other parts of the store.

The people who were best at raising the moral issues of the day were often not as useful to negotiations with practical-minded men anxious to resume business downtown. Nor did skittish politicians wish to get involved in the issue any more than was necessary. Behind the scenes Greenfield Pitts, treasurer of Harvey's and head of the Chamber of Commerce Retail Merchants Division, and John Sloan, president of Cain-Sloan, worked diligently with store owners to ease Jim Crow out of downtown. Earlier, Pitts had visited Baltimore to observe the desegregation of its stores, and he knew from that experience that the world was not going to collapse with desegregation. Harvey's and Cain-Sloan also set the example by being the first to desegregate. Pitts and Sloan went from one store owner to the next, gaining momentum as they went because the merchants they visited later felt less risk in moving ahead of the pack. Once the agreements were made and the demonstrators were informed, the actual integration of the lunch counters was carefully orchestrated, with just a few blacks and whites assigned to quietly break the color barrier with no publicity.[78]

Another temporary truce went into effect in May, while Pitts and Sloan continued their negotiations, but in November 1960 sit-ins resumed against the holdouts. Resistance stiffened at stand-alone restaurants that had never had a black clientele and were afraid that integration would drive away their white customers. At the Krystal Grill demonstrators were locked inside and punished with water hoses, cleansing powder, wet brooms, and insect spray. At the Tic-Toc Restaurant blacks were driven away at rifle point. Other restaurant owners forcibly blocked demonstrators from entering.[79]

Despite these and other pockets of resistance, by the middle of 1960 the civil rights movement in Nashville seemed to have gathered an unstoppable momentum. As one downtown store and restaurant owner after another gave into the demand for integration, others saw little advantage in holding out only to lose black business and invite continued disruptions. In February 1961 the protest shifted to segregated movie theaters downtown. Large lines of blacks formed outside the ticket booths in what came to be called stand-ins. Police arrested protesters for "blocking fire exits" and other charges, and white youths threw eggs and rocks, but the demonstrators persisted, and the theater business suffered drastically. By May 1961 the theater owners capitulated, and one more tier in Jim Crow's wall was knocked over.[80]

That summer the movement broadened again, now focusing on fair employment practices. H. G. Hill Grocery stores, accused of excluding blacks from clerical jobs, became the prime target, and pickets urged sympathizers to boycott the Hill stores. In August a group of these picketers was assaulted by a gang of white youths, and the police arrested the protesters, along with only three of their attackers. There were charges of police brutality and a sit-down strike at police headquarters.[81] More sit-in protests in January 1962 were aimed at the last holdouts downtown. In February students staged "sleep-ins" in the lobbies of the Hermitage and Andrew Jackson hotels. More sit-ins against the Krystal, Tic-Toc, and Cross Keys restaurants occurred throughout the year.[82]

By the spring of 1963 Nashville faced daily demonstrations against segregation, unfair employment, and the more general problem of racial prejudice. In March the NCLC announced a "full-scale assault" on segregation practices in Nashville. They sponsored a series of marches downtown and organized a second Easter boycott of downtown department stores, this time protesting unfair employment practices.[83] Mayor Beverly Briley, recently elected, came under heavy pressure in May of 1963 for a permanent agency to address the community's racial problem. Briley appointed black and white civic leaders, among them the leading bank and insurance company officers, to the Metropolitan Human Relations Committee.[84]

The process of desegregating the clientele of privately owned businesses now became institutionalized to some degree. Within months the Human Relations Committee was able to report a string of suc-

Figure 81. A black demonstration leader in front of Cross Keys Restaurant tries to keep his group separated from a group of taunting white youths in 1963. *Tennessean* Library.

Figure 82. Demonstrators from Pearl High School picket Krystal Grill on Church Street, April 1964. The sign in front reads, "Is Nashville the Birmingham of Tennessee?" *Tennessean* Library.

cessful efforts in dismantling racial barriers in a variety of public accommodations.[85] This development coincided with the euphoria following the inception of the new metropolitan government and gave Mayor Briley cause to congratulate the community, and its business leaders in particular, for Nashville's handling of issues that were tearing other cities apart.[86] Later, in 1965, the City Council replaced this advisory committee with a more powerful Human Relations Commission, and the mayor placed Dr. Edwin Mitchell, a black radiologist, at its head.[87]

There were still holdouts, like Morrison's and the B&W cafeterias where pickets and "sip-ins" by white protesters were used to challenge segregation during 1963 and 1964.[88] The trend was unmistakable, however. Segregation had all but disappeared in most Nashville public accommodations by 1964. After the succession of Lyndon Baines Johnson to the presidency, Congress passed the Civil Rights Act, which went into effect on July 4, 1964, banning segregation in all public places. To be sure, there were many whites who remained unhappy with the new order in Nashville, but organized resistance remained small and ineffective. A small, local White Citizens' Council was organized in April 1962, with leadership from Lambeth Mayes and John M. Aden, but it foundered as membership dwindled to about twenty-five in 1965.[89] The Ku Klux Klan came to Nashville and held recruitment rallies in 1965-66, but these were notable for their failure to arouse white Nashville. Mayor Briley openly denounced the Klan and made it clear that their point of view was altogether alien to Nashville's tradition of conciliatory race relations.[90]

Nor did black militancy and violence take firm hold in Nashville. A "new breed" of young, black militant, without the training or the commitment to nonviolent protest, emerged in organizations like SNCC by 1964. In May of that year a raucus protest, mostly by Pearl High School youths, led to a violent confrontation with police downtown.[91] But this "riot" was interpreted as an unnecessary departure from an orderly process of change that was being negotiated off the streets by the Human Relations Committee. The civil rights movement in Nashville continued attacking racial barriers, primarily in jobs and housing, and continued pursuing school desegregation.[92] The process of institutional desegregation, for the most part, proceeded quietly. Demonstrations, marches, and sit-ins increasingly gave way to negotiations behind the scenes. Nashville was widely applauded as a model southern city for its handling of desegregation.[93]

Then in April 1967 riots broke out around Fisk and the Tennessee A&I campuses, and the aura of calm that had characterized Nashville race relations was suddenly shattered. Again, it was black outside agitators who were blamed. Stokely Carmichael, the fiery leader of SNCC and an outspoken advocate of militant "black power," had been invited by Vanderbilt students to speak at the university's Impact lecture series. The invitation had met with strenuous opposition from James Stahlman's *Banner*, several patriotic organizations, and the state legislature (which recommended deporting Carmichael, a native of the West Indies). Community opposition to Carmichael intensified, but Vanderbilt chancellor Alexander Heard bravely defended the university's duty to serve as an "open forum" for all ideas. Carmichael, whose incendiary speeches had precipitated violence in other cities, came to Nashville ten days early and addressed enormous crowds of black youths at Fisk and Tennessee A&I, urging them to "organize and take over the city."[94]

Carmichael delivered a rather mild speech before his Vanderbilt audience on Saturday afternoon, April 8. But that night a minor incident at a Jefferson Street tavern brought a crowd of black protesters. When police ordered them to disperse, rocks began to fly; police sent for reinforcements, and the crowd — mostly young students — retreated to the Fisk campus, where a general melee broke out as the police advanced. Eminent black leaders, Dr. Edwin Mitchell, head of the Human Relations Commission, and the Reverend James E. Woodruff, minister of St. Anselm's Episcopal Church, tried to calm the crowd but instead became targets for rock throwers. Police led charges against the students and were met by a barrage of rocks and air-gun pellets. The next day violence broke out near the Tennessee A&I campus, where protesters hurled Molotov cocktails through store windows, set buildings ablaze, and fired guns.[95]

Fortunately, no one was killed before the disorder ended, but the confidence of Nashville's black and white leaders was shaken badly. Mayor Briley denounced Carmichael and SNCC for having deliberately planned a violent disturbance in Nashville. A *New York Times* report put part of the blame on the *Banner* and those who, in vociferously opposing Carmichael's speech at Vanderbilt, had polarized the community.[96] A federal investigation later accused Carmichael, H. Rap Brown, Eldridge Cleaver, and other black power organizers of having met in Nashville in March 1967, to plot "Operation Nashville," which included plans to teach local youths to manufacture and use Molotov cocktails and to burn white-owned businesses.[97]

Nashville's black leaders denounced Carmichael and questioned the goals of black power but quickly added that it was the underlying conditions of racial injustice that made it possible for such a riot to explode and insisted that the community focus on those conditions. Most blacks and whites alike were confounded by the meaning of black power and the apparent aimlessness of the violence in April. One year later, on April 4, 1968, the assassination of King in Memphis set off another furious burst of violence from Nashville's black youth. In the end the guns and fires of April 1967 and 1968 shook — but did not destroy — the confidence of black and white leaders in "the Nashville

Figure 83. National Guard troops in North Nashville, April 1968, following Martin Luther King's assassination. *Tennessean* Library.

way" of pragmatic, piecemeal reform. Perhaps it encouraged them to move faster, if only to avoid a future explosion.[98]

SCHOOL DESEGREGATION AFTER 1960

The school desegregation issue returned to center stage after 1968. Though Nashville had reason to congratulate itself on the successful desegregation of schools, a decade later many blacks and whites remained dissatisfied. Integration remained a legal victory with little practical effect on most Nashville schoolchildren. In 1966 the Metro school board voted to abandon its "grade-a-year" plan and proceed to integrate all grades at once. But by 1970, fifteen years after *Kelley* vs. *Board of Education* began, the overwhelming majority of whites and blacks still went to schools predominantly of their own race. The liberal transfer policy made integration a voluntary choice of parents and students, and a majority were choosing not to integrate.[99] Integration also meant that black children went to predominantly white schools with white teachers and white administrators. Beginning in 1964 faculty integration began, but this usually meant a token of one black on the faculties of integrated schools, and they were said to be selected only from the lightest-skinned black teachers.[100] Many blacks worried that integrated education under these terms would only accentuate the distance between black and white children.

Whites who were unhappy with the decision to integrate often transferred their children within the public schools to all-white neighborhood schools, or they joined the "white flight" to predominantly white suburban schools. In January 1961 the county schools started desegregation, beginning with grades one through four to catch up with the Nashville Plan.[101] In 1963 the U.S. Supreme Court ruled against the type of liberal transfer policy allowed in the Nashville Plan because it was based on racial rather than academic criteria. With that escape shut off, more whites moved into the private schools or left for white suburban schools. But some private schools had already integrated. The city's Catholic schools had been among the first to integrate, beginning with Father Ryan High School as early as 1955. Several other private schools, some established decades before desegregation, others only recently, were academically restrictive or financially prohibitive for many families. In response to the new demand, a few "segregation academies" sprang up, but before 1970 there was still room within the public school system for families that wanted to avoid integration.

By 1970 all twelve grades of the public school system had been officially integrated, but the combination of residential segregation and neighborhood school zones left all the city's formerly segregated black schools all black and about one-third of the formerly segregated white schools all white. Avon Williams, Jr., now a state senator, appealed successfully in that year to Judge Miller on behalf of the NAACP Legal Defense Fund, asking that the Board of Education prepare a new plan for desegregation. Subsequently, in prolonged hearings before federal district judge L. Clure Morton, Williams argued for racial balance in every public school, and the Board of Education defended its existing piecemeal plan. Morton referred the case to a team of experts from the federal Department of Health, Education, and Welfare, who devised a controversial plan for busing students. The aim was to create a "unitary" school system, with every school in Metropolitan Nashville integrated roughly in proportion to the percentage of blacks and whites in the whole community.[102]

The busing issue aroused a whole new level of debate over school desegregation. In the city election of 1971 Casey Jenkins opposed two-term incumbent Beverly Briley for mayor and whipped up a furor of antibusing sentiment. During Judge Morton's hearings Jenkins addressed an angry crowd of whites outside the federal courthouse and forced Morton to postpone the hearings. Jenkins linked the federal busing plan to "creeping Communism" and called for a public boycott of the schools. His Concerned Parents Association sponsored enormous rallies in the summer of 1971. One at the state fairgrounds speedway drew fifteen thousand white parents determined to stop the busing plan, by a boycott of the public schools if necessary.[103] Briley, running scared against the surprising popularity of Jenkins's appeal, vocalized his own distaste for the busing plan but argued that this was no longer an issue for local government to decide. His electoral victory in 1971 seemed to confirm that Nashville's voters also accepted busing as inevitable.

As the escape valves from desegregated schools were closed off, many whites left for distant suburbs beyond the district busing plan, and others streamed into the private school system. Between 1970 and 1979 white enrollment in schools ordered by the court to desegregate in 1971 decreased 53 percent, versus a decline of only 13 percent in the non-court-ordered schools of the county. (The school-age population was declining overall during the 1970s.) The court-ordered schools were 40 percent black; the others were only 9 percent black.[104] Simultaneously, private school enrollment in Davidson County shot up from 8,200 in 1969 to nearly 14,750 three years later. Seven new private schools were organized in 1971 alone.[105]

With the implementation of the busing plan, the racial question became confused with the cherished American tradition of the neighborhood school. An issue that had begun years earlier with young Robert Kelley's protest against being bused across town to Pearl High School had now come full circle. Adding to the confusion was the rejection by militant young blacks of the original goal of integration. Well-

Figure 84. Protesters at one of Casey Jenkins's antibusing rallies at War Memorial Auditorium in March 1971. *Tennessean* Library.

intentioned white liberals, who began with the premise that blacks wanted nothing more than the opportunity to join the mainstream of white, middle-class America, were now perplexed by a black determination to nurture a separate culture and avoid being swallowed by the dominant race. The unpopularity of busing exposed the public schools to attacks from politicians and to public opposition to increased school funding at a time when strong public support was more desperately needed than ever. The Board of Education, school administrators, and citizen groups worked diligently to restore community confidence in the public schools. But in Nashville and across America there was a growing popular perception—never fully proven but real enough in its consequences—that the academic quality and student discipline in the public schools was in serious decline. Some unmeasurable portion of the migration to private schools was due to usually unspoken fears of racial mixing, but many parents defended it by concerns about academics, drugs, physical safety, and moral environment—issues that went beyond the issue of race. By the early 1980s the public school problem was still unresolved.[106]

Though there was cause for despair, there was also good reason for pride in the Nashville experience. Nashville's race relations fell far short of perfection in terms of genuine social integration and equal justice, but the kind of fear and hatred that had led to the ugly demonstrations and the violent explosion at Hattie Cotton School in the fall of 1957 seemed no longer possible in a community where blacks and whites had apparently learned to accommodate one another within a system of laws. By 1980 a whole generation of black and white children had gone through twelve or more years of schooling together. Whatever problems remained—in Nashville and America—this generation was better prepared to solve them.

CENTURY III

Nashvillians of the 1920s would have to look hard to discover the historical continuity in the city of 1980. The provincial town that country people had flocked to after World War I was now a sprawling metropolis of more than one-half million people.[1] Nashville by 1980 was much more than the urban mecca for the surrounding rural hinterland; it was an international tourist center and a city with a public image as definite in its own way as that of Los Angeles, San Francisco, or New York. "Music City, U.S.A." projected a caricature of the city as the home of country music and quaint southern folkways. It was a public image as distorted and misleading in the 1970s as the Athens of the South image had been for the city of the 1920s.

Behind those caricatures of urban uniqueness was a city whose history reveals much about the general experience of a region undergoing enormous change in the half-century since the 1920s. The clearest indicator of change was the growth of the southern urban population. It increased 39 percent in the decade preceding 1930, 19 percent during the 1930s, then 38 percent in the decade before 1950, 40 percent before 1960, slowing down to 27 percent and 24 percent in the next two decades. Simultaneously, the rural population, which claimed over 72 percent of southerners in 1920, declined to 33 percent by 1980.[2]

For millions of rural migrants who left the farms and small towns for the cities there were a multitude of readjustments that had to be made. The city presented the rural newcomer with different kinds of work, more densely packed neighborhoods, more formal styles of worship, and a strange urban environment of unfamiliar streets, buildings, traffic, entertainment, people, and manners. Nashville witnessed the fascinating tensions that occurred between the ways of life these country people brought with them to the city and the new ways of life urban living demanded, and those strains were felt across the South as its people moved into the city during this period. The rural migrant's trials in the city may serve as an apt metaphor for Nashville and the entire South during this half-century, for the city and region were collectively reordering their economy, politics, and race relations in the face of new conditions.

In Nashville an economy that had been frustrated and consequently cautious in developing new manufacturing industries found itself ideally positioned to take advantage of the rapid expansion of the new service economy, with its emphasis on finance, government, entertainment, education, health, and religion. Those sectors of Nashville's economy, many of them planted before the 1920s, flourished amid the new affluence that came to the South after World War II.

In politics Nashville's frustrated experiments with good-government reform in the progressive era and the 1920s finally yielded to the long reign of Boss Hilary Howse. Despite the indignant accusations of corruption hurled against the Howse machine, there emerged a grudging respect for this professional politician. Howse gave poor and black citizens a sense of belonging and gave businessmen room to plan the city's economic development. The crisis of the Great Depression brought the federal government into a lasting partnership with the city. The boss and the political machine were gradually displaced by the expanded functions of government in the welfare state. The intrusion of the federal government on behalf of labor, blacks, and the poor was resented by some conservative business leaders, but they usually welcomed the federal-city partnership that brought cheap electric power, urban renewal, defense contracts, military bases, suburban home mortgages, and educational grants to the city and the region.

Howse's career as a professional politician who served twenty-one years as mayor established a pattern followed by Thomas Cummings, who served nearly fourteen years; Ben West, twelve years; Beverly Briley, twelve years; and incumbent Richard Fulton, who began as mayor in 1975 and before that had been the Nashville district's congressional representative for eighteen years. The continuity of political leadership in Nashville was, for the most part, a favorable factor in the city's adjustment to the changes the city experienced in this period. But the political structure of the city and county before and, for a time, after World War II was wracked by factional infighting and encrusted with old politicians who had been in office for years. The war and its aftermath saw a new generation of young leaders brought forward, many of them veterans and beneficiaries of the GI bill that opened new opportunities for college education. Briley, West, and Fulton were only the most notable of this generation who emerged as standard-bearers for a progressive, forward-looking Nashville. They joined with members of the Nashville academic community, from Vanderbilt and Fisk in particular, also part of a postwar generation of young professors committed to applying their knowledge as social scientists to the solution of community problems. This coalition of local politicians and academicians rose to power with a new tide of political reform in Tennessee during the 1940s and 1950s when Boss Ed Crump's political machine fell apart and new Tennessee leaders emerged in senators Estes Kefauver, Albert Gore, Percy Priest, governors Gordon Browning and Frank Clement, and others. The final success of Nashville and Davidson County's metropolitan government in 1962 was the triumph of this postwar generation of leaders in government and academe. This reform was also the legacy of the progressive era concern for efficient government and the New Deal liberal faith in government as a positive, essential instrument for rational planning of the economy and society.

Nashville's progressive political climate also boded well for the reordering of race relations that came after World War II. That blacks maintained some political leverage under the Howse regime gave them advantages when local and state politics opened up rapidly to more black political participation during the late 1940s and 1950s. Racial segregation was a serious obstacle to the economic and social progress of Nashville, and the entire South after World War II, but taking down the Jim Crow walls might have proved even more disruptive. Nashville's comparatively peaceful acceptance of the new order of race relations was the fortunate result of responsible leadership by black civil rights activists, savvy political leadership generally, pragmatism on the part of businessmen, and the willingness of churches and colleges to provide forums for discussion of the issues. The shortcomings of the movement in eradicating discrimination and black poverty were irrefutable, but those failings cannot obscure the fundamental redefinition of race relations that came with the integration of public schools, public accommodations, and politics—all within a surprisingly short time.

As Nashville approached its two-hundredth anniversary, it seemed that the changes involved in this reordering of the economy, politics, and race relations overshadowed the continuity of the city's historical traditions. In the heart of the city, old landmarks that had been in place for a century were routinely demolished to make room for sleek skyscrapers, parking lots, and freeway loops. For a time there was an unquestioned premise that a new building, a new city, was demonstrably superior to what preceded it. The new skyscrapers and freeways looked undistinguishable from those one might find in any American city of similar size. Local character also was besieged by an influx of nationally franchised hotels, fast-food eateries, and retail outlets. The southern country diet of fried meat and well-cooked vegetables now competed with a youthful breed of restaurant whose menus and decor strained toward the modern. The homogenization of local and southern culture was equally apparent in everything from music to politics by the 1970s.

The quality of social relationships seemed no less volatile than landmarks and local customs. The civil rights movement had failed to eradicate all vestiges of prejudice and inequality, to be sure, but it effected a sea change in the way the races interacted. The expectations of both races that governed blacks' place in the job market, in the political arena, at the lunch counter, or in the bus were redefined by the events of the 1960s.

Nor did traditions of southern chivalry protect Nashville from the transformation of women's roles that swept across the nation in the 1970s. More women entered the work force, no longer just in temporary or clerical jobs but more often to pursue careers in business and the professions. The country girls who came to town in the 1920s and 1930s to work in the offices, restaurants, stores, and factories a few years before settling down with a husband and children were a sharp contrast to the new breed of career-minded women that emerged in the 1970s. Male ego, like white racial prerogatives, gave way, sometimes warily, before a tide of change.

Beneath the changing skyline, the reordered social relations, and the national fashions that rippled through the city there were still deep roots of historical tradition that nurtured the city's character. But in the timeless contest between change and tradition, Nashville at two hundred years seemed bent on celebrating the former. From the earliest planning of the city's bicentennial there was an ambivalence toward the strictly historical significance of the occasion, and this was reminiscent of the one-hundredth anniversary. The 1880 Centennial had been initiated by the Tennessee Historical Society and then taken over by businessmen who geared the event to a celebration of industrial development in the New South. In the Centennial exhibition hall, historical artifacts commemorating the pioneers of Nashville competed with noisy exhibits of the latest technology, along with circus performances, a fountain filled with alligators and sea lions, beer halls, restaurants, baby shows, military drills, and horse races.[3]

The same juxtaposition of reverence for the past and jubilant celebration of the future was apparent one hundred years later. This time, however, the principal planners from the outset were business and political leaders who were concerned not to dwell too heavily upon the past, fearing it might appear unprogressive or backward looking. Mayor Richard Fulton, elected in 1975, began laying plans for Nashville's two-hundredth anniversary at the end of the national Bicentennial in 1976. By October 1977 he had appointed a Steering Committee of eleven people, carefully selected to represent different segments of the community. Fulton appointed Amon Carter Evans, president of the *Tennes-*

sean, as the committee's chairman.[4] Among the committee's first tasks was to call in no less than five public relations consultants to help cast the proper image of the city's bicentennial. "They determined that the Celebration should be more a springboard into Century III than a commemoration of the past," thus the official name for the bicentennial. The public relations people also designed an eye-catching logo that incorporated the columns and pediment of the Parthenon, and they composed a slogan that underlined the forward-looking purpose of the occasion: "Celebrating the Past While Looking to the Future."[5]

The emphasis on the future was evident in the ambitious early plans of the Steering Committee. It announced a Century III Center, which was to be an enormous complex on a 132-acre site in the Sulphur Dell area north of Capitol Hill. It would include a 50,000-seat stadium, a 100,000-square-foot exhibition hall, an indoor arena with 17,000 seats, and a large parking structure. New hotels and restaurants, it was projected, would rise up around this complex to form one of the best convention centers in the South.[6]

The Steering Committee also proposed an All-Faith Center, inspired partly by Dallas's Thanksgiving Square and conceived as "a lasting symbol of the dominant role religious institutions and spiritual leaders have played in the city's history." The restoration of Union Station was another early priority of the committee. Preservationists in Historic Nashville, Inc., a voluntary citizens' group, had begun a campaign to "Save Our Station" as early as 1975. Jay Solomon, a Tennessee real estate developer who served as administrator of the General Services Administration under President Carter, allotted $7 million in federal funds for the renovation of Union Station as a federal office complex. But the project had been stalled by political infighting, and the Century III Steering Committee determined to make the station's resurrection one of its primary objectives.[7] Finally, the committee planned to appoint a group to record the celebration of the city's bicentennial and to investigate the possibility of sponsoring a written history of Nashville's second century. This would be the bicentennial counterpart to W. Woodford Clayton's *History of Davidson County*, sponsored by the Tennessee Historical Society in 1880.[8]

In February 1978 Mayor Fulton appointed the Century III Commission on the basis of recommendations from members of the Metropolitan Council. It included two hundred members and drew from almost every neighborhood and social group in the city. More than a dozen committees were formed as new projects and events came into focus. The Century III Celebration became a yearlong extravaganza of festivals, parades, lectures, television and radio broadcasts, souvenirs of all kinds, and a continuous round of committee meetings for those involved in the planning.

Though it took responsibility for planning several key events during the year, the Century III Commission acted as a kind of clearinghouse that approved projects that sprang up in legion from the community. Railroad buffs sponsored the Century III Steam Special that ran round-trips from Union Station to Columbia in April. Nashville high schools sponsored "Graduation to Century III" at Vanderbilt Memorial Gym, with Pittsburgh Steeler quarterback and Christian evangelist Terry Bradshaw brought in as the featured speaker. Cedarwood Publishing Company produced an album with ten country-style songs commemorating Nashville's heroic past. T-shirts, tote bags, cookbooks, historical calendars, Andrew Jackson candle stands, commemorative letter openers, paperweights, cigarette lighters, and dozens of other souvenirs were sold with the Century III Commission's endorsement.[9]

The most memorable events were those sponsored directly by the commission to honor the founding of the city. On Founders Day, designated as December 23, 1979, the Sunday before Christmas, descendants of sixty-four "First Settlers" of Nashville honored those who had arrived by the overland route with James Robertson two centuries earlier. They gathered on the east side of the river and walked across the Woodland Street Bridge behind banners identifying the families of their ancestors. Two centuries earlier the Robertson party had walked across the frozen river to the bluffs where they built Fort Nashborough. In 1979 it was a rainy, bone-chilling day that tested the grit of the twentieth-century descendants. But a crowd of three thousand braved the weather and witnessed one of the least ostentatious but most moving reminders of the historical meaning behind the celebration. There, walking across the bridge, surrounded by a modern city, were hundreds of people whose genealogy stretched back two hundred years to the small band that ended their wilderness trek and began to scratch out a new settlement on the western banks of the Cumberland.

Settlement Day, April 24, 1980, honored the arrival of John Donelson's party that had come a thousand miles by river, down the Tennessee and up the Ohio and Cumberland, to meet Robertson and his overland party. In contrast to the dreary December gathering, perfect weather met the thousands of people who came to celebrate what was the climax of the bicentennial. A trumpet announced the arrival of two flatboats representing Donelson's flotilla, and a cannon volley answered.[10] Nashville City Bank executive John Hardcastle read from Donelson's journal as the boats landed. Mayor Fulton, clad magnificently in buckskin, welcomed William Stockley Donelson, descendant of the pioneer, and his crew, all in costume.

What followed had little to do with the historical event that was being celebrated, but it was enjoyed by an estimated fifty thousand schoolchildren, families, executives, and office workers who took the afternoon off to join the festivities. After a brief address by Mayor Fulton and a musical performance by country music star Tom T. Hall, the

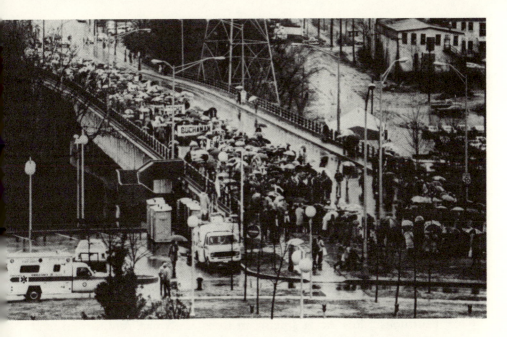

Figure 85. Founders Day, December 23, 1979. Descendants of Nashville's pioneer families celebrate the city's founding two centuries earlier by walking across the Woodland Street Bridge. *Tennessean* Library.

Figure 86. Mayor Richard Fulton in buckskin greets William Donelson, descendant of John Donelson, on the banks of the Cumberland, on Settlement Day, April 24, 1980. *Banner* Library.

audience participated in a "reverse parade." Stationed throughout the downtown were musical and dance performances that featured Tennessee bluegrass and country music along with authentic clog dancing.

The concept of the reverse parade was original but not entirely unlike the magnificent procession of April 24, 1880, which had involved nearly every organized group in the city. But the overall tone of the celebration a century earlier was notably different. In 1880 the purpose clearly was to edify the heroes of the past, the pioneer settlers, the Indian fighters, and especially Andrew Jackson. On the day Jackson's equestrian statue was unveiled in 1880, a crowd estimated by some at twenty-five thousand pressed around the capitol and perched on its ledges, listening to hours of oratory and poetry commemorating Jackson and the heroes of Nashville's past.

What was striking about the 1980 version was the nearly complete absence of any reference to the past, except in the preliminary pageantry. The dominant presences were the music stars and local television personalities—not statesmen or historians. It was Tom T. Hall at the courthouse, Roy Acuff singing in front of Ryman Auditorium, and Johnny Cash at the capitol, along with many other singers, musicians, and clog dancers, who entertained the throngs in 1980.[11] Settlement Day ended that evening, something like it had in 1880, with a magnificent fireworks display at the Parthenon, climaxed by the Century III logo emblazoned in the sky.

As the year unfolded, there were dozens of other festivities honoring the city's bicentennial. Despite the Century III Commission's interest in giving precedence to building for the future, its major projects foundered. The Century III Center in Sulphur Dell found little support, and the Opryland Hotel clouded the issue by announcing its own plans for a convention center. Efforts to go forward with a smaller convention center in another location became snarled in disagreements over rival sites. Those favoring the downtown site, across from the Ryman Auditorium, finally prevailed over those pushing for the railroad gulch next to Union Station. But this project soon fell into financial difficulties, and as of 1984 all there was to show for the Century III Center was a massive hole in the ground at Fifth and Broad.[12] By September of that year Mayor Fulton and the Metro Council had resurrected the project, and it appeared that Nashville would soon have its downtown convention center.

Union Station's restoration also became tied up in red tape and befouled by pigeon droppings. Historic Nashville, Inc., continued the long crusade on behalf of this movement after Century III disbanded, but four years after the bicentennial the future of this magnificent architectural legacy remained in the hands of an indifferent federal bureaucracy. Nor was the All-Faith Center realized. Plans to design a monument of some sort on the riverfront ran into a competing scheme for

Figure 87. Settlement Day, April 24, 1984. Chet Atkins and Roy Acuff, in front of the Capitol, protect their ears from the noise of fireworks that celebrated the arrival of the Donelson party 200 years earlier. *Tennessean* Library.

a Century III Riverfront Park, a special project of the commission that had completed its first stage by 1983. Alternative plans to attach a chapel to the Century III Center were forgotten once the commission abandoned the Sulphur Dell site.[13] The plans to produce a written history did come to fruition, and in more than one project. Plus Media, Inc., publishers of *Nashville Magazine,* produced a beautifully illustrated, large-format book written by John Egerton and several others. *Nashville: The Faces of Two Centuries* interpreted the entire two hundred years of the city's past. It came out during the bicentennial year and was one of the most coveted souvenirs of the year. Don H. Doyle's *Nashville in the New South, 1880–1930* and *Nashville Since the 1920s,* also products of Century III, interpreted the second century of Nashville's history.

With or without these publications, one of the most notable results of the bicentennial was a revival of the community's sense of history and tradition. This was apparent earlier, even before the national Bicentennial of 1976, but it came into sharper focus for many amid all the pageantry and gala celebrations of Century III. This historical consciousness was most apparent in an awakening of concern for the architectural landmarks and physical artifacts of the past. Before the 1970s, historic preservation in Nashville, and in most older cities, was directed by a dedicated corps of elder citizens and usually devoted to preserving the homes of famous local families. In the 1970s a new generation of young professional men and women became aggressive historic preservationists. Many began while rehabilitating individual residences in the older neighborhoods of the city, then came together in neighborhood associations to protect their common interests against reckless developers and speculators. In the old Edgefield and Lockeland Springs neighborhoods of East Nashville, in Germantown north of the capitol, in Belmont-Hillsboro and Richland-West End in Southwest Nashville, these neighborhood preservationists had turned declining old houses into vibrant neighborhoods full of historic architectural charm.

New legislation favoring the restoration of commercial buildings and offices brought the preservation movement into the downtown in the 1970s. Urban renewal and the downtown revival that began in the 1960s left little of old Nashville standing in the shadows of the new skyscrapers. Along Second Avenue (old Market Street), however, a remarkable stand of late-nineteenth-century commercial structures stretched almost without modern interruption from Lower Broad to the Courthouse Square. The destruction in 1974 of the beautiful Victorian stores on the square, to make room for a parking lot and roadway, spurred preservationists to protect and restore Second Avenue. There, fortunately, generations of small family firms in hardware, drugs, groceries, and manufacturing had persisted without renovating or replacing their commercial homes.

A 1976 conference focusing on the Nashville waterfront brought attention to the area and publicized plans to integrate the riverfront area into hotel and convention facilities downtown. One of the major forces behind the Second Avenue movement was the Metropolitan Historical Commission, established by Mayor Fulton in 1975 and headed by May Dean Eberling. It was the commission that won historic district status for Second Avenue. This status enhanced property values by offering attractive tax incentives to developers willing to renovate the old structures for commercial use. It was one of the ironies of the historic preservation movement that firms that had been doing business on the street for decades (at least one since antebellum times) were forced by rising property values to give way to new restaurants, boutiques, and professional offices. The Historical Commission and Historic Nashville, Inc., took offices in the renovated Silver Dollar Saloon at Second and Lower Broad. Historic Nashville sponsored the annual Market Street Festivals that drew thousands of suburbanites downtown to enjoy the fun and to rediscover an architectural heritage Nashvillians had taken for granted.[14]

Along Lower Broad another fine stand of Victorian commercial buildings had long ago yielded to honky-tonk bars and sleazy pornography stores. But as plans for the downtown convention center and the Riverfront Park began to take form, this strip of old buildings became ripe for rehabilitation. The restoration of the U.S. Customs House, on Broad near Eighth, and the drive to save Union Station tapped a popular well of enthusiasm for preserving the city's landmarks. Some of the preservationists, to be sure, were more interested in tax incentives and real estate profits than in the history they were saving. Others were willing to "gentrify" historic neighborhoods at the expense of the lower-class residents who lived or worked there. But beyond them was a broad-based shift in popular thinking in favor of preserving the physical artifacts of the past and, with them, a sense of the history they conveyed. This was no longer a movement of sentimental cranks universally opposed to change of any sort. The preservationists, however, were echoing some of the Agrarians' questions about the thoughtless surrender to the premise that modernity was automatically superior to tradition, that new was better than old, and that people had no choice but to make way for the juggernaut of progress. The preservationists were prepared to take their stand, not against Nashville's progress, but in defense of a local character and a sense of tradition that was rooted in history.

This historical consciousness that revived with neighborhood preservation, and with the national and local bicentennial celebrations, by no means prevailed in Nashville in 1980. But it did help restore a certain balance that had been evident a century earlier when the New South boosters joined the Tennessee Historical Society in the Centennial celebration. In 1980, as in 1880, Nashville seemed willing enough to look to the future but not to forsake the past. That, in the end, was the most encouraging omen for the city's future.

APPENDIXES

APPENDIX A: POPULATION AND RACE, NASHVILLE AND DAVIDSON COUNTY, 1860–1980

	Total Population				Black Population			
Year	City	% Change	County	% Change	City	% of City	County	% of County
1860	16,988	—	47,055	—	3,945	23	15,999	34
1870	25,865	52	62,896	34	9,709	38	25,412	40
1880	43,350	68	79,009	26	16,337	38	31,331	40
1890	76,168	76	108,174	37	29,382	39	41,315	38
1900	80,865	6	122,790	14	30,044	37	43,902	36
1910	110,364	36	149,478	22	36,523	33	46,710	31
1920	118,342	7	167,815	12	35,633	30	44,528	27
1930	153,866	30	222,854	33	42,836	28	51,797	23
1940	167,402	9	257,267	15	47,318	28	56,797	22
1950	174,307	4	321,758	25	58,695	34	64,381	20
1960	170,874	−2	399,743	24	72,789	43	76,832	19
1970	426,029	149	447,877	12	87,851	21	89,223	20
1980	455,651	7	477,811	7	105,942	23	106,257	22

SOURCE: City and county population figures were taken from the published reports of the U.S. census for the appropriate year, 1860–1980. Revised figures from subsequent censuses were used in favor of the originally reported figure whenever necessary. The county black population for 1970 was found in Metropolitan Planning Commission, *A Study of Nonwhite Residential Distribution in Nashville, Tennessee in 1940, 1950, 1960, and 1970* (Nashville, 1975), 3.

APPENDIX B: NASHVILLE BANK CLEARINGS, 1915–1980

Year	Clearings	Year	Clearings
1915	322,901,654	1934	584,513,170
1916	407,729,406	1935	696,558,318
1917	532,907,290	1940	1,056,329,939
1918	746,156,611	1945	2,140,405,311
1919	863,911,696	1950	3,986,631,166
1920	1,179,501,244	1955	5,864,236,090
1921	845,509,813	1960	7,920,388,575
1922	898,067,590	1965	11,337,827,789
1923	1,003,657,993	1970	17,298,729,024
1924	1,012,243,160	1971	19,133,148,520
1925	1,122,203,951	1972	21,063,810,690
1926	1,126,611,576	1973	25,013,908,295
1927	1,198,811,102	1974	32,589,314,666
1928	1,179,685,805	1975	32,510,257,059
1929	1,243,935,793	1976	39,131,389,453
1930	1,078,478,051	1977	46,764,386,337
1931	628,043,516	1978	51,941,830,411
1932	460,439,179	1979	57,044,053,209
1933	468,491,660	1980	60,102,485,356

SOURCE: *Polk's Nashville ... City Directory ...*, 1972, 1981.

APPENDIX C: NASHVILLE'S LABOR FORCE, 1950, 1980

	1950	1980	Percent Change
Agriculture, mining	2.3%	0.7%	−1.6
Construction	7.7	5.2	−2.5
Manufacturing			
Durable goods	5.3	6.8	+1.5
Nondurable goods	17.6	9.9	−7.7
Transportation, communication	8.8	8.5	−.3
Wholesale trade	4.6	5.6	+1.0
Retail trade	17.1	16.1	−1.0
Finance, insurance, real estate	4.6	7.3	+2.7
Services			
Professional, related	7.3	23.1	+15.8
Entertainment, recreation	1.0	1.6	+.6
Businesss, repair	2.5	4.2	+1.7
Personal	10.3	4.0	−6.3
Government	11.0	6.9	−4.1
Total	100%	100%	
N	(127,598)	(219,225)	+72

SOURCE: Bureau of the Census, *Census of Population: 1950*, 2, *Characteristics of the Population*, pt. 42, Tennessee (Washington, D.C., 1952), 214–28; idem, *1980 Census of Population*, 1, *Characteristics of the Population*, ch. C, *General Social and Economic Characteristics*, pt. 44, Tennessee (Washington, D.C., 1983), 153. Data based on the city population in both censuses.

NOTE: Due to rounding, totals do not always add to exactly 100%.

APPENDIX D: MUNICIPAL REVENUES AND EXPENDITURES, 1938–1971

	1938	1951	1960	1971	1981
Per capita					
Tax	$23	$68	$74	$190	$725
Expenditure	27	177	155	481	879
Indebtedness	190	205	464	692	1,442
Percentage of general revenues from					
Property tax	62%	51%	35%	35%	39%
Sales, other tax	0	5	12	18	16
Intergovernmental transfers	26	36	41	30	26
Other	12%	8%	12%	17%	19%
Total Revenue (000s)	$5,828	$11,906	$26,805	$152,765	$633,808

SOURCE: *The Municipal Year Book*, 1941, 1953, 1962, 1973; Bureau of the Census, *Local Government Finances in Selected Metropolitan Areas and Large Counties: 1980–81* (Washington, D.C., 1983), 48. The 1981 data are for Davidson County. Estimates on per capita figures were made from the closest federal census.

APPENDIX E: MAYORS OF NASHVILLE, 1915–1983

Mayor (Birth–Death)	Term
Robert Ewing (1849–1932)	1915–17[1]
William Gupton (1870–1957)	1917–21[2]
Felix Z. Wilson (1866–1951)	1921–22[3]
Percy Sharpe	1922–23
Hilary Howse (1866–1938)	1923–27
Howse	1927–31
Howse	1931–35
Howse	1935–38[4]
Thomas L. Cummings (1891–1968)	1938–39
Cummings	1939–43
Cummings	1943–47
Cummings	1947–51
Ben West (1911–1974)	1951–55
West	1955–59
West	1959–63
Beverly Briley (1914–1980)	1963–67
Briley	1967–71
Briley	1971–75
Richard Fulton (1927–)	1975–79
Fulton	1979–83
Fulton	1983–

NOTE: All of Nashville's mayors in the twentieth century were Democrats.

1. Ewing filled the remainder of Hilary Howse's term after the ouster of 1915. Howse had served as mayor 1909–1911, 1911–13, 1913–15.

2. Gupton resigned in the face of an ouster by the City Council on May 5, 1921.

3. Wilson filled the rest of Gupton's term. Wilson was ousted by the City Council on November 22, 1922. The council appointed Percy Sharpe to fill the remainder of Wilson's term.

4. Howse died in office January 2, 1938. Cummings was elected by the people to fill the remainder of his term.

NOTES

CHAPTER ONE

1. Ida Clyde Clarke, *All About Nashville: A Complete Historical Guidebook to the City* (Nashville, 1912), 144–48, describes the prominent white women's clubs. See *Tennessean*, June 25, 1916; Charlotte A. Williams, comp., *The Centennial Club of Nashville: A History from 1905 to 1977* (Nashville, 1978). Black women had their own set of clubs, with the Phillis Wheatley Club being the most eminent. *Globe*, May 3, 1912, includes a directory and description of black women's clubs.
2. See F. Garvin Davenport, *Cultural Life in Nashville, 1825–1860* (Chapel Hill, N.C., 1941).
3. Mencken, "Sahara of the Bozart," (New York) *Evening Mail*, Nov. 13, 1917, rpt., Mencken, *Prejudices: Second Series* (New York, 1920), quoted in George B. Tindall, *The Emergence of the New South, 1913–1945*, A History of the South, vol. 10 (Baton Rouge, 1967), 285–86.
4. Tate, "The Profession of Letters in the South," *Virginia Quarterly Review* 11(1935): 175–76, quoted Tindall, *Emergence*, 287.
5. Tindall, *Emergence*, 287.
6. *New York Times*, Oct. 19, 1925; Nov. 19, 1925; Edwin Mims, *History of Vanderbilt University* (Nashville, 1946), 401f; Louise Cowan, *The Fugitive Group: A Literary History* (Baton Rouge, 1959), 32–34, 206.
7. *Tennessean*, Dec. 9, 1926, gives an account of Mims's speech before the Southern Society of New York. The *Tennessean* published several excerpts from *The Advancing South* in Dec. 1926. See also *The Nation* 122(June 30, 1926): 727.
8. John L. Stewart, *The Burden of Time: The Fugitives and Agrarians* (Princeton, 1965), 13, 22, 24.
9. Stewart, *Burden*, 13–14; Cowan, *Fugitive*, 10. See also Daniel Joseph Singal, *The War Within: From Victorian to Modernist Thought in the South, 1919–1945* (Chapel Hill, 1982), 203–19; Thomas Daniel Young, *Gentleman in a Dustcoat: A Biography of John Crowe Ransom* (Baton Rouge, 1976). Virginia

Rock, "The Making and Meaning of *I'll Take My Stand*: A Study in Utopian Conservatism, 1925–1939" (Ph.D. diss., Univ. of Minnesota, 1961), 474–89, 528–36, 537–46, 555–65.

10. Stewart, *Burden*, 15–16; Cowan, *Fugitive*, 10–11; Singal, *War*, 220–230; Thomas Daniel Young and M. Thomas Inge, *Donald Davidson* (New York, 1971).

11. Stewart, *Burden*, 23–24; Singal, *War*, 232–60.

12. Robert Penn Warren, "Reminiscence," in *Nashville: The Faces of Two Centuries*, ed. John Egerton (Nashville, 1980), 205–20.

13. *Current Opinion* 55(Sept., 1913): 174–75; *Tennessean*, May 5, 1913; Stewart, *Burden*, 7–10. Hirsch's brother-in-law, James M. Frank, was president of the Nashville Retailers Association in 1922 when it also sponsored the first issue of *The Fugitive*.

14. Stewart, *Burden*, 20.

15. Ibid., 26–27. Cowan, *Fugitive*, 183, 219. "The Fugitives are busy people," Ransom explained in the final issue, "for the most part enslaved to Mammon, their time used up in vulgar bread-and-butter occupations." Quoted in Cowan, *Fugitive*, 219.

16. Stewart, *Burden*, 24; Cowan, *Fugitive*, 47f.

17. Ransom went to Kenyon in 1937, in part because Vanderbilt did not come up with an attractive counteroffer. His biographer explains Mims made an honest effort to improve Vanderbilt's offer, but he felt restricted because Ransom did not have a Ph.D. Tate led a vigorous, public campaign through the *Tennessean* in the hopes of embarrassing Vanderbilt into retaining Ransom, but it failed. Young, *Gentleman*, 273–88. Tate blamed Mims for denying him a graduate fellowship and left for New York in 1924. Singal, *War*, 237. Warren taught at Vanderbilt for three years and, in his words, was "fired" by Mims in 1934. Warren, "Reminiscence," 215. Davidson stayed at Vanderbilt; he was looking for other academic appointments during the 1920s and was not promoted to professor until 1938. He taught summer school in Vermont and wrote a weekly column for the *Tennessean* (1924–30) as part of his constant struggle to supplement his meager Vanderbilt salary, which began at $10 a week in 1920. Rock, "Making and Meaning," 474–83.

18. Cowan, *Fugitive*, 48.

19. Stewart, *Burden*, 36, 38.

20. Singal, *War*, 210–16.

21. Ibid., 237–38.

22. Davidson, *Southern Writers in the Modern World* (Athens, Ga., 1958), 42.

23. Quoted in Charles P. Roland, "The South of the Agrarians," in *A Band of Prophets: The Vanderbilt Agrarians After Fifty Years*, ed. William C. Havard and Walter Sullivan (Baton Rouge, 1982), 37–38.

24. Davidson, *Writers*, 31–41. Cowan, *Fugitive*, 208. The role of the Scopes trial as the spark for the Agrarian revolt may be overemphasized, even in connection with Davidson's own turn of mind. The rediscovery of southern identity preceded the adverse publicity of the trial, and the shift to an aggressive defense of southern society took place more gradually after the trial. As late as 1928, Davidson's article, "First Fruits of Dayton: The Intellectual Evolution in Dixie," *The Forum* (June 1928), was almost apologetic, pointing out that Dayton was not the entire South and that the region contained many progressive

elements. Both Davidson and Ransom were still considering leaving their Vanderbilt posts for jobs in the East after 1925, further evidence of their unformed commitment to the South. Louis D. Rubin, Jr., *The Wary Fugitives: Four Poets of the South* (Baton Rouge, 1978), 155, 161.

25. Stewart, *Burden*, 110, 116; Davidson, *Writers*, 41.

26. Davidson, *Writers*, 38, 44.

27. Davidson to Tate, Mar. 4, 1927, Nashville, in John Tyree Fain and Thomas Daniel Young, eds., *The Literary Correspondence of Donald Davidson and Alan Tate* (Athens, Ga., 1974), 192-93.

28. Davidson, *Writers*, 45.

29. Davidson to Tate, July 29, 1929, Saratoga Springs, N.Y., in Fain and Young, *Correspondence*, 227.

30. Twelve Southerners, *I'll Take My Stand: The South and the Agrarian Tradition* (New York, 1930), 244.

31. Mencken, "The South Astir," *Virginia Quarterly Review* 7(1931): 53, quoted in Tindall, *Emergence*, 579.

32. *Masquerader* 10(Dec. 1933).

33. Edward Shapiro, "The Southern Agrarians and the Tennessee Valley Authority" *American Quarterly* 22(Winter 1970): 791-806.

34. Several articles appeared in the *American Review*, a right-wing journal that put the Agrarians in the unfortunate company of American fascist writers in the 1930s. Stewart, *Burden*, 178-79. See Davidson's "'I'll Take My Stand': A History," *American Review* 5(1935): 301-21, for a good review of the book and its critics.

35. Singal, *War*, 250-51.

36. Ransom to Mims, June 8, 1937, Nashville, Ransom Papers, VUL, Special Collections, explains his intention to abandon writing on Agrarianism. Ransom, "Art and the Human Economy," *Kenyon Review* 7(1945): 686-87.

37. A locally popular explanation, and one Davidson would have found hard to resist, is that Yankee soldiers cut down the trees when they fortified Capitol Hill in 1862. Perhaps the trees grew back only to be permanently disposed of by Davidson's New South burghers.

38. Davidson, "'Southern Agrarians' State Their Case," *Progressive Farmer* 51(June, 1936): 5, 26. See also David Alvin Hallman, "Donald Davidson: The Development of His Poetry" (Ph.D. diss., Duke Univ., 1972), 24, 25.

39. Davidson, *Writers*, 41; Davidson, *The Tall Men* (Boston, 1927), 43, 114; Singal, *War*, 222-26.

40. Davidson, "The South and Intellectual Progress," typescript, Davidson Papers, VUL, Special Collections, 8-10.

41. George B. Moulder, *The Parthenon at Nashville, Tennessee* (Nashville, 1930), 2. See also the articles on the Parthenon in *Tennessean*, Feb. 5, 6, 7, 1930.

42. *New York Times*, Jan. 31, 1926, original quote capitalized in headlines.

43. "Tennessee's New Parthenon," *Literary Digest* 86(July 25, 1925): 28.

44. George Marvin, "Progress and the Parthenon," *The Outlook* 139(Apr. 29, 1925): 653-56.

45. Mrs. William W. Geraldton, *Social Directory of Nashville, Tennessee* (Nashville, 1911), 167; Mrs. James C. Bradford's letter to the editor, *Tennessean*, Nov. 4, 1933.

46. *Nashville This Week*, Nov. 30-Dec. 7; Dec. 14-21, 1925.

47. *Tennessean,* Jan. 30, 1927.

48. The development of music at Ward-Belmont can be traced in Ward-Belmont School of Music, *Catalog,* 1913-1914, pp. 4, 5, 32-33; ibid., 1919-1920, pp. 7-8, 39-42. Albert Wardin, Jr., interview with James Summerville, Dec. 19, 1983. See also, Gilbertine Moore, *Gilly Goes to Ward-Belmont* (Nashville, 1973), 37-39, on the musical awakening of one student.

49. On Naff see her obituary, *Tennessean,* Mar. 5, 1960; clippings in Naff Collection, Nashville Room, Ben West Public Library; John Bridges, "The Most Picturesque Manageress," *Premier Magazine,* Spring-Summer 1982, pp. 6-10. *Tennessean,* Apr. 28, 1922: editorial complained too many Ryman performers sang to empty seats and that "John McCormack alone played to capacity."

50. *Banner,* Oct. 5, 1924, cited in Germaine Gioia, "Nashville, The Athens of the South, 1920-1930" (unpublished undergraduate paper, Vanderbilt Univ., May 1981).

51. See George Pullen Jackson, "The Nashville Symphony Orchestra: What is It Worth to You, Mr. Business Man?" *Nashville Review* 3(Oct. 15, 1921):1, for a classic example of cultural boosterism. See also the editorial in *Tennessean,* July 29, 1929, refuting the notion that industrialism will degrade the civilization and traditions of the South: "It should be possible for us to retain those graces that have given Southern civilization such a delightful flavor and at the same time take advantage of the opportunities which the accumulation of wealth will present to our people for a still higher development."

52. *Tennessean,* May 24, 1920, quoted in Blaine A. Brownell, *The Urban Ethos in the South, 1920-1930* (Baton Rouge, 1975), 71.

53. Jackson was a professor of German, an expert on southern folk music and white spirituals, and music critic for the *Banner.* He was referred to as the "father of the Nashville symphony," *Tennessean,* Oct. 5, 1928. See his obituary in *Banner,* Jan. 19, 1953.

54. Nashville Symphony Orchestra, *Program* (Nov. 7, 1930), 3.

55. *Tennessean,* Oct. 4, 1925.

56. Ibid., Mar. 4, 1929. See also Harry Eugene Williams, "Music at Peabody: A Personal and Factual History" (Ed.S. thesis, George Peabody College for Teachers of Vanderbilt Univ., 1979).

57. Nashville Symphony Orchestra, *Program* (sixth concert, 1926-27 season); *Tennessean,* Oct. 5, 1928, clipping in Kenneth Rose Collection, box 1, file 1, TSLA.

58. *Banner,* Apr. 17-24, 1927.

59. Ibid., Oct. 25, 1927; *Tennessean,* Nov. 6, 1927; see also *Tennessean,* June 20, 1936, for de Luca's obituary and a summary of his musical accomplishments in Nashville.

60. *Tennessean,* Aug. 5, 1928.

61. Jeter and Smith returned to Ward-Belmont in 1932. See the Jeter-Smith Collection, Nashville Room, Ben West Public Library.

62. Geraldton, *Social Directory,* 238.

63. *Tennessean,* June 19, Sept. 15, 1921.

64. Ibid., Apr. 15, 1921; Sept. 11, 1921, cited in Margery Hollister Hargrove, "A History of the Community Theater Movement in Nashville, Tennessee, 1926-1951" (M.A. thesis, Tennessee Technological Univ., 1965), 8-10.

65. Hargrove, "Community Theater," 10-14.

66. *Tennessean*, Sept. 5, 1926, quoted in ibid., 18.
67. *Tennessean*, Apr. 29, 1928, quoted in ibid., 29.
68. Hargrove, "Community Theater," 34–41.
69. Davidson, "Here or Nowhere!" *Tennessean*, May 29, 1927.
70. *Tennessean*, Oct. 11, 1934; Sept. 13, 1936.

CHAPTER TWO

1. Blaine A. Brownell, *The Urban Ethos in the South, 1920–1930* (Baton Rouge, 1975), 138.
2. *Tennessean*, Jan. 16, 1921.
3. *Macon County Times*, Lafayette, Tenn., June 7, 1926.
4. *Carthage Courier*, Feb. 4, 1926. Thanks to Jeannette Keith of Putnam County for sharing both these items with me.
5. Homer L. Hitt, "Peopling the City: Migration," in *The Urban South*, ed. Rupert B. Vance and Nicholas J. Demarath (Chapel Hill, 1954), 54–77; Jack Temple Kirby, "The Southern Exodus, 1910–1960: A Primer for Historians," *Journal of Southern History* 49 (Nov. 1983): 585–600, deals with migration out of the region.
6. George P. Antone, "Willis Duke Weatherford: An Interpretation of his Work in Race Relations, 1906–1946" (Ph.D. diss., Vanderbilt Univ., 1969); and Wilma Dykeman, *Prophet of Plenty: The First Ninety Years of W. D. Weatherford* (Knoxville, 1966).
7. See Jessie Bernard, *The Sociology of Community* (Glenview, Ill., 1973), 33–50, for a good summary of the theories of Robert Park and the Chicago School. On Nashville's leading sociologists see Patrick Joseph Gilpin, "Charles S. Johnson: An Intellectual Biography" (Ph.D. diss., Vanderbilt Univ., 1973); Antone, "Weatherford"; Dykeman, *Prophet*. Daniel Joseph Singal, *The War Within: From Victorian to Modernist Thought in the South, 1919–1945* (Chapel Hill, 1982), chs. 5, 10, deals primarily with the Chapel Hill sociologists but is helpful in understanding their counterparts in Nashville.
8. Nashville followed the Chicago model by establishing fixed census tract boundaries beginning with the 1930 census to allow consistent area studies over time.
9. Jerry Walker Combs, Jr., "Population Migration in the State of Tennessee" (M.A. thesis, Univ. of Tennessee, 1948), 173, 176.
10. Walter J. Reckless, "Census Tract Data for Nashville, Tennessee, 1930–1940," typescript [1941?], VUL, 4. This study, based on city directory entries, probably underestimates the population turnover, since many highly mobile poor people were left out of the directories.
11. *Tennessean*, Sept. 30, 1923. See also ibid., Oct. 1, 1932.
12. Waldo Proffitt, "A Study of Social Conditions in Davidson County" (M.A. thesis, Vanderbilt Univ., 1926), 40. "Real wages," i.e., controlled for changes in the cost of living, grew 63 percent for Nashville women between 1913 and 1923.
13. The ratio of males per 100 females in 1930 was 87.8; among those 15 to 29 years of age it was 79.9. The surplus of women in this younger age cate-

gory was even greater for blacks, 73.4, compared to whites, 82.6. Bureau of the Census, *Fifteenth Census of the United States: 1930, Population*, 3, pt. 2 (Washington, D.C., 1932), 890.

14. Avis C. Wiggins, "The Migrant Girl" (M.A. thesis, Vanderbilt Univ., 1933), 34.

15. Ibid., 78.

16. Ibid., 78-79.

17. Robbie Sanford interview, by John Rumble, May 21, 1981.

18. Wiggins, "Migrant Girl"; R.E. Wicker, "A Study of the Working Women Residing in Nashville's Four Largest Semi-Charity Homes for Women" (B.D. thesis, Vanderbilt Univ., 1931), 1.

19. Wiggins, "Migrant Girl," 68-72. Over 50% of the girls' home residents had arrived within the previous two years, 30% within the past year.

20. Susie Peach Foster, "Leisure-Time Activities of Industrial Girls in Nashville" (M.A. thesis, Vanderbilt Univ., 1930), 9-10. All 1929 wage estimates are from Aline Mayne Cavanaugh, "Women Workers in Nashville: A Wage Study" (M.A. thesis, Vanderbilt Univ., 1929), 57-58. Wages dropped about $2 on average by 1933, but the cost of living dropped correspondingly, according to Anna Fay Fowler, "Economic Adjustment of Rural Unmarried Girls Working in Nashville, 1932-33" (M.A. thesis, Scarritt College, 1933), 14.

21. John Hardcastle, interview with author, May 1981.

22. Charles T. Wyatt, *History of the Development of Watkins Institute, Nashville, Tennessee* ([Nashville], 1935), summarizes the history of this important night school. Wilson E. Wood, "The Development of Watkins Institute as an Educational Service to the Community," student paper, Watkins Institute library, 1951, describes the institute's programs during the interwar years. See also James C. Booth, "Educational Backgrounds and Personality Problems of Night School Students" (M.A. thesis, Vanderbilt Univ., 1938).

23. *Polk's Nashville City Directory, 1935* (Nashville, 1935), 1312-13.

24. In 1941 she left for higher wages at the Vultee Aircraft plant where overtime wages allowed her to earn $31 a week. Robbie Sanford interview.

25. Summarized in Wicker, "Working Women," 87.

26. Company magazines, Life & Casualty's *Mirror* and National Life's *Our Shield*, include numerous references to company-sponsored recreation for the home office staffs.

27. John Hardcastle interview. These observations were based on his recollections from a later period, but the pattern could not have been dramatically different in the interwar years.

28. Douglas Carr Chavis, "The Underworld of Nashville: Its Character and Function as Based on Records of Personal Experiences of Prisoners in the Tennessee State Prison" (M.A. thesis, Fisk Univ., 1941), app. E, 4. The description that follows is drawn primarily from Chavis's detailed account, unless specified otherwise.

29. Raines had strong links to the political machine of Mayor Hilary Howse and was allegedly exchanging political support—if not money—for police protection of his club. *Tennessean*, Sept. 9, 28, 1935.

30. Chavis, "Underworld," 25-26. *Tennessean*, Dec. 7, 1938, provides a rare account of Bill James's world.

31. A 1940 survey showed about one-third of black families in the Capitol

Hill area subscribed to the *Afro,* a newspaper—even though many could not read—largely because the winning number was disguised in the paper each week. George Washington Woody, Jr., "The Natural History of a Slum Area and of its Inherent Characteristics" (M.A. thesis, Fisk Univ., 1940), 100. Woody also mentions Bill James, the numbers king, and his generosity to the poor in the Capitol Hill area. Ibid., 97.

32. Camilla Caldwell interview, by John Rumble, May 21, 1981.

33. Chavis, "Underworld," 13-14.

34. Caldwell interview.

35. Ed Huddleston, *The Bootleg Era* ([Nashville, 1957]), 6, a compilation of articles originally appearing in the *Banner. Tennessean,* Oct. 12, 1927, lists many of the prominent madams and their addresses in a report on a vice raid. The Caldwell interview also informed this portrait of the Capitol Hill vice district.

36. Woody, "Natural History of a Slum," 70.

37. "The people on the whole," the surveyor observed, "give one the impression of being a rural people. Certain characteristics of rural people are quite dominant." Ruth Wyche, "A Community Survey of a Factory District in Nashville, Tennessee" (M.A. thesis, Scarritt College, 1931), 3-6.

38. Fisk Univ. Department of Social Science, "A Social Study of Negro Families in the Area Selected for the Nashville Negro Federal Housing Project" (1934), typescript report for the Planning and Zoning Commission and Nashville Federal Housing Advisory Committee, 9-10, in VUL.

39. Council of Social Agencies, "A Social Study of White Families in the Area Selected for the Nashville Federal Housing Project" (1934), typescript, 4.

40. See, for example, Harlan W. Gilmore, "Racial Disorganization in a Southern City" (Ph.D. diss., Vanderbilt Univ., 1931), 31-32. On the racial views of two important Nashville sociologists, see Gilpin, "Charles S. Johnson," 111-97; Antone, "Weatherford"; and Dykeman, *Prophet.*

41. Gilmore, "Racial Disorganization," 48-49.

42. J.B. Williams interview, by John Rumble, May 13, 1981, and Williams's family scrapbook, courtesy of J.B. Williams.

43. John Paul McConnell, "Population Problems in Nashville, Tennessee: Based on United States Census Reports for 1920 and 1930 and Other Related Local Data" (typescript, YMCA Graduate School, 1933), 105; Gilmore, "Racial Disorganization," 49, maps the rent categories for the city.

44. Derived from McConnell, "Population Problems," 104-5. For evidence of the persistence of poor housing in the 1930s see Eli Samplin Marks, "Housing Survey: Low Income Housing Areas of Nashville, Tennessee, 1940," typescript report to Nashville Housing Authority, in TSLA.

45. W.D. Weatherford, ed., *A Survey of the Negro Boy in Nashville, Tennessee* (New York, 1932), 26-27; Charles S. Johnson, "The Negro Population of the Tennessee Valley Area," (1934) typescript, pt. 2, pp. 11-13, Fisk Special Collections.

46. Weatherford, *Survey of the Negro Boy,* 61.

47. Methodist Episcopal Church, South, Board of Missions, *A Social Survey of the Bethlehem House Community, Nashville, Tennessee, December, 1920* ([Nashville, 1920]), 40-41.

48. *Report of Studies of Health Work* (Nashville, 1930), 282.

49. Lillian Claire Kelly and Frank Goodwin, "A Study of Racial Disorganization" (M.A. thesis, Vanderbilt Univ., 1930), 11.

50. Research and Planning Division of Council of Community Agencies, Nashville, Tenn., "The People of Our Community: Population Analysis and Related Social Welfare Data, Nashville and Davidson County" (Nashville, 1945), 3. See Frances Baker, "Aspects of Health Education in Areas Served by Bethlehem Center and Centenary Methodist Institute" (M.A. thesis, Scarritt College, 1935), for a thorough review of health conditions and the efforts to improve them during the 1930s.

51. Division of Surveys and Field Studies, George Peabody College for Teachers [Frank Bachman, Director], *Public Schools of Nashville Tennessee: A Survey Report* (Nashville, 1931), 154, 156 (hereafter Bachman, *Report*).

52. Council of Community Agencies, "The People of Our Community," 16.

53. Johnson, "The Negro Population of the Tennessee Valley Area," pt. 1, 134. Black high school attendance went up from 742 in 1929 to 1,089 by 1934, due in part to a lack of jobs. The building of the new Pearl High School in the 1930s also relieved the severe overcrowding that restricted enrollment earlier.

54. Proffitt, "Social Conditions in Davidson County," 40–41.

55. Weatherford, *Survey of the Negro Boy*, 31, 65.

56. Her weekly budget included $1.50 for burial insurance, and she insisted on buying from a white salesman, perhaps from National Life or Life and Casualty. John Gordon Gay, "Negro Dependency and Delinquency in the Southern Community" (M.A. thesis, Vanderbilt Univ., 1926), 38.

57. Robert A. Woods and Albert J. Kennedy, *Handbook of Settlements* (New York, 1911); Howard P. Chudacoff, *The Evolution of American Urban Society*, 2nd ed. (Englewood Cliffs, N.J., 1981), 184.

58. Roy Lubove, *The Professional Altruist: The Emergence of Social Work as a Career, 1880–1930* (Cambridge, Mass., 1965); Allen F. Davis, *Spearheads for Reform: The Social Settlements and the Progressive Movement, 1890–1914* (New York, 1967).

59. Francis H. McLean, *Path Finding Survey of the Social Work and Its Possible Development of [sic] Nashville, Tenn.* (Nashville, 1925), 7.

60. Marvin D. Bean, "A Study of the Methodist Settlements in Nashville, Tennessee, An Example of Selected Social Service Activities Under Denominational Sponsorship" (M.S. thesis, Nashville School of Social Work, 1948), 116; "Historical Sketch, Nashville Wesley House," *The Missionary Voice*, July 1925, p. 213; Emily Olmstead, "Finding the Larger Life," ibid., Apr. 1928, pp. 152–54.

61. McCulloch, *The Call of the New South: Addresses Delivered at the Southern Sociological Conference, Nashville, Tennessee, May 7 to 10, 1912* (Nashville, 1912). Dewey W. Grantham, *Southern Progressivism: The Reconciliation of Progress and Tradition* (Knoxville, 1983), 374–85.

62. Robert D. Smith, "A Historical Sketch of Bethlehem Center" (senior paper, Tennessee A&I, 1939), 1–4. See also, Board of Missions, *Social Survey . . . 1920*, 5–7

63. Board of Missions, *Social Survey . . . 1920*, 9–13; Thelma Stevens, "Summer at Bethlehem Center," *The Missionary Voice*, Sept. 1927, p. 280.

64. Olmstead, "Larger Life," 153.

65. Ernest F. Baulch, "Centenary Methodist Institute: A Short Account of the Past and Present of Centenary Methodist Institute" (B.D. thesis, Vanderbilt

Univ., 1933), 18–21, et passim. In 1916 the Methodists began a fourth settlement. This too was designed for white mill workers and their families. Located on Humphreys St. near the May Hosiery Mill in South Nashville, it was named the Lucy Holt Moore Community Center, in honor of the recently deceased president of the Board of City Missions. Bean, "Methodist Settlements," 91–92.

66. McLean, *Path Finding Survey*, 101–2.

67. Research and Planning Division of Council of Community Agencies and Community Chest, "Social Welfare Year Book: Nashville, Tennessee, 1939," typescript, VUL, 24.

68. Idem, "Social Settlements in Nashville, Tennessee 1937 . . . ," typescript, VUL, surveys the seven settlements in detail but does not identify them. The two additional settlements could not be identified.

69. Alfred Leland Crabb, *Nashville: Personality of a City* (New York, 1960), ch. 6, provides a good overview of church life in Nashville. See also Don H. Doyle, *Nashville in the New South, 1880–1930* (Knoxville, 1985), ch. 6, on the social gospel movement.

70. J.B. Williams interview.

71. Lillie Bearden, "The Religious Situation in the Fensterwald Settlement Area of Nashville, Tennessee" (M.A. thesis, Vanderbilt Univ., 1929).

72. Howard Kester, "A Study of Negro Ministers in Nashville" (B.D. thesis, Vanderbilt Univ., 1931).

73. Ibid., 48–49.

74. Baulch, "Centenary," 101–3.

75. Federal Writers' Project, WPA, *Tennessee: A Guide to the State* (New York, 1939), 192.

CHAPTER THREE

1. Don H. Doyle, *Nashville in the New South, 1880–1930* (Knoxville, 1985), chs. 6, 7.

2. George B. Tindall, "Business Progressivism: Southern Politics in the Twenties," *South Atlantic Quarterly* 42(1963): 92–106; Blaine A. Brownell, *The Urban Ethos in the South, 1920–1930* (Baton Rouge, 1975), 125–56.

3. Doyle, *Nashville in the New South*, ch. 7.

4. *Tennessean*, Aug. 8, 14, 20, 1915.

5. Biographical material on Gupton can be found in his obituary, *Tennessean*, Aug. 13, 1957; *Banner*, Aug. 13, 1957; and in *Banner*, Sept. 2, 1946, clippings in the scrapbooks on Nashville's mayors in the Nashville Room, Ben West Public Library.

6. *Banner*, Sept. 13, 1917, quoted in Howard S. Brooks, "Nashville's Municipal Politics, 1909–1938: Hilary Howse and the Decline of the 'Moral Wave'" (unpublished undergraduate paper, Vanderbilt Univ., May 1980), 11–12. Brooks, "Nashville's Reform Constituency During the Progressive Era" (unpublished undergraduate paper, Vanderbilt Univ., Dec. 1980), is another useful analysis of Nashville politics in the Howse era.

7. *Tennessean*, Sept. 14, 1917.

8. Ibid., July 23, 1918.

9. Ed Huddleston, *The Bootleg Era* (Nashville, 1957), 2–5.

10. Christman was finally sent to jail, but his twenty-one-year sentence was commuted after three and one-half years, and he returned to the city in Dec. 1930. Huddleston, *Bootleg*, 10, 15.

11. Ibid., 22.

12. *Tennessean*, Aug. 29, 1920, includes a full account of the legislative dealings. Louise Davis, "The Women Had the Last Word," *Tennessean Magazine*, Jan. 18, 1948; George B. Tindall, *Emergence of the New South, 1913–1945*, A History of the South, vol. 10 (Baton Rouge, 1967), 222–23; see also A. Elizabeth Taylor, "The Woman Suffrage Movement in Tennessee" (Ph.D. diss., Vanderbilt University, 1943); and the briefer version published as Antoinette Elizabeth Taylor, *A Short History of the Woman Suffrage Movement in Tennessee* (Nashville, 1943); Carrie Chapman Catt and Nettie Rogers Shuler, *Woman Suffrage and Politics: The Inner Story of the Suffrage Movement* (New York, 1923).

13. *Tennessean*, Mar. 15, 27, Apr. 18, 1921. Huddleston, *Bootleg*, provides a colorful account of the Western Front.

14. *Tennessean*, Mar. 15, 1921. The hotel referred to was the Hermitage.

15. Ibid., Apr. 18, 1921.

16. Ibid.

17. Irby Roland Hudson, "Nashville's Experience with Commission Government," *National Municipal Review* 10(Mar., 1921): 156–60.

18. On municipal reform, see James Weinstein, *The Corporate Ideal and the Liberal State, 1900–1918* (Boston, 1968); Kenneth Fox, *Better City Government: Innovation in American Urban Politics, 1850–1937* (Philadelphia, 1977).

19. Irby Roland Hudson, "Nashville Plays Politics," *National Municipal Review* 10(Sept., 1921): 452. Dean Anderson, "Nashville's City Manager Government: 1921–1923" (unpublished undergraduate paper, Vanderbilt Univ., spring 1981).

20. *Tennessean*, Feb. 5, 1921.

21. Ibid., Jan. 27, 28, 1921.

22. Ibid., May 1, 1921.

23. Ibid., May 5, 6, 1921.

24. Ibid., July 17, 1921.

25. Ibid., Apr. 18, 1923.

26. Ibid., Feb. 18, 19, 21, Mar. 6, 1922.

27. Ibid., Aug. 1, 1922.

28. Ibid., Nov. 25, 26, 1922; Arthur W. Bromage, "Why Some Cities Have Abandoned Manager Charters," *National Municipal Review* 19(Nov. 1930): 764–65. See *Tennessean*, Apr. 26, 1923, for a retrospective explanation of the Wilson ouster.

29. *Tennessean*, Jan. 13, 1923.

30. Ibid., Apr. 27, May 1, 1923. Two black candidates representing the Third and Fourth wards also ran for council on Howse's slate but were unsuccessful, apparently due to voting fraud.

31. Anderson, "Nashville's City Manager Government."

32. *Tennessean*, Apr. 21, 22, 24, 26, 1923.

33. Ibid., May 11, 1923. Biographical details on Howse's career can be found in his obituaries; *Tennessean*, Jan. 3, 1938; *Banner*, Jan. 3, 1938, and other clip-

pings in the scrapbooks on Nashville mayors, in the Nashville Room, Ben West Public Library; and Hilary Howse, "Scrapbook," TSLA.

34. *Tennessean*, Jan. 3, 1938; *Banner*, Jan. 3, 1938; Paul E. Isaac, *Prohibition and Politics: Turbulent Decades in Tennessee, 1885–1920* (Knoxville, 1965, 267.

35. *Tennessean*, Jan. 3, 1938.

36. Brownell, *Urban Ethos*, 99–124, 157–90.

37. *Tennessean*, Feb. 27, 1921. This arrangement began under reform rule and was widely publicized as "the Nashville Idea."

38. Brownell, *Urban Ethos*, 173.

39. Quote in *Tennessean*, Dec. 3, 1929. See also ibid., Feb. 3, 1927; "Minutes of City Planning and Zoning Committee," Nov. 30, Dec. 12, 1928; Feb. 22, Mar. 5, Dec. 12, 1929, in "Chamber of Commerce Committee Meetings," typescript in Nashville Chamber of Commerce. The chamber feared the 1925 legislation would interfere with the City Park Commission, an early stronghold of business progressivism in Nashville city government. See the Chamber of Commerce, "Minutes, Board of Governor's Meeting," Oct. 11, 1928 (hereafter "Minutes, BOG" and date); "Minutes, Cabinet Meeting," Dec. 28, 1931; Robert James Parks, "Grasping at the Coattails of Progress: City Planning in Nashville, Tennessee, 1932–1962" (M.A. thesis, Vanderbilt Univ., 1971), 33–40.

40. Parks, "Grasping at the Coattails," 35–37, 39–40, 43–52; Brownell, *Urban Ethos*, 181–82, 188–89; *Banner*, June 30, 1932.

41. Parks, "Grasping at the Coattails," 43–44, 57–66.

42. Ibid., 67–69, 75–78; Planning and Zoning Commission, *A Traffic Safety Survey of the City of Nashville . . . Conducted under the Auspices of the Tennessee Emergency Relief Administration* (Nashville, 1934).

43. *Nashville Transportation Survey: Findings* (Nashville, 1937). This report was prepared for the Railroad and Public Utilities Commission of the State of Tennessee with the cooperation of the Nashville Planning Commission.

44. *Tennessean*, Mar. 24, 26, Apr. 9, 1925; Oct. 13, 1929.

45. Ibid., Mar. 24, 1925.

46. John Ellis, "Belle Meade . . ." (M.A. thesis, Vanderbilt Univ., 1984).

47. *Polk's Nashville City Directory, 1924* (Nashville, 1924), 7; *Polk's Nashville City Directory, 1930* (Nashville, 1930), 12.

48. *Tennessean*, Dec. 6, 18, 1925; July 22, 1925.

49. See ibid., Nov. 10, 1933, for example.

50. Ibid., Nov. 2, 3, 4, 6, 9, 10, 13, Dec. 3, 1929; July 3, 4, 1930.

51. Ibid., Jan. 8, Mar. 7, Apr. 22, Aug. 11, 1935; Dec. 4, 1936. Jennings Perry, *Democracy Begins at Home: Tennessee's Fight on the Poll Tax* (Philadelphia, 1944), 44–45.

52. *Tennessean*, Sept. 20 through Nov. 7, 1935; Mar. 14, Apr. 25, Aug. 12, 1936.

53. Ibid., May 14, July 8, 1937; Aug. 5, 1938.

54. Ibid., Nov. 10, 1937.

55. Ibid., Feb. 2, 3, 4, 9, 1937.

56. Ibid., Feb. 4, 1937. Hatcher's columns provide excellent critical commentaries on local politics in this period.

57. Ibid., Apr. 16, 17, May 2, 1937.

58. Ibid., Apr. 24, 1937.

59. Ibid., Apr. 21, 24, May 2, 1937.
60. Ibid., Apr. 25, 1937.
61. Ibid., May 28, 30, 1937.
62. Ibid., Aug. 26, 1937; Jan. 3, 1938.
63. Ibid., Nov. 10, 1937.
64. Ibid., Mar. 29, 1938.

CHAPTER FOUR

1. Don H. Doyle, *Nashville in the New South, 1880–1930* (Knoxville, 1985), ch. 9.
2. *Tennessean*, Sept. 2, Oct. 5, 1930.
3. Ibid., Dec. 28, 1930.
4. Ibid., Nov. 16, 1930.
5. Ibid., Sept. 1, Nov. 28, Dec. 13, Dec. 22, 1930; Feb. 5, May 26, Sept. 3, Nov. 1, 1931; Feb. 26, Nov. 26, 1932, contains accounts of the suicides of prominent businessmen; there were probably many others, less well known, who were driven to similar acts of despair but never received attention in the newspapers.
6. See, for example, accounts in ibid., Jan. 18, Aug. 5, Dec. 13, 1931; Aug. 30, 1932; June 27, 1935; Apr. 26, 1936; March 13, 1938.
7. Ibid., Jan. 29, May 4, June 12, 1933.
8. Ibid., Apr. 7, 1931; Oct. 2, 1932.
9. "Social Welfare Yearbook: Nashville, Tennessee, 1941," typescript, 33–34; ibid., "1937," 55.
10. Dewey W. Grantham, Jr., *The Democratic South* (Athens, Ga., 1963), 69–74; Frank Friedel, *FDR and the South* (Baton Rouge, 1965).
11. Edgar Eugene Robinson, *The Presidential Vote, 1896–1932* (Stanford, Cal., 1933), 324. The turnout in 1928 and 1932 was just below 29,000 for the county, about one-quarter of the voting-age citizens. This turnout was up from a little over 17,000 in 1924. Voting restrictions and political apathy in the one-party South kept turnouts low.
12. Jennings Perry, *Democracy Begins at Home: The Tennessee Fight on the Poll Tax* (Philadelphia, 1944), 55–58, refutes the theory that Evans bought the *Tennessean* with a Reconstruction Finance Corporation loan.
13. *Tennessean*, Aug. 1, 10, 1933; Mar. 4, 1934.
14. Ibid., Aug. 1, 1933; see also July 26, 30, 1933, for accounts of the NRA in Nashville.
15. James A. Burran, "The WPA in Nashville, 1935–1943," *Tennessee Historical Quarterly* 34(Fall 1975): 293–306.
16. Ibid.; U.S. Congress, Committee on Appropriations, *Investigation and Study of the Works Progress Administration*, Before the Subcommittee of the Committee on Appropriations, House of Representatives, on House Resolution 130, 76th Cong., 1st sess., pt. I, 1939, 525; *Tennessean*, Nov. 9, 1935.
17. Robert James Parks, "Grasping at the Coattails of Progress: City Planning in Nashville, Tennessee, 1932–1962" (M.A. thesis, Vanderbilt Univ., 1971), 75–80.

18. Paul H. Beasley, ed., *A Directory of Nashville, Davidson County Historical Markers* (Nashville, 1977), 135, 79, 176–77.
19. *Tennessean*, Feb. 2, 14, 22, May 18, June 27, 1930.
20. Ibid., Jan. 15, Mar. 28, 1931; Oct. 25, 1932; Jan. 11, 15, 1933.
21. Ibid., Oct. 22, 25, 1935; Nov. 1, 1936.
22. Burran, "WPA in Nashville," 229; *Tennessean*, June 26, July 17, Oct. 22, 1935; Oct. 25, Nov. 1, 1936; Nov. 14, Dec. 22, 1937.
23. *Tennessean*, Oct. 9, 1939.
24. U.S. Congress, *Investigation*, 975–76. Another monument to Luke Lea, erected by the officers of his 114th Field Artillery regiment, stands nearby, but it was erected later in the 1950s.
25. *Tennessean*, Jan. 9, 1939; U.S. Congress, *Investigation and Study of the Works Progress Administration*, 984–85.
26. Bachman, *Report*, 356–61, 227.
27. John Dean Minton, "The New Deal in Tennessee, 1932–1938" (Ph.D. diss., Vanderbilt Univ., 1959), 147–48.
28. *Tennessean*, Jan. 30, 1934; Feb. 2, 1936; Mar. 14, May 1, Nov. 17, 19, 1937; Mar. 6, 1938.
29. Ibid., Mar. 15, 1940.
30. Ibid., Jan. 7, 10, 1930; July 19, 1934; Jan. 8, May 19, 1935; Nov. 22, 1936; Dec. 11, 1937.
31. John Elam, "The Impact of PWA on Nashville" (unpublished undergraduate paper, Vanderbilt Univ., May 1982). George Rollie Adams and Ralph Jerry Christian, *Nashville: A Pictorial History* (Virginia Beach, Va., 1981), 132.
32. *Tennessean*, June 27, 1935; see also ibid., July 26, 1936, on shanty boat dwellers on the Cumberland River.
33. Ibid., June 8, 9, Oct. 16, 1934; July 15, 1935; Mar. 7, 1936.
34. Ibid., Jan. 24, 1937; Minton, "New Deal," 151–55.
35. Charles S. Johnson, "A Social Study of Negro Families in the Area Selected for the Nashville Negro Federal Housing Project . . . ," (1934) typescript, Nashville Room, Ben West Public Library.
36. *Tennessean*, Mar. 3, Oct. 16, 19, 1938; see also ibid., Oct. 27, 1938, and subsequent issues for Nat Caldwell's series on public housing in Nashville.
37. Ibid., Nov. 1, 1938.
38. Ibid.
39. Ibid., Nov. 2, 6, 7, 1938.
40. Ibid., Nov. 15, 1938.
41. Ibid., Nov. 7, 24, Dec. 4, 9, 10, 12, 20, 24, 27, 1938; Jan. 13, 19, June 3, 29, 1939; Minton, "New Deal," 151–57.
42. Ellen Ann Dickerson, "The Nashville Housing Authority, 1938–1941: A Case Study of Public Housing Under the New Deal" (M.A. thesis, Vanderbilt Univ., 1977).
43. James A. Hodges, "The Tennessee Federation of Labor, 1919–1939" (M.A. thesis, Vanderbilt Univ., 1959), 39, 60, 61, 183.
44. *Banner*, Sept. 3, 1919; *Tennessean*, Aug. 22, 1919; Hodges, "Tennessee Federation of Labor," 37–38.
45. *Banner*, May 4, 1920, cited in Hodges, "Tennessee Federation of Labor," 47; *Tennessean*, Jan. 28, Dec. 5, 1920; May 22, 1922.
46. *Tennessean*, June 3, 1926.

47. Ibid., Jan. 28, 1920; Hodges, "Tennessee Federation of Labor," 161; Minton, "New Deal," 234-37.
48. Hodges, "Tennessee Federation of Labor," 63-65, 92-93.
49. Ibid., 106-25; Tom Tippett, *When Southern Labor Stirs* (New York, 1931), 58.
50. George B. Tindall, *Emergence of the New South, 1913-1945*, A History of the South, vol. 10 (Baton Rouge, 1967), 444-45.
51. Hodges, "Tennessee Federation of Labor," 161, 167; *Labor Advocate*, Jan. 3, Apr. 18, 1935; see also June 3, 1937.
52. Hodges, "Tennessee Federation of Labor," 176-77, 146. Peter Goodman, "Nashville Under the National Labor Relations Act: 1935-1937 . . ." (unpublished undergraduate paper, Vanderbilt Univ., May 1982), 5-6.
53. *CIO News*, Feb. 19, 1938, quoted in Minton, "New Deal," 227; *Tennessean*, Apr. 22, 23, May 8, 10, June 3, 1937.
54. Hodges, "Tennessee Federation of Labor," 184-87, 190.
55. *Banner*, June 13, 1937; see also *Tennessean*, June 3, 7, 1937.
56. "Minutes, Board of Governors" (BOG), May 5, 1937, Chamber of Commerce.
57. Hodges, "Tennessee Federation of Labor," 188.
58. *Decisions and Orders of the National Labor Relations Board*, IV, (Washington, D.C., 1938), 977, cited in Goodman, "Nashville," 10.
59. Minton, "New Deal," 219-21; *Decisions and Orders*, 982-86; *Tennessean*, July 28, 1937.
60. "Minutes, BOG," Aug. 3, 1937, pp. 1-3.
61. *Tennessean*, Aug. 3, 1937; see also July 28, 1937.
62. *Banner*, Aug. 10, 13, 1937.
63. *Labor Advocate*, Aug. 19, 1937.
64. *Tennessean*, June 3, 28, July 1, 2, 12, 1937.
65. Alfred J. Watkins and David C. Perry, "Regional Change and the Impact of Uneven Urban Development," in *The Rise of the Sunbelt Cities*, ed. David C. Perry and Alfred J. Watkins (Beverly Hills, 1977), 19-54.
66. Quoted in Donald Davidson, *The Tennessee: The New River, Civil War to TVA*, Rivers of America, vol. 2 (New York, 1948), 214. Davidson's account of the coming of TVA is a thorough, reliable history but is highly colored by his own strong reaction against "King Kilowatt" and against the whole premise that industrial progress is beneficial. See also William Havard's spirited essay "Images of TVA: The Clash Over Values," in *TVA: Fifty Years of Grass-roots Bureaucracy*, ed. Erwin C. Hargrove and Paul K. Conkin (Urbana, Ill., 1983), 297-315.
67. Davidson, *Tennessee*, 215.
68. *Banner*, Apr. 20, 1933, quoted in Minton, "New Deal," 259-60; *Tennessean*, Apr. 22, May 21, 1933.
69. *Tennessean*, Oct. 24, 25, 1933.
70. Paul Hembree, *The Role and History of Nashville Electric Service* (Nashville, 1973), 3; Davidson, *Tennessee*, 307-11; Minton, "New Deal," 287-88.
71. Minton, "New Deal," 289-90.
72. *Tennessean*, Aug. 16, 1939.
73. Ibid., Aug. 20, 1939.
74. Ibid.; Hembree, *Nashville Electric Service*, 8-9.

75. Hembree, *Nashville Electric Service*, 8–9; *The NES News*, July–Aug. 1979.

76. *Tennessean*, Jan. 23, 1940. The other major breakthrough improving air pollution in Nashville was the advent of the natural gas pipeline in 1946.

CHAPTER FIVE

1. *Census of Population: 1950*, 1, *Number of Inhabitants* (Washington, D.C., 1952), 74; *1980 Census of Population*, 1, *Number of Inhabitants*, pt. 1, *United States Summary* (Washington, D.C., 1983), 223.

2. Carl Abbott, *The New Urban America: Growth and Politics in Sunbelt Cities* (Chapel Hill, 1981), and Richard M. Bernard and Bradley R. Rice, eds., *Sunbelt Cities; Politics and Growth Since World War II* (Austin, 1983), ch. 1, provide overviews of the rise of Sunbelt cities after the war.

3. See Louise Davis, "The Man Who Wouldn't Take 'No,'" *Tennessean Magazine*, Aug. 14, 1966, for the story of Wade Thompson and Nashville's acquisition of a natural gas pipeline.

4. *Tennessean*, Nov. 26, 1939; May 22, 1945.

5. Ibid., Nov. 26, 1939; May 4, 1941; *Banner*, May 4, 1941.

6. *Banner*, Oct. 5, 1939; Nashville Chamber of Commerce, "Economic Survey of Essential Facts About Nashville, Tennessee as a Location for Defense Projects" (1941), typescript in Nashville Chamber of Commerce.

7. *Tennessean*, May 4, 1941.

8. Ibid., Sept. 1, 1940; Aug. 17, July 20, 1945; *Banner*, Feb. 25, 1941; John Egerton, et al., *Nashville: The Faces of Two Centuries, 1780–1980* (Nashville, 1980), 237.

9. *Tennessean*, Oct. 14, 1943; May 18, 1942; Jesse C. Burt, *Nashville: Its Life and Times* (Nashville, 1959), 121.

10. *Banner*, May 15, 1941; *Tennessean*, Dec. 11, 1941.

11. *Tennessean*, July 1, 2, 9, 18, 1941; July 6, Sept. 1, 25, 26, Nov. 22, 1942; Oct. 3, 1943.

12. Ibid., May 4, 1941.

13. Burt, *Nashville*, 124.

14. *Tennessean*, July 6, 1941; Sept. 6, Oct. 4, Dec. 4, 1942; Jan. 31, 1943; Mar. 26, 1944; Oct. 14, 1945; Egerton, *Nashville*, 239.

15. *Tennessean*, May 21, Oct. 4, 18, Nov. 24, Dec. 2, 1942; Jan. 7, 1943.

16. Ibid., June 23, 1944.

17. Ibid., Nov. 17, 1943.

18. Ibid., Apr. 8, 1944.

19. Ibid., June 23, Sept. 1, 1944.

20. Ibid., Mar. 14, 1945; Aug. 15, 1944; Apr. 24, 1949.

21. Robert Lovelace, "We're Committing Suicide Downtown," *Nashville Magazine* 4(June 1966): 10.

22. See *Tennessean*, Nov. 13, 1960, for a story on Lovemans, one of the downtown's oldest firms, which closed its old store and opened a new one in the suburbs at this time.

23. Howard P. Chudacoff, *The Evolution of American Urban Society*, 2nd ed. (Englewood Cliffs, N.J., 1981), 286–87, 296–99, provides a good summary of urban renewal and its critics. See also Martin Anderson, *The Federal Bulldozer* (Cambridge, Mass., 1964); James Q. Wilson, ed., *Urban Renewal: The Record and the Controversy* (Cambridge, Mass., 1966).

24. *Tennessean*, May 29, June 1, July 21, 1949; Robert James Parks, "Grasping at the Coattails of Progress: City Planning in Nashville, Tennessee, 1932–1962" (M.A. thesis, Vanderbilt Univ., 1971), 128.

25. Nashville Housing Authority, *Capitol Hill Redevelopment Project* (Nashville, 1952), 11, 24.

26. See Gerald Gimre and C. D. Campbell, "Nashville Upgrades City's Capitol Hill," *The American City* 76(June 1961): 209.

27. Nashville Housing Authority, *Capitol Hill*, 22. See Louise Davis's article on Mrs. John Hill Eakin and Mrs. Robert F. Weakley, who led the movement to improve the Capitol Hill grounds, *Tennessean Magazine*, Sept. 18, 1966. See also *Tennessean*, Nov. 13, 1966. The view of the east side of the Capitol, framed by the State Office Building and Cordell Hull Building, would again be partially blocked when the Central Services Building went up in later years.

28. Gimre and Campbell, "Nashville Upgrades," 209.

29. Chudacoff, *Evolution*, 284–97, summarizes federal-city relations. For a fuller treatment see Mark I. Gelfand, *A Nation of Cities: The Federal Government and Urban America, 1933–1965* (New York, 1975).

30. William Alexander, "Nashville's Premium: Insurance," *Nashville Magazine*, Sept. 1963, pp. 31–33; *Tennessean*, Dec. 6, 1964.

31. Alexander, "Nashville's Premium," 32; *Tennessean*, May 14, Sept. 2, 1953.

32. Era Irene Simmons, *The Thrift Family: The Story of Life & Casualty Insurance Company, 1903–1943* (Nashville, 1943), 49.

33. On Guilford Dudley, Jr., see *Banner*, Sept. 7, 1978; "The Guilford Dudley Story, Part I," *Tennessean Magazine*, Mar. 27, 1960, pp. 10–11, 22; ". . . Part II," Apr. 3, 1960, pp. 14–15, 20.

34. Chester D. Campbell, "Standing Tall at Sixty," *Nashville Magazine*, Sept. 1963, pp. 35–38.

35. Dudley continued as president until 1969. The company was reorganized in that year as a central headquarters for several American General acquisitions in the East and South. By 1976 the "Nashville-Based Companies" of American General surpassed $8 billion insurance in force. Allan Steele, former general counsel for the company, was installed as president of the L&C in 1970. Ibid.; *Tennessean*, Sept. 27, Oct. 16, 1966; "The Guilford Dudley Story"; "1903–1978, Observing Three Quarters of a Century of Growth," in *Life & Casualty Report for the Year 1977* (Nashville, 1977).

36. *Tennessean*, Aug. 11, 1963; July 5, 1978; Jan. 27, 1979; Powell Stamper, *The National Life Story: A History of National Life and Accident Insurance Company of Nashville, Tennessee* (New York, 1968), 253, 297, 336. See also NLT Corporation, "The NLT Story: A Corporate History and Fact Book Revised Through December 31, 1975" ([Nashville, 1976]), 3–4, for a discussion of the shifting markets for insurance.

37. *Tennessean*, Sept. 24, 1968; July 18, 1977.

38. By summer, 1982, after another dramatic takeover duel in which each

company threatened to buy out the other, NLT agreed to a "friendly merger" with American General.

39. Stamper, *National Life*, 231, 234–37.

40. Ibid., 283–84, 286, 325–30.

41. Third National Bank, *Nashville, 1927–1952: Twenty-five Years of Progress* (Nashville, 1952), 34.

42. *Tennessean*, Sept. 23, 1965.

43. Eleanor Graham, ed., *Nashville: A Short History and Selected Buildings* (Nashville, 1974), 81. Graham's book is the best single guide to historic and contemporary architecture in Nashville.

44. Third National, *Nashville, 1927–1952*, 32; *Banner*, July 18, 1977.

45. On Sam Fleming see Jim Sparks and Ken Powers II, "*Advantage* Interviews Sam Fleming," *Advantage* 2(July 1979): 47–50, 74–80, which includes many personal insights on Nashville business. See also Marshall Morgan, "Man on His Toes: Sam Fleming," *Nashville Magazine*, May 1963, pp. 23–28.

46. Margaret Dick, "Survival of the Fittest: Nashville City Bank at the Crossroads," *Nashville Magazine*, July 1978.

47. *Tennessean*, Jan. 24, Aug. 5, 1964.

48. Alice Jean Landt, "Economic Aspects of the Merger of the Third National Bank in Nashville and the Nashville Bank and Trust Company" (M.A. thesis, Vanderbilt Univ., 1966), 59–61, 29. By this merger Third National closed the gap between it and front-runner First American from $60 to $20 million, and gained a trust department in the bargain.

49. In 1970 Nashville Bank and Trust merged with Capitol City Bank, founded in 1964, and became Nashville City Bank. For the text of U.S. comptroller James J. Saxon's report, see *Tennessean*, Aug. 9, 1964. Dick, "Nashville City Bank."

50. *Banner*, Sept. 24, 1968; *Tennessean*, Jan. 16, 1972.

51. *Banner*, July 18, 1977; *Tennessean*, Aug. 15, 1978; Wayne Whitt, "Banking: A Center for the Mid-South," *Tennessean Magazine*, Jan. 1978.

52. *Tennessean*, Apr. 21, 1963; First American National Bank, *Three Quarters of a Century, Annual Report for 1957* (Nashville, 1957), 28.

53. First American National Bank, "Financial Leader for 90 Years" [1973], typescript, First American National Bank, summarizes the bank's history.

54. On Andrew Benedict see *Tennessean*, Jan. 15, 1960; Jan. 11, 1981; *Banner*, Apr. 17, 1968.

55. *Tennessean*, July 17, 1964; First American, "Financial Leader"; Whitt, "Banking."

56. *Banner*, Aug. 1, 1973, Apr. 6, 1974; Graham, *Nashville*, 79.

57. James R. Kellam, Jr., *Bootstraps: A History of Commerce Union Bank, 1916–1966* ([Nashville, 1966]), 44, 58–59.

58. Jesse Hill Ford, *Mr. Potter and His Bank: A Life of Edward Potter, Jr.* (Nashville, 1978). See also *Tennessean*, Dec. 4, 1983, for a good review of Harvey's downtown store.

59. Kellam, *Bootstraps*, 61–62; Ford, *Mr. Potter and His Bank*, 194–96. On Fred Harvey see Chester D. Campbell, "Fearless Fred, the Fabulous Storeman," *Nashville Magazine*, July 1963, pp. 30–34, 38; "Nashville's Flashiest Merchant," *Business Week*, Mar. 27, 1954, pp. 124–26. When negotiations between Harvey and a Lebeck heir stalled, Cain-Sloan intervened with a higher bid than Har-

vey, which would have thrown Harvey out of the largest of three buildings his store occupied on Church. The case was thrown into the courts where it went through four decisions. It was the most exciting case since the Scopes trial, some thought. When the Tennessee Supreme Court finally decided it in Harvey's favor the *Banner* headlines announced "HARVEY'S HAS IT!"

60. Kellam, *Bootstraps*, 45, 55.

61. Ibid., 69–71, 73. Broadway National Bank was run by Potter's father until the crash of 1930, and for sentimental reasons the merger had been postponed all these years.

62. Whitt, "Banking."

63. *Tennessean*, Aug. 26, 1979; Jan. 13, 1980; *Banner*, Jan. 7, 1980.

64. On Brownlee O. Currey see obituary, *Banner*, Feb. 21, 1952; *New York Times*, Feb. 22, 1952; and "Brownlee Currey Directs South's Largest Investment Firm," *Finance*, Feb. 10, 1946. On Equitable see "The Mid-South's Investment Center," ibid., Dec. 15, 1950; *Tennessean*, May 21, 1967, a reprint of a *New York Times* profile earlier that month, and Robert Jennings, "Nashville's Investment Giant" [unidentified periodical, 1968.], in Brownlee O. Currey, Jr., clippings. I am grateful to Mr. Currey for making available several clippings on his father and Equitable Securities.

65. John Ward and Patrick Thomas, "An Interview with J.C. Bradford," *Advantage*, June 1978, pp. 33–37. *Banner*, May 20, 1977; Dec. 15, 1981; *Tennessean*, Oct. 14, 1979.

66. For an overview of Nashville as a health center, see J.L. Farringer, "A History of Hospitals in Davidson County, Tennessee," *Journal of the Tennessee Medical Association* 67(Apr. 1974): 295–306.

67. Robert M. Gibson, Daniel R. Waldo, and Katharine R. Levit, "National Health Expenditures, 1982," *Health Care Financing Review* 5(Fall 1983): 2.

68. Paul Starr, *The Social Transformation of American Medicine* (New York, 1982), 338–78, 420–49, explores the federal role in the expansion of the health industry, the health crisis of the 1970s, and the "coming of the corporation" to health, with special attention to HCA.

69. Gibson, et al., "Health Expenditures."

70. HCA, *Fifteen Years of Growing Through Caring* ([Nashville, 1983]).

71. *Tennessean*, Sept. 23, 1979.

72. Dan Ermann and Jon Gabel, "Multihospital Systems: Issues and Empirical Findings," *Health Affairs*, Spring 1984, p. 53.

CHAPTER SIX

1. *Tennessean*, Oct. 18, 1964; Nov. 9, 13, 1974. See also Wesley Rose's warning against mixing country and pop music, *Banner*, Aug. 4, 1977; and Ernest Tubbs's criticism of recent trends in country music, *Tennessean*, Mar. 14, 1980. Going the other direction was the Nashville Music Association, organized in 1980 to promote Nashville as a "complete music center," including everything "from disco to gospel"; *Tennessean*, Aug. 1, 1980.

2. Charles K. Wolfe, *Tennessee Strings: The Story of Country Music in*

Tennessee (Knoxville, 1977), 54–74, esp. 55, 64, 70. Wolfe's excellent overview of the music industry in Nashville has informed this entire section.

3. Ibid., 72–75.

4. Ibid., 75–76.

5. Bill C. Malone, *Country Music, U.S.A.: A Fifty Year History* (Austin, Tex., 1968), 336–37.

6. Wolfe, *Tennessee Strings*, 77–78; Charles Portis, "That New Sound From Nashville," *Saturday Evening Post*, Feb. 12, 1966, p. 38; Roger M. Williams, *Sing a Sad Song: The Life of Hank Williams* (New York, 1973).

7. Wolfe, *Tennessee Strings*, 79–80.

8. Ibid., 82.

9. In the summer of 1982 Columbia Records announced that it would convert Bradley's famous Quonset hut into an office. *Tennessean*, June 26, 1982.

10. Wolfe, *Tennessee Strings*, 97; Robert Shelton and Burt Goldblatt, *The Country Music Story: A Picture History of Country and Western Music* (Indianapolis, 1966), 214–15.

11. Wolfe, *Tennessee Strings*, 104–105; Chet Atkins with Bill Neely, *Country Gentleman* (New York, 1975).

12. John Woodruff Rumble, "Fred Rose and the Development of the Nashville Music Industry, 1942–1954" (Ph.D. diss., Vanderbilt Univ., 1980), 43, 45.

13. Ibid., 72, 76, 78, 117–18.

14. Ibid., 141, 127, et passim.

15. Wolfe, *Tennessee Strings*, 101; Shelton and Goldblatt, *Country Music*, 219–20.

16. Shelton and Goldblatt, *Country Music*, 223–26.

17. *Tennessean*, Oct. 19, 1965.

18. Shelton and Goldblatt, *Country Music*, 223–26.

19. SESAC also followed BMI to Nashville in 1962; ibid. "A Big New Sound Blows Out of Nashville," *Broadcasting*, Jan. 28, 1963, pp. 67, 68, 69; this is one of the best surveys of the Nashville music industry. BMI had 208 publishers in Nashville in 1963; SESAC claimed only three, and ASCAP an undisclosed "few." Ibid., 69.

20. "A Big New Sound," 70, 80.

21. Paula Becker, "The Changing Image of Nashville Music," *Nashville Magazine*, (May 1966), pp. 11, 21; *Tennessean*, Nov. 5, 1964; Oct. 21, 1965; Feb. 25, 1966.

22. *Tennessean*, Apr. 1, 1967.

23. Shelton and Goldblatt, *Country Music*, 226–29.

24. Tony Velocci, "Country Music Makes the Bottom Line Boom," *The Nation's Business*, Jan. 1979, pp. 45–49. See also Richard A. Peterson, "Single Industry Firm to Conglomerate Synergistics: Alternative Strategies for Selling Insurance and Country Music," in *Growing Metropolis: Aspects of Development in Nashville*, eds. James F. Blumstein and Benjamin Walter (Nashville, 1975), 341–57.

25. See Pete Axthelm's tribute to the Ryman from the bar at Tootsie's, *Newsweek*, Mar. 25, 1974, p. 69; Garrison Keillor, "Onward and Upward with the Arts; at the Opry," *New Yorker*, May 6, 1974, pp. 46–48.

26. See *Tennessean*, May 2, 1975, for one of many periodic reports on the emerging tourist industry.

27. Velocci, "Country Music," 48. On Nashville as a convention center, see *Tennessean*, Jan. 12, 1975.

28. *Tennessean*, Oct. 19, 1965.

29. Ibid., June 14, 1982.

30. Edwin Mims, *History of Vanderbilt University* (Nashville, 1946), 429–87; *Banner Magazine*, May 26, 1935, p. 3; *Tennessean*, Jan. 23, 1938; Sept. 26, 1966.

31. Harvie Branscomb, *Purely Academic: An Autobiography* (Nashville, 1978), 141.

32. Ibid., 127, 128.

33. Ibid., 135, 186–89, 196–98.

34. Ibid., 197.

35. See *Tennessean*, Apr. 25, 1965; Feb. 18, 20, 1973, on the protest against the University Center project. See also Charles Fels, et al., "Special Project, The Private Use of Public Power: The Private University and the Power of Eminent Domain," *Vanderbilt Law Review* 27(May 1974): 681–813.

36. Branscomb, *Purely Academic*, 155.

37. Ibid., 154–56. Rev. Joseph A. Johnson, Vanderbilt's first black student, later became a member of the Board of Trust.

38. See ch. 8.

39. Branscomb, *Purely Academic*, 164–65. The undergraduate students voted against a recommendation to the Board of Trust that Vanderbilt adopt a policy of open admissions. Paul Conkin, *Gone with the Ivy: A Biography of Vanderbilt University* (Knoxville, 1985), forthcoming, will include a full account of the university's desegregation.

40. On Alexander Heard, see Saundra Keyes's overview in *Tennessean*, June 27, July 4, 1982; also *Tennessean*, Aug. 10, 1969; Dec. 9, 1980.

41. *Tennessean*, Sept. 20, 1964; Apr. 18, Oct. 24, Dec. 2, 1965. A notable exception to Vanderbilt's response to the activism of the 1960s was the Student Health Coalition, which continued to mobilize students in the service of the Appalachian poor long after the student movements on other campuses had sputtered out.

42. Keyes quotes the *Banner* editorial in *Tennessean*, June 27, 1982.

43. *Tennessean*, Mar. 27, 1968.

44. Ibid., June 27, 1982.

45. Robert A. McGaw, *A Brief History of Vanderbilt University* (Nashville, 1973), 43; *Banner*, May 1, 1970.

46. *Tennessean*, Dec. 9, 1980; June 27, 1982.

47. Ibid., May 7, 8, June 25, 1964; Sept. 27, 1965; Feb. 18, 1966; Jan. 7, 31, Mar. 18, 1967; Oct. 23, 1964.

48. Jack Allen, "The Peabody Saga," *The Peabody Reflector*, Summer 1980, pp. 4–13, provides a good overview of Peabody's history. My thanks to Evelyn Stephenson of the Peabody Archives for her assistance on this subject.

49. "Peabody Says 'NO' to Merger," *The Peabody Reflector*, Nov. 1962, p. 185; J.E. W[indrow], "It Takes Two to Cooperate," ibid., May/June 1961, p. 65.

50. *Tennessean*, May 25, 30, June 6, 1965; Mar. 29, Aug. 17, 18, 1966; Jan. 8, Mar. 26, Apr. 5, 1967.

51. Allen, "Peabody Saga," 13; *Tennessean*, Mar. 25, 1979; June 30, 1980; *Banner*, June 30, 1979.

52. *Tennessean*, Sept. 21, 1945; Oct. 30, 31, 1946; Nov. 7, 1947.

53. Ibid., July 7, 1949; June 25, 1950; June 29, July 4, 1954; Apr. 2, 1955.

54. See ch. 8.

55. *Tennessean*, Jan. 9, 1966; Joe M. Richardson, *A History of Fisk University, 1865-1946* (University, Ala., 1980), 124-25.

56. He was not related to the James Lawson expelled from Vanderbilt during the sit-ins of 1960.

57. *Tennessean*, Nov. 4, 1967; Oct. 7, 1968.

58. *Banner*, June 27, 1975; *Tennessean*, July 25, 1975; Oct. 9, 1977. Figures on Fisk's peak endowment vary from about $11 million to as high as $15 million in these several newspaper accounts.

59. *Banner*, Oct. 1, 1976; Oct. 7, 1977; Oct. 26, 1979; Mar. 1, 1982; *Tennessean*, Nov. 6, 1976; Oct. 7, 9, 1977; Jan. 16, 1979. In the winter of 1983-84 Fisk confronted a near-fatal financial crisis and was unable to meet utility payments. Students shivered in their dormitories, President Leonard resigned, and the university desperately sought outside help.

60. James Summerville, *Educating Black Doctors: A History of Meharry Medical College* (University, Ala., 1983), 96-97. My account of Meharry has drawn extensively from Summerville's well-researched study. See also *Tennessean*, Jan. 6, Mar. 3, June 6, 1941; Apr. 15, 1944.

61. Summerville, *Educating Black Doctors*, 120-21; *Tennessean*, Oct. 24, 1947; Jan. 19, Feb. 15, May 14, Dec. 14, 1948.

62. Summerville, *Educating Black Doctors*, 101-103; *Tennessean*, June 14, 18, 22, 23, 28, 1948; Apr. 3, July 11, 14, 1949.

63. Summerville, *Educating Black Doctors*, 134-36.

64. *Tennessean*, June 10, 1968; *Banner*, Apr. 6, 1976.

65. *Banner*, Mar. 2, Dec. 14, 1978; Apr. 17, 1979; *Tennessean*, Jan. 13, Mar. 22, Sept. 19, 1980.

66. Tennessee State University, "Fact Book for the Institutional Self-Study: Southern Association of Colleges and Schools" (Nashville, 1977), 5-7. This chronology of TSU history was prepared by Samuel H. Shannon of the TSU Department of History and Geography. I am grateful to Prof. Shannon for sharing his extensive knowledge of TSU's past with me.

67. Ibid.; "Ed Temple," *The Cupolian*, Fall 1977, p. 14.

68. Tennessee State University, "Contingency Planning Committee Self-Study Report" (Apr., 1978); John Egerton, "Tennessee's Long-Running Desegregation Drama," *Chronicle of Higher Education*, Apr. 3, 1977.

69. Egerton, "Desegregation"; *Banner*, June 30, 1979.

70. *Tennessean*, Aug. 27, Sept. 8, 1979; Jan. 13, 1980; *Banner*, Feb. 6, June 30, 1980.

71. James W. Carty, *Nashville as a World Religious Center* (Nashville, 1958).

72. Sydney E. Ahlstrom, *A Religious History of the American People* (New Haven, 1972), 954.

73. Ibid., 952–53.

74. John Shelton Reed, *The Enduring South: Subcultural Persistence in Mass Society* (Chapel Hill, 1972), ch. 6; Charles P. Roland, *The Improbable Era: The South Since World War II*, rev. ed. (Lexington, Ky., 1976), ch. 7.

75. Carty, *World Religious Center*, 19; Bertil Hanson, *A Report on Politics in Nashville* (Cambridge, Mass., 1960), p. I-8.

76. Carty, *World Religious Center*, 3; *Tennessean*, Sept. 20, 1954.

77. Daisy Maryles, "Bustling Nashville: Publishing, Bookselling, Wholesaling," *Publishers Weekly* Nov. 15, 1976, p. 46. Estimates of employment and payroll compiled by Don Belcher from data in Research Division, Nashville Area Chamber of Commerce.

78. Carty, *World Religious Center*, 14.

79. Ibid., 14; Maryles, "Bustling Nashville," 47.

80. Maryles, "Bustling Nashville," 47–48; Carty, *World Religious Center*, 3–4.

81. Maryles, "Bustling Nashville," 48.

82. Carty, *World Religious Center*, 2.

83. Ibid., 1.

84. *Tennessean*, Mar. 3, 1973; Apr. 24, 1974; Sept. 11, 1977.

85. Ibid., Sept. 11, 1977; *Banner*, Apr. 6, 1976. See also Louise Davis's biography of Andrew M. Burton, which details some of his contributions to David Lipscomb College; *Tennessean*, Oct. 9, 1966. Also Alfred Leland Crabb, *Nashville: Personality of a City* (New York, 1960), 205.

86. John T. Benson, *The Trevecca Story: Seventy-five Years of Christian Service* (Nashville, 1976); *Banner*, Apr. 6, 1976; Crabb, *Nashville*, 206.

87. Crabb, *Nashville*, 196–98; *Banner*, Apr. 6, 1976.

88. *Banner*, Apr. 6, 1976.

89. Ibid.

90. Interview with Paul C. Conkin by author, Oct. 29, 1984. Conkin *Gone With the Ivy*, includes a history of the Divinity School. Carty, *World Religious Center*, 20.

91. Carty, *World Religious Center*, 15.

92. Ibid., 17.

CHAPTER SEVEN

1. *Tennessean*, Feb. 4, 1938. The total vote was 18,307.

2. Ibid., Mar. 2, 1938.

3. See Joe Hatcher's eulogy to Cummings in ibid., Mar. 31, 1968; also ibid., Mar. 30, 1968; *Banner*, Mar. 29, 1968.

4. *Tennessean*, Mar. 2, 19, 1938.

5. Ibid., Mar. 2, 1938.

6. Ibid., Mar. 24, Apr. 13, 21, 23, 1938.

7. Ibid., Apr. 15, 16, 19, 20, 26, 27, 1938.

8. Ibid., May 10, 1938. Cummings appointed Phil M. Howse, Sr., nephew of the late mayor, to fill Tolmie's post. Apparently this was a ploy to placate

Howse loyalists, who felt their late leader had been unfairly dishonored in the recent revelations regarding the relief fund. See ibid., Apr. 27, 1983, p. 2.

9. Ibid., May 13, 20, 1938.

10. Ibid., Mar. 1, 3, 16, 26, Apr. 20, May 3, 29, 31, June 1, 2, Sept. 9, 10, 26, Nov. 29, 1938.

11. Ibid., July 19, Aug. 20, 1939.

12. Ibid., June 9, 1938.

13. Ibid., Aug. 4, 6, 1938.

14. Ibid., May 12, 1939.

15. Ibid., May 17, 26, 1939.

16. Ibid., Feb. 25, 1940; e.g., Oct. 18, 19, 1940, the *Tennessean* blasted Cummings for his "liquidation" of George Cate on the Board of Education.

17. See Luton's obituary in *Banner*, Dec. 4, 1952, for details on his political career.

18. *Tennessean*, Aug. 6, 1942.

19. Ibid., Aug. 2, 1940.

20. Ibid., Aug. 6, 1942.

21. Ibid., Jan. 27, 1941; Apr. 17, 1942.

22. Ibid., Dec. 4, 12, 1942; Jan. 6, 1943.

23. Public Administration Service, *Organization and Administration of the Government of the City of Nashville, Tennessee* (Chicago, 1943), 8–9.

24. *Tennessean*, Jan. 23, 26, Feb. 23, Mar. 12, 1943.

25. Ibid., May 14, 1943.

26. Ibid., July 1, 6, Oct. 10, 1943.

27. Ibid., June 15, 1944; Jan. 10, 11, 14, Feb. 7, 1945.

28. Ibid., Dec. 31, 1944; Jan. 1, 6, 1945.

29. Ibid., Jan. 11, Feb. 7, 9, 11, 12, 16, 21, 1945. The Davidson County delegation simultaneously promoted legislation to restore the recently repealed poll tax in city elections, which would be a major setback for reformers. *Tennessean* Feb. 16, Mar. 1, 2, 1945.

30. Ibid., July 15, 1945.

31. Ibid., July 23, 1946. See the file on Windrow's speech in George Peabody College for Teachers Archives for copies of the speech, published in pamphlet form, and correspondence from mostly approving readers.

32. *Tennessean*, July 7, 14, 23, 28, 1946.

33. Ibid., Feb. 4, 1947.

34. Ibid., Apr. 20, 1947.

35. Ibid., May 9, 1947.

36. See Hatcher's insightful column in ibid., May 11, 1947.

37. Ibid., Sept. 12, 15, Oct. 5, 1948; Mar. 9, 16, 17, 18, 19, 22, 24, 31, 1950. Bertil Hanson, *A Report on Politics in Nashville* (Cambridge, Mass., 1960), prepared for the Harvard-MIT Joint Center for Urban Studies, includes an excellent summary of the 1948–51 watershed in county and city politics.

38. *Tennessean*, Mar. 30, 31, 1968; *Banner*, Mar. 29, 1968.

39. The best summaries of West's career are found in obituaries: *Banner*, Nov. 20, 1974; *Tennessean*, Nov. 21, 24, 1974. See also Dick Battle's tribute on West's retirement in *Banner*, Mar. 29, 1963.

40. Hanson, *Report on Politics*, p. I-11.

41. When a serious diarrhea epidemic broke out in the summer of 1949, coinciding with layoffs of city garbage collectors, West took the occasion to blame "this little kinkapin mayor" who "lets these little babies die while garbage is lying in the alleys in the hottest season of the year." He denounced the mayor's recent layoffs of garbage collectors as "the scurviest, lousiest, stingiest trick one man ever pulled on another," and went on the compare the mayor to Hitler and Mussolini. *Tennessean*, July 8, 1949; see also ibid., Nov. 4, 1949.

42. Hanson, *Report on Politics*, p. IV-1. Robert B. McKay, *Reapportionment: The Law and Politics of Equal Representation* (New York, 1965), 59–86.

43. *Banner*, Jan. 18, Feb. 4, 6, 17, 18, 24, 25, 1915; *Tennessean*, Mar. 25, Apr. 2, 1940; *National Municipal Review* 29(May 1940): 334.

44. See ch. 3. Maps illustrating annexations in specific years can be found in Community Services Commission for Davidson County and the City of Nashville, *A Future for Nashville: A Report* (Nashville, 1952), 23–24 (hereafter *Future for Nashville*).

45. *Future for Nashville*, 44–53.

46. See, e.g., *Tennessean*, Jan. 19, 1949.

47. Daniel R. Grant, "Urban and Suburban Nashville: A Case Study in Metropolitanism," *Journal of Politics* 17(1955): 88.

48. *Future for Nashville*, 97–100; Grant, "Urban and Suburban Nashville," 87–88.

49. Grant, "Urban and Suburban Nashville," 88.

50. *Tennessean*, Feb. 2, 5, 16, Mar. 1, 3, 5, 29, 1950.

51. Ibid., Apr. 15, 22, 23, May 8, 28, 1952.

52. Ibid., Dec. 14, 1952; Jan. 2, 1953.

53. Brett W. Hawkins, *Nashville Metro: The Politics of City-County Consolidation* (Nashville, 1966), 18; Grant, "Urban and Suburban in Nashville," 82, 83, 99.

54. Daniel J. Elazar, *A Case Study of Failure in Attempted Metropolitan Integration: Nashville and Davidson County* (Chicago, 1961), 30, cited in Hawkins, *Metro*, 34.

55. Tennessee Taxpayers' Association, *Report on a Detailed Survey of the Financial Condition and Administration of Davidson County, Tennessee*, Research Reports, nos. 86–90 (Nashville, 1951–53), report no. 90, sec. IV, 3–5; Hawkins, *Metro*, 35.

56. The CSC included Edwin F. Hunt, chairman, Edward W. McGovern, Robert T. Cochran, Hugh J. Bradley, Edward E. Bryan, L. Elmer Bryant, James C. Dale, Jr., W. Dudley Gale, Calvin L. McKissack, Athens Clay Pullias, Mary K. Todd, Charles C. Trabue IV, Ernest B. Walton, Thomas M. Woodson.

57. *Future for Nashville*, 3–4.

58. *Tennessean*, Jan. 7, 13, 1953.

59. Grant, "Urban and Suburban Nashville," 98; Grant and Lee S. Greene, "Surveys, Dust, Action," *National Civic Review* 50(Oct. 1961): 467.

60. Grant and Greene, "Surveys," 467–68. Another amendment eliminated the old system of annexation by approval of the county delegation, thus making it more difficult to annex in the future.

61. Ibid., 468; Hawkins, *Metro*, 37.

62. Hawkins, *Metro*, 39.

63. Ibid.

64. Ibid., 42; Elazar, *Case Study*, 23–25.

65. Hawkins, *Metro*, 43.
66. Ibid., 43–44; *Tennessean*, Sept. 3, 1961.
67. Hawkins, *Metro*, 45.
68. Ibid., 46; Hanson, *Report on Politics*, p. VI-8; David A. Booth, *Metropolitics: The Nashville Consolidation* (East Lansing, Mich., 1963), 19–21.
69. Booth, *Metropolitics*, 20–21; Hawkins, *Metro*, 49–50.
70. Hawkins, *Metro*, 50.
71. Hanson, *Report on Politics*, p. V-2; Robert Horton, telephone interview with author, June 28, 1984.
72. Hawkins, *Metro*, 50.
73. Ibid., 50–56, 148, includes table on 1958 vote.
74. David Grubbs, "City-County Consolidation Attempts in Nashville and Knoxville, Tennessee" (Ph.D. diss., Univ. of Pennsylvania, 1961), 354, 374, cited in Hawkins, *Metro*, 51–52.
75. Elazar, *Case Study*, 10; Hawkins, *Metro*, 54–55; Edward McDill and Jeanne Clare Ridley, "Status, Anomia, Political Alienation and Political Participation," *American Journal of Sociology* 68(Sept. 1962): 205–13, cited in ibid., 56n.
76. *Tennessean*, June 5, 1960.
77. Hawkins, *Metro*, 58.
78. Booth, *Metropolitics*, 73; Hawkins, *Metro*, 58–59.
79. Hawkins, *Metro*, 59–60.
80. *Tennessean*, May 18, 1960; Hanson, *Report on Politics*, p. VI-11.
81. *Tennessean*, Apr. 2, 1960.
82. Hawkins, *Metro*, 60–61.
83. The court ruled that the annexation was reasonable and cited the recommendations for annexation in the 1952 study *A Future for Nashville*. See Grant and Greene, "Surveys."
84. Hawkins, *Metro*, 64–67. *Tennessean*, Apr. 2, 3, 5, 14, 17, 19, 20, 30, May 1, 1960.
85. Hawkins, *Metro*, 61–63.
86. Ibid., 70. *Tennessean*, Dec. 9, 23, 1960; Feb. 17, Mar. 1, 8, 9, 14, 1961.
87. Hawkins, *Metro*, 71; see *Tennessean*, Aug. 18, 1961, for election results.
88. *Tennessean*, Aug. 18, 1961; Hawkins, *Metro*, 71–72; Booth, *Metropolitics*, 81.
89. Hawkins, *Metro*, 73–74; Booth, *Metropolitics*, 83.
90. Lillard formed an unexpected alliance with Sam Davis Bell, mayor of Belle Meade, and Lewis Frazer of Forest Hills, another wealthy white suburb, in opposing Metro in the courts. Hawkins, *Metro*, 77–78.
91. Ibid., 75; Daniel R. Grant, "A Comparison of Predictions and Experience with Nashville 'Metro,'" *Urban Affairs Quarterly* 1(Sept. 1965): 51–52. Assuming that no blacks would win the at-large seats, this arrangement gave blacks six of forty-one seats, or less than 15%. The black population rose from over 31% to almost 38% of the old central city population between 1950 and 1960, then slipped to less than 28% of the enlarged city after the 1960 annexations. Within Davidson County nonwhites were only a little over 19% of the population in 1960, approximately half their proportion in the old city. Booth, *Metropolitics*, 13; Hawkins, *Metro*, 19.

92. Booth, *Metropolitics*, 82, 92n.26; Hawkins, *Metro*, 77; see also David Booth, "New Wine in Old Bottles: Nashville's New Charter," *Municipal South* 9(June 1962): 26–30; *Banner*, Sept. 12, 1961.
93. Hawkins, *Metro*, 92–108.
94. Ibid., 93–94.
95. Ibid., 93.
96. Ibid.
97. Ibid., 96–97.
98. Ibid., 81–82, 85–90.
99. Grant, "Metro and Professional Political Leadership: The Case of Nashville," *Annals of the American Academy of Political Economic Science* 353(May 1965): 80.
100. Booth, *Metropolitics*, 87; Hawkins, *Metro*, ch. 9, includes detailed analysis of voter opinion.
101. Hawkins, *Metro*, table 20, p. 151, gives the votes by ward and district.
102. See David Halberstam, "Good Jelly's Last Stand," *Reporter*, Jan. 19, 1961, pp. 40–41, for an interesting account of this politician's uneasy alliance with West during the Metro battle.
103. Hawkins, *Metro*, 141–44.
104. The sketch of Briley that follows is drawn from *Tennessean*, Jan. 12, Aug. 31, 1975; Sept. 15, 1980; *Banner*, Sept. 16, 1980.
105. Chester D. Campbell, "Metro Mayor," *Nashville Magazine*, Jan. 1963, p. 37; *Tennessean*, Aug. 31, 1975.
106. *The Municipal Yearbook, 1972* (Boston, 1972), 87.
107. Grant, "Comparison"; Horton interview.
108. *Tennessean*, Jan. 23, 1966.
109. "Nashville Thrives on City-County Merger," *Business Week*, Sept. 25, 1971; *Tennessean*, Dec. 28, 1979.
110. *Tennessean*, Dec. 28, 1979.
111. "Nashville Thrives"; Gareth Aden and Chester Campbell, "The Upheaval Downtown," *Nashville Magazine*, Feb. 1967.
112. Horton interview.
113. Ibid.
114. Ibid.
115. Ibid.
116. *Tennessean*, May 20, 1966.
117. Ibid., Jan. 12, Aug. 31, 1975; Sept. 15, 1980; *Banner*, Sept. 16, 1980; Horton interview.
118. Loser, a conservative, apparently won the Democratic primary by 78 votes, but evidence of election fraud forced both candidates to run as independents in the general election, which Fulton swept with a 17,000-vote margin. Gene "Little Evil" Jacobs went to jail for election fraud in the primary. *The Almanac of American Politics . . . 1974* (Boston, 1973), 950, includes a sketch of Fulton's political career.
119. *Tennessean*, Aug. 5, 1975.
120. Horton interview.
121. Community Services Administration, *Geographic Distribution of Federal Funds in Tennessee* (Washington, D.C., 1979).

CHAPTER EIGHT

1. "Nashville and the Black Student Movement," panel discussion, Martin Luther King, Jr., Lectures, Vanderbilt University, Jan. 23, 1985.
2. Neil R. McMillen, *The Citizens' Council: Organized Resistance to the Second Reconstruction, 1954–64* (Urbana, Ill., 1971), 129–30.
3. Among the black Nashville elite would be Henry Allen Boyd, Dr. R. H. Boyd, M. G. Ferguson, Flem Otey, Coyness Ennix, Calvin McKissick, Dr. George S. Meadors, and Z. Alexander Looby as leaders of business, law, and the professions. Connected to Fisk and Meharry Medical College were Doctors Stephen J. Wright, Harold West, Mathew Walker, Dorothy Moore, Merle Eppse, and Mrs. Charles S. Johnson.
4. Patrick Joseph Gilpin, "Charles S. Johnson: An Intellectual Biography" (Ph.D. diss., Vanderbilt Univ., 1973), 523–35.
5. See Jack L. Walker "The Functions of Disunity: Negro Leadership in a Southern City" in *The Making of Black America*, 2, August Meier and Elliott Rudwick, eds., (New York, 1971), 342–52. According to arrest records publicized by the police, 98 percent of the protesters in the February 27, 1960 demonstrations were from "out of town." *Banner*, Apr. 11, 1960.
6. Lester C. Lamon, *Blacks in Tennessee, 1791–1970* (Knoxville, 1981), 98.
7. Jennings Perry, *Democracy Begins at Home: The Tennessee Fight on the Poll Tax* (Philadelphia, 1944), 154. Frederic D. Ogden, *The Poll Tax in the South* (University, Ala., 1958), 142, 193–99.
8. Bertil Hanson, *A Report on Politics in Nashville* (Cambridge, Mass., 1960), pp. III-2–III-7. *Tennessean*, May 14, 1937; Jan. 20, 1938; Aug. 16, 1941; Aug. 5, 1945; Feb. 2, 1947. Voting data from *Tennessean* May 14, 1943; May 13, 1955.
9. Looby had run unsuccessfully in 1943 and 1947. *Globe*, Apr. 10, 1943. Z. Alexander Looby Papers, Fisk University Special Collections, clippings.
10. Don H. Doyle, *Nashville in the New South, 1880–1930* (Knoxville, 1985), ch. 7.
11. Hanson, *Report*, p. I-11.
12. Mrs. Z. Alexander Looby interview, by Betty Grimes, May 29, 1984. The other biographical information is taken from George Barker's two-part series on Looby, "Man Behind the Move," and "No Place to Hide," *Tennessean Magazine*, Apr. 16, 23, 1961.
13. *Tennessean*, July 6, 1949; Gilpin, "Charles S. Johnson," 542–43.
14. Looby Papers, clippings; Hugh Davis Graham, "Desegregation in Nashville: The Dynamics of Compliance," *Tennessee Historical Quarterly* 25(Summer 1966): 137.
15. Stanley J. Folmsbee, Robert E. Corlew, Enoch L. Mitchell, *Tennessee: A Short History* (Knoxville, 1969), 574. McMillen, *Citizens' Council*, 308–309.
16. Casey Jenkins's popular opposition to busing in the mayoral election of 1971 against incumbent Beverly Briley may be the exception that proves this rule.
17. Hugh Davis Graham, *Crisis in Print: Desegregation and the Press in Tennessee* (Nashville, 1967), 36; Graham, "Desegregation," 139–42.

18. Metropolitan Planning Commission, *A Study of Nonwhite Residential Distribution in Nashville, Tennessee in 1940, 1950, 1960, and 1970* (Nashville, 1975), map 2.

19. Ibid., map 4.

20. John Vahaly, Jr., and Benjamin Walter, "Black Residential Succession in Nashville, 1930 to 1960," in James F. Blumstein and Benjamin Walter, eds., *Growing Metropolis: Aspects of Development in Nashville,* (Nashville, 1975), 96. The number of blacks designated by the Census Bureau to constitute a black census tract rose from 250 in 1940 to 400 in 1960, a change that may exaggerate the trend toward racial segregation as measured in these statistics. However, other measures, specifically the index of dissimilarity based on block data, indicate growing segregation of the races from 1940 to 1960, when the index rose from 86 to 91; it leveled off in the 1960s as blacks penetrated more white neighborhoods. Planning Commission, *Nonwhite Residential Distribution,* 12.

21. Vahaly and Walter, "Black Residential Succession," 98. These data apply only to blacks living in the black census tracts, defined in the previous note, but that included virtually all blacks.

22. Ibid. The rising percentage of white-collar employees and high school graduates, and the reduction in residential overcrowding, also confirmed the trend of improving conditions for black Nashville.

23. Ibid., 98, 107; Planning Commission, *Nonwhite Residential Distribution,* 39.

24. Among 2,300 employees at Ford Glass, fewer than 2% were black, and many of those were in menial jobs; at Gates Rubber, fewer than 1% were black. Henderson's report is summarized in *Tennessean,* Apr. 24, 1960. See also, Vivian Henderson, *The Economic Status of Negroes: In the Nation and in the South* (Atlanta, 1963).

25. Of Nashville's 3,650 acres of park land among 32 parks, blacks were allowed fewer than 55 acres (1.5%) among 6 parks, including 34 acres in Hadley Park near the TSU campus. Community Services Commission for Davidson County and the City of Nashville, *A Future for Nashville: A Report* (Nashville, 1952), 141.

26. J.M. Elrod, "I Invited Negroes to My Home," *Atlantic,* Jan. 1961, pp. 67–68.

27. The best point to begin the study of desegregation in Nashville is Graham, *Crisis,* and his summary article "Desegregation." See also Saundra Ivey's eleven-part series, "Desegregation," *Tennessean,* May 13–27, 1979. Nashville's racial strife won constant attention in the national press, coverage interesting not only for factual information but also for the national interpretation of Nashville's successful adjustment to integration, a theme that became a self-fulfilling prophecy to some degree. Several of these articles are cited in the notes that follow.

28. Graham, *Crisis,* 180; the numbers vary from one source to the next.

29. The quote on Davidson is taken from Russell Kirk, "A Professor of Genius," *National Review,* June 8, 1957, p. 555, quoted in Neil R. McMillen, "Organized Resistance to School Desegregation in Tennessee," *Tennessee Historical Quarterly* 30(Fall 1971): 324. McMillen's article and book, *Citizens' Council,* provide the best overview of white resistance.

30. *Christian Century,* Oct. 9, 1957.

31. *U.S. News and World Report,* Sept. 20, 1957, pp. 74–76; Benjamin Muse, *Ten Years of Prelude: The Story of Integration Since the Supreme Court's 1954 Decision* (New York, 1964), 118.

32. The second Klan of the 1920s had staged a cross-burning rally in Nashville, but they had never found sufficient popular support to sustain a local organization. *Tennessean,* June 3, 1923.

33. Muse, *Ten Years,* 118.

34. *Tennessean,* Aug. 4, 29, 1957.

35. *New York Times,* Aug. 29, 1957, quoted in Alexander Tettenborn, "The Development of Civil Rights in Nashville from 1954 to 1964" (unpublished undergraduate paper, Vanderbilt Univ., spring 1980), 8.

36. *U.S. News and World Report,* Sept. 20, 1957, p. 74; *Newsweek,* Sept. 23, 1957, p. 30.

37. *Newsweek,* Sept. 23, 1957, p. 30.

38. Muse, *Ten Years,* 119–20.

39. *Tennessean,* Aug. 18, Nov. 8, 9, 1958.

40. *Newsweek,* Sept. 23, 1957, p. 31.

41. Will D. Campbell telephone interview, by Betty Grimes, May 24, 1984.

42. Jackson Toby, "Bombing in Nashville: A Jewish Center and the Desegregation Struggle," *Commentary* 25(May 1958): 385–89; see also Lou H. Silberman's letter to the editor in ibid. (July 1958): 79–80. For a general discussion of the dynamics of race and religion in Nashville see Eugene J. Lipman and Albert Vorspan, eds., *A Tale of Ten Cities: The Triple Ghetto in American Religious life* (New York, 1962), 139–65, a chapter entitled "Nashville: Athens with an Achilles Heel."

43. Graham, "Desegregation," 152–53.

44. *Tennessean,* Nov. 13, 1960; *Banner,* June 3, 1963; Tettenborn, "Civil Rights," 13–14. See John Egerton, "De Facto Segregation: A Tale of Three Cities," *Southern Education Report* 3(Sept. 1967): 13–14; Helen Fuller, "Nashville—First Steps Firmly Taken," *New Republic,* Mar. 2, 1959, pp. 12–16; and W. A. Bass, "In Nashville Schools," *National Education Association Journal* 52(Dec. 1963): 48–50, for three optimistic assessments on Nashville's school desegregation, the last by the city's superintendent of schools. For a less sanguine view a few years later see John Egerton, "Report Card on Southern School Desegregation," *Saturday Review* 55(Apr. 1, 1972): 47–48.

45. August Meier and Elliott Rudwick, *CORE: A Study in the Civil Rights Movement* (Urbana, Ill., 1975), 75–76, 85. Nashville's CORE chapter disintegrated in 1959 when Holden left.

46. For a description of Smith's role in the Nashville movement, see *Time,* May 26, 1961, p. 17.

47. Meier and Rudwick, *CORE,* 49, 77; Guy Carawan, "The Nashville Sit-In Story," *Folkways Records* (New York, 1960), in Fiskiana Collection, Fisk University, Special Collections. The recollections of Kelly Miller Smith, John Lewis, Diane Nash, and other civil rights activists in Nashville are included on this recording. The album notes by Smith also provide details on the early planning of the sit-ins. See also, *Globe and Independent,* Feb. 20, 1959.

48. Carawan, "Sit-In," Diane Nash recollection. Information also from John

Lewis, telephone interview, with Betty Grimes, May 20, 1984. See also the interview with Lewis in Howell Raines, *My Soul is Rested: Movement Days in the Deep South Remembered* (New York, 1977), 71-74, 97-100.

49. Carawan, "Sit-In."

50. Lewis interview; *Banner*, Mar. 21, 1960.

51. *Tennessean*, Feb. 14, 19, 21, 1960. Reports of the first sit-ins were repressed in the *Tennessean*'s city editions, and buried in the back pages of the suburban and state edition on Feb. 14. The *Banner* reported none of the sit-ins before February 27. See also Julia Moore's inside report in *Fisk News* (Spring, 1960), 16, which mistakenly places the first sit-ins on Feb. 6 and 11; and Carawan "Sit-In."

52. *Banner*, Feb. 29, 1960.

53. Earl Mays, a Fisk student, testified that the police deliberately left the protesters exposed to their attackers at a point when white anger had reached a peak. He ran outside to ask a police officer for help and was told he was busy "directing traffic." The police denied this account. *Tennessean*, Feb. 29, 1960. LaPrad was a visiting student from India. James Lawson at the Martin Luther King Lectures, Vanderbilt University, Jan. 23, 1985, related behind the scenes details on the sit-ins.

54. David Halberstam, "'A Good City Gone Ugly,'" *The Reporter*, March 31, 1960, p. 19.

55. Carawan, "Sit-In"; Moore, *Fisk News*. Again, the numbers of those arrested and brought to trial sometimes vary from one source to the next. Two of the 81 were juveniles and not brought to trial. *Banner*, Mar. 4, 1960.

56. *Banner*, Mar. 1, 1960.

57. Ibid., Mar. 1, 2, 1960.

58. Ibid., Mar. 3, 4, 1960.

59. See Harvie Branscomb, *Purely Academic: An Autobiography* (Nashville, 1978), for his account of the Lawson affair. Woodrow A. Geier, "Sit-ins Prod a Community," *Christian Century* 77(Mar. 30, 1960): 379-82, includes a good summary of the Lawson affair.

60. Moore, *Fisk News*.

61. Ibid., 17; *Banner*, Mar. 4, 1960.

62. *Banner*, Mar. 1, 1960; *Tennessean*, Mar. 8, 1960.

63. *Tennessean*, Mar. 19, 1960; *Banner*, Mar. 19, 1960.

64. *Banner*, Mar. 26, 1960.

65. *Tennessean*, Apr. 6, 10, 1960. The committee members included two blacks, Dr. Steven J. Wright, president of Fisk, and Dr. W.S. Davis, president of Tennessee A&I. Two others, Lipscomb Davis of Davis Cabinet Co. and F. Donald Hart of Temco, were businessmen. B.B. Gullett, president of the Nashville Bar Association, and George Barrett, a lawyer and president of the Nashville Community Relations Conference, filled out the rest of the committee. *Banner*, Mar. 4, 1960.

66. *Banner*, Apr. 11, 1960.

67. *Tennessean*, Apr. 5, 1960. See Louis E. Lomax, *The Negro Revolt* (New York, 1962), 125-30, for an account of the Nashville sit-ins and the boycott. Lomax viewed the Nashville movement as being among the best organized and most effective in the civil rights movement up to that point. Ibid., 129.

68. *Tennessean*, Mar. 3, 1960. Greenfield Pitts of Harvey's estimated that about 15% of the store's business was from the black community. Greenfield Pitts, telephone interview, by Betty Grimes, May 29, 1984.
69. Moore, *Fisk News*, Summer 1960, p. 8.
70. *Banner*, Apr. 20, 1960; *Tennessean*, Apr. 20, 1960.
71. *Tennessean*, Apr. 19, 20, 1960; *Banner*, Apr. 19, 1960.
72. Carawan, "Sit-In"; Moore, *Fisk News*, Summer 1960, p. 9; *Tennessean*, Apr. 20, 1960. The reporter was David Halberstam.
73. *Tennessean*, Apr. 21, 1960.
74. Ibid., May 11, 1960. The six-week boycott ended at this point.
75. *Time*, May 26, 1961, p. 17.
76. Pitts, interview.
77. McMillen, *Citizens' Council*, 250.
78. Pitts, interview. *Tennessean*, May 11, 12, 1960.
79. *Tennessean*, Nov. 11, 13, 14, 23, 24, 1960. See John Lewis's account in Raines, *My Soul is Rested*, 99–100.
80. Ibid., Feb. 2, 3, 5, 10, 21, 26, May 8, 1961.
81. Ibid., Aug. 7, 9, 14, 1961.
82. Ibid., Feb. 2, 16, Nov. 25, Dec. 10, 1962.
83. Ibid., Mar. 20, 27, 31, Apr. 10, May 9, 14, 1963.
84. Ibid., Mar. 28, 30, Apr. 29, May 7, 12, 16, 17, 21, 25, 31, Sept. 15, 1963. Will Campbell recalled conferring with Mayor Briley on the membership of the committee. When he noted the absence of any ministers among all the business executives, Briley responded that "if the ministers had done their job," the committee would not be necessary. Campell interview.
85. See Edmund Willingham's optimistic report in *Tennessean*, Sept. 15, 1963; also June 11, Oct. 11, Dec. 13, 1963.
86. Ibid., Apr. 2, 1964.
87. Ibid., Oct. 28, 31, Nov. 11, 30, Dec. 23, 1965.
88. Ibid., June 25, Dec. 8, 1963; Apr. 28, 30, May 1, 2, 4, 7, 8, July 4, 1964. In a sip-in, white customers ordered a cup of coffee and tied up a table for several hours to slow down business while black protesters picketed outside.
89. McMillen *Citizens' Council*, 130; *Tennessean*, June 20, Sept. 29, 1965.
90. *Tennessean*, Oct. 15, 18, Nov. 3, 1965; Feb. 3, 1966.
91. *Newsweek*, May 11, 1964, pp. 21–22; *U.S. News and World Report*, May 11, 1964, p. 6.
92. On segregation and housing, see the excellent series by Saundra Ivey and Dwight Lewis in *Tennessean*, June 5, 6, 8, 14, 1977.
93. See, e.g., the laudatory articles in ibid., Sept. 15, 1963; Feb. 16, Apr. 2, 1964; Dec. 2, 1965. The articles in the national press, cited above and below, generally upheld a similar image of Nashville as an exceptional southern city.
94. *Tennessean*, Apr. 8, 1967.
95. Ibid., Apr. 16, 1967.
96. As reported in ibid.
97. Ibid. and June 4, 1969.
98. Ibid. and Apr. 20, May 7, 1967; Apr. 5, 6, 1968.
99. In 1970 among those students in public schools, 81% of whites and 62% of blacks went to schools with 90% or more of their own race. Ibid., May 18, 1979.

100. Ibid., May 23, 1979.

101. Ibid., May 18, 1979. There were so few blacks in the county outside the city, this had little practical effect.

102. Edwin Hale Harris, "Desegregation: Metropolitan Nashville–Davidson County Public Schools, 1955–71" (Ed.S. thesis, George Peabody College for Teachers, 1971), 26f.

103. *Tennessean,* May 20, 1979.

104. Ibid., May 27, 1979.

105. Ibid., July 22, 1973. Cf. statistics in ibid., Aug. 3, 1980, which show a less dramatic climb. Richard Pride and J. David Woodard, "The Burden of Busing: The Politics of Desegregation in Nashville, Tennessee" chs. 6, 8, includes a through analysis of the shift of white students out of public schools and into private schools, controlled for the effects of normal suburban migration and the decline of the birth rate. I am grateful to Prof. Pride for allowing me to read portions of this book forthcoming from University of Tennessee Press.

106. See Saundra Ivey's review, *Tennessean,* May 21, 24, 25, 1979. Also ibid., Apr. 10, 1977; Jan. 14, Aug. 26, 1979; Jan. 13, Aug. 3, 1980, for articles dealing with the decline in public confidence in the schools.

CHAPTER NINE

1. The 1980 census showed 518,325 in the densely settled areas of Davidson County and adjacent counties. There were 805,505 people in the eight-county SMSA. *1980 Census of Population,* 1, *Characteristics of the Population,* ch. A, *Number of Inhabitants,* pt. 1, *United States Summary* (Washington, D.C., 1983), 223, 249.

2. The federal census of 1920 showed 28.1% of the South living in settlements of 2,500 or more; the census for 1980 showed 66.9% in urban places. The U.S. figures for these years were 51.2% and 73.7%. Ibid., 1–49.

3. See Don H. Doyle, *Nashville in the New South, 1880–1930* (Knoxville, 1985), ch. 1, for an account of the 1880 Centennial celebration.

4. Others on the steering committee included: Robert J. Baltz, of Baltz Brothers meatpackers; Ruth Burkitt, head of the Cane Ridge Community Club in the Antioch area; Robert M. Eskind, with Capitol Distributors; Matthew Lynch, president of the Tennessee State Labor Council; Ira L. North, television evangelist and Madison Church of Christ minister; Diane Porter, director of public relations with the Tennessee Department of Revenue and a black television show hostess; Kelly Miller Smith, civil rights leader and minister of the black First Baptist, Capitol Hill Church; Allen M. Steele, president of Life and Casualty Insurance Company; William C. Weaver, Jr., retired chairman of National Life Insurance Company; and Eleanor Willis, wife of William Willis, a prominent lawyer connected with Mayor Fulton. North was later replaced by Robert H. Spain, district superintendent of the United Methodist Church. Weaver died in March 1979 and was replaced by Charles J. Kane, chairman of Third National Bank, who served the committee as treasurer. Russell L. Wagner of NLT Corporation worked with Kane as financial secretary. After Amon Carter Evans retired to his new home in Columbia, Tennessee, Edward F. Jones,

executive vice president of the Chamber of Commerce, took over most of the daily administrative leadership of the commission. Joan Link Armour, *Century III, Nashville: Final Report* (Nashville, 1981), 14–17.

5. Ibid., 36.
6. Ibid., 34–35.
7. Ibid., 56–57.
8. Ibid., 16, 44–45.
9. Ibid., 51–53.
10. The flatboats had been constructed earlier during the national Bicentennial when Mrs. Melville Barnes, Sr., organized Adventure II, a reenactment of the Donelson party's trip.
11. Ibid., 4–5, 47–49.
12. Ibid., 34–35.
13. Ibid., 28–29, 54.
14. Don H. Doyle, "Saving Yesterday's City: Nashville's Waterfront," *Tennessee Historical Quarterly* 35(Winter 1976): 354–57.

ESSAY ON SOURCES

References to sources on specific topics are included in the notes for each chapter and need not be repeated here. The interested reader may find it useful to know some of the most helpful published and archival materials on the history of Nashville since the 1920s.

The single most important resource for any local history is usually the newspapers. The intense rivalry between the *Tennessean* and the *Banner* persisted long after the days of Luke Lea and Edward B. Stahlman. This contentious tradition colored nearly every aspect of Nashville's politics, but this divergence of views can be very helpful to the historian as a check against the unstated biases of a single newspaper. No index is available for either paper before 1960, when the Ben West Public Library began a subject index for both newspapers. The *Globe* was a black weekly newspaper that began in 1905 and continued until 1960. Unfortunately, the files of this newspaper are very spotty and almost entirely missing for the important interwar years.

The Tennessee State Library and Archives contains few private manuscript collections of value to Nashville history since the 1920s, but its collections of photographs, maps, and vast store of published materials make it an invaluable resource on most every topic covered in this book. The Nashville Room of the Ben West Public Library is a special collection of published, manuscript, photographic, and ephemeral materials on the city's history. Its biographical clippings files are especially useful. The Jeter-Smith and Naff collections proved quite helpful to understanding the cultural life of the interwar years.

The Nashville Area Chamber of Commerce has a valuable set of historical records that reveal much of the inner workings of this organization. Many of these records are now available on microfilm at the Tennessee State Library and Archives. The Chamber's Research Division also maintains an extensive collection of files that illuminate the economic history of the city and region.

The minutes of the City Council are located in the city clerk's office in the County Courthouse. Usually the deliberations of the council were thoroughly covered in the daily newspapers, however. More valuable are the annual reports of the mayor and city departments, which reveal not only the activities of local government but the social conditions of the community. Between 1883 and 1913 these reports were published together in one convenient volume, but since 1913 city department reports have remained scattered in the individual department offices, along with other department records. Some city departments have maintained excellent historical records. The library of the Planning Commission is an example of the best standard of government record keeping. But too many other city departments, pressed for space and quite naturally concerned with current rather than historical record management, have thrown out valuable records or removed them to inaccessible storage facilities. The Nashville Room has served as the repository for city reports and publications, but the collection is spotty and shortages of space and staff have not permitted an aggressive policy of gathering past and present city records. Many of the older records of the city and county have been allowed to deteriorate in the upper floors of the courthouse. There is a desperate need for a professionally organized city archive that can serve as the repository of Nashville's valuable historical records. This city's legacy of government innovation over the past century make its city records all the more valuable. Alas, this plea only echoes the words of John Woolridge in the preface to his 1890 publication of *The History of Nashville, Tennessee*: "The labors of future historians would be rendered much more valuable if such cities as Nashville should assign to some individual especially qualified to do the work the collection, classification, and proper arrangement of everything published with reference to any department or feature of the city's life. . . ." I hope the present city government leaders will make it unnecessary for the historian of Nashville's tricentennial to plead this case again.

There is a wealth of published works on the history of Nashville more readily available to the interested reader and researcher. For a general overview of the South in this period readers should begin with George B. Tindall's monumental survey, *The Emergence of the New South, 1913–1945*, A History of the South, vol. 10 (Baton Rouge, 1967). Charles P. Roland, *The Improbable Era: The South Since World War II*, rev. ed. (Lexington, Ky., 1976), continues the story of southern development, but in less thorough fashion. The best single volume surveying Tennessee's history is Stanley J. Folmsbee, Robert E. Corlew, Enoch L. Mitchell, *Tennessee: A Short History*, 2d ed. (Knoxville, 1981), a condensed version of their four-volume history of the state.

The urban South has recently attracted the attention of scholars.

David R. Goldfield's *Cotton Fields and Skyscrapers: Southern City and Region, 1607–1980* (Baton Rouge, 1982), is a provocative interpretation of the subject. Blaine A. Brownell, *The Urban Ethos in the South, 1920–1930* (Baton Rouge, 1975), includes Nashville in a stimulating analysis of a single vital decade. Blaine A. Brownell, "The Urban South Comes of Age, 1900–1940," in Brownell and Goldfield, eds., *The City in Southern History* (Port Washington, N.Y., 1977), provides a broader survey of the subject. The recent attention in the Sunbelt has inspired some useful studies of its historical roots. Alfred J. Watkins and David C. Perry, "Regional Change and the Impact of Uneven Urban Development," in *The Rise of the Sunbelt Cities*, ed. Perry and Watkins (Beverly Hills, 1977). Carl Abbott, *The New Urban America: Growth and Politics in Sunbelt Cities* (Chapel Hill, 1981), and Richard M. Bernard and Bradley R. Rice, eds., *Sunbelt Cities: Politics and Growth Since World War II* (Austin, 1983), are two useful overviews of this phenomenon. For surveys of the history of urban America see David R. Goldfield and Blaine A. Brownell, *Urban America: From Downtown to No Town* (Boston, 1979), and Howard P. Chudacoff, *The Evolution of American Urban Society*, 2nd ed. (Englewood Cliffs, N.J., 1981).

Several popular histories of Nashville in this period are available. The best is John Egerton, et al., *Nashville: The Faces of Two Centuries* (Nashville, 1980). Several others, of less value, are listed in the essay on sources in my *Nashville in the New South, 1880–1930*. George Rollie Adams and Ralph Jerry Christian, *Nashville: a Pictorial History* (Virginia Beach, Va., 1981) is a fine visual history with informative text and captions.

Nashville's cultural history is loaded with excellent studies of the Fugitives and Agrarians, but remarkably scanty in terms of published works on music, theater, art, and architecture. On the Fugitives, Louise Cowan, *The Fugitive Group: A Literary History* (Baton Rouge, 1959), is a good starting point. John L. Stewart, *The Burden of Time: The Fugitives and Agrarians* (Princeton, 1965), provides a more critical assessment of the two movements. Daniel Joseph Singal's *The War Within: From Victorian to Modernist Thought in the South, 1919–1945* (Chapel Hill, 1982) is a highly stimulating analysis of Tate, Davidson, and Warren in the context of broader southern intellectual movements. William C. Havard and Walter Sullivan, eds., *A Band of Prophets: The Vanderbilt Agrarians After Fifty Years* (Baton Rouge, 1982), includes some interesting retrospective assessments. Thomas Daniel Young, *Gentleman in a Dustcoat: A Biography of John Crowe Ransom* (Baton Rouge, 1976), is one of several works by Young that explore the intellectual evolution of the Fugitives and Agrarians.

The story of the great southern migration from farm to city awaits its historian. This movement, and the entire history of the common folk, is always more difficult to retrieve than intellectual or political history. But in Nashville, with its universities and charitable institutions, the lives of the migrants and the poor were recorded in dozens of surveys. These works are found primarily at Vanderbilt, Fisk, and Scarritt libraries in the form of master's theses and scholarly reports. The historian must be wary of the sociological biases of these works, despite the recurrent claims of scientific objectivity. Several of these surveys are cited in the footnotes of chapter two, but these represent only a fraction of the material available. Among the more accessible examples of this survey genre are: Willis D. Weatherford, ed., *A Survey of the Negro Boy in Nashville, Tennessee* (New York, 1932); Harlan W. Gilmore, "Racial Disorganization in a Southern City" (Ph.D. diss., Vanderbilt Univ., 1931); and Methodist Episcopal Church, South, Board of Missions, *A Social Survey of the Bethlehem House Community, Nashville, Tennessee, December, 1920* ([Nashville, 1920]). Biographies of Nashville's leading sociologists proved helpful; see George P. Antone, "Willis Duke Weatherford: An Interpretation of his Work in Race Relations, 1906–1946" (Ph.D. diss., Vanderbilt Univ., 1969); Wilma Dykeman, *Prophet of Plenty: The First Ninety Years of W.D. Weatherford* (Knoxville, 1966); and Patrick Joseph Gilpin, "Charles S. Johnson: An Intellectual Biography" (Ph.D. diss., Vanderbilt Univ., 1973).

The political history of Nashville in this period must be pieced together primarily from the newspaper accounts, as the leading figures left behind no significant collections. Hilary Howse and his political machine deserve full treatment by some future historian. Ed Huddleston, *The Bootleg Era* ([Nashville, 1957]), is a popular account of Nashville's underworld during the prohibition era. Antoinette Elizabeth Taylor, "The Woman Suffrage Movement in Tennessee" (Ph.D. diss., Vanderbilt Univ., 1943), and the briefer published version, *A Short History of the Woman Suffrage Movement in Tennessee* (Nashville, 1943), provide a good starting point for the story of women as a force in Nashville politics, but this subject also begs for more thorough study. Several contemporary accounts of municipal reform in Nashville proved useful: Irby Roland Hudson's articles, "Nashville's Experience with Commission Government," *National Municipal Review* 10(Mar. 1921) and "Nashville Plays Politics," *National Municipal Review* 10(Sept. 1921), deal with the commission and city manager movements. Arthur W. Bromage, "Why Some Cities Have Abandoned Manager Charters," *National Municipal Review* 19(Nov. 1930), deals with Nashville after 1921. Robert James Parks, "Grasping at the Coattails of Progress: City Planning in Nashville, Tennessee, 1932–1962" (M.A. thesis, Vanderbilt Univ., 1971), provides an excellent historical analysis of its subject. Jennings Perry, *Democracy Begins at Home: Tennessee's Fight on the Poll Tax* (Philadelphia, 1944), looks at the poll tax battle in terms of the *Tennessean*'s war against Boss Ed Crump but does not deal sufficiently with its implications for the Howse machine.

Aspects of Nashville's experience during the New Deal are revealed in John Dean Minton, "The New Deal in Tennessee, 1932-1938" (Ph.D. diss., Vanderbilt Univ., 1959); James A. Burran, "The WPA in Nashville, 1935-1943," *Tennessee Historical Quarterly* 34(Fall 1975); Ellen Ann Dickerson, "The Nashville Housing Authority, 1938-1941: A Case Study of Public Housing Under the New Deal," (M.A. thesis, Vanderbilt Univ., 1977); and James A. Hodges, "The Tennessee Federation of Labor, 1919-1939" (M.A. thesis, Vanderbilt Univ., 1959). The *Labor Advocate*, the newspaper for the Tennessee Federation of Labor, is a useful supplement to Hodges's thesis. Donald Davidson, *The Tennessee: The New River, Civil War to TVA,* Rivers of America, vol. 2 (New York, 1948), is a fascinating polemic against TVA written by an unreconstructed southern Agrarian.

The impact of World War II on the South is just beginning to attract the attention of scholars. The books dealing with the Sunbelt cited above are all illuminating in dealing with this period. The Parks thesis, "Grasping at the Coattails of Progress," also cited above, deals with the coming of urban renewal and its impact on Nashville. James Q. Wilson, ed., *Urban Renewal: The Record and the Controversy* (Cambridge, Mass., 1966), and Mark I. Gelfand, *A Nation of Cities: The Federal Government and Urban America, 1933-1965* (New York, 1975), examine the broader context of federal involvement in urban affairs. The institutional histories of Nashville's banks, insurance companies, and other businesses cited in the notes for chapter five are all reliable sources of information. Two periodicals, *Nashville Magazine* and *Advantage,* are also filled with helpful articles on economic trends and individual business leaders in the city.

Nashville's emergence as Music City, U.S.A., has been treated in numerous scholarly and trade publications. Charles K. Wolfe, *Tennessee Strings: The Story of Country Music in Tennessee* (Knoxville, 1977), is the best starting point. Bill C. Malone, *Country Music, U.S.A.: A Fifty Year History* (Austin, Tex., 1968), paints a more comprehensive picture. Robert Shelton and Burt Goldblatt, *The Country Music Story: A Picture History of Country and Western Music* (Indianapolis, 1966), is filled with details on Nashville's Music Row entrepreneurs. John Woodruff Rumble, "Fred Rose and the Development of the Nashville Music Industry, 1942-1954" (Ph.D. diss., Vanderbilt Univ., 1980), is currently being revised for publication as a book and is an excellent analysis of the man most responsible for the popularization of country music after World War II.

The Athens of the South's education industry is treated in several institutional histories: Edwin Mims, *History of Vanderbilt University* (Nashville, 1946); Harvie Branscomb, *Purely Academic: An Autobiography* (Nashville, 1978); and Robert A. McGaw, *A Brief History of Vanderbilt University* (Nashville, 1973), treat the history of the city's largest university. Paul C. Conkin's forthcoming history of Vanderbilt, *Gone with the Ivy: a biography of Vanderbilt University* (Knoxville, 1985), provides a comprehensive analysis. Joe M. Richardson, *A History of Fisk University, 1865-1946* (University, Ala., 1980), closes before examining the important role of Fisk in redefining race relations in Nashville, a subject that demands the attention of historians. James Summerville, *Educating Black Doctors: A History of Meharry Medical College* (University, Ala., 1983), is the only reliable history of this important institution.

Nashville's historic role as a center of religion and religious publishing is best summarized in James W. Carty, *Nashville as a World Religious Center* (Nashville, 1958). On the religious publishing industry, see Daisy Maryles, "Bustling Nashville: Publishing, Bookselling, Wholesaling" *Publishers Weekly,* Nov. 15, 1976. The several small religious colleges and seminaries in Nashville have not received the kind of historical biographies they deserve. John T. Benson's *The Trevecca Story: Seventy-five Years of Christian Service* (Nashville, 1976), is an exception. The story of Vanderbilt's Divinity School is included in Paul K. Conkin's *Gone With the Ivy: A Biography of Vanderbilt University* (Knoxville, 1985).

The evolution of metropolitan government in Nashville is the subject of numerous scholarly articles and books and is recorded in several reports by outside consultants and citizen commissions. Bertil Hanson, *A Report on Politics in Nashville* (Cambridge, Mass., 1960), a report for the Harvard-MIT Joint Center for Urban Studies, is an excellent account based on extensive interviews. Daniel R. Grant, a political scientist at Vanderbilt and a participant-observer in the process of consolidation since 1954, provides his insights in: "Urban and Suburban Nashville: A Case Study in Metropolitanism," *Journal of Politics* 17(1955): "A Comparison of Predictions and Experience with Nashville 'Metro,'" *Urban Affairs Quarterly* 1(Sept. 1965); "Metro and Professional Political Leadership: The Case of Nashville," *Annals of American Academy of Political Economic Science* 353(May 1965); and, with Lee S. Greene, "Surveys, Dust, Action," *National Civic Review* 50(Oct. 1961). Brett W. Hawkins, *Nashville Metro: The Politics of City-County Consolidation* (Nashville, 1966), is the best single account of the coming of Metro and is based on numerous interviews as well as careful analysis of election data. Daniel J. Elazar, *A Case Study of Failure in Attempted Metropolitan Integration: Nashville and Davidson County* (Chicago, 1961); David A. Booth, *Metropolitics: The Nashville Consolidation* (East Lansing, Mich., 1963); and Booth, "New Wine in Old Bottles: Nashville's New Charter," *Municipal South* 9(June 1962), are also informative.

Nashville's response to the Second Reconstruction also has been the subject of several scholarly treatments. The best starting place is

Hugh Davis Graham's brief overview of school desegregation: "Desegregation in Nashville: The Dynamics of Compliance," *Tennessee Historical Quarterly* 25(Summer 1966). Graham's *Crisis in Print: Desegregation and the Press in Tennessee* (Nashville, 1967) puts the Nashville experience in a broader context. Neil R. McMillen, *The Citizens' Council: Organized Resistance to the Second Reconstruction, 1954–64* (Urbana, Ill., 1971), is a good overview of white resistance with valuable insights on the Nashville scene. Jennings Perry, *Democracy Begins at Home,* cited above, reviews the fight against the poll tax. For a survey of neighborhood segregation patterns before 1960 see John Vahaly, Jr., and Benjamin Walter, "Black Residential Succession in Nashville, 1930 to 1960," in James F. Blumstein and Benjamin Walter, eds., *Growing Metropolis: Aspects of Development in Nashville* (Nashville, 1975), and the report by the Metropolitan Planning Commission, *A Study of Nonwhite Residential Distribution in Nashville, Tennessee in 1940, 1950, 1960, and 1970* (Nashville, 1975). Guy Carawan's recorded interviews of the leaders of Nashville's 1960 sit-ins, "The Nashville Sit-In Story," *Folkways Records* (New York, 1960), with album notes by Kelly Miller Smith, is a highly valuable source for the history of those events and for an understanding of the personal sentiments behind the protest. Julia Moore's inside report on the sit-ins in *Fisk News* (Spring 1960) provides information that was either repressed or missed in the early newspaper reports. David Halberstam's eyewitness account of the sit-ins, "'A Good City Gone Ugly,'" *The Reporter,* March 31, 1960, also adds insights not available in the newspapers. Benjamin Muse, *Ten Years of Prelude: The Story of Integration Since the Supreme Court's 1954 Decision* (New York, 1964), gives considerable attention to the Nashville scene. Woodrow A. Geier, "Sit-ins Prod a Community," *Christian Century* 77(March 30, 1960), covers the Lawson affair. Eugene J. Lipman and Albert Vorspan, eds., *A Tale of Ten Cities: The Triple Ghetto in American Religious Life* (New York, 1962), includes a chapter on Nashville. An excellent film "NBC White Paper: The Nashville Sit-Ins," December 22, 1960, made available to me courtesy of John Siegenthaler, Jr., of WSM-TV, provides a vivid account of the events of 1960.

The history of a city is also recorded in the memories of the historical actors themselves. Oral history is no substitute for research in the written records, but there are many important subjects for which no formal documents exist. Many of the interviews that support the interpretations presented in this book have been cited, but there were dozens of other conversations that informed my understanding of the city's past. The Waller Collection in the Special Collections of the Vanderbilt University Library (now the Jean and Alexander Heard Library) includes transcripts of interviews of prominent people reflecting on Nashville's history between 1890 and 1910. A comparable effort to systematically record the history of Nashville since 1910 would be a valuable resource for future historians. I hope this book may inspire such an effort.

INDEX

Aberbach, Jean 153
Aberbach, Julian 153
Abingdon Press 175
Acuff, Roy 144, 146, 153, 157, 268; illustrations 147, 269
Acuff-Rose Publishing Company 153
Aden, John M. 254
Advanced Planning and Research Division 198–99
African Methodist Episcopal Sunday School Union 175
Agrarians 4, 10, 12–18, 63; illustration 16
Aikin, W.L. *See* "Kid Wolfe"
Airport. *See* Berry Field
Aladdin Industries 187
Alexander, Helen, illustration 227
Alexander, Will 34
All-Faith Center 265, 268
Allen, Jack 165
Allen, Jim 68
Allen Manufacturing 112
Altman, Robert 157
Amalgamated Clothing Workers 102
American Airlines 109
American Baptist Theological Seminary 177, 224
American Educational Life Insurance Company 129
American Express 139
American General Insurance Company 130, 131
American Legion 164
American National Bank 133, 136–37, 158. *See also* First American Bank
American Society of Composers, Authors, and Publishers (ASCAP) 154

Anderson, Thomas J. 211
Andrew Jackson Court 96
Andrew Jackson Hotel 125, 129, 252
Annexation 78, 204–6. *See also* Suburbs
Aquinas Junior College 177
Archie, James, illustration 227
Army Air Classification Center 112
Army Corps of Engineers 120
Arnold, Eddy 149
Art Commission 20
"Athens of the South" 3, 144, 157, 173, 223
Atkins, Chet 151; illustration 269
Atkinson, Richard M. 80
Automobile 76, 121
Autry, Gene 153
Aviation Manufacturing Corporation (AVCO) 110

Bachman Report 92, 94
Baker vs. *Carr* 190, 211
Banks 132–39, 274
Banner 119, 162, 190, 197, 202, 211, 229, 245, 246, 248
Baptists 174, 175, 178; black 175, 177; Free Will 177
Barrett, George 172
Barthell, Alex J. 68, 71, 73
Bartolini, C.P., illustration 25
Battle, Dick 211
Bauman, Dr. John W. 182, 184–85
Bearden, Lillie 59
Bell, Sam Davis 214
Belle Meade 92, 157, 193, 194, 195, 203; and annexation 78
Belmont neighborhood 78, 212

320

Belmont College 176
Benedict, Andrew 136, 156
Berry, Harry S. 89, 92
Berry Field 90, 109, 187; illustration 91
Berry Hill 195, 200
Bertha Fensterwald Social Center 53, 55
Bethlehem Community Center. See Bethlehem House
Bethlehem House 53; illustration 52
Bicentennial, Nashville. See Century III
Bijou theater 234
Birthright, William 99
Black Bottom 45
Blacks, and local politics 190, 224, 225; and urban renewal 125–26; illustration 232. See also Civil rights
Blackwood Field 90
Blue Cross 141
Blue Shield 141
Board of Education 82, 235, 237, 239, 243, 258
Board of Public Works 77, 183–84
Bootleggers 68, 75, 194
Bordeaux 230
Boyd, Richard Henry 175
Brackinreed, Verna, illustration 25
Bradford, James C. Jr. 140
Bradford, James Cowdon 140. See also J.C. Bradford and Company
Bradford, Mrs. James C. 20
Bradley's Barn 151
Bradley, Owen 151; illustration 152
Bradshaw, Terry 266
Bramwell, Charles 205
Branscomb, B. Harvie 160–62, 248
Branstetter, Cecil 200
Briley, Beverly 132, 134, 156, 186, 187, 197, 199, 200, 202, 206, 214, 217, 218, 221, 252, 254, 258; illustration 188
Broadcast Music, Incorporated (BMI) 154
Broadman Press 175
Broadway 120
Broadway National Bank 138
Brooks, G. Daniel 132
Brown, H. Rap 255
Brown, Ira T. 97
Browning, Gordon 187, 229, 263
Burns, Harry 69
Burton, Andrew M. 130, 176
Bush Lake 205
Business progressivism 65, 76
Busing 258, 260; antibusing demonstration, illustration 259
Butler, John Washington 32
Byrns, Joseph W. 87; illustration 88

Cabbage Hill district 45
Cain-Sloan Department Store 137–38, 245, 251

Caldwell, Camilla 44
Caldwell, James E. 133, 134, 136, 139
Caldwell, Rogers 5, 85, 132, 136, 139
Caldwell and Company 5, 15, 29, 85, 129, 138, 139–40
Caldwell School, illustration 240
Campbell, Chester D. 126
Campbell, Reverend Will 243
Candyland 40
Capers Chapel 51
Capitol Hill 42, 44, 56, 121; map 43; illustrations 122, 123, 127, 219
Capitol Hill Redevelopment Project 120, 126, 132, 191
Capitol Records 149
Carmack, Edward Ward 67
Carmichael, Oliver Cromwell 160
Carmichael, Stokely 162, 164, 254–55
Carnegie Library 125
Carr, William M. 82
Cartwright, Thomas 206
Carty, James W. Jr. 173
Cash, Johnny 268
Castle Studio 149
Castner Knott Department Store 137
Cate, George Sr. 94, 182, 184–85
Cate, George Jr. 210
Catholics 177, 178, 257
Catt, Carrie Chapman 69
Cedar Street (Charlotte Ave.) 42
Cedarwood Publishing Company 154
Centenary Methodist Institute 53; illustration 39
Centennial, 1880 264
Centennial Club 3, 26, 28, 94
Central business district (CBD). See Downtown
Central Church of Christ Home for Girls 37, 38
Century III Center 265, 268
Century III Commission 265, 268
Century III, city bicentennial 261–72
Chamber of Commerce 5, 30, 76–77, 85–86, 87, 90, 100, 101, 102, 104, 110, 119, 120, 158, 185, 202, 251
Charter Commission, 1961 207; See also Metro
Cheatham Place 96; illustration 98
Cheek, Joel 24
Cheek, John 134
Cheek, Robert 134
Cheekwood Botanical Gardens 158
Chenault, Robert N. 200
Cherokee Life Insurance Company 129
Cherry, William C. 181–82
Chicago school of urban sociology 34
Children, and poverty 49–50
Christman, Frank 68
Church membership 174. See also Religion

Church of Christ 176
Church Street 120
Citizens Committee for Better Government (CCBG), 209–10
Citizens Committee for Metro, 1958 202
Citizens Council for Industrial Peace 102
Citizens Protective Committee (CPC), 1945 186
City charter reform 71–74, 182
City Council 97, 106, 200, 202, 205, 206, 207, 228
City Manager 72
City Mission Board 51
City-County Democratic Civic League 225; illustration 227
Civil rights movement 222, 243–57; illustration 250. See also Sit-ins, Blacks
Clark Memorial Methodist Church 244
Claunch, John M. 166
Clawson, M. Don 169
Clayton, W. Woodford 265
Cleaver, Eldridge 255
Clement, Frank G. 218, 229, 263
Clinton, Tennessee 238, 242
Clouse, Ewing 200
Cochran, Carmack 200
Cockrill Bend 205
Coffee House 3
Cohen, Paul 149, 151
Cohn, Sol 68
Cold War 159, 173, 178, 203
Coleman, Baron 141
Collier, Clara, illustration 27
Columbia Records 151
Commerce Union Bank 133, 137–38
Commercial Club 30
Commission on Interracial Cooperation (CIC), 6, 34
Committee to Save Davidson County Government 202
Community Playhouse 29
Community Relations Conference 242–43
Community Services Commission (CSC) 197
Concerned Parents Association 258
Congress of Industrial Organizations (CIO) 101–2
Congress of Racial Equality (CORE) 244
Conservatory of Music 29
Cordell Hull Building 126
Cornwell, Dean 96
Council of Jewish Women 53, 210
Country music 63, 143–58. See also Music industry
Country Music Association (CMA) 144, 156

Country Music Foundation 156
Country Music Hall of Fame 156
County Court 202, 205, 206
Craig, Cornelius A. 136
Craig, Edwin W. 131
Cramer, Maude 53
Crappy Shoot 45, 230
Crawford Street 44; illustration 123
Crieve Hall 212
Cross Keys restaurant 252; illustration 253
Crownover, Sims 237
Crump, Ed 76, 181, 183, 187, 229, 263
Cumberland Law School 190, 214
Cumberland Life Insurance Company 129
Cumberland Presbyterians 174
Cumberland River 109, 115
Cummings, Patricia Ann 106
Cummings, Thomas 82, 106, 110, 180–89, 190, 262; illustration 117, 189
Curell, Marian, illustration 27
Currey, Brownlee O. 139
Curry, Walter Clyde 8
Customs House 96, 271

Dalton, May Herbert, illustration 25
Dalton, Sydney, illustration 25
Daughters of the American Revolution 94
David Lipscomb College 176
Davidson, Donald 6, 7, 8, 12, 13, 14, 15, 17, 18, 20, 28, 60, 237
Davidson, Phillip 119
Davidson County 89, 131, 183, 185, 186, 191, 197, 198, 200, 207, 214
Davidson County Public Building and Court House 94–96; illustration 95
Davis, Finley M. 72
Davis, Paul 132, 136
Davis, Willie Mai, illustration 227
de Luca, Gaetano Salvatore 21, 24; illustration 25
Death rates 48
DeBow, J.D.B. 68
Decca Records 149
Denham, T.O. 102
Denny, Jim 154
Depression, 1930s 15, 28, 46, 56, 85–107, 134, 136–37, 140, 176, 262
Desegregation, and Vanderbilt 162. See also Civil rights, Sit-ins
Dodson, K. Harlan Jr. 200
Donelson, John 266
Donelson, William Stockley 266, 267
Donelson 203, 212
Downtown 121–29, 222; illustrations 122, 127
Downtown merchants 22
Downtown Urban Renewal Project 129, 132, 137; illustration 128

Doyle, Andrew 205, 242
Doyle, Don H. 270
Drama League of America 26
Dudley, Anne Dallas 69
Dudley, Guilford Jr. 130
Dunworth, John 166
DuPont, William I. Jr. 92
DuPont powder plant 5, 85, 99
DuPont rayon plant 32, 112
Dupontonia. *See* Lakewood
Dyer, Art J. 77
Dyer, Gus 100, 103

Earthman, William F. Jr. 138
East High School 94, 235
Easter boycott 249, 251–52
Eastern Airlines 109
Eberling, May Dean 271
Economic development, post-1940 108–42, 262
Edgefield 270
Edgerton, John 100, 103
Education 92, 158–73, 176; and church colleges 175–77
Edwin Warner Park 92
Egerton, John 270
Eisenhower, Dwight 103
Elam, Lloyd C. 170
Elazar, Daniel 203
Electric Power Board 106
Electric power. *See also* Tennessee Valley Authority (TVA)
Elizabethton strike 100. *See also* Labor
Ellington, Buford 248
Elliott, William Yandell 8
Elmington Park 90
Emerson, Henry 49–50
Ennix, Coyness 228
Equitable Securities Corporation 139
Eskind, Irwin 141
Eskind, Richard 141
Estes, P.M. Jr. 130
Evans, Amon Carter 229, 264
Evans, Silliman Sr. 87, 94, 115, 181–82, 225; illustration 117
Evans, Silliman Jr. 204, 209, 229
Ewing, Robert 66
Exchange Club 76

Fair Labor Standards Act 101
Farris, Frank M. 132–34
Father Ryan High School 257
Federal government, and the South 86–87
Federal Housing Act of 1949 125
Federal-city relations 120–21, 125–26, 129, 140–42, 216–20
Federation for Constitutional Government 239
Fields, Emmett 164

Fillebrown, T. Scott 136
Fire protection 194
First American Bank 136–37, 138. *See also* American National Bank
First American Center 137
First Amtenn 138
First Baptist Church 55
First Baptist Church, Capitol Hill (formerly "Colored") 244
First Presbyterian Church 55
Fisk Jubilee Singers 28
Fisk Race Relations Institute 168, 224, 228
Fisk University 46, 159, 224, 249, 255; after 1940 166–68; illustration 54
Flat Rock 190, 193
Fleming, Sam M. 129, 134, 136
Fletcher, John Gould 14
Flexner, Abraham 169
Flexner Report 140
Foley, Gerald 99
Ford, Henry 104
Ford, Miss Theodore, illustration 227
Ford Foundation 160, 164
Ford Glass Plant 205, 234
Fort Negley 90
Founders Day, 1980 266; illustration 267
Fourth and First National Bank 133, 139. *See also* American National
Frank, James Marshall 9
Franklin Road 158
Free Will Baptist College 177
Freeman, Lurelia 210
Frierson, William 8
Frist, Thomas F. Sr. 141
Frist, Thomas F. Jr. 141
Fugitives 4–10; illustration 11
Fulton, Lyle 218
Fulton, Richard H. 156, 216–21, 262, 264–66, 271; illustrations 219, 267
Fulton, Sandra 220
Future for Nashville 197

Gabhart, Herbert C. 176
Gambling 194
Gandhi, Mohandas K. 244
Garfinkle, Elkin 82, 186–87
Garrison, Sidney C. 165
Gas pipeline 109
Gates Rubber 234
Gebhart, David R. 22
Geier vs. *Blanton* 172
General Care Corporation 141–42
General Hospital 169–70
General Services District 199
General Shoe Company 112
George Peabody College for Teachers 164–66
Germantown 270

"GI Joe" ticket 186, 214
GI-bill 165
Gillem, Aubrey D. 205
Gilliam, Maxine, illustration 227
Gimre, Gerald 77, 99, 125–26
Glendale Park Zoo 40
Goodlettsville 195, 212
Goodman, Lawrence 21
Goodyear Tire 112
Gore, Albert 229, 263
Grand Ole Opry 31, 63, 146, 156, 158; stars of, illustrations 145, 147, 148, 150
Grant, Daniel R. 197, 198, 199, 215; illustration 219
Grant's 245
Gray, Frank Jr. 172
Great Society 217, 220. *See also* federal-city relations
Greene, Lee S. 197
Green Hills 205
Green-sticker tax 204–6, 209, 212
Greyhound Bus Terminal 248
Gupton, William 66, 67, 71, 72, 74

H.G. Hill Company 135
H.G. Hill Grocery 252
Hackworth, W.S. 135
Halberstam, David 246
Hale, William J. 171
Hall, Tom T. 158, 266, 268
Hampton Field 90
Hand, Irving 198, 199
Hanley, David 99
Hardcastle, John 266
Hardin, Carl R. 198
Harvey, Fred Sr. 137, 251
Harvey's Department Store 137–38, 245, 248, 251
Harwell, Coleman 229
Hatcher, Joe 82, 187
Hattie Cotton School 239, 242, 260; illustration 241
Hawkins, Charles W. 125, 198, 199
Hays, C.M. 210
Hazel Burgess Players, 26
Head School 46
Health conditions 48, 115
Heard, Alexander 162, 164, 255
Hell's Half Acre 42
Henderson, Vivian 210, 234, 249
Hendersonville 158
Henkel, Frederick Arthur 21, 22; illustrations 25
Hermitage 158
Hermitage Health and Life Insurance Company 129
Hermitage Hotel 69, 125, 252
HEW (Department of Health, Education, and Welfare) 170

Hickman, Litton 180, 183, 187, 214; illustration 188
Hicks, Edward D. Jr. 200, 207
Hilary Howse High School 82; illustration 93
Hill, Henry A. 165
Hill, Horace G. Sr. 134
Hill, Horace G. Jr. 165. *See also* H.G. Hill Company, H.G. Hill Grocery
Hill and Range Songs, Inc. 153
Hill Burton Act of 1946 140
Hillsboro, and annexation 78
Hillsboro Theater 28
Hillsboro-Green Hills 195
Hillwood 203
Hirsch, Sydney Mttron 7–9
Historic Nashville, Inc. 265, 271
Historic preservation 270
Hobbs, Nicholas 165
Hoffman, Clare E. 102
Holden, Anna 244
Horton, Henry 100
Horton, Robert 198, 199, 217
Horton, Roy, illustration 155
Hospital Affiliates International (HAI) 141–42
Hospital Corporation of America (HCA) 141–42
Hospital management 140–42
Hotels 125
Houston, P.D. 136, 137
Houston, P.D. Jr. 136
Howse, Hilary 20, 24, 64–67, 74–83, 85, 180, 181, 221, 224, 262; illustration 81; funeral, illustration 83
Hubbard Hospital, 169–70
Hull, Cordell 87
Humane Society 158
Humphries, Frederick S. 173

I'll Take My Stand 13
Inglewood 194, 203
Ingram Book Company 175
Ingram Company 103
"Inner Citadel" 110. *See also* World War II
Insurance, 129–32

J.C. Bradford and Company 133, 140
Jackson, Andrew 268
Jackson, George Pullen 21, 22
Jacobs, Gene "Little Evil" 212
James, Bill 42
James Robertson Parkway 126
Jefferson Street 230, 255
Jenkins, Carl 149
Jenkins, Casey 218, 258
Jenkins, Sam 184–85
Jeter, Sarah 24
Jett, Leslie E. 206
Jewish Community Center 242

Jews 7, 55, 178
Jim Crow 222, 234. *See also* Segregation, Civil rights, Blacks
Johnson, Charles S. 34, 166, 168, 224; illustration 167
Johnson, Lyndon Baines 254
Johnson, Stanley 8
Johnson, Victor S. 200
Jones, Henry "Good Jelly" 212; illustration 213
Jones, Thomas 166
Jones, William T. "Bill" 180, 183, 186
Joywood-Rosebank-Dalewood 205
Justice of the peace courts 80

Kalb Hollow 45, 53, 56
Kasper, Frederick John 211, 238, 239, 242; illustration 241
Keeble, Mildred, illustration 227
Kefauver, Estes 187, 229, 263
Kelley, Alfred Z. 235, illustration 240
Kelley, Robert 235, 258
Kelley vs. *Board of Education* 257
Kerrigan Iron Works 112
"Kid Wolfe" (a.k.a. W.L. Aikin) 68
Kiger, Gus 80
Killen, Buddy 158
King, Martin Luther Jr. 244, 249, 255
King's Daughters Home 37
Kinney, Belle 18
Kirkland, James H. 6, 9, 160
Kirkpatrick, G.B. 68
Kline, Henry Blue 14
Knox, James 229
Kress's 245
Krueger, Walter 34
Krystal Grill 252; civil rights demonstration, illustration 253
Ku Klux Klan 238, 243, 254

L&C Tower 129. *See also* Life and Casualty Insurance Company
Labor 99–103
Labunska, Wanda, illustration 25
Labunski, Wiktor, illustration 25
Lafayette Street 115, 120
Lakewood 195
Lando, Albert 26
Lanier, Lyle H. 13
LaPrad, Paul 245
Lawson, Reverend James M. Jr. 162, 177, 244, 245, 246; illustration 247
Lawson, James R. 168
Lea, Luke 24, 72, 76–77, 80, 87, 92
League of Women Voters 72, 202, 210
Lebeck Brothers Department Store 137
Lechleiter, John H. 82, 94, 110
Leftwich, Irma, illustration 227
Lehman, Harry 68
Lentz, Dr. John J. 115, 194

Leonard, Walter 168
Lewis, John 177, 223, 244
Life and Casualty Insurance Company, 38, 85, 129–30
Lillard, Robert 209, 214, 225, 228
Little Theater Guild 28, 29
Lockeland Springs 78, 191, 270
Loessel, Eduard, illustration 25
Loew's Vendome Theater 26
Looby, Z. Alexander 200, 210, 224, 225, 228, 235, 243, 246, 249; illustration 236
Loser, J. Carlton 186, 218; illustration 226
Lower Broad 270–71
Luton, Luther 119, 183–84, 185, 186
Lynn, Loretta 158
Lytle, Andrew Nelson 13

McAlister, Hill, illustration 88
McClellan's 245
McConnell Field 90
McCormack, John 21
McCulloch, Reverend J.E. 51, 53
McCurrio, John 238
McGannon Hall 37
McGavock, W.H. 74, 75
McGrath, Thomas E. 202, 207
McGugin, Dan 72, 73
McKellar, Kenneth D. 99, 104
McKendree Methodist Church 55
McKonnico, Kinnard T. 80
McLean, Francis 51
McMorrough, T.J. 75
McNeilly, Warner 135
MacNevin, Evalyn, illustration 25
Macon, Uncle Dave 156
MacPherson, Joseph T. 24
Madison 193, 194, 203
Mandrell, Barbara 144, 158
Manier, William R. 104
Mann, Mrs. Delbert 94
Maps 79, 196, 231, 233
Market Street. *See* Second Avenue
Marshall, Thurgood 228, 243
Martin, Browne 25
Maryland, Dr. Ernest 74–75
Massey, Jack 141–42
Maxwell House Hotel 102, 125, 133
Mays, Seth 187
Mayes, Lambeth 254
Mayors, 1915–1983 277. *See also* individual names
Meadors, Dr. George S. 200
Medicaid 141
Medicare 141
Meharry Medical College 140, 159, 169–71, 224
Memorial Hotel 131, 132
Mencken, H.L. 4, 9, 12, 15

Mercury Records 149
Methodist Board of Education 177
Methodists 174, 175, 176, 177; and settlement houses 51, 53
Metro 179–221, 263; opposition 1958 202–3; 1962 election 212
Metropolitan Charter Commission, 1958, illustration 201
Metropolitan Charter Commission, 1962, illustration 208
Metropolitan Historical Commission 271
Metropolitan Human Relations Commission 254
Metropolitan Human Relations Committee 252
Metropolitan Nashville-Davidson County. See Metro
Migration, and Nashville's growth 35. See also Rural migrants
Miller, Roger 154
Miller, William E. 235, 237, 243, 258
Mims, Edwin 6, 9, 10, 12
Missionary Training School 51
Mitchell, Charles 24
Mitchell, Dr. Edwin 254, 255
Moore, Douglas 245
Moore, J. Washington 181
Moore, Merrill 8
Morgan, Dr. Arthur E. 104
Morgan, Joe 53
Morgan and Hamilton Bag Company 45, 53
Morrison's Cafeteria 254
Morton, L. Clure 258
Mountcastle, Paul 130
Mud Flats 46
Municipal Airport 228. See also Berry Field
Municipal Auditorium 115, 126
Municipal reform 66–74
Municipal revenues and expenditures, table 276
Murchison, Clint W. 130
Murfreesboro Road 110
Muscle Shoals 104
Music, in 1920s 21–26
"Music City U.S.A." 157, 261. See also Country music, Music industry
Music industry 143–58
Music Row 151

NAACP (National Association for the Advancement of Colored People) 210, 228, 243, 244
Naff, Lula C. 21; illustration 23
Nash, Diane 244, 249
Nashville Art Association 3, 28
Nashville Bank and Trust 38. See Nashville Trust

Nashville bicentennial. See Century III
Nashville Bridge Company 112
Nashville Christian Leadership Conference (NCLC) 244, 252
Nashville City Bank. See Nashville Trust
Nashville City Club 133
Nashville Conservatory of Music 21, 24; illustration 25
Nashville Electric Service (NES) 106
Nashville Engineering Association 76
Nashville Housing Authority 97, 125–26
Nashville, movie 157
Nashville Museum of Art 20
Nashville Plan 235, 237, 243, 257. See also School desegregation
Nashville Railway and Light Company 100
Nashville Symphony Orchestra 22, 24, 158; illustration 25
Nashville Trades and Labor Council 102, 202
Nashville Trust 134–35
Nashville Volunteers 40
"Nashville's Harlem" 42
National Baptist Convention of America 174, 175
National Baptist Convention, USA, Inc. 175
National Industrial Recovery Act 100–1
National Labor Relations Act. See Wagner Act
National Labor Relations Board 101–3
National Life and Accident Insurance Company 85, 129–32, 135, 216; workers, illustration 39, 41
National Life Center 137
National Recovery Administration (NRA) 87
Nelson, Charles 135
Nelson, Edward 139
Nelson, Harry 97
Neuhoff Packing 103
New Criticism 4, 9. See also Fugitives
New Deal 85–107, 115, 120
New York Times 255
Nichols (Harry) Building 129, 138
Nixon, Herman Clarence 13
NLT Corporation. See National Life and Accident Insurance Company
Noel Hotel 125
Noel-Palmer Mortgage Company 138
Norman, Jack 186
Norris, George 104
North Nashville 46
Numbers racket 42

Oak Hill 195, 203, 212
O'Bryan Brothers 112

Index

Office of Production Management (OPM) 112
Old Hickory 32
Old Oak 3
Opryland 130, 156
Opryland Hotel 157, 268
Opryland Productions 156
Orpheum Theater 26
Osment, Horace 185
Otey, Inman, illustration 219
Owen, Ralph 139
Owsley, Frank Lawrence 13

Page, Patti, 149
Palmer, J. Richard 176
Palmer, Joe 140
Parents School Preference Committee 237
Park Street 126
Park View Hospital 141
Park, Robert 34
Parker, Tom 149
Parks, and federal works projects 90, 92. *See also* individual park names
Parthenon 18-21, 29, 268; illustrations 19
Parton, Dolly 144, 157
Payne, Bruce R. 165
Paytes, Nathan, illustration 227
Paytes, Portice, illustration 227
Peabody College. *See* George Peabody College for Teachers
Pearl High School 94, 235, 254, 258
Pearl, Minnie 42, 157-58
Percy Warner Park 92; illustration 93
Perry, Jennings 225
Phillips and Buttorff 112
Pitts, Greenfield 251
Plan of Metropolitan Government 199
Planning 216
Planning and Zoning Commission 77, 125
Police 194
Poll tax 80, 115, 225; illustration 226
Poor 44-50; and public housing 96-99; illustrations 47, 57
Population 108, 191, 204; table 273
Potter, Ed Jr. 132, 137-38, 202
Powell, William, illustration 227
Powers, Dan 220
Presbyterians 174
Presley, Elvis 149, 151, 156
Preston, Frances Williams 154, 158; illustration 155
Priest, Percy 229, 263
Printer's Alley 68
Private schools, and desegregation 258
Prohibition 67-69, 76; and Tennessee Anti-Saloon League 80
Prostitution 44, 71, 115

"Protestant Vatican." *See* religion
Public Administration Service (PAS) 181-82, 195
Public housing 96-99, 125
Public Square 94, 121
Public Works Administration (PWA) 86, 94-96, 110
Publishing, religious 175
Pullias, Athens Clay 176

Query Club 3
Quonset Hut 151

Race relations 222-60, 263. *See also* Blacks, Civil rights movement, Segregation, Desegregation
Race relations, since World War II 222-60
Race riots, illustration 256
Radnor Yards neighborhood 193
Radnor-Woodbine 205
Railroads 109
Raines, Jim 42
Rankin, Anne 26
Ransom, John Crowe 6, 7, 12, 14, 15
RCA Victor 149, 151
Reckless, Walter J. 34, 35
Reform. *See* Prohibition, City charter reform, Hilary Howse
Religion 55-60, 63, 143, 173-78; illustrations 61-62
Religious affiliations, table 58
Religious publishing 174-75
Review Club 3
Reynolds, George 149
Richland 78, 205
Richland-West End 270
Riding, Laura 8
Riots, 1967 and 1968 254; illustration 256
Ritter, Tex 153
Riverfront Park 220, 270
Robb, Felix C. 165
Roberson, James H. 209
Robert W. Kelley, et al. vs. *Board of Education of Nashville* 235
Roberts, Albert H. 69, 73
Roberts, Kenneth 136
Robertson, James 266
Robinson, Garner 187
Roche, Nellie 73
Rockefeller General Education Board (GEB) 169
Roosevelt, Franklin D. 87; illustration 88
Rose, Fred 153
Rose, Kenneth D. 21
Rose, Wesley 153, 158
Rotary Club 199
Round Table 3

Rudolf, Wilma 171
Rural migrants 30–63
Russell Street Church of Christ Home for Girls 37
Ryman Auditorium 3, 21, 22, 24, 156–57, 220

Sanders, Mrs. J.D. 210
Sanders, Rita 172
Sanders vs. *Ellington* 172
Sanford, Robbie 40
Sarratt, Madison 160, 249
Savitch, Ramon 28
Sawyer, Sallie Hill 51
Scarritt College for Christian Workers 34, 176
Schermerhorn, H.B. 26
Scholz, Leopold 18
School attendance 49
School desegregation, 1950s 234–43; after 1960 257–60; illustration 240
Schools 207; and federal works projects 92–94
Schulman, Herbert 141
Scopes trial 6, 12
Scovel Street 46
Second Avenue (Market Street) 270
Second Reconstruction 223
Secretarial schools 38
Segregation 46, 125, 263; and public housing 99; occupational 234; proponents of 223; residential 230; maps 231, 233
Selected Editions of Standard American Catalogues (SESAC) 154
Settlement Day, 1980 266, 268
Settlement house movement 50–55
Seventh Day Adventists 175
Sewage 115, 193, 215
Shannon, Marguerite, illustration 25
Sharpe, Percy 74
Shell, Owen G. 136
Shelton, Aaron 149
Sheridan, Jake 187
Siegenthaler, John 229
Silver Dollar Saloon 271
Silverman, Rabbi William 242
Sit-ins 245–46; illustration 247
Skalowski's ice cream parlor 40
Sloan, John 251
Slums 121
Smith, Gipsy 73
Smith, James W. 73
Smith, Reverend Kelly Miller 224, 244, 246, 249
Smith, Louise 24; illustration 25
Smoke 5, 115, 179; illustration 123
Snow, Hank 158
Solid Bloc 225
Solomon, Jay 265

Sorantin, Erich, illustration 25
South, and urban population 261
Southern Baptist Convention 178
Southern Baptist Sunday School Board 175, 178
Southern Manifesto 229
Southern Manufacturing 112
Southern Methodists 174
Southern Publishing Association 175
Southern Regional Education Compact 169
Southern Sociological Congress 32, 51
Southern States Industrial Council 101
St. Cecilia Academy 177
Stagecrafters 26
Stahlman, Edward B. 72
Stahlman, James G. "Jimmy" 24, 119, 162, 164, 229, 248; illustration 118
Stahlman Building 138
Stapp, Jack 154
Starr, Alfred 9
State Insurance Company of Tennessee 129
State Library and Archives 126
State Museum 125
State Office Building 94
Steeplechase 92
Stevenson, Alec Brock 8
Stokes, Walter Jr. 186
Strickland, William 94, 126
Strikes 103. *See also* labor
Stroud, Fred 238, 239, 242
Student Nonviolent Coordinating Committee (SNCC) 244, 254
Students for a Democratic Society (SDS) 162
Suburbs 78, 121, 179, 194; and Metro 203; maps 79, 196; illustration 192
Sulphur Dell 31, 40, 45
Sunbelt 108–43
Supreme Court Building 94
Swan Ball 158
Swift and Company 103
Sylvan Park, and annexation 78

Tate, Allen 5, 6, 7, 8, 12, 13, 14, 17
Taxes 78, 132, 204
Taxpayers' League 80
Taylor, J. Frank 198
Taylor, Lark 28
Tease, Risie Lee, illustration 227
Temple, Ed 171
Tennessean 110, 115, 119, 162, 181–82, 190, 197, 202, 205, 210–11, 214, 229, 249
Tennessee Agricultural and Industrial State College. *See* Tennessee State University
Tennessee Aircraft 112

Index

Tennessee Anti-Saloon League. *See* Prohibition 80
Tennessee County Services Association 200
Tennessee Electric Power Company (TEPCO) 105–6
Tennessee Enamel Company 112
Tennessee Federation for Constitutional Government 237
Tennessee Federation of Labor (TF of L) 99–100, 102. *See also* Labor
Tennessee Historical Society 264, 272
Tennessee Manufacturers Association 102
Tennessee Municipal League 202
Tennessee State Museum 158
Tennessee State University 159, 166, 171–73, 224, 255
Tennessee Taxpayers Association 197, 202
Tennessee Valley Association 104
Tennessee Valley Authority (TVA) 103–7, 115, 182, 187; illustrations 107
Tennessee Valley Bancorp 138
"Tennessee Waltz" 153
Thayer General Hospital 112
Theater 26–28
Third National Bank 130, 133–36
Third National Corporation 138
Thomas, Rebecca 200
Thomas Nelson Company 175
Tic-Toc Restaurant 252
Tigerbelles 171
Tolmie, Verner 182
Tootsie's Orchid Lounge 157
Torrence, Joe E. 207
Townsend, Pauline 28
Trailway Bus Terminal 248
Trevecca Nazarene College 176
Trimble Bottom 45, 230
Tubb, Ernest, illustration 148
Tulane Hotel 149
Turner, Bank 69
Turner, Edward L. 169
Tyus, Wyomia 171

Underworld 42–44
Union Station 265, 268; illustration 114
Unitarian Church 243
United Methodist Publishing House 175
United Textile Workers 101
University Center Project 161
University of Tennessee at Nashville (UTN) 172
Upper Room 177–78
Urban Observatory 217
Urban renewal 125. *See also* Capitol Hill Redevelopment Project, Downtown Urban Renewal Project, University Center Project

Urban Services District 200, 212, 215–16
U.S. Customs House. *See* Customs House

V-J Day, illustration 116
Vance, Reverend James I. 71
Vanderbilt, Frederick W. 161
Vanderbilt, Harold Stirling 161
Vanderbilt Divinity School 177
Vanderbilt Glee Club 28
Vanderbilt University 5, 9, 12, 18, 131, 140, 158, 160–64, 190, 214, 255; and Fugitives 4; and James Lawson 246–48; illustration 163
Vanderbilt University Divinity School 248
Vanderbilt University Hospital 170
Vanderbilt University Law School 181
Vanderbilt University Medical School 169
Vendome Theater 3, 22
Venereal disease 115
Veterans Administration Hospital 112, 141, 161
Victory Memorial Bridge 126
Vietnam 159, 162
Vivian, Reverend C. Tindell 223, 249
Voting machines 82, 225
Vultee Aircraft 110, 187; illustrations 111

Wade, John Donald 14
Wages, and women 36, 40
Wagner Act 101, 103
Walgreen's 245
Wall, Seth 191
Wall Street of the South 5, 85, 129, 133, 136, 139
War Memorial Building 22, 125
Ward-Belmont School 176; School of Music 3, 21, 24
Warfield, Charles 207
Warioto Settlement 53
Warren, Robert Penn 6, 7, 8, 12, 14
Washington Manufacturing Company 102, 112
Water service 193
Watkins Institute 38
Watkins Park 46
Weatherford, Willis D. 32; illustration 33
Weaver, William C. 135
Welch, Sallie, illustration 227
Wells, Kitty, illustration 148
Werthan Bag Company 103, 112
Wesley Community House 51; illustration 54
West, Ben 184–85, 187, 190–214, 202, 204, 205, 206, 210–11, 218, 224, 228, 229, 239, 248, 249, 262; illustration 189

West, Harold D. 170
West End Ave. 120
West End High School 84, 93, 94. See also Hilary Howse High School
West Meade 212
West Nashville 204
Western Front 68, 71
White Citizens' Council 238, 254
Whitland Ave. 9
Whitson, Claudia, illustration 27
Who Owns America? 15
Williams, Avon Jr. 172, 210, 235, 243, 258; illustration 236
Williams, Hank 146, 149; illustration 150
Williams, J.B. 45, 46, 56
Williams, Mrs. Tommie, illustration 227
Willkie, Wendell 105
Wills, Jesse 8
Wills, Ridley 8
Wilson, David K., illustration 219
Wilson, Felix Zollicoffer 73, 74, 75, 80, 181
Windrow, John E. 185, 186
WLAC-TV 130

Women 264; and arts 3; and local politics 71–73; and Metro 210; and migration 35–42; and work force 36
Women's suffrage 69; illustration 70
Woodbine district 190
Woodruff, Reverend James E. 255
Woolwine, Emmons 96
Woolworth's 245–46
Work force, in 1950 and 1980, table 275
Works Progress Administration (WPA) 86, 89–92, 110, 171; illustration 91
World War I 165
World War II 110–15, 146, 149, 159, 173, 176, 180, 214, 262
Wright, Steven J. 168
WSM radio 130, 149, 154
WSM-TV 130

Young, Stark 14
Young Men's Hebrew Association 55, 131
Young Women's Christian Association (YWCA) 37, 94

Zolnay, George J. 18

Nashville Since the Nineteen Twenties was composed into type on a Compugraphic phototypesetter in ten point Trump Medieval with two points of spacing between the lines. Trump and Trump Bold was selected for display. The book was designed by Jim Billingsley, typeset by Metricomp, Inc., printed offset by Thomson-Shore, Inc., and bound by John H. Dekker & Sons. The book is printed on paper designed for an effective life of at least three hundred years.

THE UNIVERSITY OF TENNESSEE PRESS : KNOXVILLE